What the Bible Teaches; a Systematic Presentation of the Fundamental Principles of Truth Contained in the Holy Scriptures

WHAT THE BIBLE TEACHES

A
Systematic Presentation of the Fundamental
Principles of Truth Contained in
the Holy Scriptures

By
F. G. SMITH
Author of "The Revelation Explained"
and "Evolution of Christianity"

"Things which the Holy Ghost teacheth; comparing spiritual
things with spiritual."—1 Cor. 2:13.
"Be ready always to give an answer to every man that asketh
you a reason of the hope that is in you."—1 Pet. 3:15

Anderson, Indiana, U. S. A.
GOSPEL TRUMPET COMPANY

PREFACE

The preface of a book is usually written last, and read last—or never read at all. This one, however, was mainly written first, and I trust that it will be read first; for if the special design and object of this work is understood by the reader, its usefulness will be thereby greatly increased.

A careful study of the "signs of the times" in which we live shows the necessity of an exact statement of doctrinal truth, especially of those underlying principles known as fundamental truth. The controversial wars of the past have now given way to a compromising sentiment which demands peace and union even at the expense of true doctrinal convictions. But while we must avoid the spirit of bitter strife and controversy, still we can not consent to a course which in the end seeks to rob us of the true doctrinal standards of the Bible. The apostolic command *"Preach the Word"* comes ringing down through the ages, and every holy minister of God is obligated to respond to the best of his ability. This is important. We are exhorted to "speak the things which become sound doctrine" (Tit. 2:1); to "be able by sound doctrine both to exhort and to convince the gainsayers" (Tit. 1:9). And in language still stronger the apostle says: "Give attendance . . . to doctrine . . . take heed unto thyself and unto the doctrine; continue in them: for in doing this thou shalt both save thyself, and them that hear thee" (1 Tim. 4:13, 16).

The Word of God presents the true standard of teaching. "All Scripture is given by inspiration of God, and is profitable *for doctrine,* for reproof, for correction, for instruction in righteousness" (2 Tim. 3:16). We have no higher appeal than to the Word itself; therefore we must earnestly study the Scriptures in order that we may "rightly divide the word of truth" (2 Tim. 2:15). Many people, however, do not have sufficient time to make the prolonged investigation necessary to give them, unaided, a satisfactory insight into the deep things of God; therefore they naturally look to others for assistance. To supply this legitimate demand, many books have been written.

But the authors of these doctrinal books usually endeavor to make their treatment of the various subjects exhaustive in order to meet the requirements of special students of the Word. This course in a great measure defeats the chief object of their publications—a general perusal—for it necessarily results in a great number of specialized works which but few people in this busy age have time to read through; and if a person reads only two or three volumes of a series, he does not obtain a proper idea of the relationship that the various lines sustain to each other. Therefore the need of a general, condensed work, one which can be placed in the hands of busy people and which will, with the least amount of time and effort, impart to them the very things that they need to know.

Personal experience on the foreign missionary field has also tended to magnify greatly the above-mentioned difficulty and to emphasize the importance of a comprehensive doctrinal work of a general character. In the first place, our many excellent works are written in an American setting, particularly adapted to an advanced stage of society, and containing illustrations and comparisons that are for the most part unintelligible to Oriental readers. Furthermore, up to the present time our religious services abroad have been conducted in seven different foreign languages, and each of these nationalities, as well as scores of others, require literature in their own tongue setting forth the various lines of Bible doctrine. If recourse be had to translation, how can we, in the earlier stages of missionary work, attempt the translation and publication in many languages of a whole library of doctrinal works? Manifestly it is impossible.

Realizing these conditions, I have felt clearly directed of the Lord to write the present work, which presents in one volume all the principal lines of Bible truth, sustained by all the leading evidences relating thereto. This has been done in plain, easily understood language. Much fresh light has been thrown on these important Bible themes; therefore by the help of the Lord I have been enabled to "bring forth out of his treasure things new and old." Omitting as far as possible all local coloring, I have endeavored to deal faithfully with fundamental principles that are of universal application.

Many subjects of considerable importance are not presented in separate chapters, but are included in other chapters to which they stand particularly related, being treated under appropriate subheads. Some subjects, however, such as Prayer and Faith, are of such a nature as to make their special classification in a general doctrinal outline practically impossible. Prayer and Faith unite the human with the divine; therefore they are the life and soul of the entire gospel system; hence they belong, not to a part, but to the whole. And while a great variety of subjects are considered in this work, they are not treated in an independent and disconnected way, after the manner of an encyclopedia, but are for the most part presented in a logical order of progression from the beginning to the end.

For lack of sufficient space the digest of the subject-matter, given in the Table of Contents, has been greatly abridged; therefore it comprises but a partial amount of the real contents of the book.

The Index of Texts will enable the reader to ascertain quickly the use that is made of special scriptures pertaining to the various subjects. Furthermore, the principal scriptures frequently urged against these doctrines are also considered in the body of the work; hence the Index will be found very convenient in finding the answer given to the objections based on these particular texts.

The large diagrams entitled "The Church in Prophecy and History," which is inserted at the beginning of Chapter XVI, will be found very helpful in obtaining a correct understanding of the different lines of prophetic truth herein presented.

I trust that God will bless this work to the good of thousands of souls, and that through its humble instrumentality many may be led out into the glorious light of present truth.

Yours in Christ,
F. G. Smith.

Beirut, Syria, Nov. 1, 1918.

CONTENTS.

THE PROBLEM OF SIN
CHAPTER III
THE PROBLEM OF SIN

Sin a Fact, Notwithstanding God's Holiness and Goodness—Whence Came it? ITS ORIGIN: Three Theories Concerning—God Not the Author of Moral Evil. IS NOT A DIVINE METHOD: It Formed no Part of his Purposes or his Plans—Originated in the Finite and by Apostasy—Made Possible by Man's Essential Nature. MAN WHOLLY RESPONSIBLE: A Problem of Moral Government. SIN AND PREDESTINATION: God's Relations to Sin Always Antagonistic—Designed to Prevent, Punish, or Counteract—God's Plans and Purposes Relative to Sin Agree with Man's Free Moral Agency. NATURE OF SIN. ITS UNIVERSALITY. *—Page* 75.

REDEMPTION
CHAPTER IV
THE REDEMPTIVE PLAN

SELF-REDEMPTION IMPOSSIBLE: An Insurmountable Legal Difficulty—A Moral Difficulty—Angels Could not Accomplish It. MAN WHOLLY RESPONSIBLE FOR SIN: Therefore God Not Obligated to Redeem. WILL GOD REDEEM? Presumptive Evidences—Scriptural Intimations. A DIVINE PLAN. PROGRESSIVE REVELATION. THE ABRAHAMIC COVENANT: Two Prominent Divisions of. THE LAW. THE PROPHETS. CHRIST THE CENTER. FUTURE REDEMPTION: Relates to the Body—Consummated at the Resurrection. IMPORTANCE OF THE PROGRESSIVE VIEW: A Basis of Harmony for Facts Not Otherwise Reconcilable—Examples. *—Page* 87.

CHAPTER V
CHRIST AND THE ATONEMENT

With Sin a Universal Fact and Self-Redemption Impossible, a Redeemer is Necessary—God's Law Can Not be Ignored, therefore Redemption must be Accomplished Righteously, hence NECESSITY OF THE INCARNATION: Union of Two Natures—Human and Divine—A Middle Link—Christ the Redeemer. THE VIRGIN BIRTH: Old Testament Prophecies of—Mysterious—Other Things Mysterious—A Reasonable Thing. EVIDENCES OF CHRIST'S DIVINITY: 1. Prophecies of Incarnation; 2 Old Testament Types Fulfilled in Him; 3. He Bore the Divine Names; 4. Divine Attributes Attributed to Him; 5. He Performed Miracles and Wrought Divine Works;

CHAPTER VI
CONDITIONS FOR SALVATION

CHAPTER VII
SALVATION

CHAPTER VIII

A HOLY LIFE

New Testament Teaches a Sinless Life. WHAT IS SIN? Responsibility to Law—Must be Enlightenment, Otherwise No Responsibility—The Will involved in Actual Sin. ALL MEN BY NATURE SINNERS: The Universal Conviction—Uniform Testimony of the Scriptures—Old Testament Predictions of Salvation. CHRISTIANS ARE SAVED FROM SIN: The Gospel Standard—1. Christ Taught it—Examples; 2. Peter Taught it—Texts; 3. Paul Taught it—Scriptural Proofs; 4. John Taught it—Many Texts. THE LINE OF DISTINCTION: Sin-Preachers—Amusing Example of Consistent Application of Sin-Doctrine. THE CONTRAST: As Presented by Bible Authorities—Jesus, Paul, Peter, James, Jude, John. SOME OBJECTIONS ANSWERED: 1. Certain Texts Apparently Inconsistent with Holiness; 2. Paul's Experience in Romans 7, etc.—Proper Basis of Harmony for all such Objections. FREEDOM FROM WORLDLINESS: Occasional Meaning of the Term "the World"—God's People "Not of the World"— Implies Forsaking of All that is Essentially Worldly in Sentiment, Associations, Amusements, Dress, etc. WORLDLY AMUSEMENTS: Prevalence of—A Snare to Souls. WORDLY DRESS: God's Word Condemns Such—"Modest Apparel" the Bible Standard—What Constitutes Modest Apparel?—The Apostle Tells What it Is—and also What it is Not—Not of the World. THE POSITIVE SIDE: Put on Christ—Manifest Christ—What He is to Us—The Christian Graces—A Life of Holiness.   —*Page* 139.

CHAPTER IX

SANCTIFICATION

More for the Believer—Sanctification Describes a Result— One Phase of a Work Variously Expressed. A BIBLE DOCTRINE: Provided through the Atonement—Taught by Apostles—Is for the Church. WHAT DOES SANCTIFICATION SIGNIFY? Two Definitions—Scriptural Examples of Each. FOR JUSTIFIED PEOPLE ONLY. A SECOND WORK OF GRACE: Two Forms of Sin, Inherent and Committed—Two Degrees in the Descent into Sin; therefore Two Degrees in Redemption—Many Scriptural Proofs and Examples. TWO WORKS SYMBOLIZED: By the Tabernacle—Its Two Rooms— Two Altars for the Blood of Sin-offerings—Two-fold Services—Applied thus in the New Testament. APOSTOLIC EXAMPLES OF TWO WORKS: 1. The Apostles Themselves; 2. The Jerusalem Church; 3. The Samaritan Church; 4. The

CHAPTER X

DIVINE HEALING

RELATIONSHIP OF BELIEVERS; OR THE CHURCH: ITS MEMBERSHIP AND ORGANIZATION, ITS ORDINANCES AND ITS WORK

CHAPTER XI

UNITY OF BELIEVERS

Two-fold Relationship—With Christ and with Each Other—The Standard of the Word. UNITY ILLUSTRATED: By the Physical Body., IN ONE BODY: Salvation itself Inducts us into "One Body"—Christ the Head—He Prayed for the Perfection of this Unity—Indwelling Carnality a Hindrance—Perfect Holiness Effects Perfect Unity—Exemplified in the Apostolic Church. UNITY THROUGH RELATIONSHIP: First Basis of Unity not Knowledge or Development, but Spiritual Relationship—Illustrated. UNITY PERFECTED: Four Essentials to: 1. *"In Christ"*; 2. Kept in His Name; 3. Receive and Obey the Word; 4. Be Sanctified Wholly—All in Christ's Prayer—False Ideas Concerning Unity—Oneness the Uniform New Testament Standard. —*Page* 223.

CHAPTER XII

THE NEW TESTAMENT CHURCH

Christ its Founder. THE CHURCH IN TYPE: God's House—Prefigured by the Old Testament House of God—The Transfer—Miraculous Manifestations at the Dedication of Each. IT IS THE BODY OF CHRIST: Christ the Head—One Body Only—All True Christians Constitute it. SALVATION ITS MODE OF MEMBERSHIP: Includes Every Saved Individual —Those who Commit Sin are No Part of God's Church. CONTRASTED WITH SECTS: I. The Church was Fully Organized on Pentecost—All Sects are of Later Origin; 2. Salvation Secures Divine Membership—It Makes No One the Member of a Sect; 3. God's Church has in its Membership Every Saved Individual—No Sect Contains All the saved; 4. God's Church Contains No Unsaved People—Sects Contain many who are Unsaved; 5. God's Church Contains all of the Truth—No Sect Contains All of the Truth, else it would Not Exist—Example of one Person who was Pleading for Sectarianism; 6. God's Church Contains No Error—Every Sect Contains Much Error; 7. Salvation, which Makes us Members of the Church of God, Reconciles All "In One Body"—Sectarianism Divides God's People into Hundreds of Bodies. ITS VISIBILITY: False Claim that Sects are Necessary in order to Make the

CHAPTER XIII

BAPTISM

Authority for New Testament Ordinances—Their Perpetuity—Paul's Experience a Special Proof—Baptism—In the Last Commission. A BELIEVER'S BAPTISM: Apostolic Examples—Infant Baptism a Heresy—Originated in the Apostasy as the Result of two other Errors—No Valid Reason for—Can Only Produce Great Harm—Occasions a False Standard of Christianity—Deplorable Results of, Especially in the East. CONDITIONED ON REPENTANCE: Bible Proofs—Otherwise Invalid, even Though Performed in the Bible Manner and by a Holy Minister—Example. IS A BURIAL: "Immersion" the English Equivalent of the Greek *Baptizo*—Can be Substituted for the word "Baptism" without Destroying the Sense; whereas either *Sprinkle* or *Pour*, in many cases, would make a Ridiculous Rendering—Immersion the Primitive Practise—Admitted by Many Historians—Example, a Consistent Inconsistency—Bible Examples—Necessary Conditions for True Baptism—Following the Word. A PURIFYING ORDINANCE: Double Cleansing in the Law, Actual and Ceremonial—Twofold Cleansing in the Gospel. *Actually* by the Blood of Christ; *Ceremonially*, by Water-Baptism—Various Texts—The Outward Sign of an Inward Work. SINGLE IMMERSION: The Threefold Formula Given in the Last Commission does Not Imply Three Immersions: 1. It was Never Used by the Apostles in the Acts; 2. The Design of Baptism Precludes such Repetition.   —*Page* 267.

CHAPTER XIV

THE LORD'S SUPPER

NOT A REGULAR MEAL: Scriptural Proofs. A COMMEMORATIVE INSTITUTION: Lord's Supper and Communion Identical—Was Observed in Apostolic Church. ITS DESIGN: False Theories—The Truth—Twofold Signification of—Complete in the Church of God Only—Worthy Candidates. ITS PERPETUITY.   —*Page* 283.

CHAPTER XV

FEET-WASHING

Generally Ignored—Why?—Inconsistency. EXPRESSLY COMMANDED: Scriptural Proofs—Compared with other Obligations. A CHURCH ORDINANCE: Essentials to a Church Ordinance. OLD CUSTOM CONSIDERED. OTHER OBJECTIONS: Inconsistency of Those who Urge the "Sandal" Theory—Examples—Amusing Incident of a Preacher's Attempts to Explain Away this Ordinance. WAS PRACTISED IN THE APOSTOLIC CHURCH: Scripture Proofs. ITS LESSON TO US.   —*Page* 291.

THE CHURCH IN PROPHECY AND IN HISTORY

CONTENTS. 19

DIVINE LAW AND THE KINGDOM OF GOD

CHAPTER XX

THE TWO COVENANTS

of the Law—All was Given by God in the Same Manner—
Spoken from Heaven—Decalogue Delivered Publicly—Remainder Spoken Privately to Moses, at the Request of the People—
Difference in Recording—Why?—Decalogue, which was Delivered Publicly, Afterward Written on Stones by God Himself
as a "Testimony," or "Witness," that the Rest of the Law,
Written by Moses, and which the People did Not Hear, was
true—the *Very Law of God*—Such Visible "Testimonies," or
"Witnesses," Customary in Those Days—Other Examples of—
The Testimony, or Witness, Not Superior to the Thing Testified, or Witnessed to. A TEMPORARY SYSTEM: Proved by
Many Texts—"Not Made for a Righteous Man"—Applicable
to a Sin-age Only. A NEW COVENANT PREDICTED: A
Better Covenant—Established by Jesus Christ—Five Points
of Superiority Given. FIRST COVENANT ABOLISHED:
Direct Scripture Texts—What Was Included in this Abolished
Covenant? 1. The Decalogue as Delivered in the Wilderness—
Three *Unanswerable* Texts which Directly Affirm This; 2. All
other Commandments and Ordinances of the Mosaic Dispensa-
tion—The Entire Law System, Moral, Civil, and Ceremonial,
Only a Natural Code, hence could be Superseded—Other Plain
Scriptures.   —*Page* 403.

CHAPTER XXI
"THE LAW OF CHRIST"

NECESSITY OF LAW: As a Standard of Conduct—As a
Standard of Judgment. ONLY DIVINE LAW CAN DEFINE
SIN: What Law are Christians Under?—Revelation made *in
Various Ways* and *at Different Times*—Progressive—Folly of
Attempting to Hold to Divine Injunctions After they have
Served their Purpose or been Superseded—Particular Example.
CHRIST THE LAWGIVER: Predicted—Was to Supersede
Moses—Thus Applied by Peter—His Law to be the Standard
of Judgment, According to the Prophets—Demonstrated on
the Mount of Transfiguration—Compared with Sinai. NEW
LAW GOD'S STANDARD OF JUDGMENT: The Words of
Christ on this Point—The Directness and Authority of His
Law Shown by Six Distinct Considerations—Its Relation to
the Mosaic Law—Many Scriptural Proofs. A "PERFECT
LAW OF LIBERTY"; Perfect in that it Covers Every Phase
of Human Conduct and Character—Condemns All Wrong; En-
joins All that is Right—List of Thirty-three Sins which the
Law of Christ, as Revealed in the Gospel, Distinctly Names and
Prohibits—List of Twenty Righteous Things which the Same
Law Distinctly Names and Enjoins—Gospel Standard the Only
Standard in this Dispensation. A GRADUAL CHANGE: The

CHAPTER XXII

THE LAW OF HOLINESS

"Holy" *When* God "Blessed and Sanctified" it "Because that in it he *Had* Rested"—When did he "Bless and Sanctify" it as a Sabbath for Man?—Answered by Many Direct Scripture Texts—Twofold Object of its Institution as Revealed in the Law—Ceremonial Nature of the Sabbath Command Proved by Three Unanswerable Arguments—Observe Carefully—Impossibility of its Internal Writing in the Heart Demonstrated, therefore it Forms *No Part of the New Covenant*—Its Abolition, with all Other Ceremonies of the Law, Clearly Shown by the Plainest and Most Natural Interpretation of the New Testament Texts—Arguments for Perpetuity of the Sabbath that Concern New Testament Texts Answered—Also some Other Special Texts. OBJECT OF LAW CEREMONIES: To Serve in a Typical Relation—Imperfect Types, "Shadows"—Nature of Symbols and Types—Paul Classes the Sabbath-days as "Shadows" whose Substance is Found in Christ, Col. 2: 14-17—The Writer of the Hebrews thus Points out the Sabbath as a Type of the True Spiritual "Rest" of the Christians, which We "by Faith" Enter When "We also Cease from our Own Works as God did from His." Hebrews 4—Careful Analysis of Hebrews 4. NEW TESTAMENT CEREMONIES: New Covenant Primarily Subjective—Requires External Manifestation; hence the Necessity of Ceremonial Institutions as Channels of Expression—also Commemorative Institutions—Four Special Things to be thus Represented: 1. Our Private Acceptance of Christ and the Authority and Law of his Kingdom—Represented by Baptism; 2. The Procuring Cause of Salvation, as the Basis of all our Hopes, the Atonement—Represented by the Lord's Supper; 3. Our Deep and Special Love for the Brethren—nepresented by Ordinance of Feet-washing; 4. Our Worship and our Faith—Requires a Time and Place of Public Manifestation—Regular Meetings in Apostolic. Church—The Place of Worship Left to Private Judgment According to Conditions in All Parts of the World—The Special Time for this Public Worship is Set by Apostolic Example in the New Testament as "the Lord's Day," "the First Day of the Week"—As Commemorative Institutions, "the Lord's Supper" is Something Possessing Religious Significance, a Distinctive New Testament Ordinance Commemorating the Death of Christ; while "the Lord's Day" was, by the Apostolic Church, Devoted to Religious Worship, in Commemoration of the Greater Fact of the Resurrection—Many Scriptural Examples and Proofs—Many Historical Examples, Dating from the First Christian Centuries. PERVERSION OF NEW TESTAMENT CEREMONIES: Such Things Never Called "Holy" in the Bible—New Testament Holiness Pertains to People, Not to Days or Things—Originally "the

CHAPTER XXIII

THE KINGDOM OF GOD

DOCTRINE OF FINAL THINGS

CHAPTER XXIV

SECOND COMING OF CHRIST

CHAPTER XXV

DESTINY OF THE WICKED

CHAPTER XXVI

OUR ETERNAL HOME

PRELIMINARY.

DIVINE AUTHORITY OF THE SCRIPTURES.

The special design of this work, indicated by the title, does not necessitate an inquiry into the fact of revelation itself, but the divine authority of the Holy Scriptures is accepted presumptively as the everlasting basis of all doctrinal truth. But since the subjects considered are of such vast importance, involving the deepest and holiest interests of the human race, here and hereafter, it is fitting that we should at the outset consider briefly the character of those Scriptures to which we appeal as to the court of last resort.

The truth of the Bible is determined by its nature; while its authority is dependent altogether upon its source. The more carefully and reverentially we study the sacred Scriptures, the more deeply are we impressed with the fact that they have proceeded from one source. True, the Bible consists of many books penned by various writers during a period of fifteen hundred years, but there exists throughout a grand unity and harmony that suggests the idea of divine inspiration. The writers themselves did not claim to be the authors of the messages they delivered; but, as the apostle Peter affirms, they "spake as they were moved by the Holy Ghost" (2 Pet. 1: 21). Their writings encompass a variety of subjects— the origin of things, war, prophecy, biography, law and government, moral philosophy, ethics, theology and poetry; still there exists a remarkable harmony of sentiment and teaching such as can be found in no other col-

lection of books on the earth. Thousands of able scholars have written on all of these subjects; but if the best
of such works, by a score of different authors, were
brought together in one volume, what an assemblage of
perversions and contradictions we would have!

While visiting the splendid cathedral at Milan, Italy,
I was deeply impressed with the marvelous perfection
of its architectural design and the beauty of its execution. Standing on the roof, in the midst of a forest of
glistening marble spires, bearing hundreds of elegantly
carved statues, I was made to realize what wonders can
be accomplished by men who work in accordance with
a fixed plan. This structure was begun in A. D. 1386—
more than five hundred years ago—and it is still incomplete; thousands of workmen have been employed in its
construction; and its grandeur has excited the admiration
of the world. Could I believe that this was the result of
mere accident or chance? Impossible! To behold it
is to be convinced, without being told, that one mind
planned it all.

We witness the performance of an orchestra. The
strains and melodies delight us; the modulations and
the variations draw out the finer feelings of the soul; and
our enjoyment is supreme when the low, soft minor movement turns into the major and ends in one grand, sweeping majestic climax. But we know that this is the product
of the creative genius of a single composer, while the
beauty of its execution depends upon the ability of the
director and the skill of those assigned to the different
parts.

So with God's Word. Viewed as a unified structure,
it is the most perfect and magnificent that has ever been

reared, thus showing the hand of the one divine Master
Builder. As music, it is the grandest that has ever fallen
upon human ears. It forms the cradle lullaby of innocent
childhood, bursts forth spontaneously in the happiness of
youth, or modulates into a minor movement in seasons of
affliction and sorrow. Music for the young and for the
old, for the free and for the care-worn; for the strong
and for the dying. God the composer; his Spirit the
director of the orchestra.

The revelation that the Scripture makes of the one
true and living God testifies as to its source. While the
idea of a Supreme Being is universal, his nature, and
his relations with men, are necessarily subjects of
revelation. The history of all heathenism fails to dis-
close in one single instance the conception of a pure,
holy God, kindly disposed toward the human race. On
the other hand, the mythologies of all such nations abound
with the most shocking and disgusting details of the
actions of the gods whom they worshiped. The history
of the Hebrew people given in the Bible shows that
they, like other nations, were prone to evil of the deepest
and blackest type. Whence, then, did they derive the
idea of a God of holiness, a God who was opposed to all
of their evils, and yet gracious and full of mercy? When
even Athens was devoting thousands of her choicest
women to the lustful service of Venus; when Corinth,
according to Strabo, had one thousand sacred prostitutes
in one temple,—who, I ask, taught the Israelites the
principle of holiness and gave them such exalted moral
conceptions of God?

The special messengers of God by whom the Bible was
written were given the power of performing miracles,

by which their inspiration was attested and their messages made authoritative; but the *"more sure word of PROPHECY"* (2 Pet. 1:19) furnishes the greatest external proof of its inspiration. To this more than to anything else Christ and the apostles made their constant appeal. Matthew, narrating the deeds of the Savior, gives us the standing phrase, "that it might be fulfilled which was spoken by the prophet"; while Peter affirms, in words unmistakable, that the "holy men of God spake as they were moved by the Holy Ghost" (2 Pet. 1:21). From these facts Paul adduces his conclusion relative to the authority of the Bible, in these words: "All Scripture is given by inspiration of God, and is profitable for doctrine, for reproof, for correction, for instruction in righteousness" (2 Tim. 3:16).

Christianity is the only religion that has ever dared to base itself on prophecy, contented to stand or fall with its exact fulfilment. It is true that some heathen nations had oracles which they sometimes consulted in regard to the future, but the utterances of these oracles were so ambiguous and uncertain, so easily convicted of downright hypocrisy and deceit, that they are not worthy of comparison with the sublime prophecies of the Bible. Their construction was made to agree with whichever turn events might take. To illustrate: When Constantine was marching toward Rome, leading his victorious army, Maxentius, who was in command of the Eternal City, consulted the sibylline books as to the result of the impending conflict. He received this certain answer: "On that day the enemy of Rome will perish." Assured by this statement, Maxentius led his forces out to the conflict on the banks of the Tiber, but he was com-

pletely everwhelmed and in attempting to flee back into
the city was crowded off the Milvian bridge into the
river and drowned by the weight of his own armor. But
this result did not invalidate the ambiguous oracle; for
whichever way the event turned, it could be claimed that
the enemy of Rome had perished. So also when Croesus,
king of the Lydians, consulted the Delphian oracle as
to whether he should proceed in war against Cyrus, king
of Persia, he received the encouraging response, "You
will destroy a great empire"; he did, but it was his own.

I can not, in the space at my disposal, refer to the thousand examples of prophetic utterances recorded in the Bible, but even an infidel can see at least many of them are
not ambiguous or uncertain sayings. So many details
are given that the predictions are forever removed from
the category of mere human guess-work. One man has
said that it requires no divine foresight to predict that
a certain person will die; but if you add to this announcement the statement that his death will be occasioned by
a certain disease and will take place on a particular day,
this combination of circumstances removes it entirely
from the scope of human foresight. Now, the prophecy
of Daniel recorded in chap. 8: 1-12 contains at least
fifteen points of exact identification with the subsequent
historical facts which it portrays. When Elijah stood
before King Ahab and announced the destruction of his
entire household and declared, "The dogs shall eat Jeze-
bel by the wall of Jezreel," there was nothing ambiguous
in his prediction.

The marvelous prophecy which Christ made concerning the destruction of Jerusalem and the ruin and dis-

persal of the Jews has been fulfilled with such un-
questionable exactness that the boldest infidels dare not
deny the agreement; consequently they are forced to
shift to the ridiculous and unproved position that these
words were not spoken by Christ, but were written by
some one after the events themselves occurred. How
strange that Porphry and Celsus, those early opponents
of the Christian religion, did not think to employ this in-
genius device in order to break the power of the words of
Christ! But perhaps the events themselves were not far
enough removed from the knowledge of the people to
allow such a wretched perversion of the facts.

The fifty-third chapter of Isaiah describes Christ's
crucifixion and atonement work with such accuracy of
detail that the inspiration of the prophet is assured. As
there was no possibility of showing that this was written
after the crucifixion occurred, Bolingbroke went to the
absurd extreme of claiming that Christ, having read
this saying of Isaiah's, *brought on his own crucifixion* in
order to strengthen his cause by giving his disciples an
appeal to the supposed prophecy! One would think
that Bolingbroke would have known that deceivers and
hypocrites are not quite so anxious to die. Even these
infidels themselves are well contented to rest in the
shadow of our meeting-houses, and never trust their
precious heads among the cannibals where the consecrated
missionaries go!

The internal proofs of the divine authorship of the
Bible are many, but I shall refer only to a few.

Its moral beauty is everywhere evident. While it describes the lowest forms of sin in the plainest language,
still they are named only to be condemned. No un-

prejudiced person can read the sacred pages without realizing that the Book stands for all that is good in man, and is forever opposed to all that is evil. It pronounces the last word on moral character. So keenly is this felt that at the present day the leaders of heathen religions are attempting to adjust their moral standards to those of Christianity. This book, coming from heaven, has given the correct standard, and this is all summed up in the words of our Lord Jesus Christ, who "spake as never man spake." The mind of man has never conceived anything so noble, so elevating, so inspiring, so grand, as that one sermon on the mount. Search through all the religions of the ages, glean out every choice moral precept and delineation of human character and conduct, place the findings together in one collection, and they will bear a most wretched comparison with the divine beauty and the infinite wisdom here expressed by the Christ of the Bible. Here is given the spiritual essence of the law and the prophets. Here truth is pressed homeward to the human soul, and character and conduct are defined by the secret springs and motives of the heart. Here all pride, hypocrisy, and self-seeking stand condemned; while all the finer virtues of which the soul is capable find free expression and infinite encouragement in the incomparable Beatitudes. Here a restraining influence is brought to bear upon wicked men by the solemn assertion of a future state of punishment in hell; while the righteous are assured of a great reward in heaven.

Another beautiful feature of God's Word *is its simplicity*. While it contains the choicest wisdom of the ages, still it meets the wants and requirements of the unlearned and illiterate. "The wayfaring men though fools shall not err therein." The way of salvation, though straight and narrow, is not hidden, and there is nothing to hinder any seeking soul from coming in contact with its Maker. Blessed thought!

But one of the clearest proofs that the Bible is the word of God is the fact that *it now transforms human character* and accomplishes the regeneration of society. The promises of salvation and deliverance contained in its pages are, in millions of instances, proved to be a living reality. The words of men have never accomplished such results as these. Aristotle wrote on the "Principles of Ethics," but who has ever heard of his works' transforming the nature of a single man from sin to holiness? Thomas Paine wrote the book "Age of Reason"; has it ever been known to reclaim a man from drunkenness and debauchery, as does the holy Book which it so vilely derides? BUT THIS BOOK IS THE BOOK OF GOD. It bears on its face the stamp of divine inspiration and *performs the work of God in the world.* Millions of redeemed men and women have given their lives in its defense, and today it is loved and reverenced by the worthy ones of earth. It is the inspiration of the world's best literature, which in countless thousands of volumes have radiated from it, as the common center of everything that is lofty, upright, and good.

Furthermore, *it claims divine inspiration.* "Hear the word of the Lord," cries Isaiah. "Give ear, O earth, for the Lord hath spoken" (chap. 1:10, 2). "The Lord said unto me," are the words of Jeremiah (chap. 1:7). And we read that "the word of the Lord came expressly unto Ezekiel" (chap. 1:3). Jesus says concerning Moses,

"He wrote of me" (John 5:46). And again, "Search the Scriptures; for in them ye think ye have eternal life: and they are they which testify of me" (John 5:39). "If they hear not Moses and the prophets, neither will they be persuaded, though one rose from the dead" (Luke 16:31). "In the volume of the book it is written of me" (Heb. 10:7). "A more sure word of prophecy" (2 Pet. 1:19). "Holy men of God spake as they were moved by the Holy Ghost" (2 Pet. 1:21).

The apostles themselves were specially inspired by the Spirit, for Jesus said to them, "Take no thought how or what ye shall speak .... for it is not ye that speak, but the Spirit of your Father that speaketh in you" (Matt. 10:19, 20). Paul commended the Thessalonian brethren because they received his preaching, "not as the word of men, but as it is in truth, *the word of God*" (1 Thess. 2:13); and to the Corinthians he said, "The things that I write unto you are the commandments of the Lord" (1 Cor. 14:37). Peter refers to the epistles of Paul and classes them with "the other Scriptures" (2 Pet. 3:15, 16). Paul declares that "All Scripture is given by inspiration of God, and is profitable for doctrine" (2 Tim. 3:16).

The Bible emerges from every legitimate test, external and internal, with glories undimmed, and bearing every evidence that it is indeed the word of God. And since it is clearly proved to be the divine Word, its absolute authority is forever settled.

> "O precious Bible! burning words from heaven,
> We'll ever cherish thee in our heart.
> Sweet is the counsel by thy pages given;
> On life's dark ocean, our only chart.

"O precious volume! only in thy pages
We read the duty of all our race;
Only thy sunbeams, shining through the ages,
Reveal the wonders of saving grace."

The sweet words of Jesus that our lips were taught to frame in childhood's early morning shall cling to us forever. In the darkest hours of trial and affliction they furnish an unfailing light that leads to the brightness of a better day. When the pathway of life is pleasantest and happiest, our raptured spirits find joyous expression in thankful praise in the language of the living Word. And when the darkness of the long night gathers around us and we are about to begin our untried journey to the future land—bring us the Bible, blessed Bible! It alone can give us the clear light of immortality. "I have esteemed the words of his mouth more than my necessary food" (Job 23:12).

"Forever, O Lord, thy word is settled in heaven."

CONCERNING GOD.

CHAPTER I.

DOCTRINE OF GOD.

By the term "God" we mean a perfect, conscious, intelligent Being existing from eternity, the Cause of all created things. This idea seems so natural that the majority of men accept it as self-evident truth, without hesitating to give it any particular thought. But when able thinkers, as Kant, assert that God can not be known by means of pure reason, that he is not immediately discernible by the physical senses, we are led to reflect on the subject. If it be true that God can not be discovered by the five physical senses, we assert that there is in man a sort of sixth sense—an internal consciousness, a spiritual insight—that is able to discern our Creator, to realize his presence, and to feel his spiritual power.

But aside from this, God has not left us without a witness whose testimony is sufficiently clear to satisfy all reasonable minds that there is a God. The simple argument is this: We are conscious that we exist and that we are something. Of this there can be no doubt. We are also certain that from nothing nothing comes; therefore we know that something has existed from eternity; for everything that has not existed from eternity had a beginning and must have been produced by something else. We are also aware that anything that has been produced by another has derived all of its powers from that source; hence the eternal Being must be the most powerful. Furthermore, man possesses moral consciousness, knowledge and intelligence, from which fact we are certain that the First Cause of our existence was from eternity a moral, knowing being. Only "the fool hath said in his heart, There is no God"; and he can say this only in his heart, not with the full consent of his mind; for if it be difficult to prove by means of the reason that there is a God, it is altogether impossible to prove by this means that there is no God. The wish is the father of the thought; for such sinful characters would be happy indeed if it were true that there is really no God.

The writers of the Scriptures do not argue the existence of God. The first chapter of the Bible opens with the words "In the beginning God," and everywhere his being is assumed. But the Scriptures contain the revelation that he has made of his own nature and attributes. These attributes are so well understood and so generally acknowledged that I will merely refer to them, not giving the multitude of texts by which they are set forth in the Scriptures.

HIS ATTRIBUTES.

1. *Self-Existence.* "The Father hath life in himself" (John 5:26). "For with thee is the fountain of life" (Psa. 36:9). He is underived and inexhaustible.

2. *Eternity.* "Before the mountains were brought forth, or ever thou hadst formed the earth and the world, even from everlasting to everlasting, thou art God" (Psa. 90:2). The high and lofty One "inhabiteth eternity" (Isa. 57:15).

3. *Spirituality.* "God is a Spirit" (John 4:24).

4. *Unity*—the One true and living God. "There is no God else beside me" (Isa. 45:21).

5. *Immutability.* "I am the Lord, I change not" (Mal. 3:6). "The Father of lights, with whom is no variableness, neither shadow of turning" (Jas. 1:17).

6. *Omnipresence;* that is, he is everywhere present. "Can any hide himself in secret places that I shall not see him? saith the Lord. Do not I fill heaven and earth?" (Jer. 23:24). He is "not far from every one of us: for in him we live, and move, and have our being" (Acts 17:27, 28).

7. *Omniscience;* that is, he is all-knowing. "Known unto God are all his works from the beginning of the world" (Acts 15:18). "Neither is there any creature that is not manifest in his sight: but all things are naked and open unto the eyes of him with whom we have to do (Heb. 4:13).

8. *Omnipotence;* that is, he has unlimited and universal power. "His eternal power and Godhead" (Rom. 1:20). "With God all things are possible" (Matt. 19:26.)

9. *Wisdom.* "Blessed be the name of God forever and ever: for wisdom and might are his" (Dan. 2:20). "Oh the depth of the riches both of the wisdom and knowledge of God! How unsearchable are his judgments, and his ways past finding out!" (Rom. 11:33).

10. *Holiness and truth.* "I am holy" (1 Pet. 1:16). "Thou art of purer eyes than to behold evil, and canst not look on iniquity" (Hab. 1:13). "God that can not lie" (Tit. 1:2).

11. *Justice.* God demands righteousness of all his intelligent creatures, and deals righteously with them. "Justice and judgment are the habitation of thy throne" (Psa. 89:14). "In every nation he that feareth him

and worketh righteousness is accepted with him" (Acts 10:35).

12. *Goodness*—benevolence, love, mercy, and grace. "The goodness of God" (Rom. 2:4). "God so loved the world" (John 3:16). "His mercy endureth forever" (Psa. 136:26). "The God of all grace" (1 Pet. 5:10).

13. *Faithfulness.* "God is faithful" (2 Thess. 3:3). Sarah "judged him faithful who had promised" (Heb. 11:11).

THE TRINITY.

The theological term "trinity" signifies the union of three Persons—Father, Son, and Holy Spirit—in the Godhead. This subject was a most fruitful source of theological controversy in the past ages, and even at the present day there are not wanting professed Christians who deny it altogether. Our present limits preclude an extended discussion of the matter, but I will bring forward a few points in its favor.

The greatest controversy concerning the Trinity began to rage during the third century and continued until the Council of Nice, A. D. 325. The special emphasis of the Alexandrine, or Greek, Fathers during this period was laid on the doctrine of the incarnation of Christ; and this, of course, precipitated a warm controversy as to his nature. In the beginning of the fourth century the Unitarians were led by an able man named Arius, who contended that Christ, being the Son of God, was not eternal, but was a creation of God, the highest, however, of all created beings. This doctrine spread with great rapidity. When Constantine ascended the imperial throne and made Christianity the religion of the Roman state, he convoked the First General Council, at Nice, for the purpose of settling this great controversy. Athanaius, or Alexandrina, was the leader of those who contended for the essential divinity of Christ and his equality with the Father. This party was successful in the council, thus preserving to the world the idea of God triple in his unity, and one in his triplicity. The rejected doctrine is generally known as the Arian heresy.

To many this doctrine of the Trinity appears like an unimportant matter, but in reality it is not. If Christ, with his marvelous perfections, be not truly God, then instead of bringing man to God, he has only succeeded in revealing to us the impassable gulf that exists between us and the divine One; but if he truly is "God manifest in the flesh" for the purpose of transforming sinful man into his own image, then we are assured of our moral and spiritual correspondence and communion with the Father in heaven.

But the real cause of the rejection of this doctrine by many is its mystery or incomprehensibleness. But what of that? No one has yet shown that it involves a real contradiction. What demonstrated truth does it oppose? Are we not surrounded by many things that are in their real nature mysterious? Even man himself is a sort of trinity, possessing intellect, sensibility, and will; and yet these distinct elements are in some unexplained and perhaps unexplainable, manner wondrously blended in an undoubted unity. While this does not explain nor prove the exact nature of the Godhead, yet it should lead us to expect in the Infinite One a greater degree of mystery than exists within ourselves, and should caution us against rejecting everything that can not be brought down to the level of the finite mind.

Since the exact manner of existence in the Godhead manifestly lies above and beyond the range of mortal mind, the basis of our theology respecting God should be laid solely in what is revealed to us in the Holy Scriptures. And if we appeal directly to them, we find it is impossible to avoid the doctrine of the Trinity taught therein without doing great violence to scores of plain texts bearing on the subject. The course of argument is as follows:

1. The Father, the Son, and the Holy Spirit are represented as special persons distinct from each other.

2. They are classed together, separate from all other beings.

3. Divine titles are applied to each.

4. Divine attributes are ascribed to each.

5. Divine works are attributed to each.

Yet there is only one God.

THE FATHER.

The word "Father," referring to the Godhead, is used in Scripture in a twofold sense. First, it is applied to God without any personal distinctions. "Blessed be thou, Lord God of Israel our Father" (1 Chron. 29: 10). "Thou art my Father, my God, and the rock of my salvation" (Psa. 89: 26). So also 2 Chron. 6: 18; John 4: 21, 23, 24, etc. Second, it is applied to God in contrast with Christ, who is thus distinguished as Son in his office of Redeemer. "All things are delivered unto me of my Father: and no man knoweth the Son but the Father" (Matt. 11: 27). Jesus answered them, "My Father worketh hitherto, and I work" (John 5: 17).

So also Acts 2:33; Rom. 15:6; Gal. 1:1-4; and numerous other texts.

THE SON.

The passages already cited show that Christ is a person distinct from the Father. The following facts prove Scripturally that he is divine—equal with the Father himself:

I. DIVINE TITLES ARE APPLIED TO HIM THE SAME AS TO THE FATHER.

"Unto the Son he saith, Thy throne, O God, is forever and ever: a scepter of righteousness is the scepter of thy kingdom" (Heb. 1:8). "For unto us a child is born, unto us a son is given; and the government shall be upon his shoulders: and his name shall be called Wonderful, Counselor, The mighty God, The everlasting Father, The Prince of Peace" (Isa. 9:6). "Behold, a virgin shall be with child, and shall bring forth a son, and they shall call his name Emmanuel, which being interpreted is, God with us" (Matt. 1:23). "In the beginning . . . the Word was God." "And the Word was made flesh, and dwelt among us" (John 1:1, 14). "The church of God, which he has purchased with his own blood" (Acts 20:28). So also John 20:28; Rom. 9:5; Phil. 2:6; Col. 2:9; Tit. 1:3; 1 John 5:20; Rev. 17:14, etc.

II. DIVINE ATTRIBUTES ARE ASCRIBED TO HIM.

1. *Preexistence, or eternity.* "Before Abraham was, I am" (John 8:58). "The second man is the Lord from heaven" (1 Cor. 15:47). "That which was from the beginning" (1 John 1:1). "Who, being in the form of God, thought it not robbery to be equal with God: but made himself of no reputation, and took upon him the

form of a servant, and was made in the likeness of men"
(Phil. 2: 6, 7). "O Father, glorify thou me with thine
own self with the glory which I had with thee before the
world was" (John 17: 5). "And he is before all things"
(Col. 1: 17). "But thou, Bethlehem Ephratah, though
thou be little among the thousands of Judea, yet out of
thee shall he come forth unto me that is to be ruler in
Israel; whose goings forth have been from of old, from
everlasting [from the days of eternity, margin]" (Micah
5: 2). Nothing can be plainer than this last statement,
that the Bethlehem babe preexisted, even from the days
of eternity—coexistent with God himself. So also in
the Revelation he is representd by that symbolic title
signifying eternity, "Alpha and Omega." "I Jesus have
sent mine angels to testify unto you these things. I am
Alpha and Omega, the beginning and the end, the first
and the last" (Rev. 22: 16, 13). Therefore the statement that Christ is the Son of God does not signify that
he originated from the Father in the ages past, but
should be interpreted with reference to his miraculous
Virgin birth, thus denoting God's special relation to him
in his office-work as the world's Redeemer.

2. *Omnipotence.* "The government shall be upon his
shoulder" (Isa. 9: 6). "Jesus came and spake unto
them, saying, All power is given unto me in heaven and
in earth" (Matt. 28: 18). "I am the resurrection and
the life" (John 11: 25). "He is able even to subdue
all things unto himself" (Phil. 3: 21). He "is the head
of all principality and power" (Col. 2: 10). So also
John 10: 17, 18; Heb. 1: 3; 2 Tim. 1: 10, etc.

3. *Omnipresence.* "Where two or three are gathered
together in my name, there am I in the midst of them"

(Matt. 18:20). "Lo, I am with you alway, even unto
the end of the world" (Matt. 28:20).

4. *Omniscience.* "He knew all men, and needed not
that any should testify of man; for he knew what was
in man" (John 2:24, 25). "Lord, thou knowest all
things" (John 21:17). "Thou, Lord, which knowest
the hearts of all men" (Acts 1:24). "In whom are hid
all the treasures of wisdom and knowledge" (Col. 2:3)
Matt. 11:27; Rev. 2:23.

Also, holiness, truth, justice, goodness, faithfulness,
etc., are attributes of Christ.

III. DIVINE WORKS ARE ASCRIBED TO HIM.

1. *Creation.* "God .... hath in these last days spoken
unto us by his Son .... by whom also he made the
worlds" (Heb. 1:1, 2). "And thou, Lord, in the beginning hast laid the foundation of the earth; and the heavens are the works of thine hands" (verse 10). "All
things were made by him; and without him was not anything made that was made" (John 1:3). "For by him
were all things created, that are in heaven, and that are
in earth, visible and invisible .... all things were
created by him and for him" (Col. 1:16, etc.).

2. *Redemption.* "In whom we have redemption
through his blood, the forgiveness of sins" (Eph. 1:7).
"He entered in once into the holy place having obtained
eternal redemption for us" (Heb. 9:12). This phase
will be more fully considered hereafter.

IV. HE IS PREEMINENT—ABOVE ALL THINGS.

"He is Lord of all" (Acts 10:36). "Lord both of
the dead and living" (Rom. 14:9). "God hath ....

given him a name which is above every name" (Phil. 2:9). "He is the head of the body, the church . . . . that in all things he might have the preeminence" (Col. 1:18). "Who is gone into heaven, and is on the right hand of God; angels and authorities and powers being made subject unto him" (1 Pet. 3:22, etc.).

V. HE IS A PROPER OBJECT OF DEVOTION AND WORSHIP.

While the Scriptures denounce idolatry and enjoin the worship of the one true and living God only, they set forth Christ as A PROPER OBJECT OF DEVOTION AND WORSHIP. "Let all the angels of God worship him" (Heb. 1:6). "All men should honor the Son, even as they honor the Father" (John 5:23). "And they worshiped him" (Luke 24:52). Saints "in every place call upon the name of Jesus Christ our Lord" (1 Cor. 1:2). "At the name of Jesus every knee should bow" (Phil. 2:10). So also Rev. 5:13; 2 Tim. 4:18; et al.

THE HOLY SPIRIT.

The Holy Spirit is also divine and is a distinct person from the Father and the Son. He is called the "Spirit of God" (Rom. 8:9), because of his proceeding from God; (John 15:26) also the "Spirit of Christ" (Rom. 8:9), because he is sent to do the work of Christ.

I. HIS DIVINITY.

This is shown by many scriptures. "It is not ye that speak, but the Spirit of your Father which speaketh in you" (Matt. 10:20). Compare Ezek. 36:27 with Acts 2:17, 18. "Well spake the Holy Ghost by Esaias the prophet" (Acts 28:25). "As many as are led by the

Spirit of God they are the sons of God" (Rom. 8:14).
"Know ye not that ye are the temple of God, and that
the Spirit of God dwelleth in you?" (1 Cor. 3:16).
Eph. 1:13; et al.

II. HIS PERSONALITY.

The personality of the Holy Spirit is shown by the
following facts:

1. *He is associated with two other persons*—Father
and Son— *as their equal.* "In the name of the Father,
and of the Son, and of the Holy Ghost" (Matt. 28:19).

2. *The personal pronoun "he" is applied to him.*
"Howbeit when he, the Spirit of truth, is come, he will
guide you into all truth: for he shall not speak of himself; but whatsoever he shall hear, that shall he speak:
and he will show you things to come" (John 16:13).

3. *Personal acts are ascribed to him.* "He shall *teach
you* all things" (John 14:26). "He shall *testify* of me"
(John 15:26). "He will *guide you* into all truth"
(John 16:13). "The Holy Ghost *said*" (Acts 13:2).
"Being *sent forth* by the Holy Ghost" (verse 4).

4. *Particular attributes are ascribed to him.* For example: Knowledge, 1 Cor. 2:11; will, 1 Cor. 12:11;
power, Rom. 15:13.

III. HIS WORKS.

1. *In creation.* "In the beginning God created . . . .
and the Spirit of God moved upon the face of the waters"
(Gen. 1:1, 2). So also Job 33·4; 26:13; Psa. 104:30.

2. *In redemption.* "Salvation through sanctification
of the Spirit" (2 Thess. 2:13). God "giving them the
Holy Ghost . . . . purifying their hearts by faith" (Acts

15: 8, 9). "He saved us, by the washing of regeneration, and the renewing of the Holy Ghost" (Tit. 3: 5). So also 1 John 3: 24; Rom. 8: 9, 14, 16, etc.

The Father, the Son, and the Holy Spirit are classed together, separately from all other beings, as divine. "In the name of the Father, and of the Son, and of the Holy Ghost" (Matt. 28: 19). "The grace of the Lord Jesus Christ, and the love of God, and the communion of the Holy Ghost, be with you all" (2 Cor. 13: 14). Also Jude 20, 21; 1 Pet. 1: 2; Rom. 8: 14-17, etc.

GOD'S WORKS.

I. CREATION.

1. *Of angels.* "Bless the Lord, ye his angels, that excell in strength, ... harkening unto the voice of his word" (Psa. 103: 20). "Where wast thou when I laid the foundations of the earth . . . . When the morning stars sang together, and all the sons of God shouted for joy?" (Job 38: 4, 7). "His mighty angels" (2 Thess. 1: 7).

2. *Of the material universe.* "In the beginning God created the heaven and the earth" (Gen. 1: 1).

3. *Of man.* "So God created man in his own image" (Gen. 1: 27).

II. PROVIDENCE.

Having created all things, God now controls and conserves all things in his vast universe in accordance with his own will. His intelligent creatures are made the subjects of a moral providential government.

CONCERNING MAN.

CHAPTER II

THE NATURE OF MAN.

"What is man?" (Psa. 8:4). This is one of the greatest questions that has ever been asked. The Grecian sage whose maxim was, *"Know thyself,"* enjoined upon men a task well-nigh impossible. The problem of *man* is well stated in three questions: What am I? Whence came I? Whither am I going? To the first one of these questions partial answers at least have not been wanting; but the other two, touching man's origin and destiny, have always remained a profound mystery aside from the light thrown thereon by divine revelation.

Attempts have been made to account for man's origin by an ingenious theory of descent from lower animals, but this hypothesis utterly fails to satisfy the mind, from the fact that it does not account for the First Cause of all known things. Furthermore, it is certain that whatever is evolved must in the first place have been *involved;* that is, the highest degree of development of which any object is capable was inherent in that object in its most undeveloped form. Thus, the nature and peculiar properties of the fully developed oak-tree were all present in some marvelous manner in the acorn from which it grew. To illustrate further: If it could be really shown that man has descended from the frog by a process of development, it would be certain that that primitive frog possessed in an undeveloped form all the marvelous faculties to be manifested later in a Newton, a Humboldt, or a Bacon. Mere development can not create nor develop new properties. So when the evolutionists affirm that man has descended from the moneron or some other simple form of primitive life, the mystery of the true origin of man's nature is not even touched; for whence did this moneron derive those powers which are capable of such a high degree of development and perfection? Simply to throw these things a few million years further back does not account for the origin of anything, hence is no explanation whatever. Therefore man's origin, as well as his destiny, is a subject of revelation.

ORIGIN.

Turning to the Bible, we find the only satisfactory account of man's beginning. "So God created man in his own image . . . . male and female created he them" (Gen. 1:27). From this original pair, Adam and Eve, the entire human race has sprung; for Eve is declared to be "the mother of all living" (Gen. 3:20). The Bible writers uniformly acknowledge this common origin of man. Thus, Malachi asks, "Have we not all one Father? hath not one God created us?" (Mal. 2:10). Paul affirms that God "hath made of one blood all nations of men . . . . for we are also his offspring" (Acts 17:26, 28).

The unity of the human race has been acknowledged also by the greatest scientists and thinkers, Prof. Owen, Cuvier, Max Muller, Darwin, Locke, Humboldt, Chas. Bell, Buckland, Bunsen, Lord Brougham, James McIntosh, and others. This fact is important, for upon the unity of the race is based the one universal plan of redemption.

From whatever standpoint we view man, he appears

IN GOD'S IMAGE.

as the special workmanship of God, the highest type of
earthly creatures, made "in the image of God," to use
the language of the writer of Genesis. This expression,
"image of God," is comprehensive. It implies that
special characteristics of the Divine One not found in
other earthly creatures are made a part of man's being.
Thus, man *is a moral being.* In his normal state his
actions are not determined by mere instinct or expediency, or self-interest, but they are regarded as possessing in their own nature a clearly defined rightness or
wrongness. In this moral discrimination man is like
God. In connection with this, he possesses *freedom of
will,* so that he can of his own volition decide his course
of conduct. He is also *an intellectual being,* possessing
a mind capable of almost infinite development, one which
easily grasps the mightiest problems within the range
of finite environment. Man is also *a spiritual being,* a
being that naturally looks up to God, "the Father of
spirits," as its author, and holds sweet converse with its
Maker.

UNDER MORAL LAW.

As a moral and spiritual being in God's likeness, man
originally was of necessity in a state of holiness and
purity. According to the Word, he was placed under
moral law. To this day men everywhere are firm in the
conviction that they are the subjects of moral government, directly responsible to God. And this is also the
uniform teaching of the Scriptures. But the original
state of holiness was forfeited by sin; hence in this respect *and to this extent* the image of God was lost. In
the redemption of Christ, however, holiness is regained;

therefore we are restored to the image of God. "Lie not one to another, seeing that ye have put off the old man with his deeds; and have put on the new man, which is *renewed* in knowledge *after the image* of him that created him" (Col. 3: 9, 10). "That ye put off concerning the former conversation the old man . . . . and that ye put on the new man, which after God is created in *righteousness and true holiness*" (Eph. 4: 22-24).

A COMPOUND BEING.

The Scriptures represent man as a twofold, or dual, being, possessed of body and soul, or body and spirit. "Glorify God in your body and in your spirit" (1 Cor. 6: 20). "That she may be holy both in body and in spirit" (1 Cor. 7: 34). "His flesh upon him shall have pain, and his soul within him shall mourn" (Job 14: 22). "Though our outward man perish, yet the inward man is renewed day by day" (2 Cor. 4: 16).

The "outer man," or body, is mortal. "Your mortal body" (Rom. 6: 12). "Your mortal bodies" (Rom. 8: 11). The body was created in this mortal condition, as the following facts show: 1. It was made out of the dust of the earth (Gen. 2: 7). 2. It was given natural food to subsist upon (Gen. 1: 29). 3. Man was given natural work to perform (Gen. 2: 15). 4. Matrimony was instituted (Gen. 1: 27, 28). According to the words of Christ, marriage is an institution that does not pertain to angels nor to beings wholly immortal, such as we shall be after the resurrection (see Luke 20: 35, 36). 5. There was use for the tree of life (Gen. 3: 22). Had man been created immortal as to body, this tree of life would have been entirely useless.

But the crowning proof that man was originally mortal is the fact that he was "made" "a little lower than the angels" (Psa. 8:4, 5 with Heb. 2:6, 7). In what sense was man lower than the angels? Not morally or spiritually, for in these respects man was in God's image, and surely the angels are not higher than God is. What, then, does the expression mean? In Heb. 1:7 we read that God "maketh his angels *spirits*," that they are "all ministering spirits" (verse 14). Jesus plainly states that "a spirit hath not flesh and bones" (Luke 24:39). Therefore we conclude that man's inferiority to angels consists in his limitations due to a physical body, while the angels are wholly spirit-beings. That this inference is correct we can easily show by other scriptures. Paul asserts that in the resurrection-day "this mortal [body] must put on immortality" (1 Cor. 15:53); while Jesus says concerning his people in this "resurrection from the dead," "Neither can they die any more: *for they are equal unto the angels*" (Luke 20: 35, 36).

Now, according to the scripture cited in Psa. 8:4-8, man was "made" in this inferior condition at the time when he was given universal dominion over God's works, which shows clearly that his original condition physically was the same as now—not inherently immortal—and that no specific change took place in his bodily organism as a result of the fall. The foregoing points establish this point: it is simply unanswerable. The question now arises, Why, then, do the Bible writers state that death came upon mankind as a result of sin? The answer is simple. While man remained in the Garden of Eden

with free access to the tree of life, his continued existence without death was assured. And when, after the fall, the decree of death had been pronounced, this decree could be made effective only by depriving him of those privileges which had before sustained his life; therefore he was driven from the garden, "lest he put forth his hand, and take also of the tree of life, and eat, and live forever" (Gen 3:22). This decree did not make him mortal, for he was mortal already—taken from the ground: it did not change him from immortality to dust, but God recognized his natural condition in the words *"dust thou art."* The real sentence of God against man, resulting from the fall, is expressed in the remainder of the verse—*"Unto dust shalt thou return"* (Gen. 3:19). In other words, the curse placed upon man was not mortality, but *condemnation to the effects of mortality;* hence "by man came death."

Since the body of man is by nature mortal, we read that it can be "destroyed" (Job 19:26), "killed" (Matt. 10:28), it "perishes" (2 Cor. 4:16), and returns to the dust of the earth (Gen. 3:19).

But is this all there is of man? No! What saith the Scriptures? "Though our outward man perish, yet the inward man is renewed day by day" (2 Cor. 4:16). "There is a spirit in man" (Job 32:8). This soul, or spirit, is the creative work of God. "The souls which I have made" (Isa. 57:16). It is the Lord that "layeth the foundation of the earth, and *formeth the spirit of man within him"* (Zech. 12:1).

This is the specific sense in which God created man on the sixth day; for the physical substance out of which his body was formed was not created at that time, but it had been brought into existence previously. And for this reason the Almighty is termed "the God of the spirits of all flesh," which are made in his moral likeness (Num. 16:22), in contrast with the "fathers of our flesh" (Heb. 12:9). Our bodies partake of the nature of our earthly fathers, hence are subject to death and decay; while our spirits, made "in the image of God," partake of his essential nature, and "God is a Spirit"— "immortal, invisible" (1 Tim. 1:17). Therefore Jesus says plainly, "Fear not them which kill the body, but *are not able to kill the soul*" (Matt. 10:28). David affirms, "Your heart shall live forever" (Psa. 22:26).

In language still plainer the apostle Paul shows that the soul is in its own nature eternal. "Though our outward man perish, yet the inward man is renewed day by day . . . . While we look not at the things which are seen, but at the things which are not seen: for the things which are seen are temporal; but the things which are not seen *are eternal*" (2 Cor. 4:16-18). Language can not make the subject clearer. The very thing that he was talking about was the "outer man," in contrast with the "inner man"; and the "outer man," being one of the things which are seen, is "temporal"; while the "inner man," being "not seen," is "*eternal.*" And as if to make this truth still more emphatic, he says in the following verse: "For we know that if our earthly house of this tabernacle were dissolved, we have a building of God, an house not made with hands, eternal in the heavens" (chap. 5:1). "Therefore we are always confident, knowing that, whilst we are at home in the body, we are absent from the Lord . . . . We are confident, I say, and willing rather to be absent from the body, and to be present with the Lord" (verses 6, 8). So the "outer man" is the body that perishes; while the "inner man," the "eternal" man, is the "I" or "we" of our existence that is willing to depart from the earthly house or body, when it is "dissolved," and "to be present with the Lord."

This soul, or spirit, is the knowing, volitional, and responsible part of man. "For what man knoweth the things of a man, save the spirit of man which is in him? even so the things of God knoweth no man, but the Spirit of God" (1 Cor. 2:11). Just as the Spirit of God knows the things of God, so the spirit of man knows the things of man. "Shall I give my first-born for my transgression, the fruit of my body for the *sin of my soul?*" (Mic. 6:7). This text fixes responsibility upon the soul; and since the soul is the knowing, volitional part of man, it is the real man. In James 2:26 we read that "the body without the spirit is dead." The Scriptures represent the body as being only the instrument of the soul (see Rom. 6:12, 13). Every appeal that God makes to man is addressed to the real man—the soul.

This twofoldness of man Paul represented, in the scripture already cited, under the figure of a house and its occupant, thus showing their interdependence or relationship in the present state, wherein the spirit is in union with the natural body (2 Cor. 5:1-9). But he goes further and shows that the house is not indispensable to the existence of the occupant; that when it is "dissolved" the real man is "absent from the body" and "present with the Lord." In this scripture there are what may be termed two bodies, each the habitation of the soul. The first is the mortal body in which we now live, and "groan," while "desiring to be clothed upon with our house which is from heaven." The second house is the immortalized body that will be received at Christ's second coming, when "mortality shall be swallowed up of life." But Paul also speaks here of an interval between these two, when we shall exist *without a body;* for when this earthly house is "dissolved" in natural death, we shall be "absent from the body," and be "present with the Lord." Let materialists answer this question: When is that time that we shall be absent from our body to be present with the Lord? Will it be at natural death? Will it be at the time of the resurrection? When?

Peter also describes the present union with the natural body and the separation at death, under the same figure. "As long as I am in this tabernacle . . . . knowing that shortly I must put off this my tabernacle" (2 Pet. 1: 13, 14). Therefore the soul can exist while separated from the body—"absent from the body," but "present with the Lord."

Again, in 2 Cor. 12: 2-4 he says: "I knew a man in Christ above fourteen years ago (whether in the body, I can not tell; or whether out of the body, I can not tell: God knoweth . . . . How that he was caught up into paradise, and heard unspeakable words, which it is not lawful for a man to utter." It is sometimes affirmed that a man is nothing without his body, but it is evident from this text that Paul had no such belief; for here he describes one who was caught up to paradise, and there saw and heard, and understood certain things; yet he did not know whether the person was in the body or out of the body at that time. Paul believed that man is a dual being; that man can be separated from his body, and still be a seeing, knowing, thinking creature. What can materialists, who deny the distinct essence of the human soul, say in regard to this? Nothing, except to charge the apostle with ignorance on the subject.

Again, he says: "For me to live is Christ, and to die is gain . . . . For I am in a strait betwixt two, having a desire to depart, and to be with Christ; which is far better: nevertheless to abide in the flesh is more needful for you" (Phil. 1:21-24). No amount of human reasoning can evade the plain statement here that to die meant, to the apostle, to leave the flesh, to "depart and be with Christ."

Further, in Jesus' account of Lazarus and the rich man as recorded in Luke 16, we have this same doctrine of the survival of the spirit after death. Lazarus "died, and was carried by the angels into Abraham's bosom: the rich man also died, and was buried; and in hell he lifted up his eyes, being in torments," etc. At this time the rich man had five brethren still living upon the earth (verses 28-31). It is useless to attempt to evade the force of this scripture by asserting, as do some, that it is "only a parable." It is not so stated. *"There was a certain rich man . . . .and there was a certain beggar, named Lazarus"* (verses 19, 20). However, we have in the Gospels an account of more than thirty parables delivered by Christ, and *every one of them is based upon truth.* Now, if it be not possible for men to die and enter into a state of trouble and torment while they have brethren yet living on the earth, why should Christ invent such a misleading story as this? Some assert that the people whom Christ addressed believed in such lies and that therefore he accommodated himself to them! Strange accommodation! Why, then do we not find such convenient accommodation on other occasions? To the Sadducees, who denied the separate and distinct existence of the human spirit (Acts 23:8), also the doctrine of the resurrection, Christ said, "Ye do err, not knowing the Scriptures, nor the power of God" (Matt. 22:29). Instead of accommodating his teaching to that which was false, he said, "Woe unto you, scribes and Pharisees, hypocrites!"

When Christ took Peter, James, and John up into a mount and was transfigured before them, we are told that "there appeared unto them Moses and Elias talking with him" (Matt. 17:1-3). While the Bible records that Elias was translated, it also states that Moses "died in the land of Moab" and was 'buried in a valley' (Deut. 34:5, 6). Now, how did it happen that Moses appeared here on the mount? He had not been resurrected from the dead into this glorified state, for the Scriptures declare that Christ was the first one to receive this change. Some people who had recently died were restored to life before this time, but such was only a restoration of the natural, corruptible body *on the earth,* and these persons were subject to death again. But the true "resurrection from the dead," which places men in an incorruptible state, is different from this. Therefore Christ was the "first-begotten of the dead" (Rev. 1:5); "the first-born from the dead" (Col. 1:18); "the first-fruits of them that slept" (1 Cor. 15:20). Yea, Paul argues that according to the prophets and the writings of Moses himself, "Christ should suffer, and that HE *should be the first that should rise from the dead"* (Acts 26:22, 23).

But this transfiguration-scene was before the death and resurrection of Christ; therefore the decomposed body of Moses had not been brought forth from the dead. This fact, that Moses appeared on the mount of transfiguration hundreds of years after his death, shows clearly that his soul was not involved in the ruin of his body.

Jesus taught that the ancient prophets were still living, in the words, "I am the God of Abraham, and the God of Isaac, and the God of Jacob. God is not the God of the dead, but of the living" (Matt. 22:32). The Sadducees to whom these words were addressed denied both the spirit of man and his resurrection (Acts 23:8); while Christ, by declaring that these patriarchs were still living, taught the doctrine of the spirit and its survival, which fact assured their final resurrection; for without the survival of the spirit there could not be a resurrection, as I will clearly demonstrate in Chapter XXIV of the present work.

The apostle John in apocalyptic vision saw disembodied souls. "I saw under the altar the souls of them that were slain for the word of God . . . . and they cried with a loud voice, saying, How long, O Lord, holy and true, dost thou not judge and avenge our blood on them that dwell on the earth" (Rev. 6:9, 10). See also Rev. 20:4.

Natural death is the separation of body and spirit. To the dying thief Christ said, "Today shalt thou be with me in paradise" and in his last moment cried out, "Father, into thy hands I commend my spirit" (Luke 23:43, 46). The dying Stephen also said, "Lord Jesus, receive my spirit" (Acts 7:59). This doctrine of the

survival of the spirit is found throughout the Bible.
"And it came to pass, as her soul was in departing (for
she died)" (Gen. 35: 18). The death of Rachel, then,
was the departure of her spirit from the body. "Fear
not them which kill the body, but are not able to kill the
soul" (Matt. 10: 28). "Though I walk through the
valley of the shadow of death, I will fear no evil: for
thou art with me" (Psa. 23: 4). To the Psalmist death
was not a stopping-place, the end of conscious existence;
for he describes his relation with it as one of motion or
travel—"*I walk through.*" He was firm in the doctrine
of the survival of the spirit. He says in another place,
"The days of our years are threescore years and ten . . . .
it is soon cut off, *and WE fly away*" (Psa. 90: 10). But
where do WE go at death? Let the Word of God answer
—"Then shall the dust return to the earth as it was: and
the spirit shall return unto God who gave it" (Eccl. 12:
7). "Man goeth to his long home, and the mourners go
about the streets" (verse 5). "For me to live is Christ,
and to die is gain . . . . For I am in a strait betwixt two,
having a desire to depart, and to be with Christ, which is
far better" (Phil. 1: 21, 23). "To be absent from the
body, and to be present with the Lord" (2 Cor. 5: 8).
"Let God be true, but every man a liar" (Rom. 3: 4).

The dying testimonies of thousands of saints confirm
the doctrine of the Scriptures on this point—that at
death the soul takes its departure from the body to be in
a more sacred nearness with the Lord. In the most
solemn hour of life this truth is so firmly stamped upon
the heart that it finds expression in language unmistakable.

Now what can be brought against this solid array of

divine truth as to the dual nature of man? Nothing except a few obscure texts which generally refer to some
other subject.

OBJECTIONS CONSIDERED.

The strongest text that can be found is Eccl. 9:5—
"The dead know not anything." True, that part of man
which dies and goes into the grave knows nothing; but
what about that part of his being which flies away at
death, "returns to God who gave it," rests "with Christ,
which is far better," and is "eternal" (2 Cor. 4:18)?
This statement that the dead know not anything, however,
is qualified in the following verse by the words *"anything
that is done under the sun."* This agrees perfectly with
certain parallel expressions made in the Bible. For
example: 2 Sam. 15:11—"And with Absalom went two
hundred men out of Jerusalem, that were called; and
they went in their simplicity, and they *knew not anything"* This texts does not signify that they knew absolutely nothing, but simply indicates that they were altogether ignorant concerning the particular thing under
consideration—Absalom's conspiracy. So also 1 Sam.
20:39—"But the lad *knew not anything;* only Jonathan
and David knew the matter." So also Paul says concerning the false teacher, "He is proud, *knowing nothing"*
(1 Tim. 6:4).

So even if it be contended that the word "dead" in
Eccl. 9:5 refers to the departed spirit, as well as to the
body, the text can not signify more than this: that they
have no part in, or knowledge of, the works of man that
are being performed on the earth. They are inhabitants
of another realm; their knowledge, activities, and associations are there. Therefore this text can in no wise

invalidate the great multitude of clear texts that teach the conscious survival of the spirit.

So also it is sometimes urged that Christ "only hath immortality" (1 Tim. 6:16). The answer is simple. The terms "mortal" and "immortal" are in the Scriptures applied to bodily conditions rather than to the soul and hence have no bearing whatever on the question of the soul's inherent nature. It is the body that is mortal (the soul is *never* described by this term), and *"this mortal* must put on immortality." Christ has risen from the dead with a glorified, immortalized body, "the first-fruit of them that slept," "death hath no more dominion over him" (Rom. 6:9); therefore he *"only* hath immortality." Even God and the angels do not have this "immortality"; Christ "only" possesses it. But this has no bearing whatever on the soul's conscious existence after death, for the immortality which we do not have now and which we shall receive in the future resurrection, relates solely to a bodily condition.

Spirit is by nature a deathless entity. "God is a spirit"; the angels are "ministering spirits," and who will deny that they are deathless beings? But "there is a spirit in man," and God himself is the "Father of spirits"; therefore we must and do partake of the nature of his divine spirit in this respect. Fire is hot, and ice is cold, but these things are seldom described thus; for as it is the nature of fire to be hot and ice to be cold, all such qualifying words are manifestly superfluous. So also with spirit. It is entirely superfluous to say death-less spirit or immortal spirit, for it is by nature deathless.

The so-called *death* of the soul, often spoken of in the Bible, is not the end of its conscious existence, as every

one knows, but is simply spiritual death, spiritual separation from God *in this present world.* "The soul that
sinneth it shall die" (Ezek. 18:20). "Dead in trespasses and sins; wherein in times past ye *walked*"
(Eph. 2:1, 2). The soul dead—dead in a spiritual sense
—and yet the individual alive and walking around on the
earth. "Dead while she *liveth*" (1 Tim. 5:6). A multitude of texts could be given on this point.

Again I say, It is entirely superfluous to use "deathless" or "immortal" when speaking of the actual essential
nature of soul, or spirit, for it is by nature deathless.
If such a description is given it occurs incidentally, rather
than of necessity, as in 1 Pet. 3:4, where the "hidden
man of the heart" (the "inner man," the soul) is spoken
of as *aphthartos,* the same Greek word that in 1 Tim.
1:17 is applied to Christ and translated "immortal."

I have dwelt at some length on this point concerning
the nature of man, because of its importance in the plan
of redemption. Those who deny this doctrine are led,
by logical necessity, to deny also the doctrine of the new
birth and the reception of eternal life *in this world;* for
how can it be said that man now possesses eternal life if
death ends all until the day of resurrection?

It is the spirit of man that is born again, that thrives
on spiritual food and enjoys spiritual worship. The
soul, as well as the body, is defiled by sin, and both are
cleansed by the blood of Christ in New Testament salvation. In this happy, redeemed condition, the individual
can look forward eagerly, as did the apostle Paul,
to that time when the "earthly house" shall be forsaken
and the released soul shall take its joyful flight to the
realms of paradise "to be with Christ, which is far bet

ter," yea, to be "absent from the body," but "to be present
with the Lord," there to enjoy his favors until the resurrection-day, when, united with a risen, glorified body, it
shall dwell forevermore in the final home of the blest.
Amen.

THE PROBLEM OF SIN.

CHAPTER III

THE PROBLEM OF SIN.

The presence of moral evil in God's universe is one of the great questions that has puzzled the mind of man. The Bible represents God as a being almighty in power, intrinsically good, and holy in all of his works; still we are confronted by the stupendous fact of sin in the world. Whence came it?

ITS ORIGIN.

The subject of the origin of moral evil and the reason for its existence naturally resolves itself into one of the three following positions, each of which has been earnestly maintained by many people: 1. That God is the direct author of sin and is alone responsible for it, man being but an irresponsible agent in carrying out His will. 2. That although sin is not according to the nature of God, he has seen fit to employ it as his method in bringing about certain good results not otherwise obtainable. This is somewhat related to the first position. 3. That moral evil is in no sense according to God's will; that it forms no part of his plans, his purposes, or his ways; that it originated in the finite and by apostasy from God, and that therefore God is not responsible for it; that all his relations to it are antagonistic, and in the way of prevention, remedy, or punishment.

The first position, that God is the direct author of sin, is so opposed to every revelation which God has made of himself in his Word, so utterly irreconcilable with reason and common sense, that I will dismiss the thought with but few words.

God is the author of what is termed physical evil; therefore we read, "I make peace, and create evil: I the Lord do all these things" (Isa. 45:7). "Shall there be evil in a city, and the Lord hath not done it?" (Amos 3:6). Such evil consists of temporal punishments or judgments that God brings upon men because of their sins. God threatened the men of Nineveh with a great evil, even the entire destruction of their city; but when they turned from their wicked ways, "God repented of the *evil* which he had said that he would do unto them; and he did it not" (Jonah 3:10). But God is not the author of moral evil, or sin; he is infinitely holy. It is blasphemy to charge upon God, "that can not lie" (Tit. 1:2), all of the falsehoods that have been uttered during the ages; to state that the Holy One, who is "of purer eyes than to behold evil, and canst not look on iniquity" (Hab. 1:13), is, after all, its direct cause.

The second position, that sin is God's choice of methods for bringing about the great good, has received a larger number of supporters. In this it is assumed that, although sin is contrary to the nature of God, it is nevertheless according to his will that men should sin, in order that his glorious power may be manifested in bringing into effect the plan of redemption, so that the sinner can experience the exquisite delights and enjoyments of contrast by being saved from sin. But if all this be necessary in order to insure happiness, the angels of heaven must be perfectly miserable; for as far as we know they have never had the privilege of experiencing this blessedness of contrast!

IS NOT A DIVINE METHOD.

God is absolutely perfect. Sin is not good; hence if God must choose sin in order to accomplish right, he is limited in his choice of methods. The Bible nowhere introduces sin as God's work or method. It is contrary even to the moral sense in man. Can we be on both sides of a moral question? Can God consistently decree that we shall sin, and at the same time prohibit us from doing it and threaten us with the direst punishments if we do? It is contrary to common sense to assert that God will forbid his own appointments. If men have secret thoughts, purposes, and desires contrary to those they make public, they are charged with hypocrisy. We understand the character of men by their methods, so that when their methods embrace the wrong we conclude that wrong is in their nature. If God's laws and his purposes are not in harmony, then we can expect nothing but confusion in morality. I can not conceive that the Most High acts toward sin in any other manner than in perfect accordance with his own nature. In other words, if sin is not in his heart, it is not in his plan. He disowns it. "All that is in the world, the lust of the flesh, the lust of the eyes, and the pride of life, IS NOT OF THE FATHER" (1 John 2: 16).

The third position harmonizes with the moral sense in man, with our common sense, with the plain teachings of his Word, and with all the known facts in the case. Moral evil is contrary to God's nature, contrary to his plans, his purposes, and his ways. All of his relations to it are antagonistic. It originated in the finite and by apostasy from God.

In the preceding chapter mention was made that man

was created in God's image and is a moral being, placed
under moral law. This fact, properly considered, furnishes a rational and Scriptural solution of the entire
problem of sin, so far as it pertains to this world. "In
the image of God" he was an intelligent being; for without intelligence creation would be without an object, and
might as well exist only in the mind of God as out of it.
Now, God being holy, he could no more make a sinful
being than he could lie (which is declared to be impossible), for God is a power only in the direction of his
own nature and attributes. But an intelligent being
like himself he could and did make. Intelligence, however, implies real *cause*, that the being so endowed possesses inherently the power of acting voluntarily. Without this element of moral freedom, this power of choice
and determination of conduct, true intelligence could not
exist. Are we not conscious of a personal, responsible
"me" or "I," capable of self-activity? All through the
Bible this principle in man is recognized.

MAN WHOLLY RESPONSIBLE.

But with man possessing within himself the principle
of *cause* as truly as does his Maker, so that he must act
voluntarily, we see at once that it is within his sphere
also to act wrongly. In other words, the *possibility* of sin
inheres in all moral beings; for manifestly it is impossible to voluntarily act right without possessing the
ability also to act wrong. This is the gist of the whole
argument. The problem of sin is merely a problem of
moral government. The individual with a personal will
possesses a method and purpose exclusively his own.
God is in no wise responsible for it. Having created

man intelligent, in his own image, his responsibility in
this respect ceased. The universe as a physical unit
was incomplete, but when peopled with moral beings
capable of rendering intelligent, voluntary service to
God, the plan was perfect; therefore man stands out as
the crowning work of God's creative effort. The principles of moral government must be everywhere the same;
therefore even the angels of heaven are under the same
divine law that men are. But in this brief investigation
I choose to dwell chiefly on the part that directly concerns man.

SIN AND PREDESTINATION.

The first chapters of Genesis give an account of how
sin was introduced into this part of God's moral universe.
It occurred by the wilful choice of our foreparents, and
by this means they apostatized from God. Ever since
that time God's relations to evil have been antagonistic,
in the way of prevention, remedy, and punishment. But
it must be borne in mind that in these dealings with men
God has in all cases acted in strict harmony with those
principles of moral government which he has himself
ordained; so that even those individuals who have unconsciously fulfilled some part of God's plan in his relations to sin, have at the same time acted *voluntarily*.
God has his own purposes; men have theirs: but by infinite wisdom the Almighty is able to take advantage of
men's wilful actions in carrying out their own evil designs, and thereby accomplish his own purpose in the
world. He thus respects that moral freedom which he
has created in the individual.

These thoughts, carefully considered, explain what is

probably the most difficult text in the Bible pertaining
to this subject—Acts 2:23: "Him, being delivered by
the determinate counsel and foreknowledge of God, ye
have taken, and by wicked hands have crucified and
slain." Here the apostle Peter charges the Jews with
the most atrocious wickedness in crucifying the Son of
God, and yet in the same verse teaches that it was according to God's will that Christ should die. The purpose these men had in the act was evil, and they alone
were responsible for it; therefore God, knowing their
designs, simply delivered Christ into their hands, thus accomplishing his own purpose, without violating in the
least their free moral agency. This furnishes a rational
solution of the oft-debated subject of predestination. God
has predestinated or foreordained certain things, but
these appointments were made in view of and in harmony
with responsible human agency. A view of predestination which makes God the sole *cause,* and man only an
irresponsible or powerless agent of the Almighty, is in
open hostility to the entire Bible; for the Word of God
teaches that man has the power of choice and that his
actions are therefore praiseworthy or blameworthy.

As before stated, this principle of moral government
explains everything pertaining to the subject. God
claims no responsibility for men's methods and actions,
except in his proper relations to them. He distinctly
states, "My thoughts are not your thoughts, neither are
your ways my ways, saith the Lord" (Isa. 55:8). Yet
some would have us believe that everything that men do
is in some secret and unexplainable manner according to
the will of God. It is not true. Men's methods may or
may not be in accordance with the will of God. Through

the exercise of an overruling Providence all things are made to "work together for good to them that love God" (Rom. 8: 28), but even here the principle of free moral agency is respected, so that man's moral actions result from their own voluntary desires.

How often the question has been asked, Why did God permit sin in the first place? From the foregoing we see that God could not prevent the possibility of sin and still constitute man an intelligent, self-acting agent like himself. It is not a question of physical power, but a problem of moral government. And this system of divine government is not simply a good one nor the best of several possible methods, but it is absolutely perfect like God, its Author. In this order alone can real honor and glory be given to God. A mechanical service is no service; but the loving, willing obedience of free, intelligent beings is a service absolutely perfect and therefore well-pleasing to God.

NATURE OF SIN.

Two verses of Scripture give us a correct interpretation of sin. 1 John 3:4—"Whosoever committeth sin transgresseth also the law: for sin is the transgression of the law." Jas. 4:17—"Therefore to him that knoweth to do good, and doeth it not, to him it is sin." Sin is therefore either the direct transgression of God's law or else the wilful failure to conform to its requirements. But God's law is an infinite law; therefore its violation becomes a serious offense, involving the soul in spiritual ruin, both in time and in eternity. "Is not thy wickedness great? and thine iniquities infinite?" (Job 22:5). The first act of this character committed by our foreparents caused their banishment from Eden and the consequent train of sickness, pain, sorrow, and death.

ITS UNIVERSALITY.

The consciousness of sin is universal, all men having fallen under its dismal and blighting sway. One of the grand arguments of Paul in the Roman letter was to show that all men are sinners, in order that he might emphasize the truth of Christ's mission as the universal Savior. He charges the Jewish nation with sin, notwithstanding their revealed law of God, and quotes their Scriptures to prove the assertion. His description of the Gentile world shows their wretched condition morally. Then he proceeds to say: "For when the Gentiles, which have not the law, do by nature the things contained in the law, these having not the law, are a law unto themselves: which show the work of the law written in their hearts, their conscience also bearing witness, and their thoughts the mean while accusing or else excusing one another" (Rom. 2:14, 15).

The argument is plain. The Gentiles, independent of the written revealed law of God, possessed a revelation of God's law within their own natures sufficient to fix responsibility; therefore in transgressing this law they also became sinners. He is not teaching that men are saved by their conscience, independent of revelation, but that they are by this means all condemned and lost. Listen to his conclusion: "We have before proved both Jew and Gentiles, *that they are all under sin*" (chap. 3:9). "There is no difference: for all have sinned, and come short of the glory of God" (verses 22, 23). In another place he says, "The Scripture hath concluded all under sin, that the promise by faith of Jesus Christ might be given to them that believe" (Gal. 3:22). It is unnecessary to multiply texts on this point. The uniform testimony of Scripture is that all men are "by nature the children of wrath."

REDEMPTION.

CHAPTER IV.

THE REDEMPTIVE PLAN.

The fall of man wrought a complete change in his nature and condition; the primitive purity was lost, and sin and condemnation rested upon his guilty soul. As a result, the entire race was plunged into the depths of sin; therefore all men stood in need of redemption.

SELF-REDEMPTION IMPOSSIBLE.

But redemption would imply a return to the original perfect state, both as to character and condition, and this restoration man could not of his own will effect. In the first place, there was a legal difficulty that he could not surmount. As a moral being, he had been placed under moral law, and this law required his perfect obedience. Its requirements might all be summed up in the words, "Thou shalt love the Lord thy God with all thy heart, and with all thy soul, and with all thy mind" (Matt. 22: 37). Thus, it will be seen that, having disobeyed, he could not make reparation for his transgressions, since *no surplus obedience* is possible.

So also there was an insurmountable moral difficulty. Having lost purity and innocence, he could not by self-effort regain what had been lost. "Who can bring a clean thing out of an unclean? not one" (Job 14: 4). Yet such a restoration is indispensable to redemption. "Except a man be born again, he can not see the kingdom of God" (John 3: 3). "Follow peace with all men, and holiness, without which no man shall see the Lord" (Heb.

12:14). Self-redemption was therefore clearly impossible.

Nor could the angels of heaven effect the redemption of man; for they also are God's intelligent creatures and therefore moral beings subject to moral law, which law, as in the case of man, exacts perfect obedience. The highest love, service, and obedience that they are able to render to the Almighty is only sufficient for themselves alone. Therefore in the nature of the case God only could redeem.

MAN WHOLLY RESPONSIBLE FOR SIN.

So far as we are able to determine, God was under no obligation to attempt the redemption of fallen man. His original work was perfect. Man's constitution was such that he was not obliged to sin; therefore the entire penalty for disobedience properly rested upon him. Those who rashly charge God with responsibility concerning man's sin should hesitate long enough to consider the fact that the universe is not a physical unit: that with intelligent creatures provision must be made for the operation of moral law and government. This accounts both for the fact of sin and for the responsibility for sin. And who will dare to say that this system is not in its own nature good—the only perfect one? Could man wish for the extinction of his personal, rational self— forfeit all the privileges of honor and virtue, of happiness and joy, in time and in eternity—in order to escape the responsibility of wilful disobedience? Perish the thought!

WILL GOD REDEEM?

Since God stands acquitted of all responsibility in the fall, is there any evidence that he will redeem? In the realm of nature we observe that God distributes many of his gifts to men irrespectively of their moral character. "He hath not dealt with us after our sins; nor rewarded us according to our iniquities" (Psa. 103: 10). "Thou openest thine hand, and satisfiest the desire of every living thing" (Psa. 145: 16). "He maketh his sun to rise on the evil and on the good, and sendeth rain on the just and on the unjust" (Matt. 5: 45). The universal prevalence of sacrifices testifies that men have in all ages believed that God would redeem. It is highly probable that this practise was instituted by God's appointment (Gen. 3:21 with 4: 4). If so, then we have in this a clear evidence of God's redemptive purpose.

A DIVINE PLAN.

Revelation itself, however, makes this subject clear. There existed in the divine mind a plan of restoration for fallen man. This plan was for ages a "mystery" to men and to angels, but it was the "hidden wisdom which God ordained before the world" and which centers in the crucifixion of the "Lord of glory" (1 Cor. 2:7, 8). Yea, he was a "Lamb slain from the foundation of the world" (Rev. 13: 8).

PROGRESSIVE REVELATION.

But while this plan was from the beginning complete in the mind and purpose of God, its revelation to man was progressive. The first intimation we have is in Gen.

3:15, where it is predicted that the seed of the woman
shall bruise the head of the serpent. "The Lord had
respect unto Abel and to his offering" (Gen. 4:4). In
the days of Enos, son of Seth, men apparently had some
relations with God; for we read, "Then began men to
call upon the name of the Lord" (Gen. 4:26). A little
later "Enoch walked with God" (Gen. 5:24); while to
Noah God manifested himself particularly. These facts
are sufficient to show God's attitude toward the race.

THE ABRAHAMIC COVENANT.

But when we come forward to the time of Abraham,
we find a remarkable revelation of the plan of redemption in the special covenant that God made with the
father of the Hebrew nation. This covenant was divided
into two parts. The first part related to Abraham and
his literal seed: that God would make of him a great
nation; that his descendants should sojourn for a time
in the land of Egypt, after which God would bring them
into the land of Canaan and give it to them for their
inheritance. The second part of the covenant was of a
spiritual nature; for in Abraham and his seed all the
families of the earth should be blessed. (Gen. 12:1, 2;
13:14, 15; 15:5, 13-16; 17:1-8; 22:17, 18).

This second division of the covenant so clearly depicted Christ and his universal gospel that Jesus said,
"Abraham rejoiced to see my day: he saw it, and was
glad" (John 8:56). Paul says: "The promise that he
should be the heir of the world, was not to Abraham or
his seed through the law [of Moses], but through the
righteousness of faith . . . . therefore it is of faith, that

it might-be by grace; to the end the promise might be
sure to all the seed; not to that only which is of the law,
but to that also which is of the faith of Abraham; who
is the father of us all (as it is written, I have made thee
a father of many nations)" (Rom. 4:13-16).   And
again: "Now to Abraham and his seed were the promises
made.   He saith not, And to seeds, as of many; but as
of one, And to thy seed, which is Christ."   "That the
blessing of Abraham might come on the Gentiles through
Jesus Christ, that we might receive the promise of the
Spirit through faith" (Gal. 3:16, 14).

THE LAW.

In the fulfilment of the first part of this covenant to
Abraham's seed, God gave the law of Moses, the osten-
sible object of which was to govern and benefit the
Israelitish nation, but the greatest object of which was
doubtless to furnish a system of types and shadows—of
sacrifices and ceremonies, offerings and oblations—
pointing forward to the second division of the covenant,
when the spiritual and real worship of God should be
established among all the nations of the earth.   This
law, and the manner in which it was delivered, imparted
a clearer revelation of God's nature and character, as
well as of his plan, and thus furnished the means of
disciplining the Jews in preparation for the coming
Messiah.

THE PROPHETS.

The later prophets, however, were not limited to an
external system of types and shadows, but the Spirit of
God made known to them directly the higher standard

of revelation to be brought about by Christ. Thus Isaiah affirms that "God . . . . will come and save you" (Isa. 35:4) and that this salvation would be effected by His vicarious suffering and death (Isaiah 53). Daniel predicted that the Messiah would come "to finish the transgression, and to make an end of sins, and to make reconciliation for iniquity, and to bring in everlasting righteousness" (Dan. 9:24). Joel prophesied that in the last days God would pour out his Spirit upon all flesh (Joel 2:28, 29). Zechariah pointed to the fountain of cleansing for sin and ucleanness which should be opened in the house of David (Zech. 13:1).

CHRIST THE CENTER.

Jesus Christ brought the highest revelation of God and taught a perfect standard of human conduct; but, above all, we find in him God's perfect remedy for sin. He came "to save his people from their sins" (Matt. 1:21). The beloved apostle says, "Ye know that he was manifested to take away our sins," and, "Whosoever abideth in him sinneth not" (1 John 3:5, 6). Thus the perfect moral restoration of man to the original condition of holiness and purity is accomplished. He "gave himself for us, that he might REDEEM us from all iniquity, and purify unto himself a peculiar people, zealous of good works" (Tit. 2:14).

FUTURE REDEMPTION.

The redemptive plan was not completely fulfilled, however, at the time of Christ's first advent. So far as the soul is concerned, the means was provided for its

oral restoration. But we have seen that the fall also
ffected man physically. It was doubtless God's original
:sign "that mortality might be swallowed up of life,"
iat mortal man in the Garden of Eden should, by par-
iking of the tree of life, be immortalized and never
ie. But since through sin this purpose was frustrated,
 has now become a part of the redemptive plan "that
iortality might be swallowed up of life" (2 Cor. 5:4).
nd since, because of original sin, it has been "ap-
ointed unto men once to die" (Heb. 9:27), that part
f the redemptory scheme relative to our immortaliza--
on has been deferred until the last great day, the Jay
f resurrection, when "this corruptible must put on in-
>rruption, and this mortal must put on immortality"
1 Cor. 15:53).

Paul recognizes the fact that our bodies are included
t the redemptive work; for he says, "Know ye not that
our *body* is the temple of the Holy Ghost? . . . . For
e are bought with a price: therefore glorify God *in*
our body, and in your spirit, which are God's" (1 Cor.
:19, 20). He refers to those who have been saved, and
:aled by the Holy Spirit, and possessing an "earnest
f our inheritance until the redemption of the purchased
ossession" (Eph. 1:13, 14), thus clearly indicating a
hase of redemptive work yet future. In another place
e describes our immortalization, when mortality shall
e ."swallowed up of life," and declares that God "hath
'rought us for the selfsame thing" and *"hath given unto
s the earnest of the Spirit"* (2 Cor. 5:1-5). And again,
e says that we "which have the first-fruits of the Spirit,
ven we ourselves groan within ourselves, waiting for

the adoption, to wit, *the REDEMPTION of our body"* (Rom. 8:23). The body is now the recipient of certain redemptory blessings, which will be considered in Chapter X, but its greatest benefit is yet future.

IMPORTANCE OF THE PROGRESSIVE VIEW.

A knowledge of this progressive feature of God's redemptive work is absolutely necessary to a correct understanding of what the Bible really teaches. Since the plan itself was revealed to men by degrees, the scriptures that record these successive revelations are naturally progressive from the lower to the higher. Such a method was necessary because of man's constitution, for with him all knowledge is acquired progressively, and society can be advanced only by a gradual evolution. Due regard to these facts will furnish a standing answer to that class of Bible critics who delight in arraying one part of the book against the other. They affirm that certain personal acts of righteous men in olden times would not be tolerated in decent society now; that God's commands to Joshua, for example, are irreconcilable with the Sermon on the Mount, etc. But the Bible was not written all at one time, neither are all of its parts applicable to all men in all ages of the world. Are we not informed in the Word itself that the revelation which God made of his will to the fathers in past ages occurred "at sundry times" and *"in divers manners"* (Heb. 1:1)? His method of revelation was adjusted to the nature and the condition of men, and was therefore progressive, so that at times one part was made to succeed another part. But progress was always upward. The unity that we find in

all parts of the Bible is a *unity of purpose and plan,
which God was constantly seeking to make known to man,*
and by which man was being gradually elevated; that is,
THE REDEMPTIVE PLAN.

CHAPTER V.

CHRIST AND THE ATONEMENT.

Sin is a universal fact. We have seen that there is no self-redemption, and that even the angels of heaven, being under the same divine law that exacts perfect obedience, can have no surplus obedience to atone for fallen man. Only a being over whom the law had no jurisdiction was adequate to the task. There is no proof that God was under any obligation to undertake man's restoration; but on the supposition that he was willing to do this, the necessity of a redeemer is obvious. It is also evident that in accomplishing this result God must do it righteously. The moral law of his moral government could not be ignored or set aside, but all of its just claims must be fully vindicated; therefore the Redeemer must come under the law, under its jurisdiction and power. In this we see the

NECESSITY OF THE INCARNATION.

The word "incarnation," derived from the Latin, signifies "in the flesh." To become incarnate, then, signifies to become a man. So long as Christ remained in the sphere of absolute Godhead, he could not be subject to the jurisdiction of his own objective law; neither could he in any sense directly affect man in the way of redemption, there being no point of contact with man. He could not cease to be God and thus become a mere creature under the law's jurisdiction; but it was possible for him to come out of the sphere of absolute Godhead

into the sphere of a real manhood, by assuming the human form and human nature in connection with his divinity. In this the divine nature was not changed into the human, so as to become essentially what it was not before; but the two distinct elements, human and divine, were in some mysterious manner united in the same form of being. "Forasmuch then as the children are partakers of flesh and blood, he also himself likewise took part of the same . . . . For verily he took not on him the nature of angels; but he took on him the seed of Abraham" (Heb. 2: 14-16). "Christ Jesus . . . . being in the form of God . . . . made himself of no reputation, and took upon him the form of a servant, and was made in the likeness of men" (Phil. 2: 5-7).

The New Testament in numerous passages speaks of Christ as both human and divine. The apostle John begins his epistle with Christ as God, engaged in the work of Creation; after which he follows him through his earthly career among men. On the other hand, Matthew and Luke begin with his earthly birth and trace him through life and to his glorification and assumption of the Father's throne in heaven. But the result is the same in both cases. He was the divine One humiliated, and the human One glorified—both God and man.

THE VIRGIN BIRTH.

To reject the doctrine of the incarnation is in effect to reject the whole Bible; for not only does the New Testament revolve around the Person of Christ, as God incarnate, but the Old Testament stands committed to the same truth, as it contains direct prophecies of the incarnation. Isaiah distinctly affirmed that the "mighty God, the everlasting Father," should be born as a child, should assume divine government on the earth and sit upon the throne of David (Isa. 9: 6, 7). Micah taught that this "ruler in Israel" should come forth from Bethlehem, but that he had existed "from the days of eternity" (Mic. 5: 2). Isaiah also stated that he should not be born according to ordinary generation, but that he should be born of a virgin, thus setting forth a supernatural origin (Isa. 7: 14). The enigmatical passage in Jer. 31: 22 probably relates also to the virgin birth: "The Lord hath created a new thing in the earth, A woman shall compass a man." If the foregoing texts do not teach the earthly birth of a divine being, it would be difficult to state such a fact if desired.

The mystery of such a union of the divine and the human is no sufficient cause for its rejection, for we are surrounded everywhere with things that are in their nature mysterious to us. Some professing Christians have been rather inclined to doubt the story of the virgin birth; but it seems to me that if the divine was to become human, nothing could be more natural than that his introduction to this world of sin should occur in some extraordinary manner. The constant phenomenon of ordinary generation, which is the first principle of biology, has never received a satisfactory explanation. But one fact is certain—man is here; and it is also certain that there was a time when man was not. Why should it be difficult to believe that the Power which made the first man without either parent should now make another man with the assistance of only one parent? In no other way could Christ have become both human and divine, thus forming a middle link by which man could be united with God.

EVIDENCES OF CHRIST'S DIVINITY.

The special evidences of Christ's divinity are so numerous that an entire volume would not be sufficient for a careful treatment of the subject; therefore I can refer only to a few of them and to those in the briefest manner possible.

1. *The prophecies of the incarnation were all fulfilled in him.* He was born of a virgin (Isa. 7:14), was born in Bethlehem (Mic. 5:2), etc. The Old Testament abounds in prophecies concerning the birth, ministry, mission, death and resurrection of the Messiah—more than three hundred in all—and all were completely fulfilled in Jesus of Nazareth. To these prophecies more than to everything else the first preachers appealed in establishing the fact of the Messiahship of Jesus. Thus, Apollos "mightily convinced the Jews, and that publicly, showing by the Scriptures that Jesus was Christ" (Acts 18:28).

2. *The types of the Old Testament were fulfilled in him.* The blood of piacular victims which had from the days of Abel flowed freely in atoning sacrifices for the sins of men all pointed forward unmistakably to a great Sacrifice, even the sacrifice of our Lord.

3. *He bore the divine names.* "Jehovah," "God," "Emmanuel," "Lord of all," "the mighty God," "Everlasting Father," "the true God," "King of kings, and Lord of lords," etc.

4. *Divine attributes are ascribed to him.* (See Chapter I.—SON).

5. *He wrought divine works and miracles.* He claimed "power on earth to forgive sins," thus showing that he was God. He turned water into wine, multiplied loaves and fishes, walked on the raging waves of Galilee and stilled its storms, thus proving that he was Lord of creation. He cast out evil spirits, healed the bodies of the sick and suffering, and even raised the dead, thus demonstrating his universal dominion. These evidences were convincing to many. Even Nicodemus was constrained to acknowledge them. "Rabbi," he said, "we know that thou art a teacher come from God: for no man can do these miracles that thou doest, except God be with him" (John 3:2).

6. *Divine honors were claimed by him.* He claimed equality with the Father (John 5:18), a divine glory with the Father "before the world was" (John 17:5); and he taught that "all men should honor the Son, even as they honor the Father" (John 5:23). These claims to divine honors were all recognized by the apostles, and they united in the worship of Jesus as the only one through whom salvation could be obtained (Acts 4:12). Paul declared that "at the name of Jesus every knee should bow, of things in heaven, and things in earth, and things under the earth; and that every tongue should confess that Jesus Christ is Lord, to the glory of God the Father" (Phil. 2:10, 11).

7. *His unexampled human character.* Today there are many men like Thomas, honest skeptics, men who are not to be convinced by mere claims, but who require

something more tangible—the evidences of their senses, or clear arguments that appeal to the reason. If such men will carefully study the human character of our Lord, they will find an abundance of evidences that Christ was more than a mere man, and, like Thomas, after having put his finger in the print of the nails and thrust his hand into the pierced side, they will exclaim, "My Lord and my God!"

In the first place, his life was one of freedom from sin. Not one blot or sin rests upon his character. In the face of his enemies he could say, "Which of you convinceth me of sin?" (John 8: 46). If men do not believe in his virgin birth, let them account for his virgin life; for his life was one of absolute holiness and perfection. In this he differs from all other men, not only in degree, but also *in kind;* for all others possess the nature of evil, and "have sinned, and come short of the glory of God." Jesus was the only sinless one that has ever trod this earth of ours. In this he appears as something more than human.

Note also the profound wisdom manifested in his life and discourses. Whence did all these "treasures of wisdom and knowledge" proceed? Was he a self-made man? The successes of all self-made men can be traced to definite causes—peculiar circumstances, books, contact with learned people, etc. But Jesus had no advantage of training among the illustrious men of his day, he grew up among the illiterate folk in an insignificant and despised Galilean town, without education, without books, and without favorable surroundings. At the beginning of his ministry his own people marveled, saying, "How knoweth this man letters, *having never learned?*" (John 7: 15). Yet all the wisdom of the ages pales into insignificance in comparison with the sayings of Jesus of Nazareth. "He taught them as one having authority" (Matt. 7: 29). He spoke the final word on every moral subject. The verdict of the officers sent to arrest him has been the verdict of the ages—"Never man spake like this man" (John 7: 46).

Another thing worthy of notice is the universal character of his teachings. Himself a Jew, dressed as a Jew, living in the land of the Jews at a time when the Jews were narrow and bigoted, reared under local circumstances suited to make one still narrower, Jesus towered above all of these things and laid down the principles of universal righteousness. The gospel that he preached is applicable to all times and to every nation under heaven. Whence did he derive such a remarkable insight into human nature as is depicted even in that one sermon on the mount? Admit the divine element, and all becomes clear. "He knew all men, and needed not that any one should testify of man: for he knew what was in man" (John 2: 24, 25).

But this universal character of his doctrines is not all. *He is himself the universal model.* All other great men belong to particular nations or classes of men, and not one of them will serve as a model for all men. It has been said that the greatest men have the greatest faults and failings, just as the tallest men cast the longest shadows. But Jesus belongs to the whole race. He towers above all others, and yet he was *without sin*, and lived without fault or mistake. From whatever stand-

point one views his earthly life, he stands forth as the
greatest moral miracle of history. This fact has been
acknowledged even by men who are generally ranked as
unbelievers—Cobbe and Renan, Strauss and Diderot,
Richter and Rousseau; while Napoleon, recognizing the
nature of Christianity and of its Founder, exclaimed,
"I know men; and I tell you that *Jesus Christ was not
a man.*"

8. *His death and resurrection.* The trial and crucifixion of Jesus reveals something more than human.
Though mocked and abused, he betrayed no trace of
anger or resentment; nailed to the cross, and expiring in
frightful agonies, he pronounced no words of hatred or
revenge upon his malignant foes, but prayed instead,
"Father, forgive them, for they know not what they do."
No wonder that Rousseau the infidel, in a few of his sober
moments, exclaimed, "If the life and death of Socrates
were those of a sage, the life and death of Jesus are
those of a god."

But the resurrection of Christ is the grand climax of
all. This historical fact has never been affected by the
false reports of lying Jews and the vain reasonings of
unbelievers. All of the evidences go to sustain the
gospel narratives of this event. Fraud there could not
be. The timid disciples who fled when Christ was ar-
rested would certainly not have ventured to overpower
the Roman guard and steal the body of Jesus. Furthermore, the risen Lord appeared after his resurrection to
hundreds of people. When Paul stood before King
Agrippa and declared that Christ had suffered and risen
from the dead, he said, 'I am persuaded that none of

these things are hidden from thee; for this thing was not done in a corner' (Acts 26:26). Had the apostles desired to establish a falsehood concerning the resurrection, they would have selected some place other than Jerusalem to begin their deception, for all of the facts were easily obtainable there at the time. And it must be remembered also that these apostles and thousands of other Christians gave their own lives in defense of the doctrine of a risen Christ.

THE ATONEMENT.

"We also joy in God through our Lord Jesus Christ, by whom we have now received the atonement" (Rom. 5:11). Christianity is based upon the death of Christ, as the one great atonement for the sins of men. Many men professing adherence to the Christian faith, however, have practically dispensed with the real feature of the atonement. They tell us that it is the life of Christ, not his death, that saves men; that he set an example of right-doing, and that we are saved by following his example. They extol the beauty and excellence of his character and teaching, and end by saying that he died the death of a martyr to a good cause.

Such is only a partial view of Christ's mission and destroys the grand proportions and harmonies of the whole. The Word plainly teaches that more was required in order to effect our salvation than a mere example of piety. "For, when we were enemies, we were *reconciled to God by the death of his Son,* much more, being reconciled, we shall be *saved by his life*" (Rom. 5:10). He "was delivered for our offenses, and was raised again

for our justification" (Rom. 4:25). "For Christ also
hath once suffered for sins, the just for the unjust, that
he might bring us to God" (1 Pet. 3:18). "All have
sinned, and come short of the glory of God" (Rom. 3:23).
Therefore if sinful men were to reform and then follow
perfectly the outward example of Christ's right-doing,
this course would in no wise dispose of the sins of their
past life; for they can not have surplus obedience as a
result of their present righteousness, and thus make
reparation for the sins of the past. But "Christ *died
for our sins,* according to the Scriptures" (1 Cor. 15:3).
Those who repent and are converted have their sins
"blotted out," yea, they are washed from their sins in his
own blood (Rev. 1:5). No, the death of Jesus Christ
was not the death of a martyr. He died voluntarily as
God's own sacrifice for sins. Hear his own words: "I
lay down my life, that I might take it again. *No man
taketh it from me,* but I LAY IT DOWN OF MY-
SELF" (John 10:17, 18).

ITS NECESSITY.

According to the foregoing considerations, we see that
the necessity of incarnation and atonement lay in the fact
of sin itself and in God's plan to redeem man righteously.
God could not consistently set aside his righteous law and
pardon men at the expense of his infinite Justice; while
at the same time his infinite Love for man demanded expression; hence the necessity of atonement. I am aware
that some men ridicule the idea of an atonement which
resulted from a "schism in the divine nature," but the
Scriptural doctrine of atonement does not necessarily

imply that God is divided and that his attributes are at
war with each other. Do not we as men possess, though
in a lesser degree, these same principles of justice and
love? and do they not both find expression in our lives?
yet who ever thought of representing these principles as
a schism in the human nature—a man eternally at war
with himself? But the Bible does clearly teach that as
a result of the atonement God can be "just" and still be
"the justifier of him which believeth in Jesus" (Rom. 3:
26). This shows that God could not be just (maintain
his just and holy law) and pardon men without a ransom price. Man could not ransom himself—the price was
too great; angels could not; but, thank God! he "so
loved the world that he gave his only begotten Son, that
whosoever believeth in him should not perish, but have
everlasting life" (John 3: 16).

Christ as God could satisfy the claims of infinite
Justice; therefore the way of redemption was made possible. Being an infinite Sacrifice, he could pay the debt
to infinite Justice for all men. It is the *character of the
Sacrifice itself* that makes the atonement of such infinite
worth. In the exact use of the term, God does not
"pardon" sin at all, for infinite Justice has exacted the
infinite penalty for all committed sins. The forgiveness
of sins which God grants is "for Christ's sake" (Eph.
4: 32), "who his own self *bare our sins in his own body
on the tree*" (1 Pet. 2: 24).

While one purpose of the atonement is to change the
relations of God with men, it is also designed to change
the attitude of men toward God. When the transgressor
is made to realize the awful nature and extent of his sin,

and to see that he is deserving of infinite punishment, his heart sinks in despair; but if his attention is then turned to Calvary, to the dying agonies of the God-man, as the one who "gave himself for us," hope revives, and love for the Redeemer springs up in the sin-benighted soul, while the blood washes away the guilt of all past transgressions. Halleluiah! Then he is ready to exclaim, as did the apostle John, "We love him, because he first loved us" (1 John 4:19). Yes, it is this exhibition of God's love to us that wins back our wandering hearts' affections, and draws them out, and forever fixes them upon the Savior. This is the secret of regeneration.

ATONEMENT AND REDEMPTION.

In order to understand the subject of the atonement, we must carefully define the terms by which our ideas are conveyed. In popular usage the signification of the word "atonement" is very much the same as if it were pronounced at-one-ment, thus expressing a result rather than a cause. But in the Scriptures, as well as in critical usage, atonement is placed in the relation of cause, while redemption is the effect. Now, there are clear differences between these two, and this distinction of cause and effect must be carefully observed; otherwise all of our thinking on the subject will be chaotic. They differ both in design and in object; therefore what may be properly affirmed of the one may not be of the other.

The proper idea of atonement is the *satisfaction which Christ in his death paid to the justice of God, and by which the relations of God toward guilty men were altered.* Thus, we see that the atonement was Godward;

but redemption, on the other hand, is manward. In other words, the atonement was a sacrifice offered to God; while redemption is a benefit conferred upon men. The design of the atonement was to render God propitious, to change his relation toward men, "that he might be just, and the justifier of him which believeth in Jesus" (Rom. 3: 26); whereas the design of redemption is actually to change the relations of men toward God, thereby making them holy. So also there is a difference in their nature. The atonement was a sacrifice of inestimable value—infinite— "the precious blood of Christ." It was sufficient to satisfy God's infinite justice and *cover* the sins of the whole race; therefore it is useless to talk about any limitations here. But redemption, on the other hand, was not infinite in this respect, but definite—clearly limited to the number of those who accept it; for it stands inseparably related to man as its object. Redemption is not an offering for sin, but is the *deliverance of men from sin* by means of an offering already made; hence it is said that Christ "by his own blood" "obtained eternal redemption for us" (Heb. 9: 12). For this reason the word is used for *salvation,* which signifies our actual deliverance from sin (Eph. 1: 7; 1 Pet. 1: 18); also for the *resurrection,* which is the actual deliverance of our bodies from mortality (Rom. 8: 23; Eph. 1: 14; 4: 30).

Furthermore, the atonement was unconditional; while redemption is, on the part of man, wholly conditional. In other words, Christ made the atonement freely and unconditionally for all men, whether they believe it or do not. As a result of this he offers redemption to all, but no coercion or force is brought to bear upon man to secure his belief in it or his acceptance of it. It is altogether a matter of his own free will. Many men, indeed the most of men, either neglect it or reject it. Now, this being true, it is evident that it was *possible* that all men should have rejected it, and therefore not a single person have been saved. Why? Simply because the atonement itself did not directly confer salvation upon any man— it was Godward, a sacrifice offered to God in order to render him propitious—while redemption is entirely conditional. But the atonement is the ground of redemption.

Another thing: The atonement was made once and for all, not partially, but completely; so that it has for centuries been a finished work. "The offering of the body of Jesus Christ [was] *once for all*" (Heb. 10: 10). He "offered *one* sacrifice for sins forever" (verse 12). And when this was accomplished, he cried out on the cross, "It is *finished*" (John 19: 30). Here we see the atonement as a finished work. But the plan of redemption, which upon certain conditions bestows upon us *all of the redemptory blessings,* is in daily progress, and it will continue until the end of time, when we shall receive the "redemption of our body" as the last great benefit conferred upon men.

CHAPTER VI.

CONDITIONS FOR SALVATION.

The mission of Christ was " to save his people from their sins" (Matt. 1:21). We have seen that man is universally lost in sin, but that a way of restoration to holiness has been provided through Jesus Christ, and that it rests upon his atonement. But thus far our attention has been directed mainly to the divine side: there is also a human side to the realization of redemption blessings. Man was not lost unconditionally; therefore redemption is not unconditional. As man was originally a responsible agent under law, which he voluntarily transgressed; so also the plan of restoration is made to agree with his responsible agency, so that he must of his own volition accept the law of Christ if he desires to receive the benefits of the atonement.

It is the uniform testimony of the New Testament that salvation is a matter of individual choice. All its offers and promises are addressed to the individual himself for decision, and all the blame for its neglect or rejection is laid upon him. "Come unto me, all ye that labor and are heavy-laden, and I will give you rest," are the words of the Savior (Matt. 11:28). "If any man thirst, *let him come* unto me and drink" (John 7:37). "Behold, I stand at the door and knock: if any man hear my voice, and *open the door*, I will come in to him" (Rev. 3:20). "*Whosoever will*, let him take the water of life freely" (Rev. 22:17). "*Ye will not* come to me, that ye might have life" (John 5:40). "O Jerusalem, Jerusalem! . . . . how often would I have gathered thy children together . . . . and *ye would not!* Behold, your house is left unto you desolate" (Matt. 23: 37, 38). "How shall we escape *if we neglect* so great salvation?" (Heb. 2: 3).

Salvation is the most important subject in the world. It should concern every one of us, for without it our souls will be lost through a never-ending eternity. And since it is offered to man conditionally, how important it is that we understand these conditions in order that we may approach God in an acceptable manner and receive this greatest of gifts!

A SPIRITUAL AWAKENING.

Sin produces spiritual death to the soul. "Your sins have separated between you and your God" (Isa. 59: 2), and this separation is represented as death (Eph. 2: 1; Col. 2:13; 1 Tim. 5: 6, etc). Men become "hardened through the deceitfulness of sin" (Heb. 3: 13). "Even their mind and conscience is defiled" (Tit. 1: 15). They sink into the darkness of a sinful night, until, in many cases, there seems to be "no fear of God before their eyes," or until they appear to lose all consciousness of "the exceeding sinfulness of sin." How sad! Yet it is true, nevertheless, that many reach the state where sin does not appear to them so very bad, and righteousness does not appear very good. Their standard of conduct is not determined by God's revealed law, but is regulated wholly by the terms of human expediency. If they can succeed in keeping at least a fair reputation among men, or in conforming to the general standard of conduct observed in the particular circle of society in which they move, they seem entirely satisfied; as though there were no God in heaven who takes account of their sinful actions, thoughts, and desires. Such people *must become awakened* now from their sleep of sin, or else ere long the thunders of judgment will arouse the stupid soul when too late. *"AWAKE to righteousness, and sin not"* (1 Cor. 15:34).

The true preaching of the gospel of Christ is designed to produce this desired effect. "For the word of God is quick and powerful, sharper than any two-edged sword, piercing even to the dividing asunder of soul and spirit, and of the joints and marrow, and is a discerner of the thoughts and intents of the heart. Neither is there any creature that is not manifest in his sight: but all things are naked and opened unto the eyes of him with whom we have to do" (Heb. 4:12, 13). When an individual becomes awakened to the fact that the law of Christ is laid upon the soul itself, so that even its secret purposes of evil are recorded against him in the book of God, and that for all such evil intentions, as well as sinful acts committed, he must suffer the pangs of torment— the guilt, the remorse, the horrors of hell itself—he will then realize what an awful thing sin really is in God's sight.

DESIRE AND DECISION.

The individual thus aroused as to the condemnation resting upon his guilty soul is in a good condition to cry, as did the jailer, "What must I do to be saved?" (Acts 16:30). He must desire salvation in order to obtain it, and he must decide to pay the Bible price, in the way of meeting the required conditions as set forth in the Bible. Mere knowledge of the nature and extent of sin is not sufficient; there must be in the soul genuine

GODLY SORROW.

The sinner must give up the love of sin, despise sin because God does, and feel keenly a sense of sorrow for all the sins he has committed, "for godly sorrow worketh repentance to salvation not to be repented of: but the sorrow of the world worketh death" (2 Cor. 7:10). Here godly sorrow is contrasted with the "sorrow of the world." Under certain conditions men guilty of sin feel very sorry, but it is when they are caught in their sins and are about to suffer the just consequences of their wrong-doing. Thus, the robber sentenced to imprisonment may weep, yet if he were free and knew that he could commit the same deed again without being found out, he would do so. This kind of sorrow does not produce heart repentance. But godly sorrow does not proceed from human exposure of wrong conduct, but is an internal realization of the soul's guilt in the sight of God accompanied by a *deep sense of regret* for the wrongs committed. This kind of sorrow worketh

REPENTANCE.

The term "repentance" includes also a sense of personal guilt, of grief over sin, hatred toward it, and *a resolute turning from it;* hence all the conditions of salvation may properly be termed the way of repentance. But the most prominent idea is that of the forsaking of sin "Repent ye therefore and be converted, that your sins may be blotted out" (Acts 3:19). "Let the wicked forsake his way, and the unrighteous man his thoughts: and let him return unto the Lord, and he will have mercy upon him; and to our God, for he will abundantly pardon" (Isa. 55:7). This includes evil habits of every description, no matter of how long standing, as the drinking of . intoxicants and lustful indulgences of a more secret nature. All unnatural, filthy, and evil habits must be utterly forsaken; then God will deliver the individual from their power.

People who think that they have received the divine favor without the forsaking of their sins, are deceived. It does not matter if they have prayed every day and asked for forgiveness, they are not saved while continuing to do the works of sin; and unless they come to the point where they actually turn from every wrong, and are saved from the past, they will be lost in hell with all of the non-professing sinners. Listen to the Word: "If I regard iniquity in my heart, *the Lord will not hear me*" (Psa. 66:18). If we excuse sin in our hearts and lives and expect to continue in it, we may pray as long as we live, but God will pay no attention to our prayers. In Mal. 2:13 we read of some people who were "covering the altar of the Lord with tears, with weeping, and with crying out," and still he would not regard them, for their hearts were not right. But the "broken spirit, a broken and a contrite heart"—the truly penitent heart—God will not despise (Psa. 51:17). When men become so broken in spirit that the hot tears of remorse and sorrow flow freely, when they realize their lost and undone condition without Christ, then there is hope for them in God. Bless his name!

CONFESSION.

But confession also is required. "He that covereth his sins shall not prosper: but whoso *confesseth* and forsaketh them shall have mercy" (Prov. 28:13). Many people tremble under the Holy Ghost preaching of the Word and realize their lost condition in sin, but are unwilling to confess their sins as the Bible requires.

But to whom must confession be made? First, *to the Lord*. "If we confess our sins, he is faithful and just to forgive us our sins" (1 John 1:9). Why should confession be made to him? Does he not know all about us before we confess? Yes, he understands us altogether. But here is one reason: God has set his own standard of right and wrong, thus defining sin; but sinful men set their own standards and attempt to justify themselves accordingly. Often we find people who are living in open violation of God's Word on some point, and yet they excuse themselves, affirming that their conscience does not condemn them, etc. Now, if such people seek for salvation from God, while setting their own standard as to what constitutes sin, God will never hear them. *They must acknowledge the standard God has set.* For example, some people possess a violent temper and frequently manifest it in outbursts of anger. Now, if such a one excuses these acts as not sinful, he can not obtain salvation, for such God has declared to be sinful, and he says, "Let all bitterness, and wrath, and anger . . . . be put away from you, with all malice" (Eph. 4:31). If this person hopes for Bible salvation, he must confess his sins *as sins*— on this line as well as on other lines. He must come to the divine standard.

In the second place, *confession must be made to men* — when our sins involve them. This requirement is like bitter medicine to some who have been doing the dark deeds of Satan by wronging their fellow men, and who are unwilling to acknowledge these to the proper parties. As the object of confession of sins to God is that we may be reconciled to him, so also the object of confession to people whom we have wronged is that a perfect reconciliation may be effected. God requires us, as say the Scriptures, "to have always a conscience void of offense toward God, and toward men" (Acts 24: 16).

Such confession is plainly taught by Jesus in the Sermon on the Mount. "Therefore if thou bring thy gift to the altar, and there rememberest that thy brother hath ought against thee; leave there thy gift before the altar, and go thy way; first be reconciled to thy brother, and then come and offer thy gift" (Matt. 5: 23, 24). While this language is based on the ceremonies of the law, it contains, nevertheless, a principle that no change of dispensations can affect. "The altar" was the place where pious Israelites came with their offerings when they desired to approach God. Christ taught that when they thus approached God they must be reconciled with their brethren—with each other, as the whole nation were regarded as brethren.

So also when we come to God for pardon of the sins which we have committed against him, in order that we may be reconciled to him, we must also confess to our fellow men the sins which we have committed against them, in order that we may be reconciled to them. "He that covereth his sins shall not prosper; but whoso con-

fesseth and forsaketh them shall have mercy." We can
not cover from the eyes of the Almighty the sins which
we have committed against him, but we may cover from
men the sins which we have committed against them;
but in either case sin *must be confessed and forsaken.*
When a certain man who had wronged another saw this
requirement of the Word, he stubbornly refused to com-
ply, saying, "I will go to hell first." Such people will
certainly go to destruction, for they hope in vain for
salvation from God when they are not willing to do
straight work with their fellow men.

RESTITUTION.

But this is not all. The words of Christ were, "be
reconciled." Now, reconciliation may in some cases require more than a mere confession of wrong-doing. If
one man has defrauded another out of twenty dollars,
acknowledgment of the wrong deed may need to be accompanied by the necessary money in order to effect a
proper reconciliation. This the Word teaches. "If the
wicked restore the pledge, *give again that he had robbed,*
walk in the statutes of life, without committing iniquity;
he shall surely live, he shall not die" (Ezek. 33:15).
So God requires those who desire life to set right their
former wrongs, and then to walk before God "without
committing iniquity" any more. This is not popular
doctrine, but it is God's word, and must be obeyed. That
class of people who object to the part of the Bible en-
joining restitution, generally have some restitution to
make themselves.

In some cases, however, such restitution may be altogether impossible. If a man has wrongly taken so much

that he is unable to restore all, it is reasonable to suppose that if he will humbly do all he can God will receive him. A text of Scripture, pertaining directly to another subject, however, may perhaps cover in principle such a case as this: "If there be first a willing mind, it is accepted according to that a man hath, and not according to that he hath not" (2 Cor. 8:12).

Furthermore, many personal wrongs do not rest on a financial basis, hence can not be made right by the mere giving of money. One person may be the direct means of ruining the virtue, the honor, or the character of another, and such, in the nature of the case, can never be restored. The guilty person can acknowledge his wrong and bitterly repent of it, but this is all he can do, and if he is ever saved, he must come in on mercy alone.

> "Just as I am, and waiting not
> To rid my soul of one dark blot;
> To thee, whose blood can cleanse each spot,
> O Lamb of God! I come, I come!"

FORGIVENESS.

Sometimes the matter is reversed; instead of the seeker's having wrongs to set right, others have wronged him, and he has treasured up in his heart feelings of bitterness and enmity toward the offenders. Unless such feelings are given up, they will forever bar the soul from reconciliation with God; for he absolutely refuses to deal with us until our relations with our fellow men are of the kind set forth in the Scriptures. Hear the words of Christ: "If ye forgive not men their trespasses, neither will your Father forgive your trespasses"; but "if ye forgive men their trespasses, your heav-

enly Father will also forgive you" (Matt. 6:15, 14).
Jesus set an example of the proper attitude toward
enemies. When dying on Calvary's cross, he did not
call down upon his persecutors the fiercest maledictions
of heaven, but tenderly prayed, "Father, *forgive them,*
for they know not what they do." The salvation of
Jesus Christ leaves no place in the human heart for that
which is sinful; therefore every bad act must be forsaken,
as well as every evil affection—bitterness, hardness,
hatred, and enmity.

Meeting the foregoing conditions will not of itself
save men, but it prepares the way so that when humble
hearts are willing to measure up to the standard, the
sweet peace and joy of heaven can come into the soul.

PRAYER.

The way is now open for the seeker to find access to
God, by asking for the pardon that the soul craves. The
Lord has instructed him to ask. "Ask, and it shall be
given you; seek, and ye shall find; knock, and it shall be
opened unto you" (Matt. 7:7). "The same Lord over
all is rich unto all that call upon him. For whosoever
shall call upon the name of the Lord shall be saved"
(Rom. 10:12).

FAITH.

Our prayers for salvation must be accompanied by
definite faith. "Repentance toward God, and *faith toward
our Lord Jesus Christ*" (Acts 20: 21), is the gospel
direction for obtaining this desired blessing. When the
penitent jailer cried out, "What must I do to be saved?"
the answer was quickly given, "Believe on the Lord

Jesus Christ, and thou shalt be saved" (Acts 16: 30, 31). But if the heart is rebellious and unwilling to measure to the requirements laid down in the Word, saving faith will be impossible. We read of one class of people who repented not, that they might believe (Matt. 21: 32). But obedience to the Word places us on believing-grounds, where prayer and faith become perfectly natural. Then "if thou shalt confess with thy mouth the Lord Jesus, and shalt believe in thine heart that God hath raised him from the dead, thou shalt be saved. *For with the heart man believeth unto righteousness;* and with the mouth confession is made unto salvation" (Rom. 10: 9, 10).

CHAPTER VII.

SALVATION.

Salvation is the grandest theme of gospel story, which is the most important message ever delivered to man. Centuries before the advent of the Messiah, the prophet Isaiah predicted his coming and said, "He will come and save you" (Isa. 35:4). The angel of God, announcing his birth, said to Joseph concerning Mary, "She shall bring borth a Son, and thou shalt call his name JESUS: for he shall *save his people* from their sins" (Matt. 1: 21). This was his special mission to earth. He himself declared, "The son of man is come to seek and to save that which was lost" (Luke 19:10). The apostle Paul affirms that "Christ Jesus came into the world to save sinners" (1 Tim. 1:15). Peter declares that God hath exalted Christ "to be a Prince and a Savior" (Acts 5: 31); while according to Hebrews he is still "able also to save them to the uttermost that come unto God by him, seeing he ever liveth to make intercession for them" (Heb. 7:25). Therefore salvation must be

A PRESENT POSSIBILITY.

In Heb. 2:3 we read, "How shall we escape if we neglect so great salvation?" The fact that men can neglect the great salvation of Jesus Christ proves that it is obtainable; and if it is obtainable, then it is a present possibility. The New Testament throughout speaks of salvation as obtainable by men in their present state on the earth. When the Philippian jailer asked, "What must I do to be saved?" the answer was quickly given,

"Believe on the Lord Jesus Christ, and thou shalt be saved" (Acts 16:30, 31). And Paul says, "I am not ashamed of the gospel of Christ; for it is the power of God unto salvation, to every one that believeth" (Rom. 1:16). And again, "If thou shalt confess with thy mouth the Lord Jesus, and shalt believe in thine heart that God hath raised him from the dead, thou shalt be saved" (Rom. 10:9). To the Corinthians he declared that it had "pleased God by the foolishness of preaching to save them that believe" (1 Cor. 1:21). And in language still more emphatic he declares, "Behold, now is the accepted time; behold, now is the day of salvation" (2 Cor. 6:2).

The text last quoted shows that this "great salvation" belongs in some special manner to the present dispensation of divine grace. Many people are being deceived by Satan into believing the fatal lie that in some way or other they can obtain salvation in a future age. "Behold, *now* is the accepted time; behold, *now* is the day of salvation." May God help every honest soul to see that salvation must be obtained now or never.

SOME HAVE OBTAINED IT.

One of the best proofs that salvation is a present possibility is the fact that some have already obtained it. In 2 Tim. 1:9 the apostle Paul affirms that God "hath saved us, and called us with an holy calling." Peter writes to certain brethren to this effect: Ye have received "the end of your faith, even the salvation of your souls" (1 Pet. 1:9). Paul refers to the work Christ wrought in human hearts, saying, "According to his mercy *he saved us,* by the washing of regeneration, and renewing of the Holy Ghost" (Tit. 3:5). "By grace ye are saved" (Eph. 2:5, 8). "For the preaching of the cross is to them that perish foolishness; but unto *us which are saved* it is the power of God" (1 Cor. 1:18).

WHAT SALVATION MEANS.

But what does this term "salvation" signify? Its literal meaning is *deliverance;* hence in its spiritual usage it signifies *deliverance from sin.* Let the Word of God define its meaning: "Thou shalt call his name Jesus; for he shall *save his people from their sins*" (Matt. 1: 21). "Ye know that he was manifested to *take away our sins*" (1 John 3:5). "For this purpose the Son of God was manifested, that he might destroy the works of the devil" (verse 8). He "gave himself for our sins, that he might *deliver us* from this present evil world" (Gal. 1:4).

The Word of God is so very plain that we marvel that so many people misunderstand its teaching on this point. It is the happy privilege of every guilty soul to receive, at this very hour, a free and perfect deliverance from all sin. "If we confess our sins, he is faithful and just to forgive us our sins, and to cleanse us from all unrighteousness" (1 John 1:9, 7). Yea, he hath "loved us, and washed us from our sins in his own blood" (Rev. 1:5).

Now, while all Christians believe that the blood of Christ was shed for sin, still in many cases this provision for sin is not connected vitally with the individual believer, thus making the work of actual deliverance from all sin a present accomplished fact. If the actual re-

sults of salvation are not accomplished in the heart and
life, then it is because the person is not yet saved. Many
people who are still continuing to do the works of sin
claim to be Christians, declaring that they are "saved
by faith" or are "sinners saved by grace." Now, how
can a person be saved by faith or by grace while at the
same time he *is not saved at all?* Salvation is received
by faith, but a definite result is obtained, for we "receive the *end of our faith,* even THE SALVATION OF
OUR SOULS" (1 Pet. 1:9). Of what use is a mere
profession of religion unless one has a real experience in
the soul? But when the person really has salvation, then
testifies boldly to the fact, it has the desired effect; as
Paul says, "That the communication of thy faith may
become effectual, by the acknowledging of every good
thing which is in you in Christ Jesus" (Phile. 6).

Notice how the apostle Paul also connects salvation
with its results in the individual heart and life: "For the
grace of God that bringeth *salvation* hath appeared to
all men, teaching us that, denying ungodliness and
worldly lusts, we should *live soberly, righteously, and
godly, in this present world;* looking for that blessed
hope, and the glorious appearing of the great God, and
of our Savior Jesus Christ; who gave himself for us,
that he might REDEEM us from all iniquity, and purify
unto himself a peculiar people, zealous of good works"
(Tit. 2:11-14).

JUSTIFICATION.

In the Scriptures salvation is described by different
terms, as justification, conversion, new birth, etc., each
of which conveys a certain special idea relative to the

subject. The reader must understand, however, that all
these terms used in the remainder of this chapter relate
to but one work, the first work of grace. We are not
justified at one time, converted at another time, receive
the new birth at another time, etc.; but these terms only
express different aspects of the same work.

We will consider justification first. This is the legal
aspect. To justify signifies to absolve from guilt. We
have already discussed the matter of man's responsibility
to infinite law, and shown that, having transgressed, man
possesses no power to free himself from the law's just
claims. But Christ gave himself as a ransom for sinners,
paying a sufficient satisfaction to God's justice, by which
means our sins, when confessed in the Bible way, are
laid upon him (Christ), while his righteousness becomes
ours; so that we stand in the same relation to God as
though we had never sinned. This is justification. It
is expressed by Paul in these words: "All have sinned,
and come short of the glory of God; being justified freely
by his grace through the redemption that is in Christ
Jesus: whom God hath set forth to be a propitiation
through faith in his blood, to declare his righteousness
for the remission of sins that are past, through the for-
bearance of God; to declare, I say, *at this time* his
righteousness: that he might be just, and the justifier of
him which believeth in Jesus .... Therefore we conclude
that a man is justified by faith" (Rom. 3:23-28).

God "made him to be sin for us, who knew no sin; that
we might be made the righteousness of God in him"
(2 Cor. 5:21). "For if by one man's offense death
reigned by one; much more they which receive abundance
of grace and of the gift of righteousness shall reign in

life by one Jesus Christ. Therefore as by the offense of one judgment came upon all men to condemnation; even so by the righteousness of one the free gift came upon all men unto justification of life. For as by one man's disobedience many were made sinners, so by the obedience of one shall many *be made righteous*" (Rom. 5: 17-19).

When we meet the conditions of God's Word and by faith accept Jesus Christ as our personal Savior, this legal transfer (if we may so express it) is made, and we are now regarded as being in a state of perfect conformity to God's moral law. "Therefore being justified by faith, we have peace with God through our Lord Jesus Christ" (Rom. 5: 1).

A false and deceptive doctrine, almost universally prevalent in Christendom, is to the effect that Christians can continue in sin and disobedience every day, and still be righteous, it being believed that the righteousness and obedience of Christ is imputed to them, simply because they recognize him as the world's Savior. But we must bear in mind that the righteousness of God which Paul says is imputed to us covers only the ground of our "sins that are past," those committed before we found Christ. From the moment of our justification we must ourselves live "in holiness and righteousness before him all the days of our life" (Luke 1: 75). Paul anticipated and repudiated this false conclusion regarding the imputing of Christ's righteousness to Christians, saying, "Shall we continue in sin, that grace may abound?" The very idea was repulsive to his mind, and he answered, "*God forbid*. How shall we that are dead to sin, live any longer therein?" (Rom. 6: 1, 2).

CONVERSION.

While justification signifies primarily a judicial acquittal, the opposite of condemnation, the primary meaning of Bible conversion is a change wronght in the individual himself, thus conveying guite a different idea; both, however, relate, with equal importance, to different aspects of the same salvation.

So far as the term itself is concerned it signifies merely "a change from one state to another"; hence it is often used for a mere external or outward reformation, or it is sometimes used to signify a change of beliefs or doctrinal convictions. But Bible, or saving, conversion is more than this, for it signifies a real change of heart and life. "Repent ye therefore, and be converted, that your sins may be blotted out, when the times of refreshing shall come from the presence of the Lord" (Acts 3: 19). "Hide thy face from my sins and blot out all mine iniquities. Create in me a clean heart, O God; and renew a right spirit within me. Then will I teach transgressors thy ways; and sinners shall be converted unto thee" (Psa. 51: 9, 10, 13). This experience is made necessary by the fact of sin, and Jesus himself has said, "Except ye be converted, and become as little children, ye shall not enter into the kingdom of heaven" (Matt. 18: 3).

THE NEW BIRTH.

The experience of salvation received through Christ is also represented as a birth of the Spirit. Jesus himself introduced this doctrine. "He came unto his own, and his own received him not. But as many as received him, to them gave he power to become the sons of God, even to them which believe on his name: *which were born,* not of blood, nor of the will of the flesh, nor of the will of man, *but of God"* (John 1: 11-13). According to this text, all who during the incarnation received Christ and believed on his name were born of God.

So too, when Nicodemus came by night to interview the Savior, acknowledging him as a teacher come from God, "Jesus answered and said unto him, Verily, verily I say unto thee; Except a man be born again, he can not see the kingdom of God" (John 3: 1-7). Nicodemus understood about natural birth, but could not comprehend this idea of a second birth that even an old man might obtain. So Jesus explained: "That which is born of the flesh is flesh; and that which is born of the Spirit is spirit. Marvel not that I said unto thee, *Ye must be born again."*

This doctrine of the new birth is fundamental; for without being born again no man can truly be called a Christian; for a Christian is one who is Christlike, and sinners must be transformed from sin to grace before they can be Christlike, and this change is effected by the Spirit in what is here termed the new birth.

The prominent idea connected with birth is a bringing into life. Now, sinful man is in the Scriptures represented as being in a state of spiritual death. To know God, and to be associated with him in holiness and fellowship, is life eternal, and is the normal sphere of the soul's happiness (John 17: 3). On the other hand, to be cut off by sin and separated from that vital union with our Maker is spiritual death. "I was alive without the law once: but when the commandment came, sin revived, and I died" (Rom. 7:9). In Isa. 59:1, 2 we read of how sin separates men from God. In 1 Tim. 5:6 Paul says, "She that liveth in pleasure is dead while she liveth." "And you, being dead in your sins." (Col. 2: 13). "And you hath he quickened *who were dead* in trespasses and sins: wherein in time past ye walked according to the course of this world" (Eph. 2:1, 2). How strange to think of dead men *walking!* Yet we are surrounded by millions of living, intelligent beings who are nevertheless "dead in trespasses and sins." These are the ones who "must be born again." But Jesus has come "that they might have life, and that they might have it more abundantly" (John 10:10). In John 1:12, 13, already quoted, we read that those who *believed* on Jesus' name were born of God; and in John 5:24 he says, "He that heareth my word, and believeth on him that sent me, hath everlasting life, and shall not come into condemnation, but *is passed from death unto life.*" The Beloved Apostle states very clearly "that God hath given to us eternal life, and this life is in his Son. He that hath the Son hath life; and he that hath not the Son of God hath not life" (1 John 5:11, 12).

Notwithstanding all these plain texts, and many others bearing on this subject, certain religious teachers affirm that the new birth is not an experience to be obtained now; that we are only begotten in this world, but shall be born in the next; that everlasting life is not obtainable in the present dispensation, etc. "What shall we then say to these things?" We will read the divine Word and let it decide, then "let God be true, but every man a liar" (Rom. 3:4).

"Whosoever believeth that Jesus is the Christ *is born of God"* (1 John 5:1). "Behold what manner of love the Father hath bestowed upon us, that we should be called the sons of God. . . . . Beloved, NOW *are we the sons of God"* (1 John 3:1, 2). "Because he is born of God" (1 John 3:9). "Being born again . . . . by the word of God" (1 Pet. 1:23). "Every one that doeth righteousness *is born of him"* (1 John 2:29). "Which were born . . . . of God" (John 1:12, 13). *"Because ye are sons,* God hath sent forth the Spirit of his Son into your hearts" (Gal. 4:6). "As new-born babes, desire the sincere milk of the Word, that ye may grow thereby" (1 Pet. 2:2). "The Spirit itself beareth witness with our spirit, *that we are the children of God"* (Rom. 8: 16). "Every one that loveth is born of God, and knoweth God" (1 John 4:7). And since we are already born of God, and are now his sons, his believing children, "we know that we have passed from death unto life" (1 John 3:14). *"God hath given to us* eternal life, and this life is in his Son. He that hath the Son hath life" (1 John 5:11, 12).

We must not overlook the miraculous feature of this new birth, this bringing into life. In the natural world, life proceeds only from life. Things inanimate can never endow themselves with natural life. So it is also in the spiritual realm. Man, who is "dead in trespasses and in sins," can never endow himself with spiritual life. He may possibly reform himself in certain particulars and perform many good works; but after he has reached the end of all self-effort, he will simply be a good moral man, and not what the Scriptures describe as a Christian, for a Christian is a good man *plus something else.* The additional something is life from God, which is infused by the divine Spirit into our hearts. "He that hath the Son hath life; and he that hath not the Son of God hath not life"; for "this life is in his Son" (1 John 5: 12, 11).

Millions of people call themselves Christians and think themselves on the road to heaven, when they are not, but are deceived; for they have never been born again, and Jesus himself declares, "Except a man be born again, he can not see the kingdom of God" (John 3: 3). How important, then, that experimental salvation be held before all men, so that they may know how to meet Bible conditions and receive a real conversion, this birth of the Spirit, which endows the individual with everlasting life, happiness, and joy! What a shame—what a lasting disgrace to the fair name of Christianity—that multitudes of sin-loving people should claim to be Christians simply because they have joined some human church, or because they were in infancy subjected to a ceremonial rite called baptism! Yet this is a sad fact. May God help to undeceive these blinded multitudes, who are rushing onward to an everlasting hell! Dear reader, if you are one of this number, I pray God to awaken you before it is too late; to write upon your soul as it were in letters of fire these words of our Lord, *"Ye must be born agan."*

KNOWLEDGE OF SALVATION.

This experience of salvation taught in the New Testament is not an imaginary something, but is a blessed reality. When presenting this subject the apostles al-

ways spoke with certainty. John affirmed: *"We know* that we have passed from death unto life" (1 John 3: 14). "We know that we are of God" (chap. 5: 19). "We are of God . . . . Every one that loveth is born of God, and knoweth God" (1 John 4: 6, 7). Salvation is of such a positive nature that we can not avoid knowing when we receive it; nevertheless we will notice briefly some of the means by which we are assured of the fact.

Negatively, we are made conscious of this great change by the fact that all our sins are removed. We read that Jesus came "to give *knowledge of salvation* unto his people by the remission of their sins" (Luke 1: 77). When the seeker is made deeply conscious of his sins, and comes to Jesus heavily burdened with the load of his guilt, confesses and forsakes them according to the requirements of the Word, and the good Lord graciously sweeps them all away by the power of his grace; and the sweet peace of heaven flows into the regenerated heart,—no one is needed to inform him that he is saved, for he is the first one to realize it. The experience of freedom from sin and its guilt is now as real as was the fact of sin before. But this is not all. New feelings, new hopes, and new aspirations spring up in the soul, so that he is made to realize the truth of the scripture that says, "Therefore if any man be in Christ, he is a new creature: old things are passed away; behold, all things are become new. And all things are of God" (2 Cor. 5: 17, 18).

How well does the writer remember the night when he was "born again" and became a "new creature" in Christ Jesus! Though I should live to be as old as Methusaleh, I could never forget it. With heart broken in Bible conviction, my sins looming up before me like mountains, and their guilt resting heavily upon my trembling soul, I knelt before my Lord and sought for mercy; his dying love captured my affections; my faith reached out and grasped the promises of life and salvation, and the burden of sin rolled away, while the sweet peace of God filled and thrilled my entire being. Halleluiah! The next morning nature itself seemed to assume a new aspect. Never before had the sun appeared to shine so brightly; the carpet of green spread over the earth had never appeared so lovely; the flowers were more beautiful than ever; and even the song of the little birds, wafted from the swaying tree-tops, possessed a melody almost divine. All nature seemed aglow with celestial beauty and glory on that bright morning. Upon a little reflection, however, I knew that nature was in reality just the same as before and that the change *was in me.* "If any man be in Christ, *he* is a new creature."

Another clear evidence of our salvation is the radical change that is wrought in our affections. First, *toward God.* While living a sinful life, men do not really love God from the heart, for they are living in a state of indifference toward the claims of God upon them. Some descend so deeply into sin that they even become "haters of God" (Rom. 1:30). But when our souls become awakened to the reality of the great love which God has shown to us, the manifestation of divine affection in the death of our Lord for us wins back our wandering affections, and we are ready to exclaim with the apostle, "We love him, because he first loved us" (1 John 4:19).

Then how natural it is to obey God! "If a man love me," says Jesus, "he will keep my words" (John 14: 23).

Second, we experience a real change in our affections with reference to *those who have been our enemies.* Instead of the hatred and the bitterness that we felt for them, we now experience a sense of love reaching out toward them; yea, the very words of Christ concerning this subject are fulfilled in us: "Love your enemies, bless them that curse you, do good unto them that hate you, and pray for them which despitefully use you and persecute you: that ye may be the children of your Father which is in heaven" (Matt. 5: 44, 45).

Third, our feelings *toward God's people* are also changed, and "we know that we have passed from death unto life, *because we love the brethren*" (1 John 3:14). And "by this we know that we love the children of God, when we love God, and keep his commandments" (1 John 5: 2). "My little children, let us not love in word, neither in tongue, but in deed and in truth. And hereby we know that we are of the truth, and shall assure our hearts before him" (1 John 3: 18, 19). So great is our holy love toward all the children of God that Christ has said, "By this shall all men know that ye are my disciples, if ye have love one to another" (John 13: 35).

But the best and clearest evidence of our acceptance with God is the internal witness of his Spirit. Salvation is received by faith. Paul said to the jailer, "*Believe on the Lord Jesus Christ, and thou shalt be saved.*" And the apostle John says, "He that believeth on the Son of God *hath the witness in himself*" (1 John 5: 10). There is no such thing as exercising saving faith in

Christ without experiencing within the assurance of the Holy Spirit that we are now saved. This witnessing can not be well explained in words, but, thank God! it can be experienced.

One man among the writer's acquaintances affirmed that he was converted two years before he found it out. A conversion, however, that one might not become cognizant of for two years could not be worth much. But it is very evident from the teaching of the Word of God that this man did not receive Bible conversion; for the true believer 'in Christ "hath the witness in himself."

Another man dreamed that he was saved and preaching the gospel, and when he awoke in the morning, he felt so happy that he concluded he was saved, announced a meeting for that night, and attempted to preach to the people. Bible salvation, however, is not obtained unconsciously or through dreams, but is received by intelligent faith. The recipient must be awake and earnestly seeking God according to his Word. When these conditions are met, the believing soul will experience a real change of heart and the direct evidence of the Spirit that he is saved. "The Spirit itself beareth witness with our spirit, that we are the children of God" (Rom. 8:16). The time and the manner of this change will ever afterwards stand out clear in the memory of the redeemed child of God.

Reader, do you remember a time in your life when sin was instantly canceled and the grace of God came into your soul? If not, then let me inform you that you have never been born again; hence you are not a true Christian. You may be a good moral person, humanly speaking, bearing an excellent reputation among men and professing to be a Christian, *but you are not a Christian* when measured in the light of God's Word. "Except a man be born again, he can not see the kingdom of God."

CHAPTER VIII.

A HOLY LIFE.

In the preceding chapter we showed what constitutes real Bible conversion, what it means to be born of God. In this chapter we desire to show what the Bible teaches concerning the life of those who have been born of God. The New Testament standard for God's people is one of sinlessness. "We know that whosoever is born of God sinneth not; but he that is begotten of God keepeth himself, and that wicked one toucheth him not" (1 John 5: 18).

WHAT IS SIN?

The same writer defines sin in these words: "Whosoever committeth sin transgresseth also the law: for sin is the transgression of the law" (1 John 3: 4). As we can more appropriately treat the subject of God's law in a subsequent chapter, it will not be necessary to enter into it in this place. Suffice it to say that the law by which our conduct will be judged, the transgression of which constitutes sin, is "the law of Christ" (Gal. 6: 2). Jesus himself has said, "He that rejecteth me, and receiveth not my words, hath one that judgeth him: the word that I have spoken, the same shall judge him in the last day" (John 12: 48).

Since we shall be judged in the last day by the law of Christ, it is evident that it is the law of Christ that we are now held responsible to obey. But God is just; therefore our responsibility is limited to our degree of enlightenment, there being in the New Testament no such thing as sin in total ignorance of God's requirements. "If ye were blind [spiritually] ye should have no sin" (John 9:41). "If I had not come and spoken unto them, they had not had sin" (John 15:22). "Sin is not imputed when there is no law" (Rom. 5:13). "For where no law is, there is no transgression" (Rom. 4:15). There must be some knowledge of our obligations, so that the will is involved, otherwise we are not reckoned transgressors. "Therefore to him that *knoweth* to do good, and doeth it not, to him it is sin" (Jas. 4:17). So also, on this principle, To him that knoweth that he should not do evil, and then doeth it, to him it is sin.

ALL MEN BY NATURE SINNERS.

It is a fact that in all places and in all ages of the world men have acknowledged that they were under sin; for all realize that their wills have been involved in acts which they recognize to be in their very nature wrong. Therefore the Bible recognizes this universality of sin, saying: "There is no man that sinneth not" (1 Kings 8:46). "For all have sinned, and come short of the glory of God" (Rom. 3:23). "The Scripture hath concluded all under sin" (Gal. 3:22).

But while the Old Testament recognizes the universal prevalence of sin, it also contains predictions of a divine provision for its removal. Isaiah, speaking of Christ, said, "He will come and save you" (Isa. 35:4). And Zechariah says, "In that day there shall be a fountain opened to the house of David and to the inhabitants of Jerusalem for sin and for uncleanness" (Zech. 13:1).

Here we find special provisions for sin. Daniel predicted the coming of the Messiah, saying, "Seventy weeks are determined upon thy people and upon thy holy city, to finish the transgression, and to make an end of sins, and to make reconciliation for iniquity, and to bring in everlasting righteousness, and to seal up the vision and prophecy, and to anoint the Most Holy" (Dan. 9: 24). All these inspired prophecies met their fulfilment in that Christ who came to "save his people from their sins" (Matt. 1: 21).

CHRISTIANS ARE SAVED FROM SIN.

"And ye know that he was manifested to take away our sins; and in him is no sin. Whosoever abideth in him sinneth not: whosoever sinneth hath not seen him, neither known him" (1 John 3: 5, 6). This is the uniform gospel standard, as we shall see.

1. *Christ taught it.* "Verily, verily I say unto you, Whosoever committeth sin is the servant of sin . . . . If the Son therefore shall make you free, *ye shall be free indeed*" (John 8: 34-36). Here is promised a perfect freedom from the bondage of sin.

In the fifth chapter of John we read of a certain impotent man lying at the pool of Bethesda, whose infirmity was of thirty-eight years' duration. Jesus came along and healed him. "Afterward Jesus findeth him in the temple, and said unto him, Behold, thou art made whole: SIN NO MORE, lest a worse thing come unto thee" (verse 14). Now, it is preposterous to suppose that Christ was unjust, giving a commandment that could not be obeyed—a commandment whose violation was to bring upon the poor man a sorer punishment than he had endured during those thirty-eight long years. It could be obeyed. This man received power from the Lord to go and live without sin.

Again, in John 8: 3-11 we read of a certain woman who was brought to Christ accused of great sin. After a short conversation, during which time the scribes and Pharisees, becoming condemned by their consciences because of their own sins, went away, Jesus turned to the woman and said, "Where are those thine accusers? hath no man condemned thee [legally]? She said, No man, Lord. And Jesus said unto her, Neither do I condemn thee: GO AND SIN NO MORE."

2. *Peter taught it.* "Repent ye therefore, and be converted, that your sins may be blotted out; when the times of refreshing shall come from the presence of the Lord" (Acts 3: 19). "Christ also suffered for us, leaving us an example, that ye should follow his steps: who did no sin, neither was guile found in his mouth" (1 Pet. 2: 21, 22).

3. *Paul taught it.* "Awake to righteousness, *and sin not;* for some have not the knowledge of God: I speak this to your shame" (1 Cor. 15: 34, 35). Almost the whole of the sixth chapter of Romans is devoted to the subject of the Christians' deliverance from sin. I will notice just a few verses wherein it is stated.

"What shall we say then? shall we continue in sin, that grace may abound? God forbid. How shall we that are dead to sin, live any longer therein?" (verses 1, 2). "Likewise reckon ye also yourselves to be dead indeed unto sin, but alive unto God through Jesus Christ our Lord. Let not sin therefore reign in your mortal bodies, that ye should obey it in the lusts thereof" (verses 11, 12). *"Sin shall not have dominion over you:* for ye are not under the law, but under grace" (verse 14). "Ye were the servants of sin, but ye have obeyed from the heart that form of doctrine which was delivered you. *Being then made free from sin,* ye became the servants of righteousness" (verses 17, 18). "But now being made free from sin, and become servants to God, ye have your fruit unto holiness, and the end everlasting life" (verse 22).

Some people attempt to prove that Paul himself was a sinner and a defender of sin; but this chapter alone is sufficient to forever settle his attitude *as a Christian* toward the subject of sin. This point we will refer to again in the present chapter.

4. *John taught it.* "If we walk in the light as he is in the light we have fellowship one with another, and the blood of Jesus Christ his Son *cleanseth us from all sin.* If we say that we have no sin [to be cleansed from], we deceive ourselves, and the truth is not in us. If we confess our sins, he is faithful and just to forgive us our sins, and to cleanse us from all unrighteousness" (1 John 1: 7-9). Here a perfect cleansing from sin is taught, upon condition that we do not cover our sins up and deny them, but "walk in the light" and "confess our sins." And the same writer also shows that we must live before Christ in this sinless state, for he says, "He that sayeth he abideth in him ought himself also so to walk, even as he walked" (1 John 2: 6). How did Christ walk? Peter affirms that he "did no sin, neither was guile found

in his mouth" (1 Pet. 2: 22). Hence we must do no sin.
This is the Christian standard.

So John writes again, "My little children, these things
I write unto you, THAT YE SIN NOT" (1 John 2: 1).
In the same verse he goes on to show that "*if* any man
sin, we have an advocate with the Father, Jesus Christ
the righteous." This shows that, even if men should by
some means depart from the Christian standard by falling into sin, it is possible for them to be recovered, because Christ would be willing to forgive again. This,
however, does not in the least weaken the standard here
set forth that "he that sayeth he abideth in him *ought*
himself also so to walk, even as he walked" (verse 6).
But the apostle goes a step further; he shows not only
that Christians "ought" to walk this way, but that they
really *do*. "Whosoever abideth in him sinneth not: whosoever sinneth hath not seen him, neither known him"
(1 John 3: 6). "*We know that whosoever is born of God
sinneth not;* but he that is begotten of God keepeth himself, and that wicked one toucheth him not" (1 John 5:
18).

"Little children, let no man deceive you: he that doeth
righteousness is righteous, even as he is righteous. Whosoever is born of God *doth not commit sin;* for his seed
remaineth in him: and he can not sin, because he is born
of God" (1 John 3: 7, 9). Reader, mark this fact: John
does not say that God's people confess their sins every
day or repent of them frequently, but says that they
"DO NOT COMMIT SIN." Thousands of professed
Christians have asked the question, "Who are those
'just persons which need no repentance,' of which Christ

speaks" (Luke 15:7)? The answer is very clear: They are the Christians, those who have been born of God; for *"Whosoever* is born of God *doth not commit* sin." They need not, and hence could not, repent.

THE LINE OF DISTINCTION.

Recently the writer held a conversation with two ministers who were earnestly denying the doctrine of Christian freedom from sin, notwithstanding this solid array of New Testament texts clearly stating this doctrine in so many words. I then asked them to tell me the difference between sinners and these so-called "sinning Christians." Their reply was that the sinning Christians confess their sins and ask for forgiveness every day, whereas the sinners do not. I replied that, so far as such lives were concerned, they looked very much alike to me, and that this distinction reminded me of the following story, which I recently read, but of the truthfulness of which I am unable to vouch:

An Episcopalian clergyman that was traveling in one of the Southern States interviewed a farmer one day concerning religion. Asked concerning his religion, the farmer replied:

"I am an Episcopalian."

"By whom were you confirmed?" asked the clergyman.

"Confirmed?" said the farmer, "what is that?"

"How did you become an Episcopalian without learning about being confirmed?"

"Well, it was this way," the farmer replied: "Last summer I was visiting down in New Orleans, and one day I went to church; and there I heard the people say-

ing that they were doing many things that they ought not
to do, and were leaving undone many things that they
should do, that they were making many crooked paths
for their feet; and I said to myself, 'That's just the fix
I'm in.' When I went out I asked some one, 'What
church is this?' and he told me that it was the Episcopalian; so I have been Episcopal ever since."

He thought he had found his kind.

But God draws a distinct line of demarcation between
sinners and Christians. We have already shown by
many texts that God's people are saved from their sins,
and do not commit sin.

THE CONTRAST.

Now we will notice what the Bible has to say, by way
of contrast, concerning the other class.

JESUS: "Whosoever committeth sin is the servant of
sin" (John 8:34).

PAUL: "When ye were the servants of sin, *ye were
free from righteousness*" (Rom. 6:20).

PETER: "Having eyes full of adultery, and that *can
not cease from sin* . . . . to whom the mist of darkness
is reserved forever" (2 Pet. 2:14, 17).

JAMES: "Ye adulterers and adultresses, know ye not
that the friendship of the world is enmity with God?
whosoever therefore will be a friend of the world is the
enemy of God" (Jas. 4:4).

JUDE: "Ungodly sinners . . . . walking after their
own lusts . . . . having men's persons in admiration because of advantage . . . . These be they who separate
themselves [from the truth, and from the doctrine of a

sinless life], sensual, *having not the Spirit*" (Jude 15-19).

JOHN: "We know that we are of God, and the *whole world lieth in wickedness*" (1 John 5: 19). "Whosoever sinneth hath not seen him [Christ] neither known him" (1 John 3: 6). Mark this contrast: "He that committeth sin. *is of the devil;* for the devil sinneth from the beginning . . . . Whosoever is born of God *doth not commit sin. . . . . IN THIS the children of God are manifest, and the children of the devil;* whosoever doeth not righteousness is not of God" (1 John 3: 8-10), and "he that doeth righteousness is righteous, even as he [Christ] is righteous" (verse 7). The line of distinction which God has made is drawn between those who commit sin, and those who do not commit sin. Those who do not sin are born of God, and know God, and have his righteousness; while, on the other hand, those who commit sin are the servants of sin, and are doing the devil's work, hence belong to him —are "of the devil"—and *are not the children of God at all.* I pray God to grant that souls may "awake to righteousness, *and sin not.*"

> "Heaven is a holy place,
> Filled with glory and with grace;
> Sin can never enter there.
> All within its gates are pure,
> From defilement kept secure;
> Sin can never enter there.

> "If you cling to sin till death,
> When you draw your latest breath,
> You will sink in dark despair
> To the regions of the lost,
> Thus to prove at awful cost
> Sin can never enter there.

"Sin can never enter there,
Sin can never enter there;
  So if at the judgment-bar
  Sinful spots your soul shall mar,
YOU *can never enter there.*"

SOME OBJECTIONS ANSWERED.

When the doctrine of salvation from sin and a holy, sinless life is presented, people frequently come forward with certain objections to this standard. Now, so far as these objections are sincere, based upon certain Scripture texts, they are worthy of consideration and explanation; for when rightly interpreted, they harmonize beautifully with the general plan of redemption. There is no contradiction on this subject in God's Word when understood in relation to his progressive plan of salvation.

Objection 1. "There is no man that sinneth not" (1 Kings 8:46). "For there is not a just man upon earth, that doeth good, and sinneth not" (Eccl. 7:20).

Answer. These words were uttered by King Solomon, who lived about one thousand years before Christ, in the dispensation when it was "not possible that the blood of bulls and of goats should take away sins" (Heb. 10: 4). Many men of that dispensation possessed great faith in God and, considering the general standards of those times, lived very good lives; hence they were accepted by God on the ground of their faith, when they conformed to the highest standard of his revealed will.

But the experience of the new birth, the regeneration of the soul which makes men "new creatures," was not realized in those days; hence people then did not claim to live without committing sin. The plan of salvation from all sin through Christ was from the foundation of the world a "mystery" which was "hid in God" (Eph. 3:9), a mystery which even "the angels desired to look into" (1 Pet. 1:12), but which in the gospel dispensation "is made manifest to his saints" (Col. 1:26). Jesus said to his disciples, "Many prophets and righteous men [of the old dispensation] have desired to see those things which ye see, and have not seen them; and to hear those things which ye hear, and have not heard them. Blessed are your eyes, for they see: and your ears, for they hear" (Matt. 13:17, 16).

These prophets, however, caught a glimpse of this coming redemption, and wrote of it, though they did not themselves experience it. This is clearly stated by Peter, who wrote concerning brethren in the new dispensation: "Receiving the end of your faith, *even the salvation of your souls. Of which salvation* the prophets have inquired and searched diligently, who *prophesied of the grace that should come unto you:* searching what or what manner of time the Spirit of Christ which was in them did signify, when it testified beforehand the sufferings of Christ, and the glory that should follow. Unto whom it was revealed, that *not unto themselves* but *unto us* they did minister the things, which are now reported unto you by them that have preached the gospel unto you with the Holy Ghost sent down from heaven" (1 Pet. 1: 9-12). This makes it clear that the experience of salvation which we now receive through Christ was not experienced before his coming, even by the prophets who wrote of it.

Those who deny the sinless life are sure to quote Eccl. 7: 20, which says that "there is not a just man upon earth, that doeth good, and sinneth not." But why do they not quote 1 John 3: 9, which says that "whosoever is born of God doth not commit sin"? Do these texts appear contradictory? So they are in statement, but they are not contradictory in the plan of God, for Solomon wrote under the old dispensation, while John wrote under the new. The true basis of harmony is found in the fact that *"the blood of Jesus Christ his Son cleanseth us from all sin"* (1 John 1: 7).

Objection 2. Paul's experience in Romans 7, where he says: "I know that in me dwelleth no good thing: for to will is present with me; but how to perform that which is good I find not. For the good that I would I do not: but the evil which I would not, that I do. Now if I do that I would not, it is no more I that do it, but sin that dwelleth in me. I find then a law, that, when I would do good, evil is present with me. Oh, wretched man that I am!" etc.

Answer. A study of the entire chapter shows clearly that the apostle was describing his experience under the law of Moses, before he found Christ. He first speaks of his infantile state, when he was "alive without the law"—did not even know that the law said, "Thou shalt not covet." Afterward "when the commandment came" to him, he says, "sin revived, and I died." (see verses 7-13.) This law under which he was brought up was good in that it defined sin and revealed his condition as an actual sinner, but it did not bring to him deliverance and salvation from sin; therefore he cried out,

"Oh, wretched man that I am! who shall deliver me from the body of this death?" Then he obtained a ray of hope and answered the question himself: "I thank God through Jesus Christ our Lord" (verses 24, 25).

This sin-experience was the experience of Saul, the man who zealously defended the law and persecuted the church of God; but immediately following we have, in his own words, the experience of Paul the Christian: "There is therefore NOW no condemnation to them which are in Christ Jesus, who walk not after the flesh, but after the Spirit. For the law of the Spirit of life in Christ Jesus *hath made me free from the law of sin and death.* For what the law [of Moses] could not do, in that it was weak through the flesh, God sending his own Son in the likeness of sinful flesh, and for sin condemned sin in the flesh: that the righteousness of the law might be fulfilled in us, *who walk not after the flesh, but after the Spirit*" (Rom. 8: 1-4).

Reader, which do you desire, the experience of Saul, or the experience of Paul? After he found deliverance from sin through Christ, he taught that Christians are to live without sin. "Shall we continue in sin, that grace may abound? God forbid. *How shall we that are dead to sin live any longer therein?*" (Rom. 6: 1, 2). "For *sin shall not have dominion over you*: FOR YE ARE NOT UNDER THE LAW, BUT UNDER GRACE" (verse 14). This last text clears up the entire matter. Under the law sin had dominion over the people; under grace, God's people have dominion over sin. Under the law, it might be said, "There is not a just man upon earth, that doeth good, and sinneth not"; but under grace,

"Whosoever is born of God doth not commit sin." "The law was given by Moses; but grace and truth came by Jesus Christ" (John 1:17). Yea, "the *grace of God* that bringeth salvation hath appeared to all men, teaching us that, denying ungodliness and worldly lusts, we should live soberly, righteously, and godly, in this present world." Why? Because Christ "gave himself for us, *that he might redeem us from ALL iniquity,* and purify unto himself a peculiar people, zealous of good works" (Tit. 2:11-14).

That the sin-experience described in Romans 7 was not the experience of Paul the Christian at the time when he was writing this chapter, is shown also by other facts. This Epistle was written about the year A. D. 60. Six years before this time, or in A. D. 54, he was living a much better life than that; for he declared to the Thessalonian brethren, "Ye are witnesses, and God also, how *holily,* and *justly,* and *unblameably* we behaved ourselves among you that believe" (1 Thess. 2:10). Was he a backslider at the time when he wrote the Roman Epistle? No; for about that same year, A. D. 60, he testified before a council, "I have lived in all good conscience before God until this day" (Acts 23:1). And a few days later he said, "Herein do I exercise myself, to have always a conscience void of offense toward God, and toward men" (Acts 24:16). Neither did he dishonor God and his cause by departing into sin after this time, for in his dying testimony, given about six years later, he said: "The time of my departure is at hand. *I have fought a good fight,* I have finished my course, *I have kept the faith*" (2 Tim. 4:7).

Objections based on certain other texts of Scripture (for example, Romans 3:10) are of this same general character; for almost without exception they relate to Old Testament conditions, not to the New Testament standard of salvation.

The doctrine of sinning Christians originates either in a perverse state of the soul or else in a total failure to understand dispensational truth; for this last-named fact disposes of all the objections to holiness. A proper understanding of the difference between the old covenant and the new will forever settle the subject concerning the present relation of God's people with sin.

FREEDOM FROM WORLDLINESS.

This is simply another division of the subject of sin, for wordliness is sin. However, there are some special thoughts that I wish to present under this heading.

Since sin in its various forms has become universal, surrounding us on all sides, as real as nature itself, the Bible writers often refer to it as "the world." This includes not only the grosser forms of sin, but all manner of disobedience to God of whatsoever nature or extent. God's people must be free from all these things. Paul says to the brethren who had been quickened in Christ, "In time past ye walked according to the course of this world" (Eph. 2:2). But Christ "gave himself for our sins, that he might deliver us from this present evil world" (Gal. 1:4).

That our separation from the world in this sense is to be real, is shown by the words of Christ, "If ye were of the world, the world would love his own: but because ye are not of the world, but I have chosen you out of the world, therefore the world. hateth you" (John 15: 19). Reader, bear in mind that if you take your stand for God and for the whole truth of his Word, determined to be free from all worldliness, there will be a real separation in spirit and in life between you and the worldly-minded. You will even have opposition. "Yea, and all that will live godly in Christ Jesus shall suffer persecution" (2 Tim. 3:12).

This experience was truly realized by the first disciples, for we have the testimony of Jesus himself that they were free from the world. He said of them in prayer to the Father: "I have given them thy Word; and the world hath hated them, because they are not of the world, even as I am not of the world. I pray not that thou shouldst take them out of the world, but that thou shouldst keep them from the evil. *They are not of the world even as I am not of the world*" (John 17:14-16).

To us this means that everything which partakes of the spirit and nature of the world must be forsaken—worldly sentiments, worldly associations, worldly ambitions, worldly amusements, and worldly dress—everything that is not in strict harmony with the plain teaching of God's Word. "Love not the world, neither the things that are in the world. If any man love the world, the love of the Father is not in him. For all that is in the world, the lust of the flesh, and the lust of the eyes, and the pride of life, *is not of the Father, but is of the world*. And the world passeth away, and the lust thereof; but he that doeth the will of God abideth forever" (1 John 2:15-17).

WORLDLY AMUSEMENTS.

According to the principles of truth already laid down, it is evident that the holy people of God can not go to and participate in those amusements whose direct object is to cater to the spirit of foolishness, vanity, and sin. At the present day Satan is seeking by this means to draw the hearts of the people everywhere into the deeper ways of sin, thus causing them to forget God. Especially is this true respecting the young. How many are the forms of worldly amusement that have been devised and that serve this purpose!—shows, festivals, races of various kinds, card-parties, prize fights, theaters, etc. These things "are not of the Father, but are of the world"; and no true child of God can indulge in such things without loss to his spirituality and, if the indulgence is continued, the final loss of his soul. "Flee also youthful lusts: but follow righteousness, faith, charity, peace, with them that call on the Lord out of a pure heart" (2 Tim. 2: 22).

The Christian must live a life of prayer and devotion to God. By this means his spirit is refreshed from day to day, and he thus obtains conquering grace for trials and temptations. But this life of devotion can not exist where the spirit of worldliness is allowed sway. Those who attend worldly amusements do not feel a burden for secret prayer and devotion, and they have little or no active interest in the salvation of souls; while, on the other hand, those who are spiritual and live in prayer before God, *have no desire for such amusements*. They are dead to the world and its pleasures.

Of them, Jesus can say, "They are not of the world, even as I am not of the world."

WORLDLY DRESS.

But the Word of God comes even closer and lays down certain rules concerning the Christian's dress. The command of the Word is, "Glorify God in your body, and in your spirit, which are God's" (1 Cor. 6:20). We must "be holy both in body and in spirit" (1 Cor. 7:34). If we have holy, humble hearts, hearts free from vanity and pride, then our outward lives must in every way be consistent with the inward condition. Now, when people's hearts are full of the "pride of life," how do they manifest it? By proud actions and by worldly dress. They seek to adorn themselves with gold, pearls, diamonds, rubies, and costly array; until the beholder views a dazzling display of ear-rings, finger-rings, bracelets, lockets, and other ornaments; not to mention an immense amount of other costly, useless, and foolish array. What does the Word of God say on this subject?

"Whose adorning *let it not be* that outward adorning of plaiting the hair, and of *wearing of gold,* or of putting on of apparel: but let it be the hidden man of the heart, in that which is not corruptible, even the ornament of a meek and quiet spirit, which is in the sight of God of great price" (1 Pet. 3:3, 4). Yet how many professing Christians totally disregard the plain teaching of the Word on this point, and dress in all the pride and fashion of this world!

In the scriptures just given, the apostle Peter forbids the wearing of that outward adornment which is sug-

gested by pride; but the apostle Paul goes a step further
and shows how Christian women must be dressed. He
says, "In like manner also that women adorn themselves
in modest apparel, with shamefacedness and sobriety;
not with broided hair, or gold, or pearls, or costly array;
but (which becometh women professing godliness) with
good works" (1 Tim. 2: 9, 10). They must be arrayed
in *"modest apparel . . . .* not with gold, or pearls, or
costly array." These articles of adornment, then, are
not modest apparel. The wearing of them is prompted,
not by feelings of humility and modesty, but by pride
in the heart. It is plain from this scripture that such
things do not *"become women professing godliness."*
Reader, are you a woman "professing godliness"? Are
you adorned with these things? If so, then they do not
"become your profession," and *you are not arrayed in*
"modest apparel."

"Modest apparel" requires a dress that is clean and
neat, so as not to become immodest, through the failure
to measure up to ordinary standards of decency; but,
on the other hand, it is dress that is free from useless,
worldly trimmings and accompaniments, from ostenta-
tion and show. Ear-rings, finger-rings, necklaces, lockets,
bracelets, feathers, artificial flowers, and many other like
things, *"are not of the Father, but are of the world,"*
when it comes to the matter of the Christian's dress.
"BE NOT CONFORMED TO THIS WORLD," the
Word of God rings out (Rom. 12: 2), and all the pure
and holy in heart are ready to say amen.

These principles apply with equal force to the male
sex. The foolish, vain, and immodest styles and fash-

ions to which the worldly-minded cater are an abomination in the sight of God and in the sight of his redeemed saints. Do not deceive yourself, reader, in the belief that you can continue to wear things which the Word of God forbids, and still be a spiritual person, filled with the grace of God. It is impossible. God's children are to be "*obedient children,* not fashioning yourselves according to the former lusts in your ignorance" (1 Pet. 1:14).

How often we meet professing Christians who are living in open violation of this part of the Bible, and who, when we mention the fact to them, are ready to excuse themselves, saying, "Oh, these things are not in my heart"! Well, if they are not in the heart, then why are they carried about on the person? When we enter the city and see a display-sign outside of a store, we naturally expect to find the goods thus advertised kept in stock in that store. Now, we know that proud people manifest their pride in their dress. If you are humble in heart, free from this worldly abomination, and do not wish to be mistaken for a proud person, then *take down the sign.* If you think these things are not in your heart, then it will be a very easy matter for you to prove it by obeying God's Word and removing them from your person. When you undertake to do this, however, you may find, as thousands of others have found, that the love of such things goes deeper than you have ever imagined. Your teeth may rest so easily in your mouth that you seldom think of them; but when the dentist attempts to remove one, you become painfully aware of the fact that it has long roots and draws hard. Similarly you may be so accustomed to wearing worldly adornments that they seem perfectly natural and easy, so that you are deceived into thinking that they are all on the outside; but when you attempt to obey God's Word and discard them, you will find that they are rooted in your affections and reach down deep into the soul. But Jesus says, "If a man love me, *he will keep my words*" (John 14:23). "Why call ye me, Lord, Lord, and do not the things which I say?" (Luke 6:46).

THE POSITIVE SIDE.

Nor is holy life to be judged solely by a negative standard— by what we put off of sin and worldliness. There is a positive side. When we die to the world, we "put on Christ." Then we can say with the apostle Paul, "I am crucified with Christ: nevertheless I live; yet not I, but Christ liveth in me: and the life which I now live in the flesh, I live by the faith of the Son of God, who loved me, and gave himself for me" (Gal. 2:20). Our whole desire is to manifest Christ to the world. Being "risen with Christ," we "seek those things which are above" (Col. 3:1). We "put on therefore, as the elect of God, holy and beloved, bowels of mercies, kindness, humbleness of mind, meekness, long-suffering" (verse 12). The graces of the Spirit implanted within find outward expression in "the fruit of the Spirit," which is "love, joy, peace, long-suffering, gentleness, goodness, faith, meekness, temperance" (Gal. 5:22, 23). Our aim in life is to have always a conscience void of offense toward God and toward man. But even in this we do not allow the voice of conscience alone to dictate in matters of religious faith, but we render loving and willing obedience to all the commandments of our Lord and require our conscience to come into line with what the Word plainly says. Thus our lives are free and happy, and are made a blessing to all around us. This phase of the subject will be more fully treated hereafter.

Oh, how much it means to serve God "without fear, in holiness and righteousness before him all the days of our life" (Luke 1: 75)!

CHAPTER IX.

SANCTIFICATION.

Conversion and a subsequent life free from sin, taught in the preceding chapters, is indeed a high state of grace; nevertheless it is not the complete sum of Christian experience as set forth in the New Testament. As our object is to set forth what the Bible teaches, we will in this chapter show that the New Testament clearly teaches a second, definite work of divine grace wrought in the heart by the Holy Spirit, a work termed "sanctification." The Bible writers speak of it from various standpoints, sometimes one phase of the subject and sometimes another being emphasized, and therefore different terms are used to express it; all, however, are resolved into the same thing. When the subject is considered from the standpoint of sanctification, a *result* is thereby expressed, and the cause of this result may or may not be stated in a given instance. In this chapter we will consider it first as a result, or work in the soul, and then proceed to show the cause that produces this effect.

The first point that we will settle is the fact that sanctification is

A BIBLE DOCTRINE.

The apostle Paul states that God hath "chosen you to salvation through sanctification of the Spirit, and belief of the truth" (2 Thess. 2: 13). Sanctification is therefore a part of the work of salvation, and belongs to all of God's people. Christ prayed earnestly that his disciples might have this experience, as we read in John 17:17— "Sanctify them through thy truth: thy word is truth." He did even more than to pray for it: he gave his life that it might be accomplished. "Wherefore Jesus also, that he might sanctify the people with his own blood, suffered without the gate" (Heb. 13:12). But it is his own people that are to be sanctified, for Paul informs us that "Christ also loved the church, and gave himself for it: that he might sanctify and cleanse it" (Eph. 5:25, 26).

This was also taught by the apostles. Peter states that our election is "through sanctification of the Spirit" (1 Pet. 1:2). And Paul, writing to the Thessalonian brethren, says: "For this is the will of God, even your sanctification" (1 Thess. 4:3); and "the very God of peace sanctify you wholly; and I pray God your whole spirit and soul and body be preserved blameless unto the coming of our Lord Jesus Christ. Faithful is he that calleth you, who also will do it" (1 Thess. 5:23, 24). We must be "a vessel unto honor, *sanctified*, and meet for the Master's use" (2 Tim. 2:21). These texts, and others that might be cited, show clearly that sanctification is a New Testament doctrine.

WHAT DOES SANCTIFICATION SIGNIFY?

The term "sanctification" is defined by Webster as follows:

"1. The act of consecrating, or of setting apart for a sacred purpose; consecration.

"2. The act of sanctifying or making holy; or the

state of being sanctified or made holy; the act of God's
grace by which the affections of men are purified, or
alienated from sin and the world, and exalted to a supreme love to God; also the state of being thus purified
or sanctified."

The word "sanctify" he defines thus:

"1. To make sacred or holy; to set apart to a holy
or religious use; to consecrate by appropriate rites; to
hallow.

"2. To make holy or free from sin; to cleanse from
moral corruption and pollution; to make fit for the service of God, and the society and employments of heaven."

By the foregoing definitions it will be seen that sanctification signifies two distinct things: first, a consecrating,
or setting apart to a holy or religious use—a mere legal
or ceremonial holiness; second, a definite cleansing and
purifying of the heart and affections of men—a moral
work.

Now, the term is used in the Bible with both of these
significations; therefore we must be careful to "rightly
divide the word of truth." In the Old Testament, under
the law dispensation, sanctification is often mentioned;
but it was merely a legal sanctification, a setting apart
to a religious use. This was before the time when full
salvation could be wrought in the soul through the blood
of Christ; therefore a moral change was not under consideration at all; in fact, the objects of that sanctification were in many cases wholly incapable of receiving
any moral change, for inanimate objects, as well as
animate, received it. Thus, the tabernacle was sanctified (Ex. 40: 9), the altar (verse 10), the vessels of the

tabernacle (verse 9), the laver (verse 11), the mountain
of Sinai (Ex. 19:23). All of these objects, and others
of like nature, were incapable of moral change, but
they could be consecrated for a religious use. So also
all Israel was sanctified (Ex. 19:10, 14). This sanctification of the people, however, refers to consecration
only, not to any moral change in their natures, for the
act was performed by man (see Ex. 19:10, 14; Lev.
27:14-22).

But in the New Testament the term "sanctification"
is given the other signification—a purging or cleansing
of the moral nature of man. This is shown by the following considerations: 1. None but human beings can
receive it, for it is given only to those who obey God
(Luke 11:13; Acts 5:32; Rom. 15:16). 2. It is performed by the Holy Ghost, not by man (Rom. 15:16;
Acts 15:8, 9; Heb. 10:14, 15). 3. It is connected with
the blood of Christ (Heb. 13:12; 10:10, 14, 15; 1
Thess. 5:23). It is in this New Testament sense that
I shall use the term throughout the remainder of this
chapter.

FOR JUSTIFIED PEOPLE ONLY.

While none but human beings can receive this glorious
experience of sanctification, not all of them obtain it;
for it is reserved for those who have already been justified from their actual transgressions through the blood
of Jesus Christ. In other words, people must be genu-
inely converted to God, born again, and living the sinless
life described in the preceding chapter, before they are
Scriptural candidates for sanctification. In Christ's

prayer concerning his disciples, he said, "I pray for them: *I pray not for the world,* but for them which thou hast given me . . . . sanctify *them*" (John 17:9, 17). "Christ also loved the church, and gave himself for it; that he might sanctify and cleanse *it*" (Eph. 5:25, 26). It is the "brethren" that receive "an inheritance among all them which are sanctified" (Acts 20:32). Yea, people must first "receive forgiveness of sins" before they can obtain the "inheritance" among them which are "sanctified" (Acts 26:18). It was to the brethren at Thessalonica, to those who were "in the Father, and in the Lord Jesus Christ" (1 Thess. 1:1), that Paul wrote when he said, "It is the will of God, even *your* sanctification" (1 Thess. 4:3), and, "The very God of peace sanctify *you* wholly" (chap. 5:23).

From these Scriptural facts it will be seen that sanctification is

A SECOND WORK OF GRACE.

There is a definite reason for this twofoldness in the redemption of the individual believer. Sin exists in the human heart in two forms—actual and inherent; that is, there is a sinful disposition which we receive through natural generation, and there are wilful acts of wrong which we commit by the consent of our own will after we reach the age when we have a knowledge of right and wrong. Now, these two forms of sin are entirely different, and can not be identified as one in the individual heart without causing great confusion in this subject. We are in no sense individually responsible for possessing the evil nature that we inherit; but we are wholly responsible for our own sinful acts committed later by the consent of our own will. Repentance can apply only to our own individual acts of wrong; therefore forgiveness and conversion are of necessity limited to that ground, as we shall soon see by the Word of God. Therefore all attempts to identify in redemption these two distinct forms of sin is a gross perversion of the gospel plan of salvation.

We have no need of proving that men are guilty of actual transgressions: the fact is well-known and acknowledged. However, the Scripture asserts that "all have sinned, and come short of the glory of God" (Rom. 3:23). But concerning inherent sin, we must give the more exact statements of the Scriptures; for, although it is pretty generally admitted, it is sometimes denied.

"The wicked are estranged from the womb: they go astray as soon as they be born, speaking lies" (Psa. 58:3). While the Psalmist is here simply describing a fact, the verse contains at least a strong intimation of an inward bent to evil. But again, he says, "Behold, I was shapen in iniquity: and in sin did my mother conceive me" (Psa. 51:5). This text shows that an evil disposition is a part of man from the earliest moment of his existence. And the apostle Paul distinctly affirms that we are all "by nature the children of wrath" (Eph. 2:3).

In Rom. 7:7-13 Paul gives, in relating his own experience, a clear description of sin in these two forms. He says: "I had not known sin, but by the law: for I had not known lust, except the law had said, Thou shalt not covet. But sin, taking occasion by the commandment wrought in me all manner of concupiscence. For without the law sin was dead. For I was alive without the law once: but when the commandment came, sin revived, and I died . . . . For sin, taking occasion by the commandment, deceived me, and by it slew me . . . . But sin, that it might appear sin, working death in me by that which is good; that sin by the commandment might become exceeding sinful." Here the apostle speaks first of his experience as an infant, when he had no knowledge of God's law, did not even know that it said, "Thou shalt not covet." At this time, although he was "alive *without the law*," he had in him something that he calls sin, but "without the law sin was dead." Later, "when the commandment came" to his' understanding, and he transgressed it, then he says, "Sin revived, *and I died.*" He became "dead in trespasses and in sins" (Eph. 2: 1). In other words, the sin that existed in him by nature, while he was ignorant and innocent, afterwards manifested itself in the outward works of actual sin, for which he was responsible. How clear this twofoldness of sin! And this has been the experience of all who have reached the age of moral responsibility.

Our foreparents were created "in righteousness and true holiness," but from this lofty estate they fell, thereby plunging the world into the darkness of sin; for all have received from them, through natural generation, an evil nature, as we have already shown. From this fact it is evident that when we are born into the world though we are perfectly innocent, we are *one degree below* the line of perfect holiness, since we possess the nature of sin. When we reach the age of moral re-

sponsibility and take upon ourselves a sinful life, we fall
another degree lower, so that we are now *two steps* below the original plane of holiness.

Now, the design of Christ is to restore mankind in salvation to the high plane from which they fell; and since
they have descended two degrees in sin, there must of
necessity be two steps upward in redemption. Are there
not the same number of steps in a stairway when one
ascends as when he descends? And the last step taken
coming down will be the first one to take going up. So
in redemption. The last step in the descent was our
wilful departure from God into actual sins; so our first
step in salvation is *willingly* to return to God, leaving
behind all of the sins that we have committed. "Let the
wicked forsake *his way,* and the unrighteous man his
thoughts: and let him return unto the Lord, and he will
have mercy upon him; and to our God, for he will abundantly pardon" (Isa. 55: 7). "Though your sins be as
scarlet, they shall be as white as snow" (Isa. 1: 18). "If
we confess *our sins,* he is faithful and just to forgive
us our sins, and to cleanse us from all unrighteousness"
(1 John 1: 9). This confession and pardon relates solely
to our own sinful acts, and this is what Peter terms conversion: "Repent ye therefore, and be converted, that
your sins may be blotted out" (Acts 3: 19).

Now Jesus teaches that the converted man is like a
little child once more. "Except ye be converted, and
become as little children, ye shall not enter into the kingdom of heaven" (Matt. 18: 3). In other words, the person whose individual sins have been confessed, forgiven,
and blotted out, is "converted," and has now regained

the moral condition of spiritual life and innocency from which he departed at the age of accountability (Rom. 7: 9). But the infant is one degree below the plane of perfect holiness; so also is the converted person, who is "like" the little child; in fact, he is even called a "babe" (1 Pet. 2: 2; Heb. 5: 13), and is exhorted to "go on unto perfection" (Heb. 6: 1), "perfecting holiness in the fear of God" (2 Cor. 7: 1); and he is informed by the Word that God hath *"perfected forever THEM THAT ARE SANCTIFIED"* (Heb. 10: 14).

Natural babes do many things that they should not do; but the spiritual babes, having a better understanding and having had more experience, need not commit sin again. If, however, they do not watch carefully, and live a spiritual life, the evil nature within will assert itself and manifest its workings in the outward life, and thus lead them back into sin again.

Paul wrote thus to some of these spiritual infants at Corinth: "And I, *brethren*, could not speak unto you as unto spiritual, but as unto carnal, even as unto *babes in Christ*. I have fed you with milk, and not with meat: for hitherto ye were not able to bear it, neither yet now are ye able. *For ye are YET carnal* for whereas there is among you envying, and strife, and divisions, are ye not carnal and walk as men?" (1 Cor. 3: 1-3). These brethren had from the first of Paul's ministry there been "babes in Christ," and had been rather weak in spiritual things; and now as they were giving way to the carnality of their hearts, Paul made use of this external manifestation to prove to them that they had been carnal all the while. "Ye are *yet* carnal." Now, he did not say that this state of quarreling and division is the standard of justified lives—he rebuked them for it—but he placed the first cause for it in the fact that they were yet carnal. The whole passage, carefully studied, shows that "babes in Christ" still have the carnal nature, though it is not necessary, it is even wrong, to give way to it in the outward life as did these Corinthians whom he addressed.

So also the apostle John, in that Epistle in which he speaks so often about being born of God, teaches most clearly that these "sons of God" still stand in need of purification. "Beloved, *now are we the sons of God,* and it doth not yet appear what we shall be: but we know that when he shall appear, we shall be like him; for we shall see him as he is. And every man that hath this hope in him *purifieth himself* even as he is pure" (1 John 3: 2, 3).

Again I call attention to the text already quoted, that "Christ also loved *the church,* and gave himself for it; that he might *sanctify* and CLEANSE it" (Eph. 5:25, 26).

Furthermore, this fact can be tested in the experience of the apostles themselves. In John 1:11-13 we read that those who received Christ during his incarnation and believed on his name became sons of God by being born of God. Christ said to the seventy disciples, "Your names are written in heaven" (Luke 10:20). From these scriptures we are assured that the apostles were born of God, and that their names were recorded in the Book of Life in heaven. And the testimony of Jesus concerning them shows their spiritual condition and acceptance with God: "They are not of the world, even as I am not of the world." Yet we have in the gospel narrative clear evidences that these apostles still possessed the carnal nature, as when the ten were "moved with indignation" against the two who sought positions of authority over the others (Matt. 20: 20-24). Such desire for preeminence, and such feelings of envy and jealousy, are not consistent with perfect holiness, but are the outcropping of the sinful nature within. On another occasion they "disputed among themselves, who should be the greatest" (Mark 9: 34). On other occasions also there were unmistakable manifestations of this evil principle. Since, therefore, they needed a heart-cleansing from this inbred sin, Christ prayed to the Father, "Sanctify them" (John 17:17).

This twofoldness of salvation-work is also shown under the figure of a vine and its branches, in John 15: 1, 2—"I am the true vine, and my Father is the husbandman. Every branch in me that beareth not fruit he taketh away: and every branch that beareth fruit, he purgeth it, that it may bring forth more fruit." "I am the vine, *ye* are the branches." (verse 5). The individual Christian is a branch of the true vine—Christ. If he ceases to bear the fruit of the Spirit, he is taken away; but if he is a fruitful branch, he is to be *purged,* so that he can bring forth more fruit.

Some one has suggested that since there is nothing in Nature analagous to the purging of a branch, this word purge must signify *prune.* This can not be, however, for there is both a pruning and a purging spoken of. *Prune.* "To lop or cut off, as the superfluous branches of trees; to trim."—*Webster.* Now, according to Christ's statement, it is the worthless branches that are pruned off; while the good, fruit-bearing branches are to be *purged*. Of course, this is not exactly true to nature, but natural things and spiritual things are not always analagous in every particular.

The promise of a second work was given to the apostles in a threefold form.

1. The purging already mentioned.

2. "I will pray the Father, and he shall give you another Comforter, that he may abide with you forever; even the Spirit of truth; *whom the world can not receive,* because it seeth him not, neither knoweth him; but ye know him; for he dwelleth with you, and *shall be in you"* (John 14: 16, 17).

3. "I will pray the Father," said Christ in the text last mentioned, "and he shall give you another Comforter"; but in his prayer he did not say a word about the Father's giving the Holy Ghost to the apostles, but he did say, *"Sanctify them* through thy truth: thy word is truth" (John 17: 17).

Now, this threefold promise is identified in one experience to be received by them, the Holy Spirit being *cause,* and purging or sanctification being the *result.* Proof: "Being sanctified by the Holy Ghost" (Rom. 15: 16). So Christ's asking the Father to sanctify the apostles was virtually asking him to give them the Holy Ghost; for when the Holy Ghost was received as their Comforter, they were sanctified—*"sanctified by the Holy Ghost."* How clear!

So also the purging promised is the same, being the work of the Holy Ghost when received. "And God which knoweth the hearts, bare them witness, *giving them the Holy Ghost,* even as he did unto us; and put no difference between us and them, *purifying their hearts by faith"* (Acts 15: 8, 9). This text refers to the time when the household of Cornelius were baptized with the Holy Ghost (Acts 10), and Peter affirms that at that time God gave them the Holy Ghost, *"purifying their hearts,"* and that it was "even as he did unto us"—the apostles themselves. There is no way under heaven to evade this Scriptural fact that there is a purging of the heart, or sanctification, to be received subsequently to regeneration, and that it is obtained when the Holy Ghost is received as the abiding Comforter. Sin is twofold, and salvation also is twofold; yea, "He saved us by the washing of regeneration, and *renewing of the Holy Ghost,* which he shed on us abundantly" (Tit. 3: 5, 6).

TWO WORKS SYMBOLIZED.

This truth was typified by the tabernacle of the Mosaic dispensation. This ancient structure, the dwelling-place of God on earth, consisted of two apartments, surrounded by a court. The first apartment, which was entered from the court, was termed the "holy place"; and it contained a table of show-bread, candlestick, and the golden altar, which stood just before the entrance into the second apartment. This second, or inner, apartment was called the "holy of holies," or "holiest of all"; and it contained the ark of the covenant, wherein were deposited the stone tables of the law. In the court, directly in front of the entrance to the first apartment, stood the brazen altar, or altar of burnt offerings; also a laver containing water.

A description of the tabernacle and its furnishings is given in Heb. 9: 1-8; while the sacrifices are more particularly described in the next chapter verses, 1-4, 11. The priests ministered daily in the first apartment, "but into the second went the high priest alone once every year." This inner room was the dwelling-place of God.

This tabernacle of the old dispensation was, we are informed in Heb. 9: 9, "a figure for the time then present"; that is it was intended to symbolize something that was to come later. And according to verse 11, Christ has "come an high priest of good things to come, by a greater and more perfect tabernacle, not made with hands." This old house was a perfect type of "the house of God, which is the church of the living God" (1 Tim. 3: 15), in the New Testament dispensation; for "ye also, as lively stones, are built up a spiritual house, an holy priesthood, to offer up spiritual sacrifices, acceptable to God by Jesus Christ" (1 Pet. 2: 5). The writer of the Hebrews also asserts that Christ has "his own house; *whose house are we*" (chap. 3: 6). And Paul affirms that the multitudes redeemed by the blood of Christ are "a building fitly framed together, [which] groweth unto *an holy temple in the Lord* in whom ye also are builded together for an habitation of God through the Spirit" (Eph. 2: 16-22). Christ is the great sacrifice, the antitype of all the sin-offerings of the law, and by his blood we have redemption and thus become a part of his church or spiritual house.

But the two apartments in the type must have their counterpart in the antitype, and this we will set forth.

In the tabernacle there were two altars, as already observed, and the blood of sin-offerings was *placed on both altars* (Lev. 4: 7), thus clearly typifying *twofold cleansing*. So when we come to Christ confessing our sins, he freely forgives them all, and we are justified, receiving the first work of divine grace, which makes us "priests" in the house of God. We minister as it were in the "holy place" of God's church, as symbolized by the holy place of the old tabernacle. We do not offer sin-offerings, for Christ himself "offered one sacrifice for sins forever" (Heb. 10: 12), but we do offer sacrifices, typified by the "thank-offerings" and "peace-offerings" of the law. "By him therefore let us offer the sacrifice of praise to God continually, that is, the fruit of our lips giving thanks to his name" (Heb. 13: 15). We "offer up spiritual sacrifices, acceptable to God by Jesus Christ" (1 Pet. 2: 5). The show-bread on the table typifies our spritual food, and the candlestick, ever burning, our spiritual light.

Those who ministered in the first room of the ancient tabernacle were always before the entrance into the "holiest" place, the second room, but they did not have free access; for in that dispensation "the way into the holiest of all was not yet made manifest" (Heb. 9: 8). But when Christ expired on the cross of Calvary as a perfect sacrifice for sin, "the vail of the temple was rent in twain from the top to the bottom" (Matt. 27: 51); and thus a change was miraculously wrought in the typical house of God, in order to appropriately represent a new order of truth—the introduction of a new or spiritual house, with perfect access, even into its second, or

innermost, room. "Having therefore, *brethren*, boldness to enter into the HOLIEST by the blood of Jesus,
by a new and living way, which he hath consecrated for
us, through the vail, that is to say, his flesh; and having
an high priest over the house of God; *let us draw near
with a true heart, in full assurance of faith*" (Heb. 10:
19-22). Thus, by a twofold cleansing we receive a twofold experience, as symbolized by the double altars, twofold cleansing, and two apartments of the old house of
God.

The law of God was deposited in the second room of
the sanctuary; and so this second work of grace is the
perfecting grace, wherein God's laws are placed in our
hearts, and we are ourselves the dwelling-place of the
Most High! Halleluiah! "For by one offering he hath
perfected forever *them that are sanctified*. Whereof the
Holy Ghost also is a witness to us: for after that he had
said before, This is the covenant that I will make with
them after those days, saith the Lord, I will put my
laws into their hearts, and in their minds will I write
them" (Heb. 10:14-16). These texts, in connection with
verses 19-22 just quoted, show positively that sanctification admits us into the "holiest," where the laws of God
are inscribed in our hearts, this being accomplished by
the perfect renovation of our nature by the baptism of
the Holy Ghost as a second work of grace. "Therefore
being justified by faith, we have peace with God through
our Lord Jesus Christ [the first work of grace]: by whom
also we have access by faith into this [second] grace
wherein we stand, and rejoice in hope of the glory of God
.... because the love of God is shed abroad in our hearts

by *the Holy Ghost which is given unto us*" (Rom. 5:1, 2, 5).

APOSTOLIC EXAMPLES OF TWO WORKS.

We have now shown by many texts and considerations that there are two distinct works of grace, the first called new birth, regeneration, justification, or conversion; the second termed either the Holy Ghost reception or baptism, as *cause*, or else, sanctification, perfection, etc., as *effect*. The crowning proof of this twofoldness, however, is the recorded fact that the apostolic churches were saved according to this plan. We will notice several examples.

1. *The apostles themselves.* This point has already been considered. They were saved men; Jesus promised them the Holy Ghost, with his resultant work—purging or sanctification; on the day of Pentecost they received this baptism of the Holy Ghost (Acts 2).

2. *The Jerusalem church.* The penitent Jews on the day of Pentecost were commanded by Peter to "repent and be baptized," with the promise that they also should "receive the gift of the Holy Ghost." They repented and were baptized (Acts 2: 38, 41). Others also were saved later (verse 47; 4: 4). Still later we find the company of saved people—"the multitude of them that believed"—met together in earnest prayer. "And when they had prayed, the place was shaken where they were assembled together; *and they were all filled with the Holy Ghost*" (Acts 4: 29-31).

3. *The Samaritan church.* "Philip went down to the city of Samaria and preached Christ unto them," with

the result that many believed and were baptized (Acts
8: 5-8). "Now when the apostles which were at Jerusalem heard that Samaria had received the word of God,
they sent unto them Peter and John: who when they were
come down, prayed for them that they might receive the
Holy Ghost . . . . Then laid they their hands upon them,
and they received the Holy Ghost" (verse 14-17). Now,
these are two separate occurrences, in two meetings, held
by different ministers. There is no possibility of uniting them in one work.

4. *The household of Cornelius.* Cornelius was "a de-
vout man, and one that feared God with all his house,
which gave much alms to the people, and prayed to God
always" (Acts 10: 2). His prayers were effectual, for
an angel was sent to him, who said, "Thy prayers and
thine alms are come up for a memorial before God" (verse
4). He was accepted of God, for he knew the preaching of the gospel of Jesus Christ, which began in Galilee,
and he was a righteous man (verses 34-37). We are not
informed just how or by whom Cornelius had heard this
preaching of Jesus; but we do know this, that Philip,
who had such a stirring revival at Samaria, had also been
at Cæsarea, where Cornelius resided (Acts 8: 40). In
fact, Philip's home was there at a later date, and it may
have been there at that time, and in that city the Spirit
of God was poured out even upon his daughters (Acts
21: 8, 9).

By divine direction Peter went to visit this man, and ·
preached to him. "While Peter yet spake these words,
the Holy Ghost fell on all them which heard the Word";
and the Jews were astonished "because that on the Gen- ·

tiles also was poured out the gift of the Holy Ghost" (Acts 10: 44, 45).

5. *The disciples at Ephesus.* In Acts 18: 24-28 we read of the preaching of Apollos at Ephesus, and of there being brethren there. Afterwards Paul "came to Ephesus: and finding certain disciples, he said unto them, Have ye received the Holy Ghost since ye believed? They said unto him, We have not so much as heard whether there be any Holy Ghost" (Acts 19: 1, 2).

A number of things are implied in this question of the apostle: 1. That there is a Holy Ghost; 2. That it is possible for men to receive him; 3. That he is given to believers; 4. That he is given at a time subsequent to their becoming disciples or believers. "And when Paul had laid his hands upon them, the Holy Ghost came on them" (verse 6). Later, writing to this church at Ephesus, Paul says, "AFTER that ye believed, ye were sealed with that Holy Spirit of promise" (Eph. 1: 13).

6. *The Thessalonian church.* In Acts 17 we read that Paul went to Thessalonica and there preached for about three weeks, during which time a great multitude believed. But when certain Jews stirred up the people into a violent tumult, the brethren sent Paul and Silas to Berea. This was in the year A. D. 53. After remaining at Berea for a while, Paul went on down to Athens. Sometime later the apostle, solicitous for the welfare of the brethren at Thessalonica, sent Timothy to inquire concerning them; while he himself remained at Athens (1 Thess. 3: 1, 2). Timothy returned with an excellent report of their spiritual condition and activity (verse 6); whereupon Paul wrote the First Epistle to the Thessa-

lonians, in which he commended them very highly because of their faith and obedience to the Word. This was in A. D. 54, one year after the meeting which he held there. He exhorted them to carefully obey the things which they had received of him, in order that they might please God and abound more and more. Then he said, "Ye know what commandments we gave you by the Lord Jesus," and proceeded to enumerate some of these commandments, asserting that they were the will of God: 1. "Your sanctification"; 2. "That ye should abstain from fornication"; 3. "That every one of you should know how to possess his vessel in sanctification and honor"; 4. "That no man should go beyond and defraud his brother in any matter" (1 Thess. 4:1-6). One of these commandments was that they should be sanctified. Again, he says, "And the very God of peace *sanctify you wholly;* and I pray God your whole spirit and soul and body be preserved blameless unto the coming of our Lord Jesus Christ. Faithful is he that calleth you, who also *will do it*" (chap. 5:23, 24).

CONDITIONS FOR SANCTIFICATION.

This blessed state of perfect holiness can not be entered by sinners. The Holy Ghost is given, not to the world, but to those who are chosen out of the world —to those who are God's believing and obedient children. Therefore the first essential is that the candidate for sanctification possess a clear, definite experience of Bible justification. But this is not all. Justification brings us into a holy relation with God; therefore in our converted experience the outward life must be brought into harmony with the truth, so that we are living sinless lives; otherwise we do not remain in a justified state at all, hence are not candidates for sanctification, the second work of grace.

It is in our special effort to live a holy life that we are made painfully conscious of the presence of that evil nature within. Realizing that while fighting the devil on the outside there is also "a foe in the temple not subject to God," the soul cries out for an experience of heart-purity. The first disciples were earnestly praying when they received this experience (Acts 1: 14; 2: 1-4). So was Cornelius when the way was opened for him to receive the Holy Ghost (Acts 10); also, the congregation of believers in Jerusalem, after the day of Pentecost (Acts 4: 24-31). Without strong desire and earnest prayer one will never obtain this definite work of grace.

The seeker must make a complete surrender to the whole will of God, a perfect consecration of time, talents, and all to His service, and himself be sacredly the Lord's for time and for eternity. "I beseech you therefore, brethren, by the mercies of God, that ye present your bodies a living sacrifice, holy, acceptable unto God, which is your reasonable service. And be not conformed to this world: but be ye transformed by the renewing of your mind, that ye may prove what is that good, and acceptable, and perfect, will of God" (Rom. 12: 1, 2). When this perfect consecration is made, God will be pleased to send his Holy Spirit in sanctifying power, purging the heart from the very nature of sin, and will himself take up his abode in the pure and devoted soul. Halleluiah!

"If thy all is on the altar laid,
Guard it from each vain desire;
When thy soul the perfect price hath paid,
God will send the holy fire."

THE HOLY GHOST BAPTISM.

The baptism of the Holy Ghost taught in the New Testament is a special endowment of the Spirit of God in the heart of his believing and obedient children. Different expressions are used to convey this idea—baptism of the Holy Ghost (Matt. 3:11); the Holy Ghost given (John 7:39); receiving "the Spirit of truth" (John 14:17; 16:13); "Comforter" (John 14:16, 26; 15:26); recieve the Holy Ghost (John 20:22; Acts 8:17; 10:47); "filled with the Holy Ghost" (Acts 2:4; 4:31); "gift of the Holy Ghost" (Acts 2:38); the Spirit poured out upon men (Acts 2:17; 10:45); etc. These expressions all refer to one and the same thing, as will be shown later. They simply represent different aspects of the one subject; just as the different expressions used for the first work of grace convey various shades of meaning, though meaning essentially the same thing. But it must be regarded as *a definite experience in the believer,* for in the apostolic church it was a reality, the Holy Ghost being received some time subsequent to regeneration. The statements of Christ to his apostles that the Holy Ghost "shall be in you," that he shall be a Comforter that will "abide

with you forever"—these and other expressions show
that it is a *personal reality,* not simply ecstatic ·feelings
on the part of the individual.

THE SPIRIT'S WORK.

The work of the Holy Ghost in the heart of the believer who receives him is twofold—negative and positive. His negative work, as we have already shown, is
to purify, or sanctify. We are "sanctified by the Holy
Ghost" (Rom. 15:16). God gave them the Holy Ghost,
"purifying their hearts by faith" (Acts 15:8, 9). The
reception of him is compared to fire—"Baptize you
with the Holy Ghost *and with fire*" (Matt. 3:11)—
fire being a destructive and purifying element; and
those who have thus been "sanctified by the Holy Ghost"
are "pure in heart" (Matt. 5:8), for he "hath *perfected* forever them that are sanctified: whereof the Holy
Ghost also is a witness" (Heb. 10:14, 15). Not one
element of impurity remains in the moral nature of one
who has received the Holy Ghost: he is in this respect
"perfected forever." Praise God for heart-purity!

The positive work of the Holy Spirit is: 1. To give
power (Acts 1:8); 2. To guide (John 16:13); 3. To
comfort (John 14:16, 17); 4. To teach (John 14:26);
5. To increase spiritual fruits (John 15:2 with Gal.
5:22, 23); 6. To unify God's people (John 17:20-23
with Acts 4:31, 32); 7. To fit for service (Luke 24:
49; 2 Tim. 2:21).

IMPORTANCE OF.

The baptism and work of the Holy Spirit is of great importance, both to the individual believer and to the work of God. As to the individual, it is the perfecting grace, "the grace wherein we stand" (Rom. 5:2), and therefore completes our moral preparation for heaven. "Follow peace with all men, and holiness, without which no man shall see the Lord" (Heb. 12:14). "Blessed are the pure in heart; for they shall see God" (Matt. 5:8).

As to the work of God, this divine experience is necessary in order to properly fit us for the Lord's service. Christ commanded his apostles to tarry in the city of Jerusalem until they were endued with power from on high (Luke 24:49), and said to them, "Ye shall receive power after that the Holy Ghost is come upon you: and [then] ye shall be witnesses unto me both in Jerusalem, and in all Judea, and in Samaria, and unto the uttermost part of the earth" (Acts 1:8). So also the apostle Paul teaches that by being "sanctified" we are *"meet for the Master's use, and prepared unto every good work"* (2 Tim. 2:21). Alas! how many ministers of today are destitute of this sanctifying grace, this baptism of the Holy Ghost! Considering this, it is not surprising that the world is filled with conflicting doctrines and beliefs. It is the function of the Holy Spirit to "teach" men and "guide them into all truth"; therefore when men who have never been taught by the Spirit themselves attempt to instruct others, they only speak a "vision or their own head," as one of the

prophets has said. Since the dispensation of the Holy
Ghost began at Pentecost, God does not send out to
preach men who are not "filled with the Holy Ghost"
themselves. They may have a call of God to his work,
but his "command" to them is to "tarry" until they are
endued with power from on high. What the world needs
today is a Holy Ghost ministry. However, all of the
saved are "workers together with God" (2 Cor. 6: 1),
and all need this infilling of the Holy Spirit, that they
may indeed be "vessels unto honor, sanctified, and meet
for the Master's use, and prepared unto every good
work" (2 Tim. 2: 21).

EVIDENCE OF.

People have preached and written much about the
evidence of the baptism of the Holy Ghost. But to ask
for our evidence that we have the Holy Ghost is like
asking for an evidence of the existence of the sun over-
head. The sun does not need a witness to testify for
it: *it stands for itself;* and the work which it performs—
illuminating the earth, and kissing the face of nature
with its genial rays of light and warmth, causing vege-
tation to spring forth, bringing life and joy, happiness
and health, to the sons of men—these works proclaim
unmistakably, without further witness, the sun and his
glory. Likewise the Holy Ghost *stands for himself as the*
witness. "The Spirit *itself* beareth witness with our
spirit" (Rom. 8: 16; Heb. 10: 14, 15); while the works
which he performs—purifying the heart, teaching, comforting, guiding, unifying—show forth his power and
glory.

SPECIAL WORKS OF THE SPIRIT.

Now, the foregoing contains the New Testament teaching relative to the Holy Ghost—what he is to every individual that receives him. The Holy Spirit *himself,* being bestowed by the Father upon the individual believer, is *"the gift of the Holy Ghost."* This is shown clearly in the case of the household of Cornelius, when they received · their wonderful baptism of the Spirit. "While Peter yet spake these words, the *Holy Ghost fell* on all them which heard the word"; while the Jews were astonished "because that on the Gentiles also was poured out *the gift of the Holy Ghost"* (Acts 10: 44, 45).

But in addition to the regular office-work of the Holy Spirit when received, he sometimes performs *special works;* or rather, he confers upon certain people who receive him the ability to perform special works; hence these special endowments are termed *"gifts of the Holy Ghost."* We read of these particularly in 1 Cor. 12.

"Now concerning spiritual gifts, brethren, I would not have you ignorant" (verse 1). "Now there are diversities of gifts, but the same Spirit. And there are differences of administrations, but the same Lord. And there are diversities of operations, but it is the same God which worketh all in all. But the manifestation of the Spirit is given to every man to profit withal" (verses 4-7). Here we find that these spiritual gifts are simply manifestations of the Spirit, and that they are *not* given to all alike, even though all be in possession of "the same Spirit." [Notice the next verses: "For to one is given by the same Spirit the word of wisdom; to another the

word of knowledge by the same Spirit; to another faith
by the same Spirit; to another the gifts of healing by
the same Spirit; to another the working of miracles; to
another prophecy; to another discerning of spirits; to
another divers kinds of tongues; to another the interpretation of tongues; but all these worketh that one and
the selfsame Spirit, *dividing to every man severally AS
HE WILL"* (verses 8-11).

Now, if we will study the apostolic church as revealed
in the New Testament, we shall be able to see all these
special gifts manifested, some in one person, and some
in another; for all were necessary to the completeness
of the church. But viewed as individuals, not every one
who received the baptism of the Holy Ghost received
the special gift of prophecy or the gift of miracle-work-
ing or the gift of tongues. It is only by grossly perverting the Word of God that people can build up such
a claim that any one of these things was manifested in all
who received the baptism of the Spirit. The Word of
God in the hands of a Holy Ghost man will easily destroy the false structure.

"To one is given" one (or more) of these special
gifts; "to another," another or (others); etc.,—the
"Spirit dividing to every man severally *as he will."* "Are
all apostles? [No] Are all prophets? [No] Are all
teachers? [No] Are all workers of miracles? [No]
Have all the gifts of healing? [No] Do all speak with
tongues? [No] Do all interpret? [No] But covet earnestly the best gifts" (verses 29-31). Individuals who
have the Holy Spirit may or may not have these special
gifts, but they can "covet the best gifts," and perhaps

obtain them—if it is in accordance with the will of the
Spirit to grant their request (verse 11).

SOME FALSE OPINIONS.

As there has been in some quarters a great deal of
misunderstanding and false doctrine concerning this
subject, by which Satan has designed to bring the pure
Word of God into disrepute, I feel constrained to mention some of these false opinions.

1. *That all who receive the baptism of the Holy Ghost
speak in tongues as THE evidence.* Now, the scripture
just quoted from 1 Cor. 12 plainly contradicts this position, for it shows that the gift of tongues is no more
general among those who have received the Holy Ghost
than is the gift of prophecy or the gift of healing or
the gift of miracles or any other of the special gifts
mentioned. Nor is there any difference between the
gift of tongues and speaking with tongues; for these
expressions *are used interchangeably* in this chapter,
referring to exactly the same thing; just as the gift of
prophecy and "are all prophets?" or the gift of miracles
and "workers of miracles" are equivalent expressions.
Compare verses 4-11 with verses 29-31.

The Word does not say that the gift of tongues, or
speaking in tongues, is *the* evidence of the Spirit's reception; but it is here given simply as a "manifestation
of the Spirit," in common with other special manifestations which may or may not belong to a particular
individual. If you should receive as a present a fine-
looking horse, what would be to you the evidence of

your reception of it? Would it be the horses' ability
to draw a certain load up a hill or to perform some other
particular task? No. You would not for a moment
think of confounding the animal himself with some particular feat which he might or might not be able to perform. Possession of the horse himself would be to you
a sufficient evidence; while his works belong to an entirely different category.

Now, the Holy Spirit must not be confounded with
one of his works, so that he himself is denied unless he
chooses to manifest himself in some particular manner.
The Holy Ghost himself is the satisfactory evidence.
"Whereof the Holy Ghost also is a witness" (Heb. 10:
15). "The Spirit itself beareth witness with our spirit"
(Rom. 8: 16).

We have in the New Testament records of three occasions on which people spoke with tongues when they
received the baptism of the Holy Ghost: on the day of
Pentecost (Acts 2)—one hundred and twenty believers
(Acts 1: 15); certain disciples at Ephesus—twelve in
number (Acts 19: 1-7); and the household of Cornelius
—number unknown (Acts 10). The total number on these
three occasions was probably less than two hundred.
Now, we have in the Acts the record of thousands who
received the baptism of the Holy Ghost (as already
shown in this chapter), in which no mention whatever is
made concerning tongues. Some say that that part was
omitted. Well, if people desire to build up a doctrine they
should establish it on what the Word of God says, and
not on what was left out.

On the day of Pentecost, when the first disciples

spoke in tongues, Peter appealed for objective proof of the Holy Ghost baptism to the fulfilment of Joel's prophecy that the sons and daughters should prophesy. Prophecy, as well as tongues, is one of the special gifts of the Spirit. So also when the twelve disciples at Ephesus received the Spirit and spoke with tongues, they prophesied (Acts 19). Now, if either of these special gifts were to be accepted as *the* evidence of the reception of the Holy Ghost, then prophecy would have the advantage in the position of importance granted it, for "greater is he that prophesieth than he that speaketh with tongues" (1 Cor. 14: 5). "Desire spiritual gifts, *but rather that ye may prophesy*" (verse 1); for "he that prophesieth speaketh unto men to edification, and exhortation, and comfort" (verse 3), with the result that unbelievers become deeply convicted, fall down, and get salvation (verses 23-25).

2. *That people are first converted, afterwards "receive the Holy Ghost." Then still later are baptized with the Holy Ghost*—thus dividing God's work into three parts. This is entirely false, as will be shown by many scriptures. The only apparent proof of that position seems to be John 20: 22, where it is recorded that Christ, after his resurrection, appeared to his disciples and "breathed on them, and said unto them, Receive ye the Holy Ghost." It was several days later before they were baptized with the Holy Ghost on Pentecost.

But a particular examination of the circumstances connected with John 20: 22 shows that the disciples did not *at that time* receive the Holy Ghost, but that the verse is an allusion to Pentecost; for this was the same

occasion described in Luke 24: 33, s. q., where the reference to the Spirit is given in other language, as follows:
"But *tarry* ye in the city of Jerusalem, *until ye be endued with power from on high."* (verse 49). We know
that this refers to Pentecost (Acts 1: 8).

Another thing, if the disciples really received the
Holy Ghost at the time when Jesus breathed on them,
one of their number was neglected; for "Thomas, one
of the twelve . . . . *was not with them"* (John 20: 24).
But Thomas was ready for the Holy Ghost on the day
of Pentecost (Acts 1: 13).

But the crowning proof that there is no difference
between receiving the Holy Ghost and being baptized
with the Holy Ghost is the fact that in the labors of the
apostles themselves the two are identified—one and the
same thing. Paul asked these disciples at Ephesus, "Have
ye *received* the Holy Ghost since ye believed?" (Acts
19: 1, 2), and they replied that they had not even heard
of the Holy Ghost; therefore they did not have him in
this sense. "And when Paul had laid his hands upon
them, the Holy Ghost came upon them; and they spake
with tongues, and prophesied" (verse 6). Now, this
baptism of the Holy Ghost, accompanied by tongues and
prophecy, was identical with receiving the Holy Ghost;
and there were only two works with these disciples.

So also at Samaria. After Philip had the meeting
which resulted in the conversion of many (Acts 8: 5),
Peter and John came down and prayed for these disciples "that they might *receive* the Holy Ghost: for as
yet he was *fallen* upon none of them . . . . Then laid they
their hands upon them, and *they received the Holy Ghost.*

And when Simon saw that through the laying on of the apostles' hands *the Holy Ghost was given* he offered them money, saying, Give me also this power, that on whomsoever I lay hands, he may receive the Holy Ghost. But Peter said unto him, Thy money perish with thee, because thou hast thought that *the gift of God* may be purchased with money" (verses 15-20). There is no possible way of evading the fact that in this case the "gift of God," the "gift of the Holy Ghost," "receiving the Holy Ghost," and the Holy Ghost "falling" upon disciples, are all one and the same thing, in a *second* work upon believers.

So also with the household of Cornelius (Acts 10: 44-47). "While Peter yet spake these words, *the Holy Ghost fell* on all them which heard the word. And they of the circumcision which believed were astonished, as many as came with Peter, because that on the Gentiles also was poured out the *gift of the Holy Ghost*. For they heard them speak with tongues and glorify God. Then answered Peter, can any man forbid water, that these should not be baptized which have *received* the Holy Ghost as well as we?" Here again "the Holy Ghost," "the *gift* of the Holy Ghost," and "receiving the Holy Ghost" are all the same thing in a *second* work of grace.

Notice, also, Peter's account of this matter when he rehearsed it to the disciples at Jerusalem (chap. 11: 15-17): "And as I began to speak, *the Holy Ghost fell* on them, *as on us at the beginning* [Pentecost]. Then remembered I the word of the Lord, how that he said, John indeed baptized with water; but ye shall be *bap-*

tized with the Holy Ghost. Forasmuch then as God gave them the like *gift* as he did unto us .... what was I, that I could withstand God?" On another occasion Peter, relating this same matter concerning Cornelius, affirms that God gave "them the Holy Ghost .... purifying their hearts by faith" (Acts 15: 8, 9).

The apostles made no distinction between these different expressions concerning the Holy Ghost, but used them all with reference to the same thing—the time when converted believers are purified or "sanctified by the Holy Ghost." These "distinctions without a difference" have all been manufactured in recent years in order to prop up a false, deceptive doctrine. God help honest men and women to see the truth and to avoid error! There were just two works of grace in the apostolic church: the first, justification, or conversion; the second, sanctification, or baptism of the Holy Ghost. This is God's plan of saving men; and he always works according to his own plan, if he works at all. He "saved us, by the washing of regeneration, and *renewing* of the Holy Ghost; which he shed on us abundantly" (Tit. 3: 5, 6). People who claim an experience contrary to this truth are deceived.

THE SANCTIFIED LIFE.

This experience of entire sanctification, is indeed a blessed one. While the justified life must be kept free from outward acts of sin, the sanctified life is the complete harmony of the individual, both internal and external, with the perfect will of God. All evil affections, our spiritual enemies, are gone; the soul is pure. The

Lord grants unto us "that we being delivered out of the
hand of our enemies, might serve him without fear, in
holiness and righteousness before him all the days of
our life" (Luke 1: 74, 75). Yea, it is his will that "we
should live soberly, righteously, and godly, in this present world; looking for that blessed hope and the glorious appearing of the great God, and of our Savior Jesus
Christ; who gave himself for us, that he might redeem
us from all iniquity and purify unto himself a peculiar
people, zealous of good works" (Tit. 2: 12-14). Some
people think that such a high standard is almost too good
to be true. One man affirmed in the presence of the
writer that sanctified people could not live in this old
sinful world; that if people should obtain this experience
they would be immediately taken home to glory. However, when Jesus prayed for his disciples, "sanctify them
through thy truth," he also said, "*I pray not that thou
shouldst take them out of the world,* but that thou
shouldst keep them from the evil" (John 17: 17, 15).
This poor man did not understand that instead of sanctification taking us bodily out of this world, it takes every
element of the world out of us.

In this happy condition we are able to "bring forth
more fruit"; therefore the fruits of the Spirit are developed in us abundantly. The first thing mentioned
in Paul's catalogue of the fruits of the Spirit is love.
Now, love is felt by the justified soul; but when we enter
the second, or standing, grace (Rom. 5: 1, 2), "the love
of God is shed abroad in our hearts by the Holy Ghost
which is given unto us" (verse 5). Thus, there is a
marked increase in all the fruits of the Spirit.

TEMPTATIONS.

But I would not have the reader think that the sanctified life places the individual beyond the reach of temptation. In sanctification we are not deprived of that which is essentially human, but we are purged from the sinful, carnal element received through the fall, and our human natures are brought into line with the divine, so that our desires are wholly to please God. But we are capable of temptation along natural human lines. Christ himself "was in all points tempted like as we are," but he overcame them all as our example, and we should take courage and move forwards. One of Christ's special temptations had a perfectly legitimate basis in the natural desire for food (Matt. 4: 1-4); while another involved that which was not right—a temptation to desire great possessions for the purpose of worldly honor (verse 8).

God has a definite purpose in allowing us to be tempted. It is for our good. Be encouraged; for "there hath no temptation taken you but such as is common to man: but God is faithful, who will not suffer you to be tempted above that ye are able; but will with the temptation also make a way to escape, that ye may be able to bear it" (1 Cor. 10: 13).

One purpose God has in these things is shown by James in the words, "My brethren, count it all joy when ye fall into divers temptations; knowing this, that *the trying of your faith worketh patience.* But let patience have her perfect work, that ye may be perfect and entire, wanting nothing" (Jas. 1: 2-4).

Now, we can not be tempted and tried without *feeling* tempted and tried. Peter says that "for a season if need be, ye are in *heaviness* through manifold temptations" (1 Pet. 1:6). There is no mistake about this matter: the sanctified person who is deeply tempted or tried does not feel just the same then as at other times. On certain occasions Christ himself felt "grieved," and his soul was stirred within him; but the records of these occurrences fail to show any carnal stirring or actions proceeding from an impure heart. So, reader, it must be with you. In seasons of trial and trouble, remember that the Lord "giveth more grace. Wherefore he saith, God resisteth the proud, but giveth grace unto the humble. Submit yourselves therefore to God. RESIST THE DEVIL, *and he will flee from you*" (Jas. 4:6, 7). Pride and self-exaltation belong to carnality; humility, on the other hand, is one of the sweet graces of the Spirit, the natural fruit of the sanctified heart. A life of humility is blessed with the abundant grace of God, so that the soul can overcome. "Blessed is the man that endureth temptation: for when he is tried, he shall receive the crown of life, which the Lord hath promised to them that love him" (Jas. 1:12).

What a blessing is this life of entire sanctification! "Follow peace with all men, and holiness, without which no man shall see the Lord" (Heb. 12:14). "Blessed are the pure in heart; for they shall see God" (Matt. 5:8).

CHAPTER X.

DIVINE HEALING.

In Chapter IV we showed that the plan of redemption provides for the entire man, soul and body, but that while our souls are now delivered from the power of all sin—restored to the "image of God"—the immortalization of our bodies will not take place until the end of time, when "this corruptible must put on incorruption, and this mortal must put on immortality" (1 Cor. 15: 53). Paul says, "Ye are bought with a price: therefore glorify God *in your body* and in your spirit, which are God's" (1 Cor. 6: 20). This text shows clearly that God has a direct interest in the body as well as in the soul; in fact, our body is the "purchased possession" which will be redeemed in the future, as before stated (Eph. 1: 13, 14).

But while this greatest of physical blessings is reserved for some future time, the Lord has been pleased to grant us *divine healing* as a sort of forerunner of immortality. The will of God in this respect is well expressed in the desire of the beloved apostle: "Beloved, *I* wish above all things that thou mayest prosper *and be in health,* EVEN AS THY SOUL PROSPERETH" (3 John 2).

This blessed truth is established in the Word of God, and I trust that the reader, if afflicted, will by faith avail himself of the precious privilege of being divinely

healed. I am aware that this doctrine has been ignored
by many; but "what if some did not believe? Shall their
unbelief make the word of God without effect?"   It is
not what men believe or do not believe, that is to settle
the great facts of truth, but it is *what the Word of God
says.* As Christ said to a certain lawyer, "What is written? . . . . How readest thou?" (Luke 10:26).

IN THE PROPHECIES.

The prophets of old predicted a special maifestation
of healing power when Christ should appear. Thus
Isaiah, speaking of the coming of God's "servant," for
whose law men should wait, says that he was to be "a
light of the Gentiles" and that he should "open the blind
eyes, ... bring out the prisoners from the prison, and
them that sit in darkness out of the prison-house" (Isa.
42:7). Again, he refers to it in these words: "The
Spirit of the Lord God is upon me; because the Lord
hath anointed me to preach good tidings unto the meek;
he hath sent me to bind up the broken-hearted, to proclaim liberty to the captives, and the opening of the
prison to them that are bound; to proclaim the acceptable year of the Lord" (Isa. 61:1, 2).

Christ claimed the fulfilment of these prophecies in
himself. While preaching in the synagogue at Nazareth,
he said: "The Spirit of the Lord is upon me, because he
hath anointed me to preach the gospel to the poor; he
hath sent me to heal the broken-hearted, to preach deliverance to the captives, the recovering of sight to the
blind, to set at liberty them that are bruised, to preach
the acceptable year of the Lord . . . . And he began to

say unto them, This day is this scripture fulfilled in your ears" (Luke 4:18-21).

Again Isaiah makes mention of these things: "Say to them that are of a fearful heart, Be strong, fear not: behold your God will come with vengeance, even God with a recompense; he will come and save you. *Then the eyes of the blind shall be opened, and the ears of the deaf shall be unstopped. Then shall the lame man leap as an hart, and the tongue of the dumb sing*" (Isa. 35:4-6).

This prediction of healing manifestation by Christ was perfectly fulfilled, as we read, "When the even was come, they brought unto him many that were possessed with devils: and he cast out the spirits with his word, and healed all that were sick: *that it might be fulfilled* which was spoken by Isaiah the prophet, saying, Himself took our infirmities, and bare our sicknesses" (Matt. 8:16, 17).

When John sent two of his disciples to Jesus to inquire whether he was really the Christ or not, "Jesus answered and said unto them, Go and show John again those things which ye do hear and see: the blind receive their sight, and the lame walk, the lepers are cleansed, and the deaf hear, the dead are raised up, and the poor have the gospel preached to them" (Matt. 11:4, 5).

This healing-work was also predicted by Malachi, who said, "But unto you that fear my name shall the Sun of righteousness arise with healing in his wings: and ye shall go forth, and grow up as calves of the stall" (Mal. 4:2).

MANIFESTED BY CHRIST.

The scriptures just cited show that Christ manifested himself marvelously as a healer. This work of physical ministration went hand in hand with the message of salvation. "And Jesus went about all Galilee, teaching in their synagogues, and preaching the gospel of the kingdom, and healing all manner of sickness and all manner of disease among the people. And his fame went throughout all Syria: and they brought unto him all sick people that were taken with divers diseases and torments, and those which were possessed with devils, and those which were lunatic, and those that had the palsy: and he healed them" (Matt. 4: 23, 24).

"And behold, they brought to him a man sick of the palsy, lying on a bed; and Jesus seeing their faith said unto the sick of the palsy; Son, be of good cheer; thy sins be forgiven thee. And, behold, certain of the scribes, said within themselves, This man blasphemeth. And Jesus knowing their thoughts said, Wherefore think ye evil in your hearts? For whether is easier, to say, Thy sins be forgiven thee; or to say Arise, and walk? But that ye may know that the Son of man hath power on earth *to forgive sins* (then saith he to the sick of the palsy), Arise, take up thy bed, and go unto thine house. And he arose and departed to his house" (Matt. 9: 2-6).

"And great multitudes came unto him, having with them those that were lame, blind, dumb, maimed, and many others, and cast them down at Jesus' feet; and he healed them; insomuch that the multitude wondered, when they saw the dumb to speak, the maimed to be whole, the lame to walk, and the blind to see: and they glorified the God of Israel" (Matt. 15: 30, 31).

But why multiply texts to show this accompaniment of the gospel of Christ? The Gospels abound with such instances.

> "The blessed Christ of God I see,
> In that fair land of Galilee;
> He speaks in loving words to me,
> I am the Great Physician."

It is asserted by many that Jesus performed these works of healing for the purpose of establishing his claim as the Messiah. There is no doubt that this was *one purpose,* and a most important one; for Peter says that Jesus of Nazareth was *"approved of God* among you *by miracles and wonders and signs"* (Acts 2: 22). Such manifestations of superhuman power were necessary in order to convince men that he was no ordinary man.

The record shows, however, that another motive also figured in the case. "And Jesus went about all the cities and villages, teaching in their synagogues, and preaching the gospel of the kingdom, and healing every sickness and every disease among the people. And when he saw the multitudes, *he was moved with compassion* on them" (Matt. 9: 35, 36). "And Jesus went forth and saw a great multitude, *and was moved with compassion toward them,* and he healed their sick" (Matt. 14: 14).

Of course, these last-named instances would also serve to prove his mission; but we have clear proof in other texts that Christ sometimes used his healing power when the manifestation of it was not a demonstration intended to convince the multitudes, but was simply an outflow of his love and compassion. And this clearly shows his real attitude toward sickness and disease, on behalf of suffering humanity, during his earthly ministry. "And there came a leper to him, beseeching him, and kneeling down to him, and saying unto him, If thou wilt, thou canst make me clean. And Jesus *moved with compassion*, put forth his hand, and touched him, and saith unto him, I will; be thou clean . . . . And saith unto him, *See thou say nothing to any man*" (Mark 1: 40-44).

> "With great compassion Christ was stirred
> While he the plea of suffering heard;
> He spoke the great life-giving word,
> I am the Great Physician.
>
> "He saved the soul from sin and shame;
> He healed the sick, the blind, the lame.
> I know his power is just the same;
> Christ is the Great Physician."

MANIFESTED BY THE APOSTLES.

The same mighty power accompanied the preaching of the apostles. "And when he had called unto him his twelve disciples, he gave them power against unclean spirits, to cast them out, and to heal all manner of sickness and all manner of diseases" (Matt. 10: 1). He then sent them out, saying, "As ye go, preach, saying, The kingdom of heaven is at hand. Heal the sick, cleanse the lepers, raise the dead, cast out devils: freely ye have received, freely give" (verse 7, 8). "And they went out and preached that men should repent. And they cast out many devils, and anointed with oil many that were sick, and healed them" (Mark 6: 12, 13).

"And by the hands of the apostles were many signs and wonders wrought among the people . . . . Insomuch that they brought forth the sick into the streets, and laid them on beds and couches, that at the least the shadow of Peter passing by might overshadow some of them. There came also a multitude out of the cities round about unto Jerusalem, bringing sick folks, and them which were vexed with unclean spirits: and they were healed every one" (Acts 5: 12-16).

It is unnecessary to multiply texts on this point; for it is well-known that these signs accompanied the ministry of the first preachers of the church. We will now proceed to show that divine healing is really

A PART OF THE GOSPEL.

But the fact that salvation and healing went along together in the early church strongly suggests the idea that these divine manifestations for the benefit of men were intended to be a real part of the gospel itself. In the last commission, Jesus said to his disciples: "Go ye into all the world and preach the gospel to every creature. He that believeth [the gospel] and is baptized shall be saved; but he that believeth not shall be damned. And these signs shall follow them that believe [*the gospel*]; in my name shall they cast out devils; they shall speak with new tongues; they shall take up serpents; and if they drink any deadly thing, it shall not hurt them; *they shall lay hands on the sick, and they shall recover*" (Mark 16: 15-18).

Healing is a constituent part of the gospel; therefore believing the gospel will produce the effects mentioned. "And they went forth, and preached everywhere, the

Lord working with them, and confirming the word with signs following" (verse 20). "And there they preached *the gospel*. And there sat a certain man at Lystra, impotent in his feet, being a cripple from his mother's womb, who never had walked: the same heard Paul speak: who steadfastly beholding him, and perceiving that he had faith to be healed, said with a loud voice, Stand upright on thy feet. And he leaped and walked" (Acts 14:7-10). Now, the preaching of Paul inspired this man with faith for his healing. But what was the apostle preaching? The account says that he *"preached the gospel."* Healing, then, is a constituent part of the gospel. If ministers really preach the gospel as did the apostles, these signs will "follow them that believe." If men do not preach divine healing, so as to inspire faith for healing in their hearers, *they are not* preaching the full gospel of Jesus Christ. Nothing can be clearer than this.

Again, we read: "All them which dwelt in Asia heard the *word of the Lord Jesus,* both Jews and Greeks. And God wrought special miracles by the hands of Paul: so that from his body were brought unto the sick handkerchiefs and aprons, and the diseases departed from them, and the evil spirits went out of them. Then certain vagabond Jews, exorcists, took upon them to call over them which had evil spirits the name of the Lord Jesus saying, We adjure you by *Jesus whom Paul preacheth"* (Acts 19:10-13).. These vagabond Jews knew that the preaching of Jesus by the apostle produced these results; therefore they undertook to do the same work by making use of the same name; but of course they failed, because they were not true men of God.

So also we read that "Philip went down to the city of Samaria *and preached Christ* unto them. And the people with one accord gave heed unto those things which Philip spake, *hearing* and seeing the miracles which he did. For unclean spirits, crying with loud voice, came out of many that were possessed with them: and many taken with palsies, and that were lame were healed. And there was great joy in that city" (Acts 8: 5-8). We are not told that Philip preached anything to them except Christ; nevertheless they *heard* about miracles and mighty works; for to "preach Christ" in the Bible sense means to preach him as he really is to men—Savior, Sanctifier, and Healer.

PERMANENT IN THE CHURCH.

It is constantly asserted by the skeptical sectarian clergy of today that divine healing ceased with the apostles; but it is a historical fact, easily verified, that it *did not* cease with the first apostles, but was perpetuated in the early church. Of course, these divine works will quickly cease with unbelievers, but they "shall follow them that *believe.*" That they were intended to be permanent in the church is clearly shown by the Scriptures. The commission of world-wide evangelism given to the apostles, in which these works were promised, was to continue *"even unto the end of the world"* (Matt. 28: 19, 20 with Mark 16: 15-18). Therefore in 1 Cor. 12 we find all the special gifts of the Spirit placed in the normal church, the Spirit "dividing to every man severally as he will." "And *God hath set some in the church*, first apostles, secondarily prophets, thirdly teachers, after that miracles, then *gifts of healing*, helps, governments, diversities of tongues" (verse 28). Now, If God has placed these functions in his church who dares to deny the fact or to attempt to take them out?

This is not the place to discuss the subject of the gifts on other lines, but I will refer to the special nature of this gift of healing. It is not simply praying for sick people in the ordinary way, but signifies a special power of healing by the Spirit of God possessed by certain members of the church. Its extraordinary feature may be illustrated by the gift of tongues. In the last-named gift it is understood that the possessor himself has the power, through the Spirit, of speaking in other languages. "And *they* spake with tongues, and prophesied" (Acts 19:6). "They heard *them* speak with tongues" (Acts 10:46). Also, on the day of Pentecost "*they* . . . . began to speak with other tongues"(Acts 2), and their speech consisted of the real languages of earth, languages understood by the hearers. Likewise when Christ sent his apostles forth to preach, "he *gave them* power against unclean spirits, to cast them out, and to heal all manner of sickness and all manner of disease" (Matt. 10:1). And the apostles realized that they had this power within themselves; therefore when Peter and John met the lame man at the gate Beautiful, Peter could say to him boldly, "Silver and gold have I none; but *such as I have* give I thee: in the name of Jesus Christ of Nazareth rise up and walk" (Acts 3:1-11).

But this is not all. The ministry of healing belongs to all of God's ministers and is a part of their regular work. James knew this; therefore he could without hesitation instruct suffering men and women what to do in case of sickness. Here are his words: "Is any sick among you? let him call for the elders of the church; and let them pray over him, anointing him with oil in the name of the Lord: and the prayer of faith shall save the sick, and the Lord shall raise him up; and if he have committed sins, they shall be forgiven him. Confess your faults one to another, and pray one for another that ye may be healed. The effectual fervent prayer of a right- eous man availeth much" (Jas. 5: 14-16).

This is the truth of God. There is no use in trying to ignore it or to laugh it out of the Bible. Divine heal- ing belongs to the church of God and is to be adminis- tered by all of its elders. This doctrine was clear in the apostolic church and did not become neglected until the beginning of the apostasy and the dark ages, when men lost their spiritual hold on God.

The Christian pulpits of the world are filled with a graceless, hireling ministry, a ministry who have a greater desire to make a fine showing of intellectuality and learning than they have of preaching Christ in the good old Bible way. They are faithless and unbelieving themselves, and naturally those who hear them are like to them—"having a form of godliness, but *denying the power thereof: FROM SUCH TURN AWAY"* (2 Tim. 3: 5). But I am happy to be able to say that in these last days the pure Word of God is brushing aside the mists and darkness of the night of apostasy; for men and

women filled with the power of the Spirit are now carrying the full gospel of salvation and healing to men, as
in the apostolic times.

The following circumstance, related in substance only,
conveys very well the general lack of faith and trust
in God as regards divine healing. A sister in a certain
city, the member of a prominent sectarian church, was
suffering from a sudden affliction and was confined to
her bed. She began to read the Word of God diligently,
and received thereby light on the subject of divine healing. She decided to do her part in fulfilling the Word,
and accordingly she sent for her minister to come. When
he entered the room, he expressed great surprise at finding her in such a suffering condition and at once asked
her if she had sent for a doctor. "No," she replied; "I
was just reading in the Bible where it says, 'Is any sick
among you let him call for the elders of the church; and
let them pray over him, anointing him with oil in the
name of the Lord; and the prayer of faith shall save the
sick, and the Lord shall raise him up'; therefore I sent
for you." The minister seemed excited and replied;
"Sister, I am sorry, but I am in a great hurry just now;
I will have to go. But take my advice, and get a physician here as quickly as possible. Good-by."

The sister, however was not entirely discouraged, so
she sent for the minister of another sectarian church in
the town. When he came, he desired to know what he
could do for her, and she replied: "I was just reading
in the Bible this morning where it says, 'Is any sick
among you? let him call for the elders of the church,
and let them pray over him, anointing him with oil in

the name of the Lord; and the prayer of faith shall save the sick, and the Lord shall raise him up'; therefore I sent for you." But the minister quickly answered, "Why, then, did you not send for your own preacher?" She replied, "I did; but when he came, he would not obey the Word of God and pray for me, but left immediately." But this preacher also was in a great hurry, and he excused himself, saying, "Sister, you are in a very bad condition, and must get a physician here at once. Goodby."

"Having a form of godliness, *but denying the power thereof;* FROM SUCH TURN AWAY." This is the teaching of God's Word concerning our attitude toward these "blind leaders of the blind" who stand in the pulpits and in many cases preach more skepticism and infidelity into the people than true faith in God. "Have faith in God" (Mark 11:22). "And what if some did not believe? shall their unbelief make the faith of God without effect? God forbid; yea, let God be true, *but every man a liar*" (Rom. 3:3, 4).

Divine healing is not mind-healing or Christian Science (?) healing. It is healing wrought by the direct power of God. Most of the healings performed by these counterfeit healing-movements are easily accounted for on psychological grounds, being *subjective*—the natural result of the power of mind over matter. Therefore they may succeed to a certain extent in treating functional disorders, but they are not successful in dealing with organic diseases. But this principle is not new. Physicians in all ages have known how important it is to secure the favorable action of the mind of the patient, encourag-

ing him in the belief that he will be restored to health;
for when the patient despairs of life, it is difficult to do
anything for him along natural lines.

Now, Christian Science could perform just as great
healing without the word "Christian" and without any
claims whatever to being a church, if the minds of the
patients could be held in the same believing way. The
deception of the thing lies in its claims to being *Christian.*
Its healings are not in any sense divine; most of them,
if not all of them, are nothing more than psychological
phenomena. However, the devil also manifests his power
to deceive through the thing, and thus it becomes in his
hand a powerful instrument for evil. And there is such
a thing as direct devil-healing, as we shall see later—
"The spirits of devils, working miracles" (Rev. 16:14).

But divine healing is *objective—it is from without.*
It is the power of God bestowed directly upon the individual. Organic diseases yield to the mighty power of
our Christ as readily as mere functional disorders. "Jesus
Christ *the same* yesterday, and today, and forever" (Heb.
13:8). He has lost none of his power; he has not forsaken his people; and he is therefore able and ready to
fulfill his Word.

But is it certain that it is his will to heal? First of
all, let me say that the will of God is revealed in his
Word, for his Word is his will. "And behold, there came
a leper and worshiped him, saying, Lord, *if thou wilt*
thou *canst* make me clean." This man was sure of
Christ's ability to do the work, but was not certain of
his will in the matter. "And Jesus put forth his hand,
and touched him, saying, I WILL; *be thou clean.* And

immediately his leprosy was cleansed" (Matt. 8: 2, 3).

Yes, dear reader, it is his will to heal. "We *have not* an high priest which can not be touched with the feeling of our infirmities . . . . let us therefore come boldly unto the throne of grace, that we may obtain mercy, and find grace to help in time of need" (Heb. 4: 15, 16). It can still be said of him, "He was *moved with compassion* toward them, and he healed their sick" (Matt. 14: 14). The words of the apostle John exactly express the desire of Christ concerning this matter: "Beloved, I wish above all things that thou mayest prosper, and be in health, even as thy soul prospereth" (3 John 2).

The subject of divine healing appears to be somewhat complicated by the revelation of God's will in a twofold manner, contrary to each other. Thus, he has revealed his willingness to heal, saying that "the prayer of faith shall save the sick, and the Lord shall raise him up" (Jas. 5: 15); but he has also declared that "it is appointed unto men once to die" (Heb. 9: 27), showing thereby that a time will come in every life when the person will not be "raised up." This of course does not mean that in the last earthly hours the individual can not receive physical help in the way of alleviation of pain and suffering; but he will not be "raised up."

The question for the person who believes in divine healing, then, is, "Is it God's will at this time to heal me?" Can we find out God's will in this matter? Yes. "Be not unwise, but *understanding what the will of the Lord is*" (Eph. 5: 17). It is by the "prayer of faith" that the person is raised up to health again; and faith for healing requires the special inspiration of the Holy Spirit. In fact, in many cases "we know not what we should pray for as we ought: but the Spirit itself maketh intercession for us with groanings which can not be uttered" (Rom. 8:26). We may be sure that the real "prayer of faith" for perfect healing and restoration can not be offered when it is to the glory of God to take the person home to himself. But in other cases (which the Spirit of God will make clear to those who are spiritual, believing, and obedient) *it is God's will to heal;* and we should "come boldly to the throne of grace" for this blessing.

CONDITIONS FOR HEALING.

The plan of healing set forth in the New Testament is not arbitrary, but is conditional. We must understand and conform to the standard of the Word if we hope to receive its benefits. Faith is always required, either the faith of the individual himself, when he is capable of exercising it, or the faith of some one else. For confirmation of this statement consult Matt. 9:29; Mark 5:34, 36; Matt. 8:5, 13; John 4:50; Matt. 9:2; Mark 9:23, etc.

But there are other conditions of a more particular nature, and these are dependent upon the source from which the disease came. Of course, sin in the beginning was the first cause of this calamity; but the Scriptures plainly teach that sickness and disease are now brought upon us by causes proceeding from three different sources: (1) Nature, (2) Satan, (3) God himself. These we will consider separately.

1. *Natural causes.* "His bones are full of the sins of his youth, which shall lie down with him in the dust"

(Job 20:11). Overwork and mental strain, as in the cases of Daniel and Epaphroditus. "And I Daniel fainted and was sick certain days" (Dan. 8:27). "He [Epaphroditus] was sick nigh unto death: but God had mercy on him . . . . because *for the work of Christ* he was nigh unto death, not regarding his life, to supply your lack of service toward me" (Phil. 2:27-30). "In the day of our king the princes have made him sick with bottles of wine" (Hos. 7:5). A large part of the afflictions of men are directly traceable to these natural causes.

2. *Satan afflicts.* "And ought not this woman, being a daughter of Abraham, whom Satan hath bound, lo, these eighteen years, be loosed from this bond?" (Luke 13:16). "How God anointed Jesus of Nazareth with the Holy Ghost and with power: who went about doing good, and healing all that were oppressed of the devil; for God was with him" (Acts 10:38). "So went Satan forth from the presence of the Lord, and smote Job with sore boils, from the sole of his foot unto his crown" (Job 2:7).

3. *God sometimes afflicts directly.* The afflictions which God administers are not always permissive, as in the case of Job, but are frequently *direct.* God is not the author of moral evil, but he is the direct author, in many cases, of physical evil; either in the entire destruction of wrong-doers, as in the threatened overthrow of the Ninevites (see Jonah 3:10), or in the destruction or affliction of individuals, as a direct punishment for sin. God has always dealt with men thus. "Behold, therefore, the goodness and severity of God; on them which fell severity" (Rom. 11:22).

The cases of this kind are numerous. "Oh full of all subtility and all mischief, thou child of the devil, thou enemy of all righteousness, wilt thou not cease to pervert the right ways of the Lord! And now, behold, *the hand of the Lord is upon thee, and thou shalt be blind,* not seeing the sun for a season. And immediately there fell upon him a mist and a darkness; and he went about seeking some one to lead him by the hand" (Acts 13:10, 11). "Because of the wickedness of thy doings, whereby thou hast forsaken me, the Lord shall make the pestilence cleave unto thee" (Deut. 28:20, 21). "But if ye will not hearken unto me, and will not do all these . . . . but that ye break my covenant: I also will do this unto you; I will even appoint over you terror, consumption, and the burning ague, that shall consume the eyes and cause sorrow of heart" (Lev. 26:14-16). "For now I will stretch out my hand, that I may smite thee and thy people with pestilence" (Exod. 9:15). "I will put none of these diseases upon them which *I have brought* upon the Egyptians" (Ex. 15:26). "And the anger of the Lord was kindled against them . . . . and behold, Miriam became leprous, white as snow" (Num. 12:9, 10). "The Lord will make thy plagues wonderful, and the plagues of thy seed, even great plagues, and of long continuance, and sore sickness . . . . also every sickness and every plague . . . . *will the Lord bring upon thee*" (Deut. 28:59-61). "And the Lord struck the child that Uriah's wife bare unto David, and it was very sick" (2 Sam. 12:15). "And after all this the Lord smote him in his bowels with an incurable disease" (2 Chron. 21:18).

Other texts could be given on this point, but it is unnecessary.

In view of these three causes of sickness and disease,
how\precious are these words of the Psalmist! "Bless
the Lord, O my soul; and all that is within me bless his
holy name. Bless the Lord, O my soul and forget not all
his benefits: who forgiveth all thine iniquities: *who
healeth ALL thy diseases"* (Psa. 103: 1-3).

It is evident that God is the only one who can heal all
diseases.   If an affliction or sickness originates in natural causes, it may possibly be cured by natural means.
*Such diseases -constitute the special province wherein
earthly physicians are able to operate.*   If a disease is
a direct imposition of Satan, he may remove his hand of
affliction, thus effecting a cure of the individual. It is also
possible that Satan may remove afflictions originating in
natural causes. But when God himself punishes men by
affliction, because of their sins, he alone can reach such
a case and effect a cure.

This makes clear the special conditions that the appli-
cant must meet in order to obtain divine healing.   If
by intemperance or carelessness we are ourselves responsible for our afflictions, then when we call for the elders
of the church we are instructed to *"confess our faults
one to another, and pray one for another, that we may
be healed"* (Jas. 5: 16). If we are living to please God,
and Satan imposes sickness upon us, we can rebuke the
devil in the name of the Lord, and God will grant healing.   But when God has himself laid the hand of affliction upon us, because of our own sins, then conditions
are entirely different. Neither man nor Satan can reach

such cases. The conditions for divine healing in such
cases are well set forth in the circumstance concerning
Miriam already cited. Before healing can be obtained,
sin must be confessed. "And the anger of the Lord was
kindled against them . . . . and, behold, Miriam became
leprous, white as snow . . . . And Aaron said unto Moses,
Alas, my Lord I beseech thee, lay not the sin upon us,
wherein we have done foolishly and wherein *we have
sinned* . . . : And Moses cried unto the Lord, saying, *Heal
her* NOW, O God, I beseech thee" (Num. 12: 9-13).

So also the instruction given in James covers this point;
"*If he have committed sins,* they shall be forgiven him"
(Jas. 5: 15). "Fools because of their transgression,
and *because of their iniquities,* are afflicted . . . . and
they draw near unto the gates of death"; but when "they
cry unto the Lord in their trouble, he saveth them out of
their distresses. *He sent his word AND HEALED
THEM,* and delivered them from their destructions. O
that men would praise the Lord for his goodness, and for
his wonderful works to the children of men!" (Psa. 107:
17-21). `

"Bless the Lord, O my soul, and forget not all his
benefits: Who *forgiveth all thine iniquities;* WHO
HEALETH ALL THY DISEASES; who redeemeth
thy life from destruction; who crowneth thee with lov-
ing-kindness and tender mercies; who satisfieth thy
mouth with good things; so that thy youth is renewed
like the eagles' " (Psa. 103: 2-5).

I can not close this chapter without saying that at the
present time these signs are following "them that believe." The pure light of the primitive gospel of salva-

tion and healing is now proclaimed by a Holy Ghost ministry with the results set forth in the Scriptures. To testify personally, the writer has witnessed the healing of many thousands of people, and of almost all the diseases that have a name. From childhood I have known this truth, and I have frequently been healed myself; in fact, until the present hour I do not even know the taste of medicine. I will also refer to some others who have been divinely healed, giving names, also addresses when these are known. These cases are for the most part selected from the book "200 Genuine Instances of Divine Healing," where the original testimonies themselves are given in detail. Every one of these people referred to is known personally by the writer, though of course I was not present in every case to witness the healing mentioned. Many of these are indeed marvelous.

1. *Instantaneous healing of total blindness.* Mrs. Emma Miller Elwood, Burlington, Mich.

2. *Cancer, and healing of broken bones.* Mrs. Della Fry, Fennville, Mich.

3. *Chronic diarrhea, acute indigestion, dyspepsia,* and *general debility.* James Bamford, 3906 Woodland Park Ave., Seattle, Wash.

4. *Catarrhal Consumption.* J. Grant Anderson, Franklin, Pa.

5. *Muscular rheumatism.* W. N. Meyers, 2700 W. Main St., Louisville, Ky.

6. *Instantaneous healing of consumption.* Louie M. Bennett, Anderson, Ind.

7. *Catarrh.* D. F. Oden, 2500 Ninth Ave., Bessemer, Ala.

8. *Pneumonia.* Merton Merica, Huntington, Ind.

9. *Poisoning.* A..J. Byers, Newark, Ohio.

10. *Pneumonia and many other afflictions.* Mary Cole, Anderson, Ind.

11. *Dropsy of heart and lungs.* George Q. Coplin, Anderson, Ind.

12. *A large cystic growth.* C. B. Sheldon, Charlevoix, Mich.

13. *Quick consumption.* Mattie B. Wilson, Woodsboro, Tex.

14. *Dog bite and hydrophobia.* Annie H. Martin, Battle Creek, Mich.

15. *Blindness, deafness, and rheumatism.* Child of Mabel C. Porter, Forbes, Mo.

16. *Healed after intense suffering.* Orval E. Line, Pierceton, Ind.

17. *Sore eyes, female trouble and nervousness;* also child of *diphtheria and bad abscess.* Mrs. S. S. Moyer, Berlin, Ontario, Can.

18. *Consumption and appendicitis.* J. N. Howard, Anderson, Ind.

19. *Chronic Catarrh and typhoid fever.* G. T. Neal, 361 Failing St., Portland, Ore.

20. *Deafness and cancer.* M. J. Howard, Anderson, Ind.

21. *Black diphtheria.* Child of I. P. Hamerick, Cowen, W. Va.

22. *Serious internal injuries* caused by a fall. John H. Merica, Topeka, Ind.

23. *Complication of diseases.* Mrs. Addie P. King, Union City, Pa.

24. *A most remarkable healing.* L. H. Morgan, M. D., Herrin, Ill.

25. *Complication of diseases and mad-dog bite.* Lena Nelson, Jamestown, Ohio.

26. *Eczema, Tuberculosis of bone, and nervous breakdown.* E. Faith Stewart, Cuttack, India.

27. *An invalid restored to health.* Jessie M. Osborne, Decatur, Mich.

28. *Cancer dropped off.* T. J. Brundage, Farmersville, Cal.

29. *Brain-fever.* David Gerig, Auburn, Ind.

30. *Bright's disease, indigestion, female troubles, spasms, catarrh and a bad liver.* Sarah B. Hallman, 5758 South Park Ave., Chicago, Ill.

31. *Spinal disease.* Ethel J. M. Williams, Corbetton, Ontario, Can.

32. *Ovarian trouble.* Emma J. Rothman, 2010 Broadway, Pittsburg, Pa.

33. *Rheumatism.* David Koroch, St. Joseph, Mich.

34. *Cerebrospinal meningitis.* A. G. Pontious, Mt. Pleasant, Mich.

35. *Typhoid fever.* D. T. Koach, 208 Frank St., Akron, Ohio.

36. *Curvature of the spine and tuberculosis.* Ethel J. Pearl, Eastport, Mich.

37. *Copperhead bite.* Mrs. Anna Cheatham, 77 Enfield St., Belfast, Ireland.

38. *Typhoid fever and other afflictions.* J. W. Byers, Oakland, Cal.

39. *Serious intestinal trouble.* M. Near, Pentwater, Mich.

40. *Heart-failure.* T. A. Phillips, Denver, Colo.

41. *Broken bones.* The writer's father, Joseph F. Smith, Lacota, Mich.

42. *Crushed arm restored, and instantaneous healing of fever.* Lodema Kaser, La Paz, Ind. This case is attested by Dr. S. G. Bryant, Neosho Falls, Kan., who is also known to the writer.

But why continue to multiply instances? They could be related by the hundred. And in addition to those already mentioned, they run through the whole list of diseases—whooping-cough, insanity, erysipelas, neuralgia, cholera infantum, paralysis malaria, measles, nervous prostration, many injuries by accident, etc.

"Oh that men would praise the Lord for his goodness, and for his wonderful works to the children of men"; for he is the one "who forgiveth all thine iniquities, who healeth all thy diseases." Amen.

RELATIONSHIP OF BELIEVERS
OR, THE CHURCH: ITS
MEMBERSHIP AND OR-
GANIZATION, ITS ORDI-
NANCES AND ITS WORK.

CHAPTER XI.

UNITY OF BELIEVERS.

In the previous chapters we have considered the plan of redemption merely from the standpoint of the relationship of the individual with God. In this chapter we purpose to show by the Word of God that the same experience of salvation which brings the person into living touch with Christ also brings him into vital relationship, through the Spirit, with all others who have received a like experience.

As we have already shown, the definite and instantaneous experience that makes us living members of Christ is the new birth; and as we thus become members of the family of God, we also by the same act and experience become members of all those who are members of the divine family. "We are members one of another" (Eph. 4:25). "One is your Master, even Christ; and all ye are *brethren*" (Matt. 23:8). "Behold, how good and how pleasant it is for brethren to dwell together *in unity!*" (Psa. 133:1). "Endeavoring to keep the unity of the Spirit in the bond of peace" (Eph. 4:3).

So complete and perfect is this Bible standard of divine relationship, of unity among all the saved, that they are declared to constitute one body in Christ. We are reconciled "unto God *in one body* by the cross" (Eph. 2:16). "Ye are called *in one body*" (Col. 3:15). "For by one Spirit are we all baptized into one body, whether we be Jews or Gentiles, whether we be bond or free; and have been all made to drink into one Spirit" (1 Cor.

12:13). Christ "is the head of the body" (Col. 1:18); while "we are members of his body, of his flesh, and of his bones" (Eph. 5:30). This represents the closest possible union, both with Christ and with one another.

UNITY ILLUSTRATED.

In different scriptures the apostle Paul uses the natural body to illustrate the spiritual body, composed of all the truly saved. "For as we have many members in one body, and all members have not the same office: so we [Christians], being many, are one body in Christ, and *every one members one of another*" (Rom. 12:4, 5).

There is perfect harmony in a normal body, for its unity is not effected by external means, but is *organic*. Many and diverse though the members be, still they are all necessary for the completeness and harmony of the whole. So it is with the body of Christ. We are many members, differing in age, in sex, in intellectual attainments, in social advantages, in nationality; still it can truthfully be said, "There is neither Jew nor Greek, there is neither bond nor free, there is neither male nor female: *for ye are all one IN CHRIST JESUS*" (Gal. 3:28).

The body of Christ is "subject unto Christ," its head (Eph. 5:24); therefore we all have "one mind" (2 Cor. 13:11), "the mind of Christ" (1 Cor. 2:16); hence are able "to be likeminded one to another," and "with one mind and one mouth [to] glorify God, even the Father of our Lord Jesus Christ" (Rom. 15:6). We "stand fast in one spirit, with one mind striving together for the faith of the gospel" (Phil. 1:27).

IN ONE BODY.

The person who contends for division or seeks to justify division among the people of God, is opposing every
principle of truth on this subject revealed in the New
Testament. Everywhere we find this same glorious standard of unity. One purpose of Christ's death was that
"he should gather together *in one* the children of God
that were scattered abroad" (John 11: 52). Jesus himself said, "Other sheep I have [Gentiles] which are not
of this [Jewish] fold: *them also I must bring*, and they
shall hear my voice; AND THERE SHALL BE ONE
FOLD [flock], AND ONE SHEPHERD" (John 10:
16).

In the second chapter of Ephesians we read how these
two classes of people were made one. Although "in times
past" the Gentiles were "strangers from the covenants
of promise, having no hope, and without God in the
world," in Christ they were "made nigh by the blood."
"For he is our peace, who hath made both [Jews and
Gentiles] ONE, and hath broken down the middle wall
of partition between us . . . . that he might reconcile
both unto God *in one body* by the cross, having slain the
enmity thereby." Since this glorious reunion through
Christ, the Gentiles "are no more strangers and foreigners;
but fellow citizens with the saints, and of the household
of God; and are built [together with the Jews and all
other believers] upon the foundation of the apostles and
prophets, Jesus Christ himself being the chief corner-
stone"; and this "holy temple in the Lord" is the "habitation of God through the Spirit" (verses 11-22). This uni-

fication of peoples so diverse was not effected by Jews
becoming Gentiles, or by the Gentiles becoming Jews,
but was brought about by both accepting Christ as "the
way, the truth and the life," and by rejecting all that was
antagonistic to Christ and his truth.

The prayer of Christ recorded in John 17 shows the
sacredness of this doctrine of unity. In the most solemn
hours that the Savior spent during his personal ministry
his heart was burdened for the unification of his disciples. He acknowledged that they had believed on him,
received his word, and been kept in his name; also that
they were not of the world even as he was not of the
world; still he prayed, "Sanctify them through thy truth:
thy word is truth . . . . that they all *may be one*; as thou,
Father, art in me, and I in thee, that they also may be
one in us: that the world may believe that thou hast sent
me . . . . I in them, and thou in me, that they may be
made *perfect in one*" (verses 17-23).

While salvation itself brings us into a divine relationship with each other, the indwelling carnal nature pre-
vents that pefect unity which Christ so much desired.
The apostle Paul, writing to the church at Corinth, mentions the strife and division over preachers manifested
among certain brethren there and attributes it to the fact
that they were "yet carnal" (1 Cor. 3: 1-5). But sanctification purifies the heart, destroying carnality, and therefore makes the people of God "perfect in one," as Jesus
prayed, "Both he that sanctifieth, and they who are
sanctified, are all of one: for which cause he is not
ashamed to call them brethren" (Heb. 2: 11). And
while Jesus prayed for the sanctification of his disci-

ples, that they might be made perfect in one, in order that the world might believe, we find that this result was reached in the apostolic church. "And when they had prayed, the place was shaken where they were assembled together; and they were all filled with the Holy Ghost, and they spake the word of God with boldness. And the multitude of them that believed *were of one heart and of one soul* . . . . and great grace was upon them all" (Acts 4: 31-33). "And believers were the more added to the Lord, multitudes both of men and women" (chap. 5: 14).

In the early church, purity and unity went hand in hand; in fact, they can not be separated; for wherever perfect holiness is, there is unity of believers. In other words, there is no true and perfect unity without heart-purity, and there is no true heart-purity without Bible unity: *there is no true Bible holiness without both.*

Even the idea of division among Christians was foreign to the pure apostolic church. Paul says to the Roman brethren, "Mark them which cause divisions and offenses contrary to the doctrine [of unity] which ye have learned, *and avoid them*" (Rom. 16: 17). To the Corinthians he says, "I beseech you, brethren, by the name of our Lord Jesus Christ, that ye all speak the same thing, and that there be *no divisions among you;* but that ye be *PERFECTLY JOINED TOGETHER* in the same mind and in the same judgment" (1 Cor. 1: 10). Can we entertain the idea of disunion and inharmony among the members of our natural body, when it is in a normal state? Impossible! So the body of Christ, represented by this figure, is a perfect organism, and in its normal state exhibits the most perfect unity among all its members—the truly saved in Christ Jesus.

UNITY THROUGH RELATIONSHIP.

But I must say something more concerning the basis of Christian unity. The underlying foundation of true unity is *relationship,* not development or attainments. This we might illustrate by a human family. There may be many children in the family, differing in sex, age, and intellectual development; still there exists a real standard of unity. The son in college never thinks of judging his relationship with his brother in the primary school or with his sister in the cradle by an intellectual standard. The tie that binds them together is invisible; it is in no sense proportioned by their respective degrees of development, but has its basis in *blood-relationship.* But while this is the primary basis of union still development is the law of normal humanity; therefore as all the members of the family develop in intellectual capacity and learn the great facts of truth surrounding them, they will also become *one in this respect,* so far as the ability of each one will allow.

So also in the spiritual relationship. We are "all one in Christ Jesus." But what does it mean to be *in Christ?* First of all, it means to be "born again," for without this experience we are not Christians at all and "can not see the kingdom of God" (John 3: 3). "There is therefore now no condemnation to them which are in Christ Jesus" (Rom. 8: 1). Why? Because they have been "made free from the law of sin and death" (verse 2). To be in Christ, then, signifies to be born of God and to have our sins removed by his grace. "Therefore if any man be *in Christ*, HE IS A NEW CREATURE: old things are passed away; behold, all things are become new." "Whosoever abideth *in him* sinneth not: whosoever sinneth hath not seen him neither known him." (1 John 3:6). By this spiritual birth we enter the spiritual family, where we possess the divine life which flows in all its members, and are thus "all one in Christ Jesus" by virtue of a spiritual blood-relationship.

UNITY PERFECTED.

But we must also develop along spiritual lines in such a practical, visible manner "that the world may believe." We must "dwell together in unity"; we must "all speak the same thing." Now, how is this possible? How can those who are one in spirit, by virtue of spiritual birth, be made "perfect in one" before the world, so as to convince unbelievers of the truth of Christianity? The conditions for this perfect unity are:

1. *We must be "in Christ,"* which signifies salvation from sin: "not of the world."

2. *We must be kept in his name,* which means to reject all other spiritual names.

3. *We must receive the Word of God and keep it,* which means to reject all the doctrines and commandments of men.

4. *We must be sanctified wholly,* which removes from the heart the cause of carnal divisions.

All these conditions are expressly stated in the seventeenth chapter of St. John, where Christ prayed for the unification of his people.

There is a false standard of so-called unity made prominent throughout Christendom, which is simply an attempt to bring together by external organization the professed followers of Christ. But such can never be more than a miserable counterfeit. True unity can be effected only by meeting the Bible conditions already mentioned. Mere external organization—bringing together multitudes of people the majority of whom know nothing about a saved experience and sinless life, who never have been born again—such, I assert, is not in any sense Bible unity. Reader, do not be deceived by such a combination of diverse elements. Bible unity is based on spiritual life and is in perfect accordance with the Word of God. The truly saved have spiritual fellowship with each other, and know each other, and have no spiritual affinity with those who are not of God. They "have no fellowship with the unfruitful works of darkness, but rather reprove them" (Eph. 5:11). They are instructed to "stand fast in one spirit, with one mind striving *together* for the faith of the gospel" (Phil. 1:27).

Not one text in the New Testament teaches that division among God's people is right; but everywhere unity is enjoined and division denounced. We read of one Lord, one salvation, one God, one faith, one Spirit, one mind, one mouth, one body, one baptism, one new and living way, one Bible, and one heaven. And in order to serve this one God aright, follow this one Lord according to his one new and living way, obey his one revealed Word, and go home to this one heaven, *we must be* "ALL ONE IN CHRIST JESUS."

CHAPTER XII.

THE NEW TESTAMENT CHURCH.

The New Testament sets forth the truth respecting the church as clearly as it does any other subject. The introduction to this subject is found in the words of Jesus, "I say also unto thee, That thou art Peter, and upon this rock I will build my church; and the gates of hell shall not prevail against it" (Matt. 16:18).

There has been much discussion relative to the meaning of "rock" in this text, some affirming that the word means the revelation mentioned in verse 17; others that it means Peter himself; still others that it means Christ. But this point is immaterial: for we know that through divine revelation the church was established; that Peter, together with the other apostles, was a foundation-stone in that church; and that Christ himself is declared to be the "chief corner-stone." So even admitting that the church was built on Peter, the Word shows that Peter was not special in this sense, for it was "built on the foundation of the *apostles and prophets*, Jesus Christ himself being the chief corner-stone" (Eph. 2:20). In John's apocalyptic vision the foundations of the wall of the New Jerusalem contained "the names of the *twelve* apostles of the Lamb" (Rev. 21:14).

But it is the fact of the church itself that I wish to consider. "I will build my church," says Christ. Over and over again men have affirmed that Christ did not organize a church, but left this part of the work for men to arrange in accordance with their ideas and inclinations. But this text clearly represents Christ as a church-builder, and, furthermore, shows that it is an exclusive church—"I will build *my* church." Laying aside all the biased opinions of men on the subject, let us appeal directly to the Word of God and see what it teaches concerning the church.

THE CHURCH IN TYPE.

The church of God is often referred to as the house of God, his spiritual dwelling-place on earth. In Old Testament times the house of God was an earthly structure: first the tabernacle, constructed in the wilderness (Exod. 25: 8); afterwards the temple at Jerusalem (1 Kings 8: 10). When the first house, or tabernacle, was completed, God manifested himself in it, on the occasion of its dedication, in such a glorious manner that "Moses was not able to enter into the tent of the congregation because . . . . the glory of the Lord filled the tabernacle" (Exod. 40: 35). So also at the dedication of Solomon's temple, "the priests could not stand to minister because of the cloud: for the glory of the Lord had filled the house of the Lord" (1 Kings 8: 11).

Now, while such were the houses of God in that dispensation, the prophets clearly predicted the coming of the Messiah, and said that he should build another house of God. Jeremiah refers to him as "a righteous Branch and a King . . . . and this is his name . . . . THE LORD OUR RIGHTEOUSNESS" (Jer. 23: 5, 6). There is no mistaking the personage here referred to. And Zechariah says, "Behold the man whose name is The Branch; and he shall grow up out of his place, and *he shall build*

the temple of the Lord: even he shall build the temple
of the Lord; and he shall bear the glory, and shall sit
and rule upon his throne" (Zeph. 6: 12, 13). In fulfilment of these prophecies, Christ says, "I will build
my church."

The writer of the Book of Hebrews affirms that the
Old Testament house of God was "a figure for the time
then present," pointing forward to and meeting its antitype in "a greater and more perfect tabernacle" introduced by Christ and dedicated by his own blood (Heb.
9: 1-14). Paul distinctly states that the "house of God
. . . . is the church of the living God, the pillar and
ground of the truth" (1 Tim. 3: 15); while Peter just as
distinctly affirms that it is a spiritual institution, composed of spiritual people: "Ye also, as lively stones, are
built up a spiritual house, an holy priesthood, to offer
up spiritual sacrifices, acceptable to God by Jesus Christ"
(1 Pet. 2: 5). Yea, all of God's redeemed saints are a
"building fitly framed together, which groweth unto *an
holy temple in the Lord*: in whom ye are also builded
together for an habitation of God through the Spirit"
(Eph. 2: 20-22).

The transfer of God's sanction and approval from the
Old Testament house to the New Testament house took
place at the death of Christ, when all the rites, ceremonies, and appointments of the former ended. Just
before this occurrence, Jesus, weeping over the sad condition of rebellious Jerusalem, said, "Behold, your house
is left unto you desolate" (Matt. 23: 38).   Having
promised to build his own church and complete a new
order of spiritual worship, he cried, as he hung on the

cross of Calvary "It is finished." Immediately "the veil of the temple was rent in twain from the top to the bottom" (Matt. 27: 51), and God forsook the old house, nevermore to dwell in temples made with hands. A few days later the infant church, his future earthly house or temple, being fully prepared and set in order, was dedicated by the marvelous Pentecostal baptism of the Holy Ghost and fire. How perfectly this fulfilled, in an antitypical sense, what occurred at the dedication of the former temple! And when this organization and dedication of the church took place, "the same day there were added unto them about three thousand souls . . . . and the Lord added to the church daily such as should be saved" (Acts 2: 41, 47). So the church was built and dedicated, and souls were added to it. Praise the Lord!

Now let us notice the Bible characteristics of this church.

IT IS THE BODY OF CHRIST.

"And hath put all things under his [Christ's] feet, and gave him to be the head over all things to the church, *which is his body*, the fulness of him that filleth all in all" (Eph. 1: 22, 23). Christ is the head of this body. "And he is the head of the body, the church . . . . that in all things he might have the preeminence" (Col. 1: 18). "For his body's sake, which is the church" (verse 24). Christ is head of but one body. "There is *one* body" (Eph. 4: 4). In these texts the church and the body are used interchangeably, referring to one and the same thing. The body of which Christ is the head is the church that he built; yea, "the church of God which he hath purchased with his own blood" (Acts 20:28).

This is the only church taught in the New Testament. We can find out exactly what constitutes this church by reading the Bible statements about what constitutes the body of Christ, which only is the church. "For as we have many members in one body, and all members have not the same office: so we [true Bible Christians], being many, are *one body in Christ*, and every one members one of another" (Rom. 12:4, 5). The universal body of true believers constitutes the church for which Christ died. You can not have salvation, can not be a member of Christ, without being thereby a member of the body of Christ; for "now hath God set the members *every one of them* in the body, as it hath pleased him" (1 Cor. 12:18). Inversely, it is impossible to be a member of the body of Christ without being a member of Christ himself.

SALVATION ITS MODE OF MEMBERSHIP.

As we have just shown, we become members of the body of Christ, the church, by becoming members of Christ. "For by one Spirit are we all baptized [or inducted] into one body, whether we be Jews or Gentiles, whether we be bond or free; and have been all made to drink into one Spirit" (1 Cor. 12:13). This text has no reference to the literal rite of water-baptism, but is the work of the "Spirit" by which we are inducted into Christ and into his body the church. *"God hath set the members* every one of them, in the body"

(verse 18). Now, since this induction into the body, or
the church, is the work of the Spirit of God himself, it
is evident that no one but the saved can possibly find
admittance. Under a little different figure Christ conveys the same truth, "I am the door: by me if *any man*
enter in, *he shall be saved"* (John 10:9).

Who are the members of Christ? Manifestly, those
who are members of God's family. How do we become
members of the divine family? Answer: "Except a
man *be born again* he can not see the kingdom of God"
(John 3:3). "As many as received him, to them gave
he power to become the sons of God . . . . which were
born . . . . of God" (John 1:12, 13). "Beloved, now
are we the sons of God" (1 John 3:2). Now, according to Paul, in Ephesians 2, the "one body" (the church)
mentioned in verse 16 is composed of "the household of
God," the same being likened to "an holy temple in the
Lord . . . . builded together for an habitation of God
through the Spirit"; while he distinctly affirms in
another place that this spiritual temple or "house of
God . . . . is *the church of the living God"* (1 Tim.
3:15).

What can be plainer? All the truly saved are members of the body of Christ, his church; for the Spirit
inducts us into one; yea, "now hath God set the members every one of them in the body" (1 Cor. 12:13, 18).
On the other hand, all who are still in their sins are
outside of the body, hence no part of the church of God.
"There is one body" (Eph. 4:4); we are "called in one
body" (Col. 3:15); we are reconciled unto God "in one
body by the cross" (Eph. 2:16)—*and this one body is*

the church (Eph. 1:20-22; Col. 1:18, 24). Hence there is but one divine church. It is both inclusive and exclusive; for it includes all the saved, and excludes all the unsaved; thus it is "a glorious church, not having spot, or wrinkle, or any such thing," but is *"holy and without blemish"* (Eph. 5:27). Reader, this is the church of the New Testament. In this pure, holy state she shone forth in the days of her pristine glory.

The unity of believers in one body, set forth in the preceding chapter, shows the beautiful divine standard of unity and harmony in this church that Christ purchased with his own blood. But when men apostatized from the truth and lost sight of this simple divine standard, they began to organize human churches according to their own likes and dislikes; and the result is the Babel of sectarianism everywhere manifest. Oh, how changed from the apostolic order!

CONTRASTED WITH SECTS.

Let us contrast the primitive church with sects.

1. *The church was fully organized and set in order on the day of Pentecost*, about A. D. 33.

All sects have originated since that time; therefore not one of them is the church of God; and, furthermore, all of them combined do not constitute the church of God.

2. *Salvation makes men members of the church of God.*

Salvation does not make any person the member of any sect: people become members of sects by some other

means. Some people get salvation first and for lack of
better light join a sect afterward; some others join a
sect first, and afterward become awakened to their sinful condition and get saved; while the vast majority of
people either grow up from childhood in a sect, or else
join a sect later, without Bible salvation, and never get
salvation, but die in their sins and are lost.

3. *The church of God contains in its membership
all the saved of earth,* as well as the ransomed in paradise—"the whole family in heaven and earth" (Eph.
3:15).

A sect at the very best contains but a small portion of
the truly saved of earth, and that small remnant is not
in its normal condition, for it is separated by sectarian
walls from other truly saved people, while the church
of God was originally one.

4. *The church of God does not contain in its membership a single unsaved person;* for Christ is the door,
and if we enter through him we "shall be saved" (John
10:9). If we sin again, we are expelled (Exod. 32:33).

The door of entrance into every sect is human; therefore multitudes gain admittance without Bible salvation.
And even those who are saved may lose their salvation
through sin without losing their sect membership.

5. *The church of God contains all the truth,* yea,
is "the pillar and ground of the truth" itself (1 Tim.
3:15).

No sect contains all the truth, for the whole truth
destroys sectarianism. One time a certain minister
held a conversation with a person who was pleading
for sects. The minister stated that no sect contained

all the truth. At first the individual contended that some of them did. He was asked where he could find the Bible standard concerning baptism taught, and he quickly named a particular sect which holds the Bible standard in this respect, so far as the mode is concerned. He was then asked whether that sect also held the Bible standard concerning divine healing, and he was obliged to admit that it did not, that one would have to go somewhere else to find that. He was then asked concerning the Bible doctrine of sanctification as a second work of grace, accompanied by the baptism of the Holy Ghost; and he had to admit that one would have to go to another place in order to find it. He had to make the same admission regarding other Bible doctrines. Finally the minister asked, "How can you obtain all the truth in sects unless you join all the sects?" He acknowledged that this would be necessary. Then the preacher added: "But even then you would not have all the truth; for the Word of God condemns sects and divisions of every character, and says, 'Come out from among them, and be ye separate' (2 Cor. 6:14-17)."

6. *The church of God was free from error, and possessed the truth itself.*

Every sect was conceived in error, born in wrong, nurtured in falsehood, and survives in heresy. We do not deny the elements of truth scattered about here and there in sects, and these portions of truth have in the past accomplished considerable good, in spite of the errors with which they were surrounded. But while some men lay the whole world of sects under tribute in an effort to exhibit the truth; other men, more inclined to

doubt and unbelief, are gathering together the false
doctrines and errors contained therein, and presenting
to the world a horrible picture of darkness, superstition,
and heresy. This, we must admit, is working incalculable harm to the precious cause of Christ.

7. *Salvation, the mode of membership in the church*
of God, reconciled men together "in one body," and in
the Word of God we find that the church of God possessed every necessary provision for their complete and
perfect unification in the one church.

Sectarianism scatters and divides the true sheep of
the Lord, mixes and mingles them with the filthy goats
and ravenous wolves of false professors, in hundreds of
separate folds, and leaves them a prey to every foul
spirit sent forth by the destroyer to blind, mislead,
and deceive honest souls.

ITS VISIBILITY.

Men who are blinded to the truth and can see nothing
but human churches or sects, generally state that the
church of God is invisible and that therefore it was
necessary to have sectarian organizations in order to
make it visible before the world. But the superficial
character of this argument is easily seen by all of the
spiritually-minded. Where was the church of God during the early centuries before the rise of human ecclesiasticism? Paul said, "I persecuted the church of God,
and wasted it" (Gal. 1:13). Was he chasing a ghost
or a shadow, or was there a real, living, visible church of
God that he was opposing? The answer is clear to all.
He addressed his Corinthian Epistles "Unto the church

of God which is at Corinth," and he asked them, "Despise ye the church of God?" (1 Cor. 1:2; 11:22; 2 Cor. 1:1). Many times this expression concerning the church is used in the New Testament, but it is never used of an invisible something up in the air, but is *in every case* applied to *the visible body of worshipers on the earth.* Still salvation itself is clearly shown to be the mode of induction into the body of Christ, the church; and salvation, we know, is in its nature invisible, though not invisible in its effects upon men.

Now, the harmony between these two apparently discordant facts is found in the one fact that in the apostolic church the spiritual body of true believers in Christ and the collective body of worshipers *were identical.* "And the same day there were *added unto them* about three thousand souls . . . . and the Lord *added to the church* daily such as should be saved" (Acts 2:41-47). "And of the rest durst no [unsaved] man *join himself* to them. . . . . And believers were the more *added to the Lord,* multitudes both of men and women" (Acts 5:13, 14). There was no difference between being added to the Lord and being added to the apostles and disciples; for the same act of receiving salvation did both.

Now, when this identity between the body of Christ and the body of worshipers existed, the apostles did not need to write and preach about a spiritual, invisible something as the church of God, but could point to the congregation of worshipers as the church of God and call it the church of God. This they did, as we have shown.

This identity was manifested to the world in organic form *as the normal church*. It was obtained and maintained in those days by the following means: 1. All the truly saved were naturally members of the body of worshipers. 2. The spirit of holy power, discernment, and judgment which filled the church purged out all hypocrites, thus keeping the congregation clean and pure. When Ananias and Sapphira hypocritically sought to deceive, the Spirit of God revealed their condition, and even laid special judgment upon them, with the result that "of the rest durst no man join himself to them" (Acts 5: 1-13). At that time "sinners could not stand in the congregation of the righteous" as God's people. Later, when the apostasy set in and men through unfaithfulness lost their spiritual discernment, judgment, and holy power, the congregation became mixtures of saints and sinners, as was the case with the seven congregations in Asia Minor, mentioned in the opening chapters of the Revelation. But God was highly displeased with this state of affairs, which shows that it was an abnormal condition; therefore he reproved them sharply, and to the church at Laodicea he said, "I will spue thee out of my mouth" (Rev. 3: 16).

From the foregoing facts we adduce these conclusions: 1. That a congregation of the church of God is one in which the Spirit of God has the ascendency; one in which sin is rebuked and exposed, so that a clear line of distinction is drawn·"between the righteous and the wicked, between him that serveth God, and him that serveth him not" (Mal. 3: 18). 2. That whenever the Holy Spirit is no longer allowed the leadership, and good and bad mingle together undistinguished, such a congregation is rejected by Christ and therefore ceases to be a congregation of God, regardless of its name and profession.

Following the pure apostolic period of the church such wholesale apostasy took place that the church of God *in its organic form* no longer existed in any prominence on the earth, its few spiritual members being scattered among the human institutions called churches. This condition has led to the ridiculous assertion made by certain sectarian divines (?), that the visible church of Christ is filled with the precious and the vile. This may be very true of human sects, but they do not constitute the visible church of Christ.

In Chapter XIX the reader will find information concerning how God is now restoring a pure church with the Bible characteristics, a church that stands clear and clean from the entire Babel of sectarianism.

ITS ORGANIZATION.

The church of God, as revealed in the New Testament, is a perfectly organized institution, and no human tinkering is necessary in order to make it right.

Organize is defined by Webster as follows: "1. To form with suitable organs; 2. To construct so that one part may cooperate with another; 3. To distribute into suitable parts, and appoint proper officers, that the whole may act as one body." These conditions of organization are all fulfilled in the church of God, and the organizing is the work of the Spirit himself.

1. *"To form with suitable organs."* Fulfilment: "But now hath God set the members, every one of them, in the body as it hath pleased him" (1 Cor. 12: 18). Then, the parts of which the body of Christ is composed are "suitable." The manner in which this is accomplished is described in verse 13: "For by one Spirit are we all baptized into one body .... and have been all made to drink into one Spirit."

2. *"To construct so that one part may cooperate with another."* This condition of organization is fulfilled in the perfect union of all true believers in one body, according to the text last quoted. "God hath tempered the body together .... that there should be no schism in the body; but that the members should have the same care one for another. And whether one member suffer, all the members suffer with it; or one member be honored, all the members rejoice with it" (1 Cor. 12:24-26). While this was spoken with direct reference to the physical body, it was used by the apostle to set forth the spiritual body and its close association of members; for in the next verse he says, "Now ye are the body of Christ, and members in particular."

3. *"To distribute into suitable parts, and appoint proper officers, that the whole may act as one body."* This condition of organization is also perfectly fulfilled in the spiritual church of God. "*God hath set some in the church,* first apostles, secondarily prophets, thirdly teachers, after that miracles, then gifts of healing, helps, governments, diversities of tongues" (1 Cor. 12:28). "*And he gave* some apostles; and some, prophets; and some, evangelists; and some, pastors and teachers; for

the perfecting of the saints, for the work of the ministry, for the edifying of the body of Christ: till we all come in the unity of the faith, and of the knowledge of the Son of God unto a perfect man, unto the measure of the stature of the fulness of Christ" (Eph. 4: 11-13). Take heed therefore unto yourselves, and to all the flock, over the which *the Holy Ghost hath made you overseers*, to feed the church of God, which he hath purchased with his own blood" (Acts 20: 28).

Thus, all these conditions of organization were fulfilled perfectly, with the result that in the early church "the whole" was able to *"act as one body."* What sectarians palm off on the world as church organization is in reality church disorganization; for instead of allowing the entire church of God to "act as one body," as in apostolic days, their so-called organization has torn it asunder and caused it to act in hundreds of opposing bodies. Such is *sect organization,* but not organization of the church of God, for the church of God was a perfectly organized institution before sects arose. Even its officers were called to their official positions by the Spirit of God—*"the Holy Ghost hath made you overseers."* They did not enter the ministry as a profession, and seek training in theological seminaries in order to be fitted for the work; but they were saved men, filled with the Holy Ghost, and under the anointing and inspiration of the Spirit of God they governed the church and converted the multitudes. I do not wish to be understood as opposing education; for when education is used, not abused, it is indeed a great blessing. But no amount of mere human education can fit a man for the position of a New Testament minister. In addition to all natural endowments and acquirements such a position requires the reception of the Holy Ghost—the leadership and instruction of the Spirit himself.

No conference of men gave Paul his position in the church; but the Lord Jesus said unto him, "I have appeared unto thee for this purpose, *to make thee a minister*" (Acts 26:16). Therefore Paul asserted that he was "an apostle, not of men, neither by man, *but by Jesus Christ*" (Gal. 1:1). However, he was not independent of the church of God; for he afterwards went up to Jerusalem to them which were apostles before him, and submitted himself "privately to them which were of reputation" (Gal. 2:2). But it was the province of the Holy Spirit to appoint the apostolic ministers. The church and the older ministers had nothing to do but to recognize these appointments of God, which they did in an official manner by the laying on of hands by the elders; and this was called ordination.

PARTICULAR FEATURES.

In order to show more clearly how perfect was the divine organization of the church, I will enumerate some particular features, some of which, however, have already been mentioned.

1. *It was a spiritual organization,* the entire body of believers being bound together by a divine relationship.

2. *This spiritual body of believers was exhibited to the world in the form of various local congregations* of worshipers, geographically distributed. This gave rise to the plural use of the term "church"; hence we read

of the seven churches in Asia, etc. But these churches were not different kinds of churches, but were simply local congregations of the one universal church of God. Paul could travel about from place to place ordaining elders "in every church," because these churches were all alike (Acts 14: 23).

3. *It had conditions of membership.* "And the Lord added to the church daily such as should be saved," or, as the Revised Version renders it, *"such as were being saved"* (Acts 2: 47). "By one Spirit are we all baptized into one body" (1 Cor. 12: 13). "I am the door; by me if any man enter in, he shall be saved" (John 10: 9).

4. *It had a class-book*—not on earth in the hands of fallible men, however. "Whose names are in the book of life" (Phil. 4: 3). "Rejoice because your names are written in heaven" (Luke 10: 20). "And of Zion it shall be said, This and that man was born in her. . . . . And the Lord shall count *when he writeth up the people,* that this man was born there" (Psa. 87: 5, 6). "Whosoever hath sinned against me, him will I blot out of my book" (Exod. 32: 33).

5. *It had a name.* "Holy Father . . . . I kept them *in thy name"* (John 17: 11, 12). As individuals the followers of Jesus are called friends, disciples, brethren, saints, etc.; but we never read in the Bible of a Friends' church, Disciple church, Brethren church, Saints' church: but as a church the disciples took the name of the Father; therefore we read: "Unto the church of God" (1 Cor. 1: 1; 2 Cor. 1: 1). "I persecuted the church of God" (Gal. 1: 13). "Despise ye the church of God?" (1 Cor. 11: 22). "Give none offense . . . . to the church

of God" (1 Cor. 10:32). "Take care of the church of
God" (1 Tim. 3:5). "Feed the church of God, which
he hath purchased with his own blood" (Acts 20:28).

6. *It had a discipline.* "I have given them thy word"
(John 17:14). "All Scripture is given by inspiration of
God, and is profitable for doctrine, for reproof, for correction, and for instruction in righteousness: that the
man of God may be perfect, throughly furnished unto
all good works" (2 Tim. 3:16, 17).

Doctrine, reproof, correction, and instruction, cover
all the ground that any discipline can reach; therefore
the Word of God is the only necessary rule of faith
and practise. In fact, the disciplines of most of the
Protestant sects state that the Bible is to be accepted as
the supreme word of God; so that whatever is not contained therein or can not be proved thereby is not to be
required of any man. Then, why not throw away all
the disciplines of men, which contain a multitude of
unscriptural doctrines, rules, and regulations, and just
accept the Bible as the all-sufficient rule of faith? However, the Word was intended as a discipline for the
church of God and therefore is not suitable as a discipline for a sect. The members of the church of God
are instructed in case of sickness to send for the elders
of the church and be anointed by them and healed
through the prayer of faith. How will this rule work in
a sect, whose ministers do not believe this part of the
Word and who have no faith for healing? Now, "all
Scripture" is profitable and constitutes a "perfect law
of liberty"; therefore a discipline that does not contain
all the Word of God is not large enough; and, on the

other hand, one that contains more than the Word of God contains too much.

One of my brethren in the ministry once held a conversation with a sectarian minister who was opposing the truth concerning the church of God. When asked if his church taught and practised all the Word of God, the sectarian said it did, and he exhibited his discipline as proof. The brother asked him why they had a discipline other than the Bible itself if it contained all of the Word; and he replied that it contained all of the Word in a *condensed and more convenient form.* The brother then asked him to read out of his discipline the thirteenth chapter of St. John in its condensed and more convenient form; and he was obliged to refer to the Bible itself in order to find out what the thirteenth chapter of St. John is about, thus proving that the Bible is the most convenient, after all. But he was obliged to admit that the injunction given in that part of the Bible was not in his discipline. When asked whether he would obey it if it was in his discipline, he replied, "Yes." Now, this hireling minister of sect-Babylon was not ready to obey this commandment because it was in the Bible, but he would have been perfectly willing to obey it if man had only put it in his little sect discipline; thus showing that he, like thousands of others, was bound by the doctrines and commandments of men more than by the Word of God. The Word itself gives sufficient instruction along spiritual lines, and we need no legislation of a human character.

7. *It had officers properly distributed.* I have already referred to the ministers of God's church and to the

divine call and appointment to their official work. I will not attempt, in the limits of the present work, to set forth in completeness the primitive form of church government. The ministers of the Word, however, were of two classes, which I will denominate general and local. Those who were called of God to the general work were specially used in raising up new churches and in exercising a general oversight of their spiritual affairs after they were raised up; while the local ministers had the particular care of their own congregations. Thus, we find Paul and Barnabas, as general ministers, visiting the local congregations they had raised up, and ordaining elders in every church (Acts 14: 22, 23). So also Paul writes to Titus: "For this cause left I thee in Crete, that thou shouldest set in order the things that are wanting, and ordain elders in every city, as I had appointed thee" (Tit. 1: 5).

Now, these general ministers had a general burden, care, and responsibility of all the work of God. The apostles and elders at Jerusalem felt it to be their duty and responsibility to counteract the influence of certain law-teachers who were troubling the Gentile brethren; and this they did by repudiating the doctrines taught, saying, "to whom *we gave no such commandment*" (Acts 15: 24). Paul states that he was burdened daily with "the care of all the churches" (2 Cor. 11: 28).

The local elders, however, were chiefly limited in responsibility to their own congregations; and Peter exhorts them, saying, "Feed the flock of God which is among you, taking the oversight thereof, not by constraint, but willingly; not for filthy lucre, but of a ready

mind; neither as being lords over God's heritage but
being ensamples to the flock" (1 Pet. 5:2, 3). And
Paul thus instructed the local elders of the church of
Ephesus: "Take heed therefore unto yourselves, and to
all the flock, over the which the Holy Ghost hath made
you overseers, to feed the church of God, which he hath
purchased with his own blood" (Acts 20:28). The ministers whom God called and set in his church were such
as possessed spiritual gifts and qualifications fitting them
for the great work to be accomplished; their ministry
was therefore under the direct authority and inspiration
of the Holy Ghost.

There was also a special class of officers called deacons,
whose specific work was the ministration of temporal
affairs connected with the local church (1 Tim. 3: 8-13
with Acts 6: 1-6).

I have already shown that there was but one body,
therefore only one divine church, and that its members
were bound together by the closest tie of spiritual relationship and sympathy; but it is fitting that we also
observe some particular points of the relation of members to each other. There was

EQUALITY OF MEMBERS.

Men have always been prone to divide the race into
clans; classes; and castes. But the Word of God recognizes the essential unity of the human race; it teaches
that all are in one sense on the same plane, because of
universal sin, and that hence all stand in need of redemption; therefore it lifts up a standard of spiritual
equality for all those who are redeemed. "Let the

brother of low degree rejoice in that he is *exalted:* but the rich, in that he is *made low*" (Jas. 1:9, 10). This places all on the same plane in Christ. "For by one Spirit are we all baptized into one body, whether we be Jews or Gentiles, whether we be bond or free" (1 Cor. 12:13). "There is neither Jew nor Greek, there is neither bond nor free, there is neither male nor female; for ye are all one in Christ Jesus" (Gal. 3:28). The apostle James strongly reproves those who would respect a rich man more than a poor man (Jas. 2:1-4).

EQUALITY OF MINISTERS.

To the first ministers Christ said, "Be not ye called Rabbi: for one is your Master, even Christ; and all ye are brethren" (Matt. 23:8). And when some of their number sought for a position of preeminence over the rest, Christ referred to conditions among the Gentiles, how the great men domineer over the others, and said, "*It shall not be so among you:* but whosoever will be great among you let him be your minister; and whosoever will be chief among you let him be your servant: even as the Son of man come not to be ministered unto, but to minister" (Matt. 20:20-28).

While the greater gifts and qualifications of some of the apostles made them more useful than others and placed greater responsibilities upon them, still this humble standard of equality was maintained until the apostasy began to develop. The apostle John was one of the chief men among the first apostles, and that he exercised general oversight and authority is shown by the attitude which he took toward the proud and bigoted

Diotrephes, an unworthy and overbearing local elder. "I wrote unto the church: but Diotrephes, who loveth to have the preeminence among them, receiveth us not. Wherefore, if I come, I will remember his deeds which he doeth, prating against us with malicious words: and not content therewith, neither doth he himself receive the brethren, and forbiddeth them that would, and casteth them out of the church" (3 John 9, 10). But notwithstanding the general oversight and responsibility of this apostle, he humbly and affectionately writes to the churches of Asia Minor, "I John also am *your brother, and companion in tribulation,* and in the kingdom and patience of Jesus Christ" (Rev. 1:9). No minister in the early church possessed such great gifts and spiritual qualifications as did the apostle Paul, and his responsibilities were doubtless greater than all; nevertheless he humbly acknowledges himself to be "less than the least of all saints" (Eph. 3:8).

EQUALITY OF MEN AND WOMEN IN THE CHURCH.

This is a feature which, of all the religions of the world, belongs to Christianity. In heathenism women are regarded as greatly inferior to men and generally have little or no place in religion, unless, indeed, it is in some dishonorable connection, as in some of the licentious orgies. But among the Jews even the laws of Moses made special provision for women, and they were honored and respected; some of them even rose to positions of prominence, as Deborah, who held an official position in Israel. "And Deborah, a prophetess . . . . she judged Israel at that time" (Judges 4:4). She also led the armies of Israel to victorious conflict (Judges 4). Christ delivered one of his greatest sermons to a single woman by a well-side in Samaria (John 4); and a woman was the first messenger sent to proclaim the great fact of the resurrection. The apostle Paul distinctly recognizes the equality of women with men, in the words, "There is neither Jew nor Greek, there is neither bond nor free, *there is neither male nor female*: for *ye are all one in Christ Jesus*" (Gal. 3:28).

WOMEN IN OFFICIAL POSITIONS.

This equality of women with men in the apostolic church extended even to official positions.

1. *As deaconesses.* The original Greek of Rom. 16:1 clearly shows that Phebe, a woman, was a deaconess of the church at Cenchrea. Now, "the office of a deacon" was a distinct, public *official position* in the church, and its candidates were publicly ordained by the laying on of the hands of the apostles (1 Tim. 3:8-13 with Acts 6:1-6).

2. *As ministers.* Nor was the ministry of women limited to temporal affairs. We read in different texts of Priscilla and her husband Acquilla (the name of the woman usually standing first), and find that on one occasion they jointly took Apollos, a powerful minister of the gospel, and "expounded unto him the way of God more perfectly" (Acts 18:26). The first sermon concerning the Christ was preached in the temple to the people of Jerusalem by Anna the prophetess —a woman (Luke

2: 36-38). The Samaritan woman whom Jesus met at the well-side went into her city and proclaimed Christ to the people with the result that "many of the Samaritans of the city believed on him *for the saying of the woman*" (John 4: 39). On the day of Pentecost the Spirit of God was poured out publicly upon the women, and they prophesied in the presence of the wondering multitudes. Philip the evangelist "had four daughters, virgins, which did prophesy" (Acts 21: 8, 9).

Now, what does it mean to prophesy? The primary signification of the term is *to speak forth,* to tell out the message or the mysteries of God. Its secondary meaning (in some respects the outgrowth of the first) is *to foretell future events.* Paul clearly shows that the "gift of prophecy" is to "understand all mysteries, and all knowledge" (1 Cor. 13: 2). To prophesy, then, is to proclaim the mysteries and knowledge of God. The same apostle declares that redemption itself was a "mystery," "the hidden wisdom . . . . which none of the princes of this world knew"; and yet it is revealed to us by the Spirit of God: "*which things also we speak,* not in the words which man's wisdom teacheth, but which the Holy Ghost teacheth"; for "the natural man receiveth not the things of the Spirit of God: for they are foolishness unto him: neither can he know them, because they are spiritually discerned" (1 Cor. 2: 7-14).

To preach the gospel of Christ, then, under the inspiration of the Holy Ghost is to proclaim the "mysteries," the "hidden wisdom" of God—*to prophesy.* This is the application which the apostle himself makes of it; for he says, "He that prophesieth *speaketh unto men to edification, and exhortation, and comfort"* (1 Cor. 14:3). This prophecy is the public proclamation of the gospel; for he further says in the same chapter, "If therefore *the whole church be come together in one place,* and all speak with tongues, and there come in those that are unlearned, or unbelievers, will they not say ye are mad? *But if all prophesy,* and there come in one that believeth not, or one unlearned, he is convinced of all, he is judged of all: *and thus are the secrets of his heart made manifest;* and so falling down on his face, he will worship God, and report that God is in you of a truth" (verses 23-25). What is it that reveals the secrets of men's hearts and brings conviction upon their souls? It is the preaching of the word of God. "For the word of God is quick and powerful, sharper than any two-edged sword . . . . *and is a discerner of the thoughts and intents of the heart"* (Heb. 4:12). No one can deny, without twisting the Scriptures, that the prophecy of which Paul speaks is nothing else than the Holy Ghost public preaching of the gospel itself when the church is "come together in one place." (1 Cor. 14:23, 24).

Now, the prophet Joel declared, "On my servants and on my *handmaidens* I will pour out in those days of my Spirit, and *they shall prophesy* (Joel 2:28, 29); and Peter declares that the Pentecostal experience, when the women spoke publicly "as the Spirit gave them utterance," was a fulfilment of this prediction (Acts 1:14, 15; 2:4, 14-18).

From many considerations it is evident that Paul recognized woman's place in the gospel; for he wrote to the Philippians, "Help those women *which labored with me in the gospel,* with Clement also, with other my fellow laborers, whose names are in the book of life" (Phil. 4:3). Clement was a minister, and these women are ranked with him and others as Paul's *fellow laborers* in the gospel of Christ. "Fellow laborers" means laborers together on the same plane and in the same work. This was only carrying out in a practical way the doctrine of the apostle himself, that in Christ Jesus there is "neither male nor female."

The great Tertullian, after the apostolic age, recognizes this same equality of men and women, in the Word: "Together they pray, together prostrate themselves, together perform their fasts; *mutually teaching,* mutually exhorting, mutually sustaining. *Equal are they both found in the church of God."—Part IV, Book II, Chap. 8.*

NECESSARY EXCEPTIONS.

In this connection it is necessary to notice some exceptions to this general standard. In planting the gospel among different nations, varying in customs and social conditions, the apostle Paul on many occasions found it necessary *as a matter of expediency* to accommodate himself to their particular ways and social standards. This accommodation he expresses in these words: "Unto the Jews I became as a Jew, that I might gain the Jews; to them that are under the law, as under the law, that I might gain them that are under the law; to them that are without law, as without law (being not without law to God, but under the law of Christ) that I might gain them that are without law. . . . . I am made all things to

all men, that I might by all means save some. And this
I do for the gospel's sake" (1 Cor. 9:20-23).

In this same Epistle Paul admits that he wrote some
things to the Corinthians that were, in his opinion, "good
for the present distress" (chap. 7:26); hence these
things were not a standard for all people and for all
ages. One of the things to which he found it necessary,
as a matter of expediency, to accommodate himself was
their social standard concerning women. This church
was in a heathen environment, to the social standards of
which some deference had to be paid if the church hoped
to win souls to Christ. In this heathen city women were
regarded as vastly inferior to men and had no honor-
able place in the heathen religion; but, as Strabo informs
us, one of their temples had one thousand consecrated
prostitutes. Now, with such a social standard and such
public sentiment concerning women's place in religion,
what course could the apostle take other than what he
did take—command the Christian women *there* to "keep
silence in the church" (1 Cor. 14:34)?

I Tim. 2:11-15 does not cover the subject of women's
official position in the church as set forth in the other
Scriptures. It applies to the proper relationship of the
woman with her own husband. This is shown by the
example given—Adam and Eve—and by its connection
with "childbearing," etc. The design of this scripture is
to maintain the proper domestic relationship, wherein
the wife is to recognize the fact that her husband is by
nature her "head" in this respect. "For the husband
is the head of the wife, even as Christ is the head of the
church" (Eph. 5:23). But in spiritual things the hus-

band is not the head of the wife. "Christ is the head of the church," and "the church is subject unto Christ" (Eph. 5: 23, 24); therefore in spiritual things the woman's subjection, first of all, is to Christ, and she "ought to obey God rather than men." Thus Sapphira was accountable directly to God, and not to her husband, in a matter which concerned the church (Acts 5: 1-10).

THE WOMEN'S HEAD-COVERING.

When these heathen women at Corinth appeared in public, they were always heavily veiled, in accordance with a very ancient custom (Gen. 24: 65), and the same custom exists among many Oriental peoples until this day. By the people it was regarded as a shame for them to appear otherwise, and as a matter of disgrace particularly to the husband. Therefore the apostle said, "Every woman praying or prophesying with her head uncovered dishonoreth her head"—*her husband*, "for the head of the woman is the man" (1 Cor. 11: 4, 5).

Under these conditions Paul instructed the Christian women at Corinth to retain their veils, in accordance with the common custom (not of the church, *but of the country*), even while in prayer. He did not instruct women who had never worn such a veil to put one on while praying, but taught that those who had the custom of veil-wearing already *should not uncover* when they prayed; in other words, they should *wear it all the while*, as the custom of the people demanded.

The words of the apostle himself show clearly that the head-covering mentioned was based on conditions existing before the establishment of the gospel and was therefore no part of the gospel itself. He says: "The man is not of the woman; but the woman of the man. Neither was the man created for the woman; but the woman for the man. For this cause ought the woman to have power [Margin, a covering, *in sign that she is under the power of her husband*] on her head because of the angels" (1 Cor. 11: 8-10). In other words, the veil-wearing was based on the idea of the inferiority of women and was a special sign that she was "under the power of her husband."

Now, woman's Edenic condition was not one of inferiority to her husband, but she was created as his *"helpmeet"* (Gen. 2: 20). But on account of her prominent part in the fall, rushing forward into things which she ought not, and influencing her husband wrongly, she was afterwards placed in a dependent position. "In sorrow shalt thou bring forth children; and thy desire [submission] shalt be to thy husband, *and he shall rule over thee*" (Gen. 3: 16).

But the gospel restores matrimony to its original state —the union of one man and one woman for life (Matt. 5: 32; Rom. 7: 2, 3; 1 Cor. 7: 10, 11, 39). And more than this, under the gospel standard the wife becomes once more a true "helpmeet," according to the original design, the husband even being specially instructed to dwell with her "according to knowledge, *giving honor unto the wife,* as unto the weaker vessel, and as being *heirs together* of the grace of life" (1 Pet. 3: 7). Under this standard the husband is no longer to "rule over" his wife in a domineering way; they are *"heirs together* of the grace of life." In the Christian family the law of love is the only law. "Husbands love your wives," says the apostle Paul (Eph. 5: 25), and in another place he says that the younger women are to be instructed "to love their husbands" (Tit. 2: 4). The obedience of wives to their own husbands, which is frequently mentioned, is only such obedience as will harmonize with this greater law of love. The idea, then, that woman must wear a head-covering "in sign that she is *under the power of her husband*" is foreign to the gospel standard. Such might be consistent under the old order of things, but not under the gospel.

In the very next verses of 1 Cor. 11, following the ones already quoted (in which woman's inferiority to man, under the old order, is implied), the apostle shows the true standard of equality: "Nevertheless neither is the man without the woman, neither the woman without the man, IN THE LORD. For as the woman is of the man, so is the man also by the woman; but all things of God" (verses 11, 12). So all the arguments concerning woman's inferiority based on the fact of her being created last (which is the very argument for the head-covering made in verses 8-10) are in verses 11 and 12 contradicted by the apostle and shown to be without any weight "in the Lord"; for man is now by the woman just as truly as the woman is by the man—there is no difference. Furthermore, if this creation argument rested upon a solid basis in fact, it would prove woman's superiority rather than her inferiority; for in the natural order the greatest things were created last. If this be not true, then, according to the nature argument, man must admit that he is inferior to the horse, because the horse was created first! "There is neither .... male nor female; for ye are *all one in Christ Jesus*" (Gal. 3:28).

The idea that the wearing of the woman's head-covering is an ordinance or observance of the New Testament church is contrary in its nature to the general tenor of the gospel itself. Such an ordinance, or requirement— that women must cover their heads, while men must not —could have no other object than to *force a distinction between the sexes* and place one inferior to the other. But all the other ordinances apply to men and women alike, and indicate unity and equality. We do not read: "Let your men be baptized, but your women not," nor "Let your women partake of the communion, but your men not." On the other hand, when Philip preached the gospel in Samaria the believers were "baptized both men and women" (Acts 8:12). Even the ordinance of feet-washing is for both sexes. It was begun among the apostles, who were all men (John 13); but afterwards we read concerning the widow, "If *she* have washed the saints' feet" (1 Tim. 5:10). And even though custom and propriety suggest that the men wash the feet of the men, and the women the feet of the women, as we practise, the ordinance itself does not force a distinction between the sexes; for the command is the same to both sexes, and both sexes obey it alike.

But the great proof that the apostle Paul was not establishing among the Corinthians women's head-covering as an ordinance of the New Testament church is the fact, easily shown, that neither Paul nor any other apostle could establish an ordinance of the church. In

Heb. 9: 15-18 the apostle treats the new covenant as a will which was made effective by the death of Christ. "For where a testament is, there must also of necessity be the death of the testator. For a testament is of force after men are dead: otherwise it is of no strength at all" (verses 16, 17).

Now, Christ himself was the "mediator of a better covenant" (chap. 8: 6). He delivered it during his ministry, and it was brought into effect by his death— "the death of the testator." And the same apostle distinctly affirms that if a "covenant be confirmed, no man disannulleth *or addeth thereto*" (Gal. 3: 15). It was not in the power of Paul or any one else to add to the new covenant after its dedication by the death of Christ. The apostle and other God-chosen persons could execute the terms of the covenant and explain its relations with the covenant which preceded it, and this they did; but they could not add one new ordinance to that covenant: *"no man* disannuleth *or addeth thereto."* It is evident that the apostle who wrote these facts would not himself attempt to establish woman's head-covering as a New Testament rule or ordinance twenty-five years after the "death of the testator."

John 16: 12 indicates that there were many things for the apostles to learn after the crucifixion of Christ, but these pertained to the relationship of the old covenant with the new, which things they could not at that time understand; but the Spirit made all clear afterwards. The entire book of Hebrews was written in order to make this relationship between the old and the new covenants clear, and still the Jews were scarcely able to "bear it." Therefore the writer says, "We have many things to say, and hard to be uttered, seeing ye are dull of hearing" (chap. 5:11).

Now, all the New Testament ordinances are found in the Gospels, and were established either by the direct command or by the personal example of Christ himself; and therefore they were delivered by the apostles to the churches. But there is no woman's head-covering in the Gospels. That is something that does not relate to the church of God, but to custom, and that custom was based on the old order of things. The apostle says, *"Judge in yourselves, is it comely that a woman pray unto God uncovered?"* (1 Cor. 11:13). A positive New Testament ordinance, binding upon all people, is not left to the private judgment of individuals. But concerning the head-covering they could "judge in themselves." In this case, those people who have the custom would probably "judge in themselves" that it would be good for their women to continue what custom demands; while, on the other hand, those of us who "have *no such custom*" (verse 16) *"judge in ourselves"* that this custom is in no wise profitable or essential for us in our altered state of society.

The foregoing instances, however, were not the general standard of the apostolic church, as a multitude of scriptures prove, but were simply accommodations to certain local conditions among the heathen Gentiles. Jewish women did not "keep silence in the churches," but prophesied in public, as we have already shown, and "labored in the gospel." But although the Word of God allows and teaches a perfect equality of men and women in spiritual things, yet in the church local conditions and adverse public sentiment may sometimes interfere for the time being with the possession of these liberties. "He that winneth souls is wise."

WORK OF THE CHURCH.

The work of the church of God is twofold: 1. To care for and perpetuate itself; 2. To evangelize the world. It can prosper only as it keeps this twofold mission in view. A congregation that becomes self-centered, that cares for nothing but local prosperity, is almost sure to decline spiritually, and misses its mission of assisting in carrying the gospel to a lost world. Missionary work was prominent in the apostolic church, and was steadfastly pursued in obedience to Christ's command: "Go ye into all the world, and preach the gospel to every creature" (Mark 16: 15). But the accomplishing of this great work required the sacrifice of men and of means. A noble army of consecrated men and women who "loved not their lives unto the death" went forth to struggle against the powers infernal and win the triumphs of the cross. The churches of God poured out their money in order to meet the demands of the hour, even going so far in some cases, as at Jerusalem, to sell all their property and devote it to the interests of the cause of God.

The same thing is needed today. The work of God needs men and women who are consecrated to evangelize the world, even at the cost of personal comforts and advantages; and the church of God must awaken to the fact that giving of means for the support of God's work is both their privilege and their duty, and that it must be done. "Even so hath the Lord ordained that they which preach the gospel should live of the gospel" (1 Cor. 9: 14). Those who minister to the people in "spiritual things" must receive the benefit of the people's "carnal things" (verse 11). The work demands this; God demands it; and all the pure and holy in heart will say amen to the will of God.

The present conditions and work of the church will be considered more fully, however, in Chapter XIX. My special object in the present chapter has been to set forth what the apostolic church was, as revealed in the New Testament. The subject of the Ordinances of the Church will be considered in the following three chapters.

CHAPTER XIII.

BAPTISM.

The observance of ordinances in the New Testament church rests upon the last commission Christ gave to his apostles: "Go ye therefore, and teach all nations, baptizing them in the name of the Father, and of the Son, and of the Holy Ghost: teaching them to observe all things whatsoever I have commanded you: and, lo, I am with you alway, even unto the end of the world" (Matt. 28: 19, 20). In this text we find ordinances expressly commanded, and their observance is to be perpetuated *"unto the end of the world."*

Some religious teachers oppose the observance of all ordinances, claiming, through a misapplication of Col. 2: 4, that these were abolished at the death of Christ. But the text thus misapplied clearly shows that the abolished ordinances were those which belonged to the Mosaic law, and they are stated to be meats, drinks, holidays, new moons, and sabbaths (verses 16, 17). These were the "carnal ordinances, imposed upon them until the time of reformation" (Heb. 9: 10). "But Christ being come" (verse 11), the reformation was brought in; the Mosaic institutions were antityped and thus abolished, through his death; and the New Testament house, or church, of God, with its ordinances and institutions, succeeded.

This commission authorizing ministers to go and baptize was given *after the death of Christ,* and was consistently obeyed by the apostles afterwards, as the book of Acts abundantly shows. Some have foolishly affirmed that Paul did not believe in the ordinances, and therefore was quite indifferent to the subject at Corinth (see 1 Cor. 1: 13-17); and that he baptized Crispus and Gaius and the household of Stephanus merely because they required it of him. But the inspired record shows that when Paul raised up this congregation *"many* of the Corinthians hearing, believed, *and were baptized"* (Acts 18: 8). Now, if Paul himself did not do much of this baptizing, he had others do it, which shows his attitude toward the subject. Furthermore, he wrote to this same congregation, *"I have received of the Lord* that which I also delivered unto you, That the Lord Jesus the same night in which he was betrayed took bread," etc., referring to the ordinance of the Lord's Supper, as the context shows (1 Cor. 11: 23). Paul was not an antiordinance preacher.

It must also be borne in mind that Paul did not receive the gospel from those who were apostles before him, but received it by direct revelation from God, *after the crucifixion and resurrection of Christ.* Here are his own words: "I certify you, brethren, that the gospel which was preached of me was not after man. For I neither received it of man, neither was I taught it, but by the revelation of Jesus Christ." When God "called me by his grace, to reveal his Son in me, that I might preach him among the heathen, immediately I conferred not with flesh and blood: neither went I up to Jerusalem to them which were apostles before me" (Gal. 1: 11, 12, 15-17). Where, then, did Paul get his authority to baptize, institute the Lord's supper, etc.? Not from the apostles, but by the revelation of Jesus Christ—"for *I have received of the Lord* that which also I delivered unto you" (1 Cor. 11:23) This proves positively that these ordinances were not abolished at the cross, for the apostle was not even converted at the time of the crucifixion. Furthermore, the ordinances were not intended only for the Jews, because they loved ordinances so well, for the special commission of Paul was to preach among the Gentiles (Acts 26:15-18).

A BELIEVER'S BAPTISM.

The last commission of Christ, as given by Mark, is: "And he said unto them, Go ye into all the world, and preach the gospel to every creature. He that *believeth* and is baptized shall be saved; but he that believeth not shall be damned" (Mark 16:15, 16). This scripture clearly limits the subjects of baptism to those who are capable of hearing and believing the gospel; and this standard was invariably maintained by the apostles in their ministry. For example, we read concerning the multitude who received the word of God at Samaria, "And when they *believed* Philip preaching the things concerning the kingdom of God, and the name of Jesus Christ, they were baptized, *both men and women*" (Acts 8:12). No children were baptized, but only persons who *believed*—"men and women."

The entire practise of giving a so-called baptism to young children originated in an apostate church and is positive heresy. It is nowhere taught in the Bible, either by a single text or by a single example. Nor is infant baptism found in any other book outside of the Bible until near the close of the second century, and then it was introduced as a result of two other errors that were being taught: 1. That infants are totally depraved and therefore guilty and lost; 2. That baptism itself regenerates from sin. These two false doctrines believed, the baptism of infants naturally followed, as the only means of removing their depravity and preventing their going to hell in case of death.

There is no valid reason, either in the Bible or outside of it, for the observance of this infant rite. The statement often urged, that the apostles must have baptized infants, because they sometimes baptized households, has no bearing on the subject; for there is no proof in a single instance that there were infants in these households. Furthermore, in most cases, the context itself shows that believers only were baptized. For examples, see the records concerning the household of Cornelius (Acts 10) and the household of the jailer (Acts 16: 31-34). Baptism is "the answer of a good conscience toward God" (1 Pet. 3: 21), but infants have no conscience whatever.

If one ordinance of the church is applicable to infants, why not all of the ordinances? The Scriptures no more teach infant baptism than they teach infant communion. Some of the Eastern churches, such as the Greek, Syrian, and Armenian, do give communion to the infants that are baptized (?) by them. The Armenian Church also practises the ordinance of feet-washing, after a certain fashion, once each year, on which occasion the priest who performs the mass selects twelve boys and goes through a form of washing the right foot of each. But the Armenians are inconsistent in that they exclude the infants from this.

Nor does this rite of infant baptism decrease in any sense the parental obligation to endeavor to "bring them up in the nurture and admonition of the Lord." No good can possibly come to infants by this senseless rite; on the contrary an incalculable amount of harm results. One writer urges infant baptism in order that the children "should never be allowed to believe that they were naturally aliens from the household of faith." This is the very harm and deception that comes through infant baptism; for at this very day millions who were baptized (?) in infancy believing that they have always been the children of God, though they have never been "born again," and are *on the road to hell*. The entire so-called Christian East—Papal, Greek, Gregorian, Coptic, Abyssinian and others—is cursed by this delusion; while many forms of Protestantism have borrowed it from the great church apostate and are perpetuating it in the West.

When people grow up in sin believing that they are Christians because of a so-called baptism in infancy, it is almost impossible to convince them that they are not Christians at all; yet they must understand this truth before they can ever be definitely converted to God. I assert without hesitation, in the fear of God, that it is my firm conviction that no other false doctrine ever introduced under the name of Christianity has been the means of sending such a great number of people to hell as this one delusion—infant baptism. Not that the so-called act of baptism itself is so harmful, but it is the accompanying belief that such candidates are Christians from their infancy. This belief is especially strong in the East, where all baptized people (irrespective of moral character) are called Christians; while those who have not had the rite are, by the so-called Christians, generally termed heathen. The doctrine of Christ is that "except a man *be born again* he can not see the kingdom of God" (John 3:3). "He that *believeth* and is baptized shall be saved."

I wish it were in my power to arouse the millions who are sleeping under the delusion that they were really baptized when they were babes and are therefore Christians. Unless such become awakened, "believe" the gospel and are saved thereby, and then are "baptized *both men and women*" (Acts 8:12), they will all be lost forever.

CONDITIONED ON REPENTANCE.

"In those days came John the baptist preaching . . . . and saying, Repent ye: for the kingdom of heaven is at hand. . . . . Then went out to him Jerusalem, and all Judea, and all the region round about Jordan, and were baptized of him in Jordan, confessing their sins" (Matt. 3:1-6).

Not only did John teach that the people should repent and then be baptized, but he actually required repentance of them, refusing to baptize them if they did not repent. "And when he saw many of the Pharisees and Sadducees come to his baptism, he said unto them, O generation of vipers, who hath warned you to flee from the wrath to come? *Bring forth therefore fruits meet for repentance"* (verses 7, 8). We read in another place that "the Pharisees and lawyers rejected the counsel of God against themselves, being not baptized of him" (Luke 7:30). Because of their unwillingness to meet the required conditions for baptism, it is said that they "rejected the counsel of God." And so it is with all antiordinance people; by rejecting Bible baptism they are rejecting God's Word.

In his Pentecostal sermon Peter taught the same truth concerning the necessity of repentance first and baptism afterwards: "Repent, and be baptized every one of you" (Acts 2:38). Unless the heart is brought into the right attitude through repentance, the simple act of baptism amounts to nothing, even though performed in the Bible manner and by a true minister of God. Simon, the sorcerer at Samaria, was baptized with the other believers; yet when Peter and John came down the unregenerate condition of the man's heart was revealed. His baptism in water, even though performed by Philip, a man "filled, with the Holy Ghost," did not take away from his heart the love of preeminence, which had possessed him in the past. Peter said to him plainly, "Thou hast neither part nor lot in this matter: *for thy heart is not right in the sight of God"* (Acts 8:21).

IS A BURIAL.

The mode of baptism is a subject that has been much controverted by theologians. But the Word of God is very plain on this subject; and a few Scriptural considerations will be sufficient to show the humble follower of Christ that immersion is the Bible mode of baptism.

In fact, almost without exception theologians admit the validity of immersion; the chief controversy has arisen over the effort on the part of many to prove that sprinkling or pouring also is valid.

All scholars admit "immersion" to be the plain English equivalent of the Greek word *baptizo*. "Sprinkle" and "pour" are not equivalent, as the lexicons testify. There are three words in the Greek language that are equivalent respectively to the three English words "immerse," "sprinkle," and "pour." Now, whenever the Bible speaks of baptism as a literal Christian rite, it *always employs the Greek word that is the equivalent of the English word "immerse."* If the Bible writers, using Greek, desired to convey the idea of "pour," why did they not use the Greek word that signifies "pour," instead of the word that signifies "immerse"? or use a word for "sprinkle" if they meant "sprinkle"? The reason is clear to all fair-minded men: they said what they meant, and, I may add, *meant what they said.*

This distinction is so clear that wherever the literal Christian rite is spoken of one can substitute the word "immerse" without in any sense changing the meaning; whereas in many cases if we can substitute the word "sprinkle" or "pour," the passage is made ridiculous. There is no mention of sprinkling or pouring for baptism during the first two centuries, when it was introduced in case of sickness and was not regarded as regular. Furthermore, all the facts and circumstances concerning baptism, recorded in the New Testament, harmonize with the doctrine of immersion, but not on any other supposition.

The great historians, as Neander, Mosheim, Wall, Weiss, Ewald, Geikie, Eidersheimer, De Pressense, Conybeare, Stanley, Schaff, and many others, all testify that immersion was the primitive practise. This was also affirmed by the great reformers, as Luther, Calvin, Wesley, and others.

A few years ago a noted American minister, whose name is familiar in almost every household and who belonged to a church that always sprinkles for baptism, made a trip to the Holy Land, where he had his photograph taken in the act of *immersing* a candidate in the river Jordan. Why was this? Because he knew, as all well-informed men know, that *immersion was the primitive practise.* It is probably because the act of immersion is a little inconvenient, and rather humiliating to vanity and pride, that such great efforts are made to substitute something else.

Baptism is a ceremonial representation of the burial and resurrection of our Lord; therefore only immersion is appropriate. In fact, the individual believer symbolically follows Christ in his death, burial, and resurrection. First he dies the death to sin, is "crucified with Christ" (Gal. 2:20); then he is *"buried* with him in baptism, wherein also ye are *risen* with him through the faith of the operation of God, who hath raised him from the dead" (Col. 2:12). Baptism thus becomes to the individual an outward sign of an inward work. First we are "circumcised with the circumcision made without hands, in *putting off the body of the sins of the flesh"* (verse 11); then we are "buried with him in baptism," as just quoted (verse 12).

The same idea is alluded to in that remarkable passage in Rom. 6:1-4: "How shall we that are *dead to sin* live any longer therein?" "Therefore we are buried with him by baptism into death: that like as Christ was raised up from the dead by the glory of the Father, even so we also should walk in newness of life."

"Buried *with him*." Was Christ buried in baptism? Yes. John was baptizing "in Jordan" (Matt. 3:6), "In the river of Jordan" (Mark 1:5). "Then cometh Jesus from Galilee to Jordan unto John, to be baptized of him. . . . . And Jesus, when he was baptized, *went up straightway out of the water;* and, lo, the heavens were opened unto him, and he saw the Spirit of God descending like a dove, and lighting upon him: and lo, a voice from heaven, saying, This is my beloved Son, in whom I am well pleased" (Matt. 3:13-17). Jesus evidently went down into the Jordan in order to be baptized; for after his baptism, he "went up straightway out of the water." Here we have the highest authority for immersion in water, which is thus shown to be heaven's plan: 1. *Jesus himself,* the Son of God, set the example. That of itself should be sufficient. 2. *The Holy Spirit,* the third person in the Trinity, bore witness, by appearing visibly in the form of a dove and lighting upon Christ. 3. *The Father Himself* declared in audible tones, "I AM WELL PLEASED."

Reader, if you desire Bible baptism, follow the example of the Son of God, and you will receive a witness of the Spirit; while the Father himself, speaking to your heart, will say, "I am well pleased."

This is the way baptism was administered in the apostolic church. In the eighth chapter of Acts we read about Philip's meeting a certain eunuch and holding a conversation with him concerning the Scripture. "And as they went on their way, they came unto a certain water: and the eunuch said,·See, here is water; what doth hinder me to be baptized? . . . . And he commanded the chariot to stand still: and they *went down both into the water,* both Philip and the eunuch; and he baptized him. And when they were *come up out of the water,* the Spirit of the Lord caught away Philip, that the eunuch saw him no more: and he went on his way rejoicing" (verses 36-39). This passage would be meaningless and ridiculous connected with the idea of sprinkling or pouring; but it is perfectly consistent with the Bible standard, for we are "buried with him in baptism." (Col. 2: 12).

So in order to fulfil the Word of God perfectly and secure a valid baptism the candidate must observe the following: .

1. He must know or hear the gospel; which is usually through a minister (Mark 16: 15).

2. He must repent of his sins and believe the gospel, the doing of which will effect his salvation (Acts 3: 19; 16: 31; 2: 38). .

3. He must find a minister of God that is ready to baptize him (Acts 8: 36, 37).

4. Preacher and candidate must go together to a place where there is *"much water"* (John 3: 23).

5. Then they must go *"down both into the water"* (Acts 8: 38), thus following the example of Christ in his baptism (Matt. 3: 16).

6. Then he must be *"buried with Him in baptism."*

7. Both preacher and candidate can then "come up out of the water" (Acts 8:39).

8. Then the candidate, having obeyed the Word and followed his Lord, can go "on his way rejoicing" (Acts 8:39).

Reader, have you met Bible conditions and been baptized in this way? If not, you have not been baptized at all; for nothing short of this constitutes a valid baptism.

Some humble ministers of Christ may not be able to follow the learned scholars into the Greek language in order to understand all about the meaning of *words;* but after reading the plain accounts of how baptism was performed by the apostles, they can be satisfied to *do as they did.*

A PURIFYING ORDINANCE.

To the Jewish mind baptism appealed very strongly as a purifying ordinance. They had long been accustomed to "divers washings" and ablutions of a ceremonial nature, and on this account were led to regard baptism in a similar light. Therefore when John came baptizing in Enon near Salim, presenting a new cleansing ceremony, straightway "there arose a question between some of John's disciples and the Jews about purifying" (John 3:23-25).

The apostles also presented the subject in the light of a purifying ordinance. Thus, Peter said to the penitent Jews, "Repent and be baptized every one of you in the name of Jesus Christ, *for the remission of sins*" (Acts 2:38). The language clearly implies that baptism, as well as repentance, is for the remission of sins. So also Ananias said to Saul, "And now why tarriest thou? arise, and be baptized, and *wash away thy sins*, calling on the name of the Lord" (Acts 22: 16).

This appeared very clear and natural from the Jewish standpoint, for they were accustomed to the idea of double cleansing—actual and ceremonial. By consulting Lev. 14: 2-7, where the law concerning the cleansing of the leper is given, the reader will see that the actual healing of the leper is one thing and that his ceremonial "cleansing" is another thing. "The priest shall look, and, behold, if the plague of leprosy *be healed.* . . . . Then shall the priest command to take for him *that is to be cleansed* two birds alive and clean," etc. (verses 3, 4). This double cleansing was recognized by Christ; for when he granted a leper perfect healing (the actual work), he said to him, "Go thy way, show thyself to the priest, and offer the [ceremonial] gift that Moses commanded, *for a testimony unto them*" (Matt. 8: 1-4).

Now, baptism as a purifying ordinance does not cleanse the soul from sin actually, but ceremonially, being "a *testimony unto them*"—the people; the outward sign of an inward work of grace. We are "dead to sin," "therefore buried with him by baptism" (Rom. 6: 2, 4). The actual cleansing of the soul from sinful elements can not be effected by literal water, but it is "the blood of Christ" that is able to "purge your conscience from dead works to serve the living God" (Heb. 9: 14). Yea, he hath washed us from our sins in his own blood" (Rev. 1: 5). "The blood of Jesus Christ his Son cleanseth us from all sin" (1 John 1: 7).

Peter also shows the figurative nature of baptismal cleansing or salvation. He says: "The long-suffering of God waited in the days of Noah, while the ark was a preparing, wherein few, that is, eight souls were saved by water. The like figure whereunto baptism doth also now save us (not the putting away of the filth of the flesh, but the answer of a good conscience toward God), by the resurrection of Jesus Christ" (1 Pet. 3:20, 21). Baptism is not our actual salvation, but our figurative one; it is not the actual "putting away of the filth of the flesh, but *the answer of a good conscience toward God.*" How do we obtain this good conscience? Answer: "The blood of Christ . . . . purifies our conscience" (Heb. 9:14). Therefore we have blood-cleansing first, and ceremonial, or water-, cleansing afterwards, as the "answer of a good conscience toward God."

The manner in which Noah and his family were "saved by water" represents the manner in which "baptism doth also now save us." But it was necessary for Noah's household to *get into the ark* FIRST, before they were ready for that water-salvation. So also we must *first* get into the antitypical ark, CHRIST, before we are ready for the ceremonial salvation of water-baptism. In the days of Noah what happened to those who got in the water first? And what will be the result if we now seek water-baptism before we find safety in Christ?

SINGLE IMMERSION.

From the formula given by Jesus—"Go ye therefore and teach all nations, baptizing them in the name of the Father, and of the Son and of the Holy Ghost."

(Matt. 28:19), some have inferred that a threefold action is necessary; one immersion in the name of the Father, one in the name of the Son, and one in the name of the Holy Ghost. But in the Acts of the Apostles this threefold formula is never employed: the people were simply baptized "in the name of Jesus Christ," or "in the name of the Lord Jesus" (Acts 2:38; 10:48; 8:16; 19:5), which shows that the apostles did not understand that it was necessary to perform a triple action. The Father, Son, and Holy Ghost are one; therefore one action is sufficient.

Furthermore, the object and design of baptism precludes the idea of repetition. It is the outward sign of an inward work; it represents our salvation from sin. Now, this salvation is represented as the work *of God* (2 Tim. 1:8, 9), as the work *of Christ* (Matt. 1:21), and as the work *of the Holy Spirit* (John 3:5); yet it is *a single act,* and therefore can be appropriately represented only by a *single immersion;* and this single immersion is in the threefold name just as truly as the single conversion is the work of the divine Trinity. If we were converted three times, once by each person of the Trinity, then trine immersion in three separate names would properly represent it. So also the symbolic reference baptism bears to the burial and resurrection of Christ necessitates the single action. Christ was buried once and raised once; and we are "buried with him [once] in baptism, wherein also we are risen [once] with him"; yea, we arise to "walk in newness of life."

CHAPTER XIV.

THE LORD'S SUPPER.

The New Testament clearly teaches the observance of an ordinance termed "the Lord's supper." This expression, however, is used only once: "When ye come together therefore into one place, this is not to eat the *Lord's supper*" (1 Cor. 11:20). As there has been considerable misunderstanding in certain respects regarding this ordinance, I shall refer to what the Bible really teaches concerning it. First of all, it is

NOT A REGULAR MEAL.

The Corinthian church, it appears, had a misunderstanding of this subject, and in Paul's absence they either substituted something else for the Lord's Supper or else added something to the proper rite; therefore Paul wrote to them for the purpose of correcting the matter. This is shown by the following Scripture: "When ye are come together therefore in one place, this is not to eat the Lord's supper: For in eating every one taketh before other his own supper: and one is hungry, and another is drunken. What? have ye not houses to eat and to drink in? or despise ye the church of God, and shame them that have not? What shall I say to you? Shall I praise you in this? I praise you not" (1 Cor. 11:20-22).

They were coming together for a full meal, very much the same as the idolatrous feasts of the heathen in that city, and their excesses on these occasions were a reproach to the church of God. Paul severely condemned them for this practise; declared that their coming together for a full meal, or feast, was *NOT* "the Lord's supper," but was only their *"own* supper"; that the proper place for eating their own supper was in their own houses, not in the church of God. "If any man hunger," he wrote, *"let him eat at home;* that ye come not together unto condemnation" (verse 34). Those sects of the present day who meet together for the purpose of eating a full meal, calling it the Lord's Supper, are doing the very thing that the apostle condemned. They refuse to obey his word and "eat at home," and thus they "despise the church of God" by eating their "own supper" in the church; and *"this is not the Lord's supper."*

A COMMEMORATIVE INSTITUTION.

After Paul had condemned the Corinthian church for doing what he had not authorized, in thus having a public church-meal, and had denied that such was the Lord's Supper, he proceeded to show what the true Lord's Supper really is. "For I have received of the Lord *that which also I delivered unto you,* That the Lord Jesus the same night in which he was betrayed took bread: and when he had given thanks, he break it, and said, Take, eat: this is my body, which is broken for you: this do in remembrance of me. After the same manner also he took the cup, when he had supped, saying, This cup is the New Testament in my blood: this do ye, as oft as ye drink it, in remembrance of me. For as often as ye eat this bread, and drink this cup, ye do show the Lord's death till he come" (verse 23-26).

So, according to the apostle, the Lord's Supper is the eating of the bread and the drinking of the cup, after the example set by Christ. Therefore the Lord's Supper and the communion are the same. "The cup of blessing which we bless, is it not the *communion* of the blood of Christ? The bread which he break, is it not the *communion* of the body of Christ?" (1 Cor. 10:16). Hence this ordinance is properly termed either the Lord's Supper or communion.

Now, as Paul states, this ordinance was instituted by Christ himself. "And as they were eating, Christ took bread, and blessed it, and break it, and gave to the disciples, and said, Take, eat; this is my body. And he took the cup, and gave thanks, and gave to them, saying, Drink ye all of it; for this is my blood of the New Testament, which is shed for many for the remission of sins" (Matt. 26:26-28).

Following the example and commandment of Christ, the apostolic church observed the ordinance. As we have seen, Paul delivered it to the Corinthians in the proper manner and disclaimed all responsibility for their perversion of it. It was observed in the church at Troas, for we read, "And upon the first day of the week, *when the disciples came together to break bread,* Paul preached unto them" (Acts 20:7). This clearly refers to the ordinance, as nearly all commentators agree. The language, applied as it is to a religious gathering, implies the identity of that gathering with the communion service. "The *bread which we break,* is it not the *communion* of the body of Christ?" (1 Cor. 10:16).

"The Lord Jesus the same night in which he was betrayed *took bread;* and when he had given thanks, *he break it"* (1 Cor. 11:23, 24). The testimony of the earliest church fathers is to the effect that this ordinance was observed regularly by all Christians; and the observance has continued among true Christians until the present day.

ITS DESIGN.

The communion service has an object; it is intended to teach something; for Christ would not establish an ordinance in his church without a distinct purpose in view. Much of the original design, however, has evidently been lost or covered up by the accumulation of human rubbish in the form of theological opinions and false notions. Thus, I might refer to the Roman Catholic doctrine—that the bread and the wine are, at the time of consecration, converted into the actual body and blood of Christ; or to the doctrine of certain Protestant sects concerning the real presence of Christ in the eucharist; or to the doctrine of nearly all sects— that in some mysterious manner Christ attaches himself to the consecrated elements, so that the communicants receive directly some special "grace" thereby,—some even going so far as to state their sins are forgiven at the moment when they partake of the holy elements. But my purpose is not to show what the Roman Catholic sect teaches, nor what the Greek church teaches, nor what Protestant sects teach and believe; it is to show WHAT THE BIBLE TEACHES. All these so-called "exalted ideas," these theories which practically make the communion a substitute for the Savior himself or a substitute for the definite experience of salvation accompanied by a life of perfect holiness—all are without foundation in the Word of God. "Add thou not unto his words, lest he reprove thee, and thou be found a liar" (Prov. 30: 6).

The special design of this ordinance is shown in the words of Christ when commanding its observance: "This do *in remembrance* of me" (Luke 22: 19). If the ordinance is "in remembrance" of Christ, as stated, then it is not actually Christ himself (though it symbolically represents him in his atonement), but is a commemorative institution by which the sufferings of Christ for our sins are brought vividly before the mind, thus bringing us into closer fellowship with his sufferings and death. "For as oft as ye eat this bread, and drink this cup, ye do show the Lord's death till he come" (1 Cor. 11: 26). In observing it, we do not obtain spiritual life, but we "show the Lord's death."

> "Born away in mind and spirit
>   To the solemn, awful scene
> Of mount Calvary's sacred summit,
>   Where we see the crimson stream
> Flowing from the side of Jesus,
>   That has washed us snowy white;
> Here we seem in awe to compass
>   Round the reeking cross tonight.
>
> "Round thy table here we gather
>   And commune, dear Lord, with thee,
> In the consecrated emblems,
>   Lo! thy precious blood we see—
> See thy dear atoning passion
>   And our holy unity.
> Oh! we'll keep thy blest memorial,
>   Till anew we sup with thee."

"Wherefore whosoever shall eat this bread, and drink this cup of the Lord, unworthily, shall be guilty of the body and blood of the Lord. But let a man examine himself, and so let him eat of that bread, and drink of that cup. For he that eateth and drinketh unworthily, eateth and drinketh damnation unto himself, not discerning the Lord's body" (1 Cor. 11:27-29). People who do not discern the Lord's body—his sacrificial body—in its true character as a sin-offering, and who are not thereby actually redeemed from their sins, are unworthy to partake of this ordinance which "shows the Lord's death"; therefore if they "eat this bread and drink this cup," they are "guilty of the body and blood of the Lord"—eat and drink damnation to themselves. Oh, how many sinning professors are, every week, "guilty of the body and blood of the Lord"! "Let a man examine himself." Those who are truly saved, and such only, have a right to this sacred commemorative ordinance of the house of God. Let all others beware of attempting to thrust themselves in upon its sacredness, and thus "despise the church of God" and bring it into disgrace by partaking unworthily.

While the Lord's Supper is commemorative of the sufferings and death of our Lord, representing symbolically his crucified body, it also has another important signification: it represents the collective and unified body of believers in Christ. "The cup of blessing which we bless, is it not the communion of the blood of Christ? The bread which we break, is it not the communion of the body of Christ? For we [saved believers] being

many are *one bread, and one body*: for we are all partakers of that one bread" (1 Cor. 10: 16, 17).

The loaf of bread used in the communion service, in
its unbroken state represents very beautifully the one
body of saved believers. The flour out of which it was
made was ground from many kernels of wheat, which
possibly were grown in many separate fields; yet these
grains have all been brought together and by a certain
process have been unified in one loaf: even their nature
has been changed by the process of baking. So also
we as individuals are many, and we have been widely
separated; yet through Christ we have been "perfectly
joined together" by his Holy Spirit, our natures have
been changed from sin to holiness, and we are indeed
"all one in Christ Jesus." As a unified body in Christ,
the one loaf perfectly represents us. So when in communion service among God's true saints the consecrated
loaf in its undivided state is presented, it stands as the
representation of our unity in the body of Jesus Christ
—his church. From this Scriptural fact it will be seen
that the sects, even at their best, can never represent,
through their communion services, more than one-half
of the New Testament ordinances of the Lord's Supper; for the unity of God's church in one body is not
exhibited in sects. But in the apostolic church the
ordinance was perfect, for it represented both the sacrificial body of Christ and the perfect unity of all believers in him.

ITS PERPETUITY.

That the ordinance of the Lord's Supper was intended to be observed throughout the Christian dispensation is made clear by the Scriptures themselves. We have already seen that it was observed in the apostolic church. Now, the commission of Christ was that his ministers should go and "teach all nations." Teach them what? "Teaching them to observe *all things* whatsoever I have commanded you" (Matt. 28: 19, 20). Did he command this observance? "This DO in remembrance of me" (Luke 22: 19). How long was this to continue? "Teaching them to observe all things whatsoever I have commanded you: and, lo, I am with you alway, *even unto the end of the world."*

This is clear. So long as the gospel is to be preached, just so long the people are to observe all things that Christ commanded—*"even unto the end of the world."* So also we read in another place, "For as often as ye eat this bread, and drink this cup, ye do show the Lord's death till he come" (1 Cor. 11: 26). Then, it is to be observed by the true followers of Christ in all periods of the Christian dispensation, yea, "till he comes" again. Amen.

CHAPTER XV.

FEET-WASHING.

Feet-washing as an ordinance is not generally observed by professing Christians; in fact, by many it is spurned, misrepresented, and ridiculed as is no other saying of Christ recorded in the gospel history. Notwithstanding the fact that Christ said we "should" do it, that we "ought to wash one another's feet," they never observe it, either as a public ordinance or as a private duty. If those who reject feet-washing as a church ordinance were faithfully observing it as a private duty, their attitude would appear less inconsistent; but not to observe it in any form shows a disposition to reject the plain word of Christ. This is a serious matter, one that is not to be lightly turned aside or laughed out of the Bible. "He that is of God heareth God's words." "His commandments are not grievous." "Ye therefore hear them not because ye are not of God" (John 8:47). "If a man love me, he will keep my words" (John 14:23). "Ye believe not, because ye are not of my sheep . . . . my sheep hear my voice, and I know them, *and they follow me*" (John 10:26, 27). Jesus says, "Observe *all things* whatsoever I have commanded you" (Matt. 28:20). Now, if it can be shown that feet-washing was established as an ordinance, then we must "observe" it as an ordinance. We will appeal to the Word of God.

"And supper being ended, the devil having now put into the heart of Judas Iscariot, Simon's son, to betray him; Jesus knowing that the Father had given all things into his hands, and that he was come from God, and went to God; he riseth from supper, and laid aside his garments; and took a towel, and girded himself. After that he poureth water into a basin, and began to wash the disciples' feet, and to wipe them with the towel wherewith he was girded. Then cometh he to Simon Peter: and Peter saith unto him, Lord, dost thou wash my feet? Jesus answered and said unto him, What I do thou knowest not now; but thou shalt know hereafter. Then Peter said unto him, Thou shalt never wash my feet. Jesus answered him, If I wash thee not, thou hast no part with me. Simon Peter saith unto him, Lord, not my feet only, but also my hands and my head. Jesus saith unto him, He that is washed needeth not save to wash his feet, but is clean every whit: and ye are clean, but not all. For he knew who should betray him; therefore said he, Ye are not all clean. So after he had washed their feet, and had taken his garments, and was set down again, he said unto them, Know ye what I have done to you? Ye call me Master and Lord: and ye say well; for so I am. If I then, your Lord and Master, have washed your feet; ye also ought to wash one another's feet. For I have given you an example, that ye should do as I have done to you. Verily, verily, I say unto you, The servant is not greater than his Lord; neither he that is sent greater than he that sent him. If ye know these things, happy are ye if ye do them" (John 13: 2-17).

EXPRESSLY COMMANDED.

Before proceeding to show why this is an ordinance of the church, we will observe that it is here **expressly** commanded; and this fact shows at the very least *that it must be practised in some form.* "If I then, your Lord and Master, have washed your feet, ye also *ought* to wash one another's feet. For I have given you an example, that ye *should* do as I have done to you . . . . If ye know these things, happy are ye *if ye do them*" (verses 14, 15, 17).

Many attempt to evade this part of the Word by saying that it does not assert that we must do it, but merely that we *should* or *ought.* Now, the New Testament law of liberty does not consist of "thou shalt," as did the Mosaic law, but is, instead, a law of love, and Jesus says, "If a man love me, *he will keep my words*" (John 14:23). The true, humble-hearted Christian needs no further coercion than the simple knowledge that he "ought" to do a thing, yea, "should" do it. These are the strongest words in our language expressing moral obligation or duty, as every one must admit. Their true application and force is admitted in every other case where they are employed; for example, "Men *ought* always to pray" (Luke 18:1). "We *ought* to obey God" (Acts 5:29). "So *ought* men to love their wives as their own body" (Eph. 5:28). "We *ought* also to love one another" (1 John 4:11). "Ye also *ought* to wash one another's feet" (John 13:14). Now, does this word "ought" mean the same in the last verse as it does in all the others, or just the reverse?

"And this is his commandment that we *should* believe

on the name of his Son Jesus Christ, and love one another" (1 John 3:23). "Ye *should* do as I have done
to you," that is, "wash one another's feet" (John 13:
15). The commandment is clearly stated: *"Wash one
another's feet."* Men may reject these words of Christ;
they may try to explain them away; they may substitute something else for this ordinance or call it non-
essential: but still the scripture remains to mock all
their efforts: "Ye also *ought* to *wash one another's feet";*
"do as I have done to you." "He that saith, I know him,
and keepeth not his commandments, is a liar, and the
truth is not in him" (1 John 2:4).

A CHURCH ORDINANCE.

The reasons why the act described in John 13:2-17
is to be regarded as a church ordinance is so well set
forth by H. M. Riggle in his book "Christian Baptism,
the Lord's Supper, and Feet-Washing"* that I will simply
quote, at some length, his own words:

"We have here every essential to an ordinance—

"1. *The acknowledged authority of him who delivered it,* our 'Master and Lord.'

"2. *His example.* After washing their feet he said
to them, 'I have given you an example.' Example means
model, pattern, or copy. This is so simple and plain
that we can not mistake it. He washed the disciples'
feet with literal water and wiped them with a literal
towel. This is the copy, pattern, or model that we are
to follow.

, *Published by Gospel Trumpet Co., Anderson, Ind. Price,
$1.00.

"3. *His practise.* He first did the thing himself. That which he did was something which had never been practised before as he here practised it.

"4. *Jesus gave this observance a religious character.* He made it a test of fellowship between him and a beloved apostle. If Peter had continued his refusal to let Jesus wash his (Peter's) feet, he would have cut himself off from fellowship with his Master. 'If I wash thee not, thou *hast no part with me.*'

"5. *An observance commanded.* While Christ himself was washing his disciples' feet, they did not understand the nature and the purpose of the practise (verse 7). But he told them that they should understand it later (verse 7). So after washing their feet, he asked them, 'Know ye what I have done to you?' Do you understand the purpose for which I have washed your feet? Then he proceeds at once to tell them. 'If I then, your Lord and Master, have washed your feet, ye also ought to wash one another's feet. For I have given you an example, that ye should do as I have done to you . . . . If ye know these things, happy are ye if ye do them.' In washing your feet, I have given you an example, model, pattern, or copy; and now I enjoin upon you to 'wash one another's feet.'

"6. *The good to be derived from the observance not a literal benefit, but a spiritual blessing.* 'Happy are ye if ye do them.'

"The six foregoing facts, when carefully considered, prove beyond question that feet-washing as practised by Christ is a rite, or ordinance, of the New Testament. If language is of any use at all, the words of Christ

clearly show that feet-washing is a thing to be observed
by Christians. The fact that he called it an example
proves that he intended it for imitation. It rests upon
the same foundation with baptism and the Lord's Supper.
All three are established by the precept and the example of the Savior. All three were instituted from
elements and practises common to all. From time immemorial it has been the custom of all cleanly people
to bathe their bodies frequently in water. In olden
times people wore loose garments, and consequently
it was necessary to bathe their bodies in water very
often. This was usually done by going down into pools
or streams and dipping themselves in the water. Now,
as far as mode is concerned, there was some similarity
between this custom and baptism. But who will say
that baptism is simply the perpetuating of this custom?
No one. When Jesus instituted Christian baptism, he
took the element water and a practise common to all,
and connected his word with them, thus instituting one
of the sacred rites of the gospel. In this ordinance these
elements are elevated to a place where, in their application, they assume a religious character. The benefits derived and the lessons taught are conducive to our
spiritual welfare.

"The same is true of the Lord's Supper. It has been
customary, as far as we know, for people of all lands
to. eat supper. Bread and the fruit of the vine have
always been considered common articles of food. In
instituting the sacred ordinance of the communion supper, Jesus did not go out of the ordinary. He selected

common articles of food. With these he connected his word and established a divine ordinance. Although he selected common articles of food, he elevated the practise above the eating of a common meal. He first broke bread himself, and gave to his disciples of the bread and of the cup, then commanded them thus: 'This do in remembrance of me.' What he did was 'an observance commanded'—an ordinance. The lesson that it teaches, gives to the observance a *religious* character.

"Now, what is true of the two rites mentioned above is also true of feet-washing. Among all people of all nations, in all ages, it has been customary to wash feet for cleanliness; at least, this has been the custom of all cleanly people. This was true in ancient times, and it is true yet today. As with baptism and the Lord's Supper, Jesus selected something common to all—washing feet with literal water—connected his word with the same, washed his disciples' feet, and then commanded them to 'wash one another's feet.' Thus he elevated it above the common custom into a religious rite. In the same prepared room and on the same night in which he instituted the communion supper, he washed his disciples' feet and then commanded them to wash one another's feet. Speaking of both these rites, he said, 'Happy are ye if ye do them.' Jesus gave to feet-washing a religious character. By his precept and example he exalted it to the place of a religious rite, or ordinance, in the church.

"Note carefully the analogy. Christ set before us the ordinance of baptism by both precept and example. He first instituted and practised it himself (John 3:

22, 26-30; 4: 1); then he commanded the church to observe it (Matt. 28: 19, 20). He did the same with the communion supper. He first instituted and observed it himself (Matt. 26: 26-29; Mark 14: 22-25); then he commanded the church to observe it (Luke 22: 19, 20; 1 Cor. 11: 23-26). The same thing is true of feet-washing. He first instituted and performed it himself (John 13: 2-7); then he commanded the church to practise it (John 13: 12-16; Matt. 28: 20). In baptism Jesus did not invent a mode entirely different from the common custom of the people, nor select an uncommon element. This is also true of the communion and of feet-washing. Literal water is used in two of these rites; the other consists in the eating of bread and the supping of wine. A religious significance is attached to the rite of baptism (see Mark 16: 16; 1 Pet. 3: 21); likewise to the observance of the Lord's Supper (Luke 22: 19; 1 Cor. 11: 26-29); and the same is true of feet-washing (John 13: 8, 9, 16, 17). Feet-washing rests upon the same foundation with baptism and the communion supper. All three are observances commended, established rites of the gospel of Christ. Webster says that an ordinance is 'an observance commanded.' Then feet-washing is an ordinance.

"Another thought. Jesus washed his *disciples'* feet. He did not wash strangers' feet; nor have we one single hint that previous to this time he was in the habit of washing anybody's feet. . . . . The very fact of Peter's refusal, astonishment, and ignorance of the purpose Christ had in view (verses 6-9), proves that Christ had never done this before. Then, it was not a mere

custom with the Savior. Neither did he wash their
feet for cleanliness; for that would have been done before entering the house. They had already entered
the house and had seated themselves around the table
in the very room prepared for the occasion. In this
room he broke the communion bread with his disciples
and washed their feet. In this room he commanded
them to break the bread and also commanded them to
wash one another's feet. These commands were given
to his disciples—yes, his *disciples*," Pp. 196— 201.

Another reason, probably the strongest one of all,
why feet-washing is to be regarded as a positive ordinance of the Christian church is given in Chapter XXII
of the present work, under the subhead *"New Testament
Ceremonies."*

OLD CUSTOM CONSIDERED.

Again I quote from H. M. Riggle. "About all opposers of feet-washing refer the people to the common
custom of washing feet for cleanliness. They take great
pains to show that the Jews had this custom and then
declare that because they wore sandals it was necessary. This, dear reader, is all for effect. I very much
doubt if any of them really believe that the feet-washing Jesus performed in that room in Jerusalem was the
same as the old Jewish custom. This reference to the
common custom of feet-washing is simply to draw the
people's attention away from the sacred rite which
Jesus instituted.

"The old 'sandal' theory originated in sectarian
Babylon and became threadbare long ago; yet it is

repeated over and over again. It would be just as consistent to assail the Lord's Supper on the ground that it was an old custom to eat supper; that bread and the fruit of the vine have always been common articles of food; and that, therefore, what Jesus did was only to follow the old custom of eating supper. The fact is, the old custom of washing feet for cleanliness has no more to do with the feet-washing performed and commanded by the Savior on the solemn night of his betrayal than the old custom of bathing for cleanliness has to do with baptism or the old custom of eating supper has to do with the sacred Lord's Supper. I will submit a number of facts which clearly prove that there is no identity between the custom of washing feet and the ordinance of feet-washing.

"1. *The old custom is still the custom.* By having one's attention called away from the ordinance that Jesus instituted, as recorded in John 13, and its true character, back to the ancient custom of washing feet, one is more easily duped. Thus, false teachers speak of it as a thing of the past—a thing that passed away with the wearing of sandals, which belonged only to Eastern and ancient people. Now, the real truth is, all cleanly people of all nations, ancient and modern, Eastern and Western, sandal-wearers and shoe-wearers, have washed, and do wash, their feet for cleanliness. It is a universal custom.

"2. *The feet-washing of John 13 was not this custom.* Is it not strange that if this was the common custom, Christ had not been in the habit of doing it before? During his entire ministry, which covered a period

of three and one-half years, he had never before washed
his disciples' feet. This is clearly proved by the fact
that Peter had never seen such a thing and knew nothing about it. So, you see, that despite the assertions
of modern teachers to the contrary, it was not a common
custom.

"3. *The manner of the ancient custom.* For the
benefit of the reader I will quote the scriptures where
the ancient custom is mentioned. 'Let a little water,
I pray you, be fetched, and wash your feet, and rest
yourselves under the tree' (Gen. 18:4). 'And he said,
Behold now, my lords, turn in, I pray you, into your
servant's house, and tarry all night, and wash your feet,
and ye shall rise up early, and go on your ways' (Gen.
19:2). 'And the man came into the house: and he
ungirdled his camels, and gave straw and provender
for the camels, and water to wash his feet, and the
men's feet that were with him' (Gen. 24:32). 'And
the man brought the men into Joseph's house, and gave
them water, and they washed their feet; and he gave
their asses provender' (Gen. 43:24). 'So he brought
them into his house, and gave provender unto the asses:
and they washed their feet, and did eat and drink'
(Judges 19:21). 'And David said to Uriah, Go down
to thy house and wash thy feet. And Uriah departed
out of the king's house, and there followed him a mess
of meat from the king' (2 Sam. 11:8). 'And when
the servants of David were come to Abigail to Carmel,
they spake unto her, saying, David sent us unto thee,
to take thee to him to wife. And she arose, and bowed
herself on her face to the earth, and said, Behold, let

thine handmaid be a servant to wash the feet of the servants of my lord' (1 Sam. 25:40, 41).

"You will observe that in practising the custom each one washed his own feet. Only one exception to this rule is mentioned—the case of Abigail, who offered to wash the feet of the servants of David. Any one can see at a glance that the object was one of comfort and cleanliness. Now, I affirm in the fear of God that the feet-washing mentioned in John 13 is not this custom, but differs from it both in manner and in design.

"4. *Feet-washing under a new aspect.* In the cases referred to above water was brought, and the guests washed their own feet, or in one case the servant of the house offered to do it. Now, in the case of the feet-washing of Jesus, it was neither of these. 'The disciples were to wash *one another's* feet. It was neither the least among them that was to wash the feet of the others, nor the greatest. Among them there was to be no least and no greatest. This fact of indiscriminate service presents feet-washing to us under a new aspect.' Christ did not say to his disciples, 'When you get homes of your own and get all domestic affairs well settled about you, and some of your saved brethren come along and remain with you over night, you must wash their feet for their comfort and cleanliness.' Nor did he say, 'The least of you must perform this service,' nor, 'He that is greatest,' etc. This is not the manner in which Christ gave the commandment. Without waiting to dispute as to who is greatest or who is least, we are to wash one another's feet; for we are all alike, all brethren together, all members of one spiritual family—

the family of the Lord, who set us this beautiful example.

"5. *The custom and the ordinance contrasted.* 'While this custom is not practised as extensively as it was in ancient days, in many respects it is the same now as then. The design is the same—cleanliness—and the ancient people practised this custom in the same way that modern people do; that is, each one washed his own feet (Gen. 18:4; 19:2; 24:32; 43:24). So in that particular the custom has never changed; but ancient and modern, Eastern and Western, people, those who wore sandals or shoes and stockings, and those who went or go with bare feet, that is, all decent people of every age or nation that we know of, washed, and do wash, their feet when necessary for cleanliness or comfort. Any Christian, sinner, or heathen will wash the feet of those who are not able to wash themselves. And thus the custom of washing feet has existed from time immemorial and is still going on in the world among saints, sinners, and heathen also, and will go on as long as there is a cleanly people on the earth. But while this is true of this custom, we still see the ordinance of feet-washing, instituted by the Lord recorded in St. John 13, practised in the church of God as our Lord commanded (verses 14, 15) and as St. Paul demanded (1 Tim. 5:10). The saints still wash one another's feet according to the Lord's example and teaching. And God is still fulfiling the promise that Jesus made to us. Hence we see that the custom of washing feet and the ordinance of feet-washing are two different things, as we will more clearly prove hereafter—different in manner, practise, and design.'

"In the custom, each one washes his own feet; in the ordinance, we are commanded to wash one another's feet. A difference in manner. In the custom, the design is cleanliness and comfort; in the ordinance, the design is to impress some spiritual lessons, to testify publicly to certain blessed truths. A difference in design. The benefit received from the custom is a literal benefit—cleanliness; the benefit received from the observance of the ordinance is a spiritual benefit. 'If ye know these things, *happy are ye if ye do them.*' A difference in the benefit received. People wash feet as a custom, simply out of necessity. Propriety suggests it. But in the ordinance, we wash one another's feet because Jesus, our Lord, set the example and commanded us to follow it. Modern people wash their feet as a custom of cleanliness. None of them claim that they do it in obedience to the instructions that Jesus gave in the thirteenth chapter of John. There is a vast difference, you see. The custom is practised by Christians, Mohammedans, infidels, sinners, and heathens; the ordinance is observed only by 'saints' (1 Tim. 5: 10). The two can not be the same.

6. *Positive argument that there is no identity between the custom and the ordinance.* The Savior washed the disciples' feet. He did not wash his own, and they did not wash his. If it had been a mere matter of cleanliness, would not Christ have needed the washing as well as they? Although he had walked with them all day, not a word is said about his own feet. You see, he was there instituting a new rite for the church. 'If I then, your Lord and Master, have washed your feet, ye also

ought to wash one another's feet.' There is no proof
that they were wearing sandals at this time. It was
rather a cold time to go bare-foot. On that very night
Peter went to the fire and 'warmed himself' (John 18:
25). The people wore shoes as well as sandals.

"Another thought worthy of note is this: it was the
custom to bathe immediately before eating the Passover.
No doubt Jesus and his disciples had bathed before
entering that prepared room. If there was any washing feet for cleanliness, it was done on entering the
room or before entering it. Jesus very clearly showed
the disciples that the object of his washing their feet
was not cleanliness. 'He that is bathed needeth not **save**
to wash his feet, but is clean every whit: and ye are
clean' (verse 10, Revised Version). The words 'save'
and 'his feet' are not to be found in ancient authorities;
they are omitted. The words Jesus spoke were these:
'He that is bathed needeth not to wash, but is clean every
whit: and *ye are clean.*' They were 'every whit' clean.
That means feet and all. If he had washed them **for**
cleanliness, he would have included their hands and their
heads, as Peter suggested; but they had been to the bath
and were *'every whit'* clean. He was washing for a
different purpose. He was instituting a Christian rite,
the rite of feet-washing; hence it was not necessary to
wash them, *'save their feet.'*

. . "Peter was a Jew and he was well acquainted with
Jewish customs and ordinances; but he was astonished
at what Jesus was doing. He had never seen the like
before. That proves conclusively that what the Lord
did was not a Jewish custom. Again, Jesus said to him,

'What I do thou knowest not now.' He knew the Jewish custom well enough, but he knew nothing of the feet-washing that Jesus was there performing. So it was not the custom.

"There is a penalty attached to the refusal or neglect of the feet-washing that Jesus performed and commanded. When Peter said, 'Thou shalt never wash my feet,' Jesus replied, 'If I wash thee not, thou hast no part with me.' Here was one who refused to take any part in the feet-washing in the assembly of the saints. He was unwilling that Christ should wash his feet. But the Master gave him to understand that if he would not submit and take part, he would be cut off from his (Christ's) union and fellowship. 'Thou hast no part with me.' It meant separation. Such is the penalty. It means just as much to you, dear friend, as it did to Peter. But when we come to old universal customs, there is never any penalty attached for their non-observance. Jesus would not for a moment make some old Jewish rite a test of fellowship between him and a beloved disciple. This adds another strong proof in favor of feet-washing as an ordinance of the New Testament." Pp. 243—251.

OTHER OBJECTIONS.

When people are unwilling to obey the Word of God on this point, they offer all sorts of objections; but their theories can not stand the test of eternal truth. But this "sandal" theory is about the most foolish of all the objections offered. The writer is at the present time engaged in missionary work in the Orient, and I find the custom of sandal-wearing still in existence; but I do not find that it is a custom for the natives to "wash one another's feet." Furthermore, I have observed that those religious people who in America claim that Christ washed the disciples' feet because their wearing sandals made cleansing necessary, do not obey the injunction, *"Wash one another's feet,"* when engaged in missionary work among these sandal-wearing natives. If the feet-washing Christ practised and commanded was founded on sandal-wearing, why do they not obey it, at least in the same country and under the same conditions? The reason is clear—they are not humble enough. And they also know that the theory of sandal-wearing is not an explanation, but *only an excuse.*

A true sister in Christ of my acquaintance was once visited by a sectarian preacher, who asked why she did not attend his meetings; and she replied that it was because his church did not believe and practise all the Word of God. He insisted that it did. She then asked about this ordinance; and he began, in the usual manner, to attempt to explain it away. First he brought up this old sandal theory; but the sister knew the truth and was able to refute it by the Scriptures. He then shifted to the substitution theory—that Christ intended to teach merely that we should perform good works; and he explained that if we give assistance to the ministers of Christ, or if we visit the sick and suffering, or take food or a basket of fruit to some poor person, we are thereby obeying this scripture. The sister admitted that these good works were a necessary accompaniment of pure religion; but she also said, "Jesus did not say, 'If I then, your Lord and Master, have washed your feet, ye also ought to give to the preacher, visit the sick and suffering, or take a basket of fruit to a poor person'; but he said, 'If I then, your Lord and Master, have *washed your feet,* ye also ought to *wash one another's feet.* For I have given you an example that ye should do *as I have done to you.'* " The truth made the preacher uncomfortable; so he shifted to another position, and said that Christ did this in order to rebuke the spirit of strife and exaltation that existed among the apostles, and to show them their true position with reference to each other. He proceeded to cite from the Gospels examples of the manifestation of a desire for preeminence on the part of certain of the apostles, and concluded with the assertion that Christ chose this admirable method of *bringing them down to one common level,* where they belonged. The sister then replied: "If feet-washing was such a good thing in those days, in order to bring the apostles to one common level, I should think it would be a very good thing for you preachers today; for when you are a pastor, you seek to become a presiding elder; and the presiding elder seeks to become a bishop [the form of organization in that sect]—all for the purpose of securing preeminence and *authority over the rest."* Then the preacher was ready to say good-by. Such hireling ministers do not want this humble equality.

Some years ago I read in an antiordinance paper an article against feet-washing. The writer first attempted to weaken it as a command by saying that we simply "should" or "ought" to do it—that is all. Then he proceeded to produce what he regarded as a most powerful argument against the ordinance: he said that the only reason for its observance was the one word "if," and that it was indeed a precarious situation for a great church ordinance to be suspended on such a little, insignificant word as "if." He argued that "if" implied doubt and uncertainty; therefore no such thing as a church ordinance could be established upon it. But this "false prophet" or "blind guide" of sect-Babylon did not notice that in this case the "if" is altogether *positive*. *"If* I then, your Lord and Master, have washed your feet, ye also ought to wash one another's feet." The "if" refers to the fact of Christ's performing the act. Now, did Christ really wash their feet? Every one admits that he did. Therefore, since it is unquestionably a fact that he *did* wash their feet, it is unquestionably a fact that we *"ought to wash one another's feet."*

Let us notice another great doctrine of the Word that is hinged on the same kind of an "if," in language almost identical with that just considered. "Beloved, *if* God so loved us, we ought also to love one another" (1 John 4: 11). *If* God has loved us, then we ought to love one another. Now, is it a settled fact that God has loved us? Yes, for he has proved it. "God *so loved the world* that he gave his only begotten Son" (John 3: 16). Since it is a positive fact that God has loved us, then it is a positive fact that we "ought to love one another."

"If I then, your Lord and Master, have washed your feet, ye also ought to wash one another's feet." There is no evading this truth without wilful perversion of the Word of God. Let every one be careful how he deals with the question of eternal truth.

WAS PRACTISED IN THE APOSTOLIC CHURCH.

First, Christ himself set the example, instituted the practise, and then commanded its observance. That is sufficient to establish it. It is not mentioned many times in the Word, but why should it be? Must the Word of God be repeated over and over in order to make it authoritative? The new birth is set forth clearly only in the same Gospel, that of John, in the conversation Christ held with Nicodemus; yet this doctrine is all-important—the very foundation of true Christianity itself. So also the communion service, observed in some form by nearly all Christians, is mentioned only twice in the Epistles (1 Cor. 11 and Acts 20:7); yet no one denies that it was generally practised in the apostolic church.

The apostles preached the whole Word of God in the churches that they raised up; hence when they wrote epistles to them afterwards, they had no special reason for setting forth doctrine specifically, unless some special conditions required it. It will be seen, therefore, that the doctrine set forth in these epistles occurs rather by accident, one might say—the result of circumstances. It is not at all likely that Paul would have mentioned the communion in his letter to the Corinthians had it not been for the misunderstanding and perversion of the subject that existed there. So also feet-washing is mentioned in the same casual way—*but it is mentioned.* Writing to Timothy relatively to certain conditions under which widows should be taken under the financial care of the church and provided for, he says she should be "well reported of for good works; if she have brought up children, if she have lodged strangers, if she have *washed the saints' feet,* if she have relieved the afflicted, if she have diligently followed every good work" (1 Tim. 5: 10).

The statement that this refers to some sort of hospital nurse, whose duties required her to wash the feet of others, is almost too foolish for serious thought. The instructions were not concerning hospital nurses, but concerning "widows" who were not able to provide for themselves and had nobody else to care for them. Furthermore, she was only to wash *"the saints' feet"*; whereas no such discrimination on the part of a nurse would be allowable or thought of by any sensible man or woman. And the fact that this service was extended only to "the saints" is positive proof that it was no ordinary act of regular duty or hospitality, but that it possessed a religious and churchly significance.

Let us connect this fact with the circumstances under which the practise was instituted. On the same night and on the same occasion when, and in the same room where, Christ instituted the ordinance of the communion, himself setting the example and then commanding its observance, he also instituted feet-washing, himself setting the example and then commanding its observance. But who were to observe it? The disciples —"wash one another's feet." Not the feet of strangers or sinners, but *"one another's feet."* How clear! So also Paul mentions the ordinance in connection with the widow—"if she have *washed the saints' feet."* This ordinance was not limited to widows, however, though they are here mentioned accidently, as it were; but

Christ said to his apostles, all of whom were men, "YE ought also to wash one another's feet." "If ye know these things, happy are ye if ye do them."

The idea that feet-washing as an ordinance was practised in the apostolic church gains further support from the fact that the oldest churches, such as the Greek, the Roman Catholic, and the Gregorian (Armenian), have retained the rite in their religious systems until the present day. There is no reasonable way to account for the origin of this practise among these old and independent sects except by acknowledging that it was the practise of the original church. True, they have peculiar ways of observing it, but they have perverted the other ordinances as well; yet they keep them all in some form or other. It has remained for Protestants who profess to believe the Bible to discard this sacred ordinance of the gospel.

ITS LESSON TO US.

The ordinance of feet-washing, like the other ordinances, is intended to teach us some important lessons. In the first place, it teaches a real lesson of humility, made very clear to us when we undertake to practise it. It sets forth our position of equality in the church, showing that we all, as brethren and sisters, belong on the same common level. Jesus himself, our Lord and Master, humbled himself and washed the feet of his disciples; therefore how much more reasonable it is that we should wash one another's feet. And it also shows that we are properly servants of each other, that we must minister to the good of each other. However, we must observe the proper sex distinctions, as recognized in the Word of God and by society. Let the sisters wash the feet of the sisters, and the brethren the feet of the brethren. "Let everything be done decently and in order" (1 Cor. 14: 40). Oh, how real this all becomes when we humbly obey the Word! "If ye know these things, happy are ye *if ye do them.*" In the last great day our Lord will say, "As ye have done it unto one of the least of these, my brethren, ye have done it unto me."

THE CHURCH IN PROPHECY
AND HISTORY.

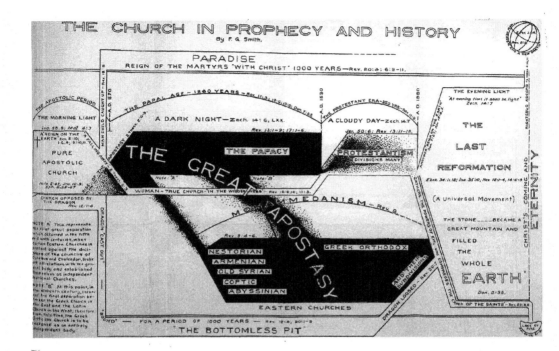

THE CHURCH IN PROPHECY AND HISTORY
By F. G. Smith.

PARADISE

REIGN OF THE MARTYRS "WITH CHRIST" 1000 YEARS—Rev. 20:4; 6:9-11.

THE APOSTOLIC PERIOD

THE MORNING LIGHT

Isa. 58:8; Mal. 4:2

A REIGN ON THE EARTH *Rev. 5:10; I. C. 3; 9:10,11.*

PURE APOSTOLIC CHURCH

Acts 2:47; Jno. 10:9; Eph. 5:25-27

CHURCH OPPOSED BY THE DRAGON *Rev. 12:1-4.*

THE PAPAL AGE — 1260 YEARS —*Rev. 11:3; 12:6; 13:5; Dan. 7:25*

A DARK NIGHT—Zech. 14:6, LXX.

THE PAPACY

Rev. 13:1-9; 17:1-6.

Note "A"   Note "B"

WOMAN—"TRUE CHURCH-IN THE WILDERNESS"—*Rev. 12:6,14; 11:3.*

THE GREAT APOSTASY

MOHAMMEDANISM—*Rev. 9*

Rev. 9:4-6.

NESTORIAN
ARMENIAN
OLD SYRIAN
COPTIC
ABYSSINIAN

GREEK ORTHODOX

EASTERN CHURCHES

"BOUND" — FOR A PERIOD OF 1000 YEARS — *Rev. 12:9; 20:1-3*

THE BOTTOMLESS PIT

A.D. 270

A.D. 1530

THE PROTESTANT ERA-350 YRS.—*Rev. 11:1*

A CLOUDY DAY—Zech. 14:7

Jer. 50:6; Rev. 13:11-18.

PROTESTANTISM
DIVISIONS MANY

A.D. 1880

THE EVENING LIGHT
"At evening time it shall be light"
Zech. 14:7

THE

LAST

REFORMATION

Ezek. 34:11,12; Isa. 35:10; Rev. 18:1-4, 14:6-9

(A Universal Movement)

THE STONE___BECAME A
GREAT MOUNTAIN AND
FILLED
THE
WHOLE
EARTH
Dan. 2:35.

"END OF THE SAINTS"—*Rev. 20:9.*

DRAGON "LOOSED"—*Rev. 20:7*

CHRIST'S COMING AND ETERNITY

NOTE "A" This represents the first great separation which occurred in the fifth and sixth centuries, when certain Eastern Churches in protest against the decisions of the councils of Ephesus and Chalcedon, broke off all relations with the general body and established themselves as independent National Churches.

NOTE "B" At this point, in the eleventh century, occurred the final separation between the Greek Church in the East and the Latin Church in the West; therefore from this time the Greek Orthodox Church is to be regarded as an entirely distinct body.

CHAPTER XVI.

THE APOSTOLIC PERIOD.

In previous chapters I have given a description of the establishment of the church of God in the apostolic age, showing its divine organization and characteristics. This description was drawn principally from the Gospels and the Acts of the Apostles. But the mission of the church was not to be limited to the period of the apostles; it was designed to be worldwide in its extent and perpetual, "even unto the end of the world." This being the case, it was fitting that the future history of the church should be described *prophetically*, in order that we might have definite knowledge concerning the operations of the Divine Hand in working out the great problem of the church's destiny after the close of the sacred canon. In fact, if inspiration had not given us information of this character, much of the history of the Christian dispensation, wrapped in superstition and ignorance, would indeed appear gloomy. But since in the word of prophecy, we see streaks of divine light breaking at intervals through the thick darkness, we are assured that the church did not fail through inherent weakness, but that God foresaw all its vicissitudes and portrayed them in advance for our encouragement and hope; until, finally, in the evening time of the world the whole scene lights up once more in glorious day.

The prophets of the old dispensation wrote concerning the dawn of the gospel era. The church of that period is described by Daniel as a "stone cut out without hands"—the divine kingdom of God (Dan. 2:34, 44). Isaiah says: "For, behold, darkness shall cover the earth, and gross darkness the people: but the Lord shall arise upon thee, and his glory shall be seen upon thee. And the Gentiles shall come to the light, and kings to the brightness of thy rising" (Isa. 60:2, 3). So also Malachi: "But unto you that fear my name shall the Sun of righteousness arise with healing in his wings; and ye shall go forth, and grow up as calves in the stall" (Mal. 4:2). This light of primitive Christianity was ushered in by John who "came for a witness, to bear witness of the light" (John 1:7).

With the breaking forth of this glorious light of pristine Christianity arose the church of God, established in unity, spotless in purity, glorious in power, and adorned with all the rich graces of the Holy Spirit. Who can describe her? "Her ways are ways of pleasantness, and all her paths are peace" (Prov. 3:17). She is the *bride of Christ* (John 3:29), *the heavenly Jerusalem* (Rev. 21:9, 10 with Heb. 12:22, 23), which is "the mother of us all" (Gal. 4:26).

THE SYMBOLIC WOMAN—PURE CHURCH.

John saw her in Apocalyptic vision, and describes her thus: "And there appeared a great wonder in heaven; a woman clothed with the sun, and the moon under her feet, and upon her head a crown of twelve stars: and she being with child cried, travailing in birth, and pained to be delivered" (Rev. 12:1, 2).

The beloved apostle was caught up to heaven, where he beheld in vision a great panorama portraying future events relative to the church's history, all of which, however, were to take place actually _upon the earth_ (Rev. 4: 1). So in the vision of chapter 12. The woman appears as the symbol of the church of God in its early glory. She was arrayed in the most splendid manner, all the brightest luminaries of heaven being gathered around her, thus symbolizing the divine light, and glory, and exaltation of the primitive church. But she had enemies.

"And there appeared another wonder in heaven; and behold a great red dragon, having seven heads and ten horns, and seven crowns upon his heads. And his tail drew the third part of the stars of heaven, and did cast them to the earth: and the dragon stood before the woman which was ready to be delivered, for to devour her child as soon as it was born. And she brought forth a man-child, who was to rule all nations with a rod of iron: and her child was caught up unto God and to his throne. And the woman fled into the wilderness, where she hath a place prepared of God, that they should feed her there a thousand two hundred and three score days" (verses 3-6).

In the Revelation, symbols drawn from the department of human life invariably refer to ecclesiastical affairs; while those drawn from the natural world or inanimate nature refer to civil or political affairs, and thus a proper correspondence of character and quality is kept up.* Therefore this woman—a pure woman—

---

*For a thorough treatment of this subject see my book entitled "The Revelation Explained," introductory chapter, "The Nature of Symbolic Language;" also for a clear explanation of the prophecies themselves. Published by Gospel Trumpet Co., Anderson, Ind. Price, $1.00.

is properly chosen to represent the pure church. This application of the symbol is further confirmed by the fact that in a subsequent chapter of the Revelation (17) a vile harlot is clearly chosen as the representative of an apostate church.

THE GREAT DRAGON—PAGAN ROME.

The dragon of this vision is a beast from the natural world, and therefore properly symbolizes a tyrannical, persecuting power or government. This we must identify in order to understand the nature of the opposition to the woman, the church.

It was a "red dragon, having seven heads and ten horns, and seven crowns upon his heads." In the following thirteenth chapter of the Revelation we read that John saw a beast rising up out of the sea with the same number of heads and horns, but ten crowns on his horns. "And the dragon gave him [the beast] his power, and his seat, and great authority" (verse 2). So far as the heads and the horns are concerned, the only difference between the two is that the crowns—a symbol of supreme authority and power—have been transferred from the heads to the horns. In chapter 17 John saw the same beast again, and there received the following explanation of the seven heads: "And there are seven kings: five are fallen, and one is, and the other is not yet come; and when he cometh he must continue a short space" (ver. 10). Concerning the horns he was told, "The ten horns which thou sawest are ten kings, which have received no kingdom as yet" (verse 12).

With this explanation before us, it will be easy to

identify the dragon of chapter 12 and the beast of chapters 13 and 17 as the Roman Empire; the first under the pagan and the second under the papal form. The seven heads signify the seven distinct forms of supreme government that ruled successively in the Empire. The five that had already fallen when John received the vision were the regal power, the consular, the decemvirate, the military tribunes, and the triumvirate. "One is" —the imperial. The seventh head we will identify later. The ten horns, or kingdoms, which had not yet risen when the Revelation was given were the ten minor kingdoms that grew out of the Western Roman Empire during its decline and fall. These are as follows:

1. Ostrogoths	6. Burgundians
2. Visigoths	7. Heruli
3. Suevi	8. Anglo-Saxons
4. Vandals	9. Huns
5. Franks	10. Lombards

The dragon is described with the horns, although they were not yet in existence and did not rise until nearly the time when the dragon became the beast, as we shall see later. Likewise he is represented with seven heads, although he really possessed only one head at a time, and five had already fallen and one was yet to come. He is described with all the heads and horns that he ever had and was to have.

The tail of this dragon "drew the third part of the stars of heaven, and did cast them to earth." This description is not literal, as some people foolishly try to imagine, but is symbolic. And with our knowledge

of the proper use of symbols this dragon is easily identified with the Roman Empire under its pagan form;
while the casting down of the stars, which are doubtless
used as symbols of ministers, as in chap. 1: 20, signifies the warfare which this awful beast-power waged
against the church of God, in which her ministers were
always a shining mark for the first persecution and suffered terribly for the cause they represented.

SIGNIFICATION OF THE MAN-CHILD.

The man-child is the next object that claims our attention. What does it signify? It is evident that it can
not signify a definite, single personage; for after he
is caught up to God, there is still a remnant of the woman's seed left upon earth (see chap 12: 17). A careful study of the facts brought out in the New Testament
shows that the man-child symbolizes the mighty host
of new converts, or children, that the early church by
her earnest travail brought forth. The seeming incon-
gruity that the church, or mother, and her children are
alike only serves to establish the point in question when
rightly understood. The child is of the same substance
as its mother and is designed to perpetuate the race.
So also the new-born babes in the church are just the
same spiritually as those who are older, and are intended
to perpetuate the church of God on earth. This is also
a distinct reason why the church of God in this dispensation should be represented by two individuals—
a woman and her son. In chapter 17 we find another
double symbol, a vile woman and her daughters being
chosen to symbolize *two distinct phases of apostasy.*

So also in the vision before us it was necessary that a double symbol, such as a woman and her son, should be chosen to set forth *two phases* of the church brought to view in this chapter. If but a single symbol were used, how could the church be thereby represented as continuing on earth and fleeing into the wilderness, and at the same time be represented as "overcome," persecuted 'to the death, and "caught up unto God and to his throne"? This double phase of the church in this dispensation—the experience of the saints on earth and the reign of the martyrs in paradise—will be referred to in a subsequent chapter and should be remembered by the reader.

But there is also direct Scripture testimony concerning the identity of this man-child. "Before she travailed, she brought forth; before her pain came, she was delivered *of a man-child*. Who hath heard such a thing? who hath seen such things? Shall the earth be made to bring forth in one day? or shall a nation be born at once? for as soon as Zion travailed, she brought forth her children" (Isa. 66:7, 8). According to Heb. 12:22, 23, this Zion, or Sion, referred to in the New Testament church, and the man-child that she is said to bring forth is interpreted by Isaiah as "a nation born at once." Such language perfectly describes the rapid increase in the church on Pentecost and shortly afterwards, when thousands were added in one day. According to the apostle Paul, the host of Jews and Gentiles reconciled unto God through Jesus Christ constituted "one new man" in Christ Jesus (Eph. 2:15). See also Gal. 3:28, R. V.

THE HOLY WAR.

"And there was war in heaven: Michael and his angels fought against the dragon; and the dragon fought and his angels, and prevailed not; neither was there place found any more in heaven. And the great dragon was cast out, that old serpent, called the devil and Satan, which deceiveth the whole world; he was cast out into the earth, and his angels were cast out with him. And I heard a loud voice saying in heaven, Now is come salvation, and strength, and the kingdom of our God, and the power of his Christ: for the accuser of our brethren is cast down, which accused them before our God day and night. And they overcame him by the blood of the Lamb, and by the word of their testimony; and they loved not their lives unto the death" (Rev. 12: 7-11).

This was not a literal conflict fought in the real heaven, as some imaginative poets have pictured, but was a conflict which was symbolically pictured in heaven, but which took place actually upon the earth. This is proved by the kind of weapons employed in overcoming the dragon: "They overcome him by the *blood of the Lamb,* and by the *word of their testimony.*" The blood of Christ was shed upon earth, and here it was that his devoted followers proclaimed the blood and testified to its power to save, and "loved not their lives unto the death." The whole scene is highly symbolic of the fierce conflict that took place between the early followers of Christ and the hosts of paganism; and so sweeping was the victory gained by the soldiers of the cross that the cry was heard, "Now is come salvation, and strength, and the kingdom of our God, and the power of his Christ; for the accuser of our brethren is' cast down, which accused them before our God day and night." Well has Butler said: "The final victory of Christianity over heathenism and Judaism, and the mightiest empire of the ancient world, a victory gained without physical force, by the moral power of faith and perseverance, of faith and love, is one of the sublimest spectacles of history, and one of the strongest evidences of the divinity and indestructible life of our holy religion."

But the fact that many Christians lost their lives in this conflict (verse 11), insomuch that the man-child is represented as caught up to God (verse 5), shows that the dragon employed also the arm of civil power in his opposition to the growing truth. But Christianity increased rapidly notwithstanding the violent opposition and persecutions of the pagans. An example of its progress is given in the nineteenth chapter of Acts, where it is said that the entire city of Ephesus was stirred over the preaching of Paul. Before the death of the apostles, according to the younger Pliny, the temples of the gods in Asia Minor were almost forsaken. In this golden period the true church of God shone forth in all her glory and beauty.

CHAPTER XVII.

THE GREAT APOSTASY.

The pure church of the apostolic period was not to continue ever with glories undimmed. It was God's will that she should remain the same, but conditions among men were destined to bring about a great change in her spiritual affairs; therefore inspiration has given us in advance a description of the great apostasy.

Peter refers to this subject in these words: "But there were false prophets also among the people even as there shall be false teachers among you, who privily shall bring in damnable heresies, even denying the Lord that bought them, and bring upon themselves swift destruction. And many shall follow their pernicious ways: by reason of whom the way of truth shall be evil spoken of" (2 Pet. 2:1, 2).

Jesus described the same as follows: "Take heed that no man deceive you. For many shall come in my name, saying, I am Christ; and shall deceive many." "And many false prophets shall arise and shall deceive many. And because iniquity shall abound, the love of many shall wax cold" (Matt. 24:4, 5, 11, 12).

A FALLING AWAY.

But Paul gives us a more particular description of the apostasy. Certain teachers had been troubling the minds of the Thessalonians with the announcement that the second coming of Christ was imminent; so the apostle wrote: "Let no man deceive you by any means:

for that day shall not come, except there come *a falling away first,* and that man of sin be revealed, the son
of perdition; who opposeth and exalteth himself above
all that is called God, or that is worshiped; so that he
as God sitteth in the temple of God, showing himself
that he is God" (2 Thess. 2:3, 4).

By consulting the historical facts in the case we find
that these predictions were only too true. Even before
the death of the apostles themselves the apostasy was
beginning to work, and its effects were noticeable in
certain places. Thus, in the seven churches in Asia
Minor, addressed in the opening chapters of the Revelation, we find proof of this sad deflection The church
at Ephesus had left its first love (Rev. 2:4). The church
at Pergamus was compromising with false teachers
and was being ruined by false doctrines (Rev. 2:14, 15).
Thyatira had lost the spirit of judgment against wrong-
doing, and was tolerating immorality to a shocking degree (Rev. 2:20-23). Sardis had lost its spiritual life;
therefore the message to it was, "Thou hast a name that
thou livest, *and art dead*" (Rev. 3:1). Laodicea had
lost spiritual warmth and fervor, and was lukewarm";
therefore the Lord said to her, "Because thou art lukewarm, and neither cold nor hot, I will spue thee out of
my mouth" (Rev. 3:15, 16). This church was fast
approaching the condition described by Christ in the
words, "Because iniquity shall abound, the love of many
shall wax cold."

The writer has in his possession the writings of the
church fathers that succeeded the apostles, and these
clearly show how the simple apostolic truth was being

lost sight of and how rapidly the dark night of spiritual apostasy was coming on. The churches of that age were filled with multitudes of nominal professors, while errors and heresies were gradually creeping in. Nor was this condition limited to one locality; *it was universal.* The churches, East and West, Greek and Latin, experienced this great "falling away" and plunged into the darkness and gloom of spiritual night.

One historian refers to it thus: "Almost proportionate with the extension of Christianity was the *decrease in the church of vital piety.* A philosophising spirit among the higher, and a wild monkish superstition among the lower orders, fast took the place in the third century of the faith and humility of the first Christians. Many of the clergy became very corrupt, and excessively ambitious. In consequence of this, *there was an awful deflection of Christianity."—Marsh's Church History,* p. 185. The italicizing is mine.

THE APOSTASY UNIVERSAL.

Concerning this monkish superstition, as an example of apostasy, Dowling says, *"It actually affected the church universal,* so far as the extent materials of ecclesiastical history enables us to trace its rise and progress." —*History of Romanism* p. 89.

Now, the history of the church since it first became extensive has always been closely interwoven with the political affairs of nations and kingdoms. In the early ages its expansion was limited to the boundaries of the Roman Empire; therefore its development and character were largely bound up with the fortunes of that empire itself. From the time of the permanent separation of the empire into Eastern and Western divisions, the churches East and West gradually became more and more separated from each other, and they came to be designated by the term "Greek" in the East and the term "Latin" in the West, on account of the prevailing languages. Finally the rupture became complete, and all relations between the East and West were broken off.

But we must remember that before this separation took place, and while the churches East and West were closely united, the great apostasy set in and, as we have already shown, *"affected the church universal."* Therefore since the separation we have simply two great divisions of the one great apostasy. Out of the one division of the apostasy developed the churches of the East —Greek, Old Syrian, Gregorian (Armenian), Abyssinian, Nestorian, Coptic, etc.; while from the other division arose the papacy in the West, and out of it Protestantism with its many divisions, as we shall see presently. But since the fortunes of the West, political and ecclesiastical, were destined to rise to greater heights, and overshadow and eclipse the fortunes of the East, the prophecies are naturally directed more particularly to the Western Empire and bring into special prominence the development of ecclesiasticism there. Hence during the Middle Ages the *papacy* forms the chief subject of prophetic interest.

THE PAPACY.

In the scripture already referred to, 2 Thess. 2:3, 4, it is the papacy that the apostle so graphically de-

scribes, as any reader possessing historical knowledge
can easily see. The description is so real that one
could almost think that it was written after the development of the papacy itself: "That man of sin should
be revealed, the son of perdition; who opposeth and
exalteth himself above all that is called God, or that is
worshiped; so that he as God sitteth in the temple of
God, showing himself that *he* is God."

In this connection the apostle shows that the seeds of
apostasy out of which the papacy was to grow were already planted; for he says, "The mystery of iniquity
doth already work" (verse 7). While this church apostate grew up by degrees in the West, it finally attained
great dominion and authority, civil and ecclesiastical;
so that Rome became as thoroughly Christian (so-called)
as it had previously been pagan. In fact, it was simply
the Roman Empire in the West in another form, arrayed
in a Christian instead of a heathen garb. It is therefore
described in the prophecies of the Revelation as the
successor of the dragon, or heathen Rome, reigning in
his stead and exercising his dominion and power.

In the previous chapter we have shown from Revelation 12 how primitive Christianity in its pure form
(symbolized both by Michael and his angels, and by the
pure woman) waged war against the prevalent paganism and succeeded in overthrowing it, thus obtaining
a wonderful victory. But by consulting verses 14-17 of
chapter 12 it will be seen that the woman is afterwards
represented as the defeated party and that she fled into
the wilderness. This represents the period of the apostasy now under consideration. We next have, in chap-

ter 13, a description of the papal church reigning supreme with civil and ecclesiastical power in the place of the dragon, or heathen Rome.

"And I stood upon the sand of the sea, and saw a beast rise up out of the sea, having seven heads and ten horns, and upon his horns ten crowns, and upon his heads the name of blasphemy. And the beast which I saw was like unto a leopard, and his feet were as the feet of a bear, and his mouth as the mouth of a lion: and the dragon gave him his power, and his seat, and great authority. And I saw one of his heads as it were wounded to death; and his deadly wound was healed: and all the world wondered after the beast. And they worshiped the dragon which gave power unto the beast: and they worshiped the beast, saying, Who is like unto the beast? who is able to make war with him? And there was given unto him a mouth speaking great things and blasphemies; and power was given unto him to continue forty and two months. And he opened his mouth in blasphemy against God, to blaspheme his name, and his tabernacle, and them that dwell in heaven. And it was given unto him to make war with the saints, and to overcome them: and power was given him over all kindreds, and tongues, and nations. And all that dwell upon the earth shall worship him, whose names are not written in the book of life of the Lamb slain from the foundation of the world" (Rev. 13: 1-8).

The heads and horns of this beast prove his substantial identity with the dragon of chapter 12, as already explained. In verse 3 of this chapter we find that one of his seven heads was wounded, then healed, after which nearly the whole world wandered after the beast and worshiped him. The explanation of this fact is to be found in Revelation 17, where the same beast appears again with its seven heads and ten horns (verse 3). Here the seven heads are represented as seven kings, or powers—the seven distinct forms of government that ruled successively in the Roman Empire; and John was thus informed: "Five are fallen, and one is [exists at the present time—the time when the Revelation was given], and the other is not yet come; and when he cometh he must continue a short space" (verse 10).

The five fallen heads I have already named; the one that existed when the Revelation was given was the *imperial,* and it was the head that was wounded as it were to death, which occurred when the hordes of barbarians from the North overran and subverted the Western Empire. Afterwards another head arose, the *patriciate,* the empire of Charlemagne, which lasted only "a short space," about twenty-six years when Charlemagne was crowned Emperor of Rome, thus reviving the empire of the West wholly under the papal form, which continued as the *Holy Roman Empire* down to the time of the French Revolution, or the time of Napoleon the First.

John was informed that the beast of chapter 17 "was, and is not, and yet is" (verse 8), which is equivalent to saying that it existed, then it did not exist, but it afterwards existed again. This was the historical fact, and herein we have the wounding and the healing of the beast. First it appears in the Revelation under its sixth, or imperial, head, which was wounded, or destroyed, as I have already shown; then for a time it did not exist; but afterwards it was revived, in which condition John saw it in Revelation 17, and was told, "The beast that was, and is not, even he is the eighth, and is of the seven and goeth into perdition" (verse 11). As "healed," and in its papal form, the head of the beast was what might be termed by successive numbers the eighth; but this eighth form was "of the seven," being simply the imperial form revived under a Christian garb.

A VIOLENT PERSECUTING POWER.

These heads and horns, however, referred to the beast simply as a political power. The ecclesiastical part is in this seventeenth chapter described under the symbol of a corrupt woman sitting on this beast and directing it, which thus describes the papacy to the very letter. "And I saw a woman sit upon a scarlet-colored beast, full of names of blasphemy, having seven heads and ten horns. And the woman was arrayed in purple and scarlet color, and decked with gold and precious stones and pearls, having a golden cup in her hand full of abominations and filthiness of her fornication: and upon her forehead was a name written, MYSTERY, BABYLON THE GREAT, THE MOTHER OF HAR-LOTS AND ABOMINATIONS OF THE EARTH. And I saw the woman drunken with the blood of the saints, and with the blood of the martyrs of Jesus: and when I saw her, I wondered with great admiration" (Rev. 17:3-6).

This agrees with chapter 13, where this beast-power is represented as exercising dominion and trampling

upon the people of God. "And it was given unto him
to make war with the saints, and to overcome them; and
power was given unto him over all kindreds, and
tongues, and nations" (verse 7).

The fearful persecutions of Christians in the past
history of papal Rome is well known, and to describe
it here would be to write another book of martyrs. It
has been estimated that at least sixty million people
suffered death by the power of papal Rome under the
authority and direction of this apostate church. It is
useless for Romanists to attempt to shift responsibility
from themselves by saying that it was the civil power
that did this; for everybody knows that in the Middle
Ages the civil power was merely a tool in the hands of
the church. If the beast did the actual work of slaughter, the prophecy represents the woman as also "drunk-
en with the blood of the saints, and with the blood of
the martyrs of Jesus," which shows that she also de-
lighted in this abominable work. It is the doctrine of
the church of Rome that she has the lawful right to
exterminate heretics by death, and this doctrine has
been confirmed again and again by the great general
councils of that church, with the popes themselves in
full accord and sometimes present in person.* This
church also boasts that she never changes her doctrine.

ITS IDENTITY WITH HEATHENISM.

"And all the world wondered after the beast. And
they worshiped the dragon which gave power unto the

*For an extended discussion of this subject and full
historical proofs see "The Revelation Explained," pp. 336-344.

beast: and they worshiped the beast" (Rev. 13:3, 4).

That this beast-power should be an object of worship and devotion is no matter of surprise, but how could its devotees "worship the dragon" which preceded the beast? This was accomplished by the Romish church adopting and perpetuating the rites and ceremonies of heathenism, or paganism. I have already shown that the dragon and the beast as temporal powers were about the same in reality, except the change of sovereignty from the heads to the horns; so also there was a remarkable similarity in spirit between the two, the one simply being the successor of the other, thus perpetuating under the Christian name many forms and ceremonies purely pagan in their origin. I will mention a few of these.

1. The high priest of the pagan religion was called Pontifex Maximus, and he claimed spiritual and temporal authority over men. The Pope of Rome borrowed the title and made the same claims, even being clad in the same attire.

2. The heathen wore scapulars, medals, and images for personal protection. Romanists wear the things and for the same purpose.

3. Pagans, by an official process called *deification,* raised men, after their death, to a dignified position and accorded them special honors and worship. Papists, by a similar process called *canonization,* exalt men after their death to the dignity of *saints* and then offer up prayers to them.

4. Papists' adoration of idols and images was also

borrowed direct from the heathen; for all such practises were absolutely forbidden by the Mosaic law and had no place in primitive Christianity.

5. Their religious orders of monks and nuns were also in imitation of the vestal virgins of antiquity.

The manner in which the Pantheon at Rome was re-consecrated for the use of the church of Rome shows clearly the heathen origin and nature of many of that church's principles. ˋ This old temple is still standing, and has been visited by the writer. It was built by Marcus Agrippa in, 27 B. C. and consecrated *to all the gods.* Pope Boniface IV, about A. D. 610, reconsecrated it to "the blessed Virgin and all the saints." From that time the Romanists prostrated themselves in the *very same temple* and before the *very same images,* and devoutly implored them by the same form of prayer and for the very same purposes, as did the heathen of old. Of course, the names of the idols were changed. The same idolatrous worship is still conducted there at the present day.

Well has Dowling said, "The scholar, familiar as. he is with the classical descriptions of ancient mythology, when he directs his attention to the ceremonies of papal worship, can not avoid recognizing their close resemblance, if not their absolute idenity."—*History of Romanism,* p 109.

The "great things" and "blasphemies" (Rev. 13:5) spoken by this beast are doubtless the prerogatives and rights belonging to God alone which are claimed by this apostate church, especially through her regularly constituted head. In fact, the pope is the real mouth of this beast, the one who dictates her laws with great authority. He claims to be the vicar of Christ on earth and supreme head of the church, even, as in the case of Pope Innocent, denominating himself the one before whom every knee must bow, of things in heaven, and things on the earth and things under the earth. He claims power over the souls of all men on earth and even after their departure from earth. If this is not blasphemy against God, his tabernacle, or church, and "them that dwell in heaven," then I am wholly unable to imagine what would fulfil the prediction. Among the blasphemous titles assumed are these: Lord God the Pope, King of the World, Holy Father, King of Kings, and Lord of Lords, Vicegerent of the Son of God. He claims infallibility (which was acknowledged by the General Council of 1870), and he has claimed such for ages. Further, he claims power to dispense with God's laws, to forgive sins, to release from purgatory, to damn, and to save.

The prophet Daniel also saw the rise of this ten-horned beast and the development of the papacy, and he describes its terrible work as continuing for the same length of time described in the Revelation (Dan. 7:7, 8, 19-25).

THE PAPAL REIGN—PROPHETIC TIME.

The reign of the papacy is symbolically described in different parts of the Revelation, but the limits of the present work preclude an extensive treatment of the subject. So also the true church or people of God, is represented, and forms a most interesting subject

.to all lovers of prophetic truth; but only a brief treatment is here possible.

The time periods specified are all the same. In Rev. 12:14 the woman, or true church, is secluded in the wilderness for a "time, and times, and half a time." A "time" signifies one year (Dan. 4:25); "times" (plural, without a designating number) would signify two years; and "half a time," one-half year: or three and one-half years—forty-two months; or, counting thirty days to the month, 1260 days. So also the beast-power made war with the saints during this period of "forty and two months" or 1260 days. In Revelation 11 the true church appears symbolized as Jerusalem, with its temple and altar, but the same was to be trodden down by a profane multitude for "forty and two months" (verse 2); while God's true witnesses were to "prophesy a thousand two hundred and threescore days, clothed in sackcloth" (verse 3). ALL are the same—1260 days.

The 1260 days are prophetic time, each day signifying one year. It is appropriate that days should symbolize years, for they are analagous periods of time, the diurnal revolution of the earth being taken to represent the earth's annual movement. Such a system of reckoning time was known many centuries ago. When Jacob complained to Laban because the latter had given him Leah instead of Rachel, "Laban said: it must not be so done in our country, to give the younger before the first-born. Fulfil her *week*, and we will give thee this also for the service which thou shalt serve me yet *seven other years*. And Jacob did so, and fulfilled her week . . . . seven other years" (Gen. 29:26-30). In this case it will be seen that a day was used to represent a year, since seven days, or one week, represented seven years. When the law was given, Moses recognized the week of seven natural days, the last day of which was constituted a Sabbath-rest for Israel; but he also instituted a week of seven years, the last year of which was a Sabbatical year of rest to the land. This last fact will explain such expressions as "forty days, *each day for a year*" (Num. 14: 34), and "I have appointed thee each day for a year" (Ezek. 4: 6).

THE CORRECT STARTING-STAKE.

Now, this time period of 1260 years in the Revelation covers two distinct lines of prophetic truth—the time of the seclusion of the woman, or true church, in the wilderness, also the reign of the beast-power, or church apostate, which made war against the saints. Therefore the time selected for the beginning of this period, or the starting-stake, must be a date that will agree with both of these facts. But as we have observed, the false church did not rise abruptly in one year, but was a gradual growth; so also, on the other hand, the true church was not driven out abruptly, but there was a gradual "falling away." First there was perfect light; later, total darkness: as the one increased, the other diminished. The division must therefore be located half-way between the two extremes, and this forms a proper and consistent date for the beginning of the time-prophecy under consideration.

The beginning of the Christian era was one of perfect light, when pure Christianity shone forth in all

her beauty and glory; about the middle of the sixth
century we find total darkness, the papacy reigning supreme in the West. The middle line between the two
extremes lies in the latter part of the third century.
Let us appeal to the historical facts.

"The living church retired gradually within the lonely
sanctuary of a few solitary hearts, an external church
was substituted in its place, and all its forms were declared to be of divine appointment. Salvation no longer
flowing from the Word, which was henceforth put out
of sight, the priests affirmed that it was conveyed by
means of the forms they had themselves invented, and
that none could obtain it but by these channels . . . .
The doctrine of the church and the necessity of its
visible unity [in this apostate form], which had begun
to gain ground in the third century, favored the pre-
tentions of Rome."—*D' Aubigne History of the Reformation*, Book I, Chap. I.

"We have found it almost necessary to separate, and
indeed widely to distinguish the events of the two first,
from those of the third century, for nearly at this point
we are disposed to place the FIRST CRISIS in the
internal history of the church."—*Waddington's Church
History*.

By this time the bishop of Rome had already attained
a great degree of authority. Concerning this the Encyclopedia Britannica says, "Before the termination of
the third century the office was held to be of such importance that its succession was a matter of interest to
ecclesiastics living in distant sees," Vol. XIX, p. 488.

George Fisher says, "The accession of Constantine

[A. D. 312] found the church so firmly organized under the hierarchy that it could not lose its identity by being absolutely merged in the state."—*History of the Christian Church,* p. 99.

As the hierarchy had thus advanced to such an important stage before the end of the third century, so the church, on the other hand, had "fallen away" to a great depth of apostasy. In the year A. D. 270 Anthony, an Egyptian, the founder of the monastic institution, fixed his abode in the deserts of Egypt and formed monks into organized bodies. Dowling shows, as already quoted, that great multitudes of people immediately followed this example, insomuch that monkery "actually affected the church universal." This clearly shows the advanced stage of the apostasy at that time.

The church historian, Joseph Milner, refers to it thus: "We shall, for the present, leave Anthony propagating the monastic disposition, and extending its influence not only into the next century, but for many ages afterward, and conclude this view of the state of the *third century,* with expressing our regret that the faith and love of the gospel received toward the close of it a dreadful blow from the encouragement of this unchristian practise." Century III, Chap. XX.

Again, the same writer says: "Moral, and philosophical, and monastic instructions will not effect for men what is to be expected from evangelical doctrine. And if the faith of Christ was so much declined (and its decayed state *ought to be dated from about the year* 270), we need not wonder that such scenes as Eusebius hints at without any circumstantial details, took place in the

Christian world." Century IV, Chap. I. The words in parentheses are Milner's also.

END OF 1260-YEAR PAPAL REIGN.

The year 270, pointed out by Milner, is a consistent dividing-date between the morning-light age and the papal age; for at this period the "falling away," or apostasy of the church, on the one hand and the rising power of the hierarchy on the other hand were about equal. Measuring forward the allotted period of 1260 years brings us to the exact date of the first Protestant creed *(the Augsburg Confession)* in A. D. 1530. To this date we must point both for the end of Rome's universal spiritual supremacy and for the rise of Protestantism.

D' Aubigne, in his "History of the Reformation," says when he comes to this period: "The conflicts hitherto described have been partial; we are entering upon a new period, that of general battles. Spires (1529) and Augsburg (1530) are names that shine forth with more immortal glory than Marathon, Pavia, or Marengo. Forces that up to the present time were separate, are now uniting into one energetic band." Book XVIII, Chap. I. "The first two books of this volume contain the most important epochs of the Reformation—the protest of Spires, and the Confession of Augsburg . . . . I determined on bringing the Reformation of Germany and German Switzerland to the *decisive epochs* of 1530 and 1531. The history of the Reformation, properly so called, is then in my opinion almost complete in those countries. The work of faith has there attained its apogee: that of conferences, of interims, of diplomacy begins . . . . The movement of the sixteenth century has there made its effort. I said from the very first, It is the history of the Reformation and not of Protestantism that I am relating."—*D'Aubigne: Preface to Volume V.*

CHAPTER XVIII.

THE PROTESTANT ERA.

The Reformation of the Sixteenth Century broke the power of Rome's spiritual supremacy. Europe was shaken from end to end by a power which it had never known before. The great secret of the early successes of the reformers was their appeal from the decisions of councils and the regulations of men to the Word of God itself. And so long as the Word and the Spirit of God were allowed their proper place as the governors of God's people, the power and inspiration of God rested upon the work of the Reformation. But, unhappily, this state of affairs did not long continue. Within a few years the followers of the reformers were divided into hostile sects and began to oppose and persecute each other. Luther denounced Zwingle as a heretic, and "the Calvanists would have no dealings with the Lutherans."

The first Protestant creed was the Augsburg Confession, 1530. This date marks an important epoch. From this time the people began to lose sight of the Word and Spirit of God as their governors. They organized themselves into sects, made their own regulations, creeds and disciplines; and these they upheld by every means possible. Thus, we find Calvin, at Geneva, consenting to the burning of Servetus because of a difference of religious views; and in England the Anglican Protestants waged a most bitter, cruel, and relentless war not only against Catholics but against all Protestants who refused to conform to the established church.

The Protestants placed armies in the field and fought
for their creeds, as during the Thirty Years' War in
Germany and the long period of the Hugenot wars in
France. From this it will be seen that the rise of Protestantism (organized sectarianism) in 1530 introduced
another period of apostasy, or rather *another form of the
apostasy,* as distinct in many of its features as was that
of Romanism before it. The quotation from the historian D'Aubigne given in the preceding chapter, shows
that he regarded the real work of the Reformation as
ending at the "DECISIVE EPOCHS of 1530 and
1531," and that the history of Protestantism there has
its beginning.

PROTESTANTISM IN PROPHECY.

This great system of Protestantism that succeeded
Romanism, taking the first place in all of the affairs of
the modern world, was also described in the prophecies.
Historically, it arose at the expiration of the 1260-year
period of the reign of the beast (1530); therefore the
Revelator, after symbolically describing the beast and
its reign, continues:

"And I beheld another beast coming up out of the
earth; and he had two horns like a lamb, and he spake
as a dragon. And he exerciseth all the power of the
first beast before him, and causeth the earth and them
which dwell therein to worship the first beast, whose
deadly wound was healed. And he doeth great wonders,
so that he maketh fire come down from heaven on the
earth in the sight of men. And deceiveth them that
dwell on the earth by the means of those miracles which

he had power to do in the sight of the beast; saying to them which dwell on the earth, that they should make an image to the beast, which had the wound by a sword, and did live. And he had power to give life unto the image of the beast, that the image of the beast should both speak, and cause that as many as would not worship the image of the beast should be killed. And he causeth all, both small and great, rich and poor, free and bond, to receive a mark in their right hand, or in their foreheads: and that no man might buy or sell, save he that had the mark, or the name of the beast, or the number of his name. Here is wisdom. Let him that hath understanding count the number of the beast: for it is the number of a man; and his number is Six hundred threescore and six" (Rev. 13: 11-18).

The symbolic description of this beast directs us to a political and religious system. He stands as the symbol of *Protestantism* in Europe, although his power and influence afterwards extended into "the whole world" (chap. 16: 14). He was to exercise "all the power of the first beast before him." In another chapter of the Revelation (17: 16) it is predicted that the ten horns of the beast, or kingdoms of Europe, after supporting the papacy during the Dark Ages would later turn against her. This prophecy has met a remarkable fulfilment under the reign of Protestantism.

The first two nations to turn violently against popery were England and Germany. They have ever been the chief supporters and defenders of Protestantism, and they are doubtless the two kingdoms symbolized by the two horns of this second beast. Protestantism gained its position and influence in the world largely through political power. This can not be denied.

In this description given by the Revelator, however, the special actions ascribed to this beast—*speaking,* working miracles, deceiving, making an image, imparting life to it, etc., which all belong properly to the department of human life—show conclusively that it is the character of this beast as an *ecclesiastical power* that is the chief point under consideration. He had political power, it is true, but he was, not to become such a terrible beast politically (for his horns were only *like a lamb*); but "he *spake* as a dragon." As soon as we enter the department to which *speaking* by analogy refers us, we find this beast to be a great religious power; and it is in this character alone that he is delineated in the remaining verses of the chapter. That the description of a religious system is the main burden of this symbol is also shown by the fact that this beast is in every case in subsequent chapters of the Revelation referred to as the "false prophet" (16: 13; 19: 20; 20: 10).

THE IMAGE OF THE BEAST.

This second beast, or Protestantism as a religion, was to make an image to the [first] beast. "Image" is defined to be "an imitation, representation, similitude of any person or thing; a copy, a likeness, an effigy." The second beast, then, is to manufacture something in *imitation* of the first beast. But which phase of the first beast, political or ecclesiastical, is to be copied? "The image of the beast should . . . . *speak.*" This directs us by analogy to religious affairs; therefore the copy is an *ecclesiastical organization* in imitation of the hierarchy of Rome. This shows a remarkable similarity between the two. In a subsequent chapter (17) of the Revelation they are represented as bearing the close relationship of mother and her daughters. In that chapter the symbol of the church of Rome is that of a corrupt *prostitute;* while the symbol of Protestantism is that of her *harlot daughters.* Later we shall see that this relationship is acknowledged even by leading Protestants.

The Roman church is a humanly organized institution, governed by a set of fallible men, all claims of infallibility to the contrary notwithstanding. Protestant sects, likewise, are all human organizations (even though they may sometimes deny it), and are governed by a man or a conference of men. The Roman Catholic church makes and prescribes the theology that her members believe. Protestant churches also make their own disciplines and prescribe rules of faith and practise. The Word of God inspired by his Spirit could not be enforced in Romanism without destroying it. So, too, the whole Word in Protestantism would soon annihilate her God-dishonoring sects; for they are all contrary to its plain teachings, which condemn divisions and enjoin perfect unity and oneness upon the redeemed of the Lord.

As the beast signifies Protestantism as a general religious system, what is said concerning the image of the beast applies to the entire body of sects, regardless of the differences that exist between them as individual institutions. As the single symbol of the dragon set forth the multitudinous forms of heathen worship, since they were all of the same general character; so the single symbol of an image to the first beast represents all the human organizations called churches, for they are all built on the same general principles and are unbiblical.

We freely acknowledge that during the Protestant era there have been great reformations in which God worked mightily in the salvation of men and women and from which great good has accrued to the race. But looking back from the present point of view, we can see that these reformations were only partial. They did not restore all of the primitive truth of Christianity, and therefore they were not permanent. In fact, when these various movements became thoroughly established and widely known, their people, made confident of God's approval through past successes, were thereby deceived into taking another step—*making an image*—and organizing themselves into ecclesiastical bodies with their own disciplines and rules. Whenever this was done spirituality rapidly declined, and soon the movement was nothing but a cold, formal sect. However, by far the greater number of Protestant sects were not preceded by truly spiritual reformations, but were deceptive movements from the beginning. It was the nature of this "false prophet" to perform mighty works for the express purpose of deceiving the people into taking the next step —making an image.

A PERSECUTING POWER.

Now, as this beast-power was responsible for the "image"—the organization of these sects—he also sought to make them possess authority over men; therefore he is represented as a persecuting power. It must be remembered that John saw this beast *"coming up* out of the earth"—which signifies the apocalyptic earth, or that portion of the earth made the subject of prophetic vision— the Roman Empire. It was at the period when he rose and *in the place* where (as symbolized by the two horns) his political influence was exercised that he did his work of persecuting and compelling men to accept the image.

The first Protestant sects in Europe, after they first became established and obtained power, acted much in the same manner as the church of Rome had acted before them, persecuting, banishing, imprisoning, and even putting to death those who refused to receive their tenets or to conform to the system of religion they had adopted. The Lutherans were at first a pious people, but on becoming numerous and exalted by the favor of the great they established a certain system of religion and then, when it was in their power, persecuted, banished, imprisoned, or put to death those who dissented. As early after the Reformation as 1574, in a convention at Torgaw they established the real presence in the eucharist and instigated the Elector of Saxony to seize, imprison, or banish all the secret Calvanists that differed from them in sentiment, and to induce their followers, by every act of violence, to renounce their sentiments and to confess ubiquity. Peucer, for his opinions, suffered ten years of imprisonment in the severest manner. Crellius, in 1601, was put to death.

In Switzerland, before the city of Zurich itself was entirely safe from the encroachments of Romanism, its Protestant council condemned a young man named Felix Mantz to be drowned because he insisted that the baby-sprinkling of Romanism was not baptism and that all who had received this rite ought to be immersed if they became true believers in Christ. This sentence was carried into effect. The severest laws were passed in different countries of Europe against the Anabaptists, and large numbers were banished or burnt at the stake.

King Henry VIII, founder of the Established Church in England, adopted the most stringent laws to enforce its doctrines. Certain articles of religion were drawn up, known in history as the "Bloody Six Articles." Concerning these the People's Cyclopedia says: "The doctrines were substantially those of the Roman Catholic Church. Whoever denied the first article (that embodying the doctrine of transsubstantiation) was to be declared a heretic, and burnt without opportunity of abjuration; whosoever spoke against the other five articles should, for the first offense, forfeit his property; and whosoever refused to abjure his first offense, or committed a second, was to die like a felon." Article Henry VIII. "The royal reformer persecuted alike Catholics and Protestants. Thus, on one occasion, three Catholics who denied that the king was the rightful head of the church, and three Protestants who disputed the doctrine of the real presence in the sacrament . . . . were dragged on the same sled to the place of execution."

In speaking of that period of history and of the religious persecutions of the times, Myers says: "Punishment of heresy was then regarded, by both Catholics and Protestants alike, as a duty which could be neglected by those in authority only at the peril of Heaven's displeasure. Believing this, those of that age could consistently do nothing less than labor to exterminate heresy with axe, sword, and fagot."—*General History,* p 558

That religious intolerance even at a later date was practised in England, witness the twelve years' imprisonment of John Bunyan and the hundreds confined in jails throughout that country for not conforming to the established religion. It was such persecution by that early Protestant sect that drove the Puritans from England's fair country to the then inhospitable shores of America, that they might have an opportunity to worship God according to the dictates of their own conscience.

In Scotland the Covenanters "insisted on their right to worship God in their own way. They were therefore subjected to most cruel and unrelenting persecution. They were hunted by English troopers over their native moors and among the wild recesses of their mountains, whither they secretly retired for prayer and worship. The tales of the suffering Scottish Covenanters at the hands of the English Protestants form a most harrowing chapter of the records of the ages of religious persecution." That the persecution and the tyranny of Protestantism, however, should never reach the enormous extent of those of Romanism before her seems to be indicated by the fact that her horns were "like a lamb."

"THE MARK OF THE BEAST."

The "mark of the beast" next claims our attention. The beast referred to is the papacy. How did the papacy mark its subjects? Undoubtedly by the false spirit which animated that organization, branding them all with its delusive doctrines and errors. In making the sect image in imitation of the papal original, then, the principle of marking subjects has also been copied. The members of every sect organization are indelibly marked. You can not become one of them without solemnly agreeing to believe the doctrines taught in their discipline and accepting the government of their manmade institution. Subscribing to the rules of faith and practise that originated with the sect shows how its members worship the image. They are also said to worship the first beast, the original of the image. How is this fulfilled? In the same manner that the worshipers of the first beast worshiped the dragon that preceded it; namely, by accepting and believing false principles of faith that originated in the system immediately preceding. Protestant sects have transferred many of the false doctrines of Romanism to their own creeds; hence they worship the first beast just as truly as the papalists worship the dragon by accepting heathenish principles. The greatest principle of false doctrine that originated with Catholicism, and one that has been trans ferred to *every Protestant sect*, is, that a human organization is necessary to complete the church of Christ on earth. The church of Rome has an earthly head and a human government; and Protestants also firmly believe the unscriptural doctrine that they must bow to an organization of men and thus be under a visible human headship: they receive the mark of the beast. Many sects have also copied other popish doctrines, such as infant baptism, the destruction of all outside the pales of the church (?), infantile damnation, sprinkling etc. Thus, they worship the first beast as well as his image.

THE "NAME OF THE BEAST."

They also received the "name of the beast." Here again "beast" refers to the papacy. The papal beast was represented as being full of the names of blasphemy, which blasphemy we have shown to signify the usurpation of prerogatives and rights belonging to God alone. The greatest ecclesiastical usurpation reached by the Romish hierarchy was that of claiming to be the head of the church and to possess the right to prescribe and enforce their doctrines, naming their organization the *Holy Catholic Church.* In making their organizations in imitation, Protestants, as above stated, have transferred the same principle, and they make the same blasphemous claim of the right to make disciplines to govern God's people, and then name their sect machinery a *church* of God. The name may be Methodist, Baptist, Episcopalian, or what not, it is only a *"beast" name,* yet a name that you must accept if you desire to become one of them.

THE "NUMBER OF HIS NAME."

Sectarians not only receive the name of the beast, but also receive the "number of his name." It will be necessary first to explain what is meant by the number of a name. "The modern system of notation by the nine digits and the cipher, was not introduced until the tenth century, but on account of its superior excellence, has since superseded every other. Previous to this great discovery, the letters of the alphabet were used to denote numbers, each letter having the power of a *number* as well as a *sound.* The same system is still retained among us for certain purposes. The Roman letters I,

V, X, L, C, D, M, have each the power of expressing a number. This however, was the common and the best mode of notation that the ancients possessed." The number of a name therefore, was merely the number denoted by the several letters of that name.

The number of the name of the beast—the first beast —is said to be the number of *man*. When we enter the Romish hierarchy and search for a man the number of whose name will be six hundred and sixty-six, where should we go more appropriately than to the pope himself, its authorized head? The Scriptures point him out particularly as the *"man* of sin," "the son of perdition" (2 Thess. 2: 3, 4). Has the pope of Rome a name the letters of which, used as numerals, make six hundred and sixty-six? Yes. He wears in jeweled letters upon his miter the following blasphemous inscription: *Vicarius Filii Dei*—Vicar of the Son of God. Taking out of this name all the letters that the Latins used as numerals, we have just six hundred and sixty-six. U and V were both formerly used to denote five.

V	5	F	0
I	1	I	1
C	100	L	50
A	0	I	1
R	0	I	1
I	1	D	500
U	5	E	0
S	0	I	1
			666

In some manner the worshipers of Protestant images also receive the number of this name—six hundred and sixty-six. The name is that of "Vicar of the Son of God." In all Protestantism the true Vicars of Christ on earth—the Word and the Spirit of God—have been set aside, as we shall see presently, and conferences of men have taken their place in all the official acts relative to spiritual affairs. Hence the number of the name applies to Protestants as well as to Romanists. That number probably symbolizes *division*. While the policy of Romanism has been that of unity, still the false claims made by one individual can be as well made by another, and by many, which has been the case, as just explained; therefore it would not be improper at all to make the pope's number symbol of the whole, since his system has been so largely copied by the rest. The whole structure of sectarianism is built on the principle of division, and it so happens that there is always enough left to divide again. It is just like an indeterminate decimal. Dividing twenty by three gives six, but does not come out even; annexing a cipher and making another division adds another six to the result (sixty-six), and still it is not even; repeating the operation gives still another six (six hundred and sixty-six). The result is always the same—enough left to divide again. So this special number is perhaps the symbol of endless division, signifying the great number of human organizations claiming to be churches of Christ. The church of God, however, is built on the principle of unity; division is destructive to its true nature and life, for it is Christ's body.

It is further said that "no man might buy or sell, save he that had the mark, or the name of the beast, or the number of his name." To *buy or sell* is to engage in the ordinary pursuits of life and have intercourse with human society. Applying this as a symbol to the analogous department of the church, we have the fact set forth that those without the special mark have no more recognized standing in the so-called churches than men that are not allowed to buy or sell have in a community. But *selling*, as a symbol, would specially indicate the dealing out of truth, or the preaching of the gospel. A Holy Ghost minister in the clear light of Heaven's truth, independent of all the creeds of sectarian Babylon, will not be allowed the privilege of laboring among them or preaching in their houses. And if he holds meetings in the community, the members of the sects are warned by their leaders against "*buying*"—receiving—his doctrine, because of his not having the mark or name of the beast. Sectarian ministers are specially marked; for they come out of their colleges and theological seminaries with the stamp of their respective doctrines upon them and licenses from the various sects to enter the ministry; and those not thus marked‾ or designated have no place among them.

While writing this part of the present chapter in Bucharest, Roumania, the author postponed his work of writing long enough to attend a Seventh-Day Adventist service in company with another brother. After the sermon another brother requested that we be given the opportunity to speak a little, but the request was absolutely refused. An explanation was made, that we would say

nothing against them or their work, but only speak a
little about salvation; but we were not permitted even to
testify in a few words. The difficulty was that we did
not have either the "mark of the beast" or its "name."

The fact just stated is also well illustrated by the following circumstance. A few years ago a brother in the
ministry went into a certain town to find a place to conduct a series of holiness meetings. He was directed by
a Presbyterian lady to her pastor, who, she said, was
a believer in the doctrine of holiness, and who would
therefore, she felt sure, give his place. When the brother
called on the minister and made known his errand, the
first question asked him was this, "Are you a member of
the Presbyterian Church?" The brother answered in the
negative. He did not have the *name of the beast*. The
next question that greeted him was this: "Do you believe
the Westminster Confession of Faith to be orthodox?"
He answered, "No, sir." He did not have the *mark of
the beast*. The last question asked was, "Do you belong
to any of the various orthodox Protestant denominations?" The brother said, "No." He did not have the
number of his name. The answer was, "You can not
have our house."

The length of the reign of the first beast of Revelation
13 is given as 1260 (symbolic) days, thus covering the
period of 1260 years extending from A. D. 270 to 1530,
when Protestantism arose. But the length of the reign
of the second beast is not stated in Revelation 13. In
chapter 11, however, we have another series of prophecy
covering the period of the reign of these two beasts, and
it gives us an understanding concerning the length of

the reign of each. I will not, however, attempt within my present limits to give a complete explanation of chapter 11.

THE TWO WITNESSES.

In the first part of the chapter we have the fact stated that the holy city (New Testament church) should be trodden under foot "forty and two months," and that during this period God's "two witnesses" should "prophesy a thousand two hundred and threescore days, clothed in sackcloth" (verses 2, 3). Now, this covers the exact length of the reign of the first beast of chapter 13. These "two witnesses" are represented as "the two olive-trees and the two candlesticks standing before the God of the earth" (verse 4). In this reference is made to the fourth chapter of Zechariah, where two olive-trees are represented one on each side of a golden candlestick, distilling into it their oil for light. When asked for the signification of the two olive-trees and two candlesticks, the angel answered, "This is the *word* of the Lord . . . . by my *Spirit*, saith the Lord" (Zech. 4:6). That the Word of God and Spirit of God are special witnesses is proved by many texts. Jesus said, "Search the Scriptures . . . . they are they which *testify* of me." (John 5:39). This gospel of the kingdom shall be preached in all the world for a *witness* unto all nations" (Matt. 24:14). "The Holy Ghost also is a *witness*" (Heb. 10:15). "The Spirit itself beareth witness" (Rom. 8:16). "It is the Spirit that beareth *witness*" (1 John 5:6). All salvation-work is effected by the Spirit of God acting in conjunction with the Word of God.

That the mission of these two witnesses was divine is

proved by their work, in which allusion is made to the miraculous works of Moses and Elijah by which their mission was attested, etc.

In the beginning of this dispensation these two witnesses were the Vicars of Christ in his church upon earth. The Word of God and the Spirit of God were the governors of his people. At that time they had perfect freedom of action among the people of God. But when the apostasy arose, the governing power of the Word and Spirit of God in the church was gradually usurped by the rising hierarchy; until, finally, men had entire authority in what was called the visible church. This was brought about when, to quote the words of the historian Mosheim, the bishops grasped the power and authority "to prescribe authoritative rules of faith and manners." D'Aubigne explains it thus: "Salvation no longer flowing from the *Word,* which was henceforward put out of sight, the priests affirmed that it was conveyed by means of the forms they had themselves invented. . . . . Christ communicated to his apostles, and these to the bishops, the unction of the *Holy Spirit;* and this Spirit is to be procured only in this order of succession. . . . . Faith in the heart no longer connected the members of the church, and they were united by means of bishops, archbishops, popes, miters, canons and ceremonies." —*History of the Reformation,* Book I, Chap. I.

During this 1260-year reign of the beast-power there existed certain bands of people who stood in opposition to the abounding corruption and iniquity of the church of Rome; a people who rejected the established hierarchy and gave heed to the Word and Spirit of God. Among

these were the Cathari, Lombards, Albigenses, Waldenses, Vaudois, etc. The names Waldenses and Albigenses
have frequently been loosely applied to all of these
bands. But these faithful people were comparatively
few in number; therefore the operations of the two witnesses were greatly limited; hence they are represented
as being clothed in sackcloth, a symbol of melancholy
and mourning.

SLAUGHTER OF THE WITNESSES.

"And when they shall have finished their testimony,
the beast that ascended out of the bottomless pit shall
make war against them, and shall overcome them, and
kill them. And their dead bodies shall lie in the street
of the great city which spiritually is called Sodom and
Egypt, where also our Lord was crucified. And they
of the people and kindreds and tongues and nations shall
see their dead bodies three days and an half, and shall
not suffer their dead bodies to be put in graves" (Rev.
11: 7-9).

Here we find that the "beast that ascendeth" at the
expiration of the 1260-year period is to slaughter the two
witnesses, and they shall lie exposed for three and one-
half days. Now, according to chapter 13, the 1260-year
period marks the reign of the first beast, or the papacy;
therefore the "beast that ascendeth" at the expiration of
that period *must be* the second beast of chapter 13,
namely, *Protestantism*. That Protestantism should accomplish the slaughter of the two witnesses may seem a
hard saying to some, but I request that the matter be
given the most careful attention in the light of prophecy
and divine truth.

It is true that the Sixteenth Century Reformation at first brought the witnesses out of the wilderness of seclusion where they had remained during the long night of Romanism and exhibited them to the public view; but when thus placed upon exhibition, they were soon robbed entirely of their position as the Vicars, or Governors, of God's church.   Since creed- and sect-making first began, the Word and Spirit have not possessed governing power and authority in Protestantism; but men have usurped that place and prescribed authoritative rules of faith and practise for the people.   While they will not for a moment allow the blessed Bible to be hidden out of sight—put into a grave—still they will not allow it that place it should occupy as the sole discipline of faith—it is a dead letter to them.   Let a true minister of righteousness step into the pulpit of almost any Protestant denomination and preach a straight sermon on the Bible doctrine of divine healing of the body, and he would be instantly expelled from their midst or looked upon as a fanatic or heretic.   Why?   Not because the Bible makes a man a heretic for preaching the Word by the Spirit of God, but because their man-made discipline by which *they are governed* does not teach the entire Word.   That all-glorious doctrine of Bible *unity*, which fills the whole New Testament, has no place whatever in the Babel of sects, for it strikes a death-blow to all these carnal divisions and institutions, and with one accord all sectarians unite in *fighting it*.   "Oh, the good old blessed Bible! we could not do without it," say they; yet, as everybody knows, they are governed by the disciplines and laws that they or their representatives have formulated.   Thus, the Word and Spirit of God are brought out into the public gaze, only to be treated with such indignity in God's sight, and killed; while infidels look on and tauntingly remark, "Either the religion of today is no Christianity, or the Bible is a lie."

In the beginning of this dispensation the church of God not only consisted of all those who were spiritual, but constituted a visible, organic body as well, made up of numerous local congregations that were separate in the management of their local affairs, yet interrelated with each other, and were directed by humble pastors, who were, in reference to each other, *equal.* The Word of God was their only discipline, and the Spirit of God, their great Teacher and Guide. Thus, the two witnesses were active in their official position, in the public view, as the Vicars, or Governors, of God's shurch upon earth. When, however, men usurped the place of these Vicars by ignoring the Spirit and rejecting the Word and making their own rules of faith, the effect was a national hierarchy—the church of Rome, which for twelve hundred and sixty years stood in the public view. Yet the two witnesses were still alive, though driven into obscurity and "clothed in sackcloth"; for they still acted in their official position in the congregations of the medieval Christians already referred to, who resisted the doctrines of men and to the best of their light and knowledge clung tenaciously to the simple, primitive form of church government and allowed the Spirit and Word authority supreme.

But during the Protestant era Christians the world over became indentified with the various sects, hence represented to the world the beast-power instead of the true church. Thus, during the Protestant period, the church of God, *in its organic form,* was not represented in any particular numbers anywhere on the earth; for its members were scattered among those who were "worshiping the beast and his image." Hence during this era the two witnesses had no place to operate in their official capacity as the Governors of God's church and are therefore represented as slain. The government of Protestant sects is not effected by the Word and Spirit; for the institutions themselves are of human origin, and men are their lawmakers and governors.

In the description before us in chapter 11, this city in which the two witnesses are slain is "spiritually [or mystically] called Sodom and Egypt, where also our Lord was crucified." It is a mystical Sodom, Egypt, and Jerusalem—a Sodom for wickedness and lewdness, an Egypt for the captivity and oppression of God's people, and a Jerusalem for the crucifying of the Son of God afresh and putting him to an open shame. Thus, this city mystically combines the wickedness of the three most wicked places on the earth—Sodom, Egypt, and Jerusalem. These facts we shall notice more particularly hereafter.

LENGTH OF PROTESTANT ERA—PROPHETIC TIME.

"And after three days and an half the Spirit of life from God entered into them, and they stood upon their feet; and great fear fell upon them which saw them" (verse 11). This indicates a great spiritual reformation at the end of the three and one-half day period, the nature of which we shall show, with additional proofs, in the next chapter of the present work. But the point of importance just now is the fact that these three and one-half days cover the length of the reign of the beast which came up at the expiration of the 1260-year period; or, in other words, the Protestant period. Now, as we have shown, the 1260-year reign of the first beast, or papacy, ended in 1530, when organized Protestantism arose. This last date, then, marks the beginning of the period signified by the three and one-half days; while the period is to be succeeded by a reformation that will *undo the bad work of Protestantism;* for the two witnesses will then be raised.

But what is the length of the period symbolized by these three and one-half days? Evidently not three and one-half natural days; nor yet are they year-days, according to the ordinary prophetic time; for the reign of Protestantism has been longer than three and one-half natural years. The *facts* oblige us to look for another explanation.

The time-prophecies of the Bible are by no means confined to the year-day manner of interpretation. Many times in the Old Testament the expression occurs, "And it shall come to pass *in that day,*" which expression is admitted by all to have reference to the gospel day, or the entire gospel dispensation. No one supposes that a short period of only one week was specified when the church of Philadelphia was promised deliverance from the *hour* of temptation that was to come upon all the world (Rev. 3:10). The rulers of the ten kingdoms were "to receive power as kings *one hour* with the beast"

(Rev. 17:12); this "one hour" really covered many years.

At this juncture the question may be asked, "Why, then, is the length of the reign of the second beast stated definitely as *three and one-half days?*" To this I reply, Probably because of similarity and analogy. The second beast is in many respects like the first beast, and even make an *image* to the first beast. Now, the length of the reign of the first beast is given as forty-two months, which is exactly three and one-half *years;* therefore it is appropriate that the reign of the second beast, its son and successor, made in its own likeness, should be represented as three and one-half *days*—an analogous period of time.

Historically, the reign of Protestantism, from A. D. 1530, has been exactly three and one-half *centuries;* for in the year 1880 a mighty holiness reformation was begun, and it is now sweeping over the earth, gathering together the people of God from their scattered condition in sect-Babylon; and in the church of God the two witnesses are at last restored to their official and original position as Governors of God's people. This work we shall notice more particularly in the following chapter, showing also the special prophecies of the Revelation which describe it.

The general trend of events following the reformation of Protestantism naturally divides the succeeding centuries into separate periods. The first (sixteenth) was a fierce conflict for the establishment of Protestantism; the second (seventeenth) was a violent reaction, wherein the church of Rome nearly triumphed over her hated opposers; while the third (eighteenth) is specially noted in history as the period of infidelity, or so-called reason. The division of time was so noticeable that D'Aubigne, who wrote about 1835, refers to it in the following remarkable language: "It has been said that the three last centuries, the sixteenth, the seventeenth, and the eighteenth, may be conceived as an immense battle of *three days' duration*. We willingly adopt this beautiful comparison. . . . . The first day was the battle of God, the second the battle of the priest, the third the battle of reason. What will be the fourth? In our opinion, the confused strife, the deadly contest of all these powers together, TO END IN THE VICTORY OF HIM TO WHOM TRIUMPH BELONGS."

—*History of the Reformation*, Book XI, Chap. IX.

CHAPTER XIX.

THE LAST REFORMATION.

In the two preceding chapters we have explained the first and second beasts of Revelation 13, showing that they symbolize two great systems of religion—Roman Catholicism and Protestantism. But the same twofold form of the apostasy is also described in other parts of Revelation under the general term BABYLON, as we shall now show; and in this connection a final reformation is also predicted.

A REFORMATION PREDICTED.

In the seventeenth chapter of Revelation, to which reference has already been made, a beast with seven heads and ten horns is brought to view, agreeing with the first beast of chapter 13. Here it refers to the Western Roman Empire under the papal form; while the papal church is symbolized by a corrupt woman seated upon this beast and directing its course. Outwardly the woman, richly adorned, presented a splendid appearance, but her true character was symbolized by the contents of the golden cup she held in her hand, it being "full of abominations and filthiness of her fornication." "And upon her forehead was a name written, MYSTERY, BABYLON THE GREAT, THE MOTHER OF HARLOTS AND ABOMINATIONS OF THE EARTH" (chap. 17:3-5).

The remaining verses of the chapter describe the manner in which the beast should support the woman for ages, after which the ten horns (or minor kingdoms) should turn against her, "and shall make her desolate and naked, and shall eat her flesh and burn her with fire. For God hath put it in their hearts to fulfil his will, and to agree, and give their kingdom unto the beast, *until the words of God shall be fulfilled.*" (verses 16, 17). That Rome possessed and exercised this temporal power during many centuries all historians know, and the last part of this prediction was fulfilled when King Victor Emmanuel entered Rome in 1870 and established the free government of United Italy, at which time the last vestige of the pope's temporal power was forever lost.

This brings us to another point. We have already seen that the ecclesiastical dominion of the first beast of Revalation 13 continued for 1260 years—from A. D. 270 to A. D. 1530, when his spiritual supremacy was broken by the Reformation and the rise of Protestantism. But in chapter 17 the woman is the church (of Rome), while the beast is the civil power, the one supporting the other. Now, this interrelation of the civil with the ecclesiastical power continued for ages. From a very early period the popes of Rome began to claim absolute dominion and authority, temporal as well as spiritual; but of course for a long time they were not able to secure the full realization of these ambitions. As early as the fifth century, however, their influence was being strongly exerted in political affairs, as is shown by the fact that when Attila with his fierce Huns threatened Rome the Emperor Valentinian *requested* pope Leo the Great to intervene; and the pope met the invader and secured the evacuation of Italy. After the downfall of the Western empire, when the head was *as it were* wounded to death (Rev. 13:3), the popes had considerable power in this respect.

In the year A. D. 606 Emperor Phocas conferred the title "Universal Bishop" upon the pope of Rome. When we consider the ambitions of the popes to obtain universal dominion, both spiritual and temporal, such recognition from the emperor of the East (coming at a time when there was no strong, settled civil power in the West) is significant. It is not likely that Phocas had any intention of advancing the pope's claims to temporal rule; nevertheless such official recognition had its influence. In the next century when Pepin subverted the Lombard kingdom in Italy (756) and gave a large part of their dominion to Rome, the pope actually became a temporal ruler. Temporal power was claimed and to a considerable degree exercised in a rather indirect way before this time, but this was the pope's first acquisition of *territory*. And when Charlemagne confirmed this grant of his father Pepin, the pope in grateful return publicly crowned Charlemagne in St. Peters as the Emperor of Rome, thus reviving the empire of the West under its "eighth" head, in which form it is portrayed as the beast of Revelation 17. But the pope was recognized as having this dominion before; therefore he could bestow it upon whomsoever he chose.

Now, the time that elapsed between the date when the pope received this *official* recognition from Phocas, in A. D. 606, to the time when the last vestige of his temporal power was lost in A. D. 1870, was approximately 1260 years also. Though the 1260 years of spiritual supremacy ended in 1530, when the second beast of Revelation 13 arose, yet the beast himself did not end then. For this reason we read concerning the second beast, or Protestantism, "And he exercised all the power of the first beast *before him*" (chap. 13:12). This same fact is conveyed in chapter 17, where the ten horns are represented as turning against the woman. These have done so one by one; and the pope's dominion as a temporal ruler ended completely in A. D. 1870. And this last event answers to the fifth vial of wrath in Rev. 16:10, 11: "And the fifth angel poured out his vial upon the seat of the beast; and his kingdom was full of darkness; and they gnawed their tongues for pain, and blasphemed the God of heaven because of their pains and their sores, and repented not of their deeds." So this last date, 1870, marks the time when the woman was indeed made "desolate and naked," the time when "*the words of God shall be fulfilled.*" Now observe:

"And after these things I saw another angel come down from heaven having great power; and the earth was lightened with his glory. And he cried mightily with a strong voice, saying, Babylon the great is fallen, is fallen, and is become the habitation of devils, and the hold of every foul spirit, and a cage of every unclean and hateful bird. For all nations have drunk of the wine of her wrath of her fornication . . . . . And I heard another voice from heaven, saying, COME OUT OF HER, MY PEOPLE, that ye be not partakers of her sins, and that ye receive not of her plagues" (Rev. 18:1-4).

A spiritual movement of mighty power is symbolized

in these verses; and as it was to take place *after* the fulfilment of the things described in chapter 17, it could not take place before the year 1870, when the temporal power of the pope ceased. This movement agrees with the sixth vial of Rev. 16:12, which vial was poured out "upon the great river Euphrates, and the water thereof was dried up, that the way of the kings of the East might be prepared." In this allusion is made to the capture of literal Babylon by Cyrus, who diverted the Euphrates from its bed in order to accomplish his purpose, and whose victory thus gained resulted finally in the liberation of the Jews from their Babylonish captivity. So also this spiritual movement in Revelation 18 calls forth the people of God from spiritual Babylon, which is "fallen."

By comparison it will be seen that this movement synchronizes with the movement symbolized by the resurrection of the two witnesses in chapter 11, which event took place after the 350-year reign of Protestantism, or, in other words, A. D. 1880. Moreover, the term "Babylon," as we shall show clearly from the prophecies themselves, included both forms of the apostasy, Papal and Protestant; and therefore this reformation, or heavenly movement against Babylon, properly occurs at the expiration of the prophetic time marking the Protestant era.

WHAT BABYLON INCLUDES.

Protestants generally endeavor to limit the designation "Babylon the Great" in the verses quoted to the church of Rome, because the woman symbolizing the apostate church in the preceding chapter is denominated

"Babylon the Great" (verse 5). But the same verse also declares her to be the *"mother* of harlots"; and if she as a degraded woman stands as the representative of a corrupt church, her unchaste daughters must at least symbolize churches that are her descendants; and if the real name of the mother is Babylon, as stated, the proper name of her harlot daughters must be Babylon also. Whether, therefore, the mother or the daughters are mentioned in a given instance, the reference is to "Babylon," because it is all the *same family,* connected with that "GREAT CITY" which reigneth over the kings of the earth" (chap. 17:18).

But the term "Babylon" doubtless has even a more extensive application even than papacy and protestantism. So far as the papacy in connection with civil power is concerned, that was well represented by the symbol of the first beast in Revelation 13; therefore, it seems to me, there must be some special reason for giving another representation of this great fact here in chapter 17. Here the woman, representing the papacy, is termed specifically "Babylon *the Great."* Why is she pointed out comparatively as "the Great"? Verse 18 says that she is "that great city, *which reigneth over the kings of the earth."*

It must be evident to all that in this designation clear reference is made to the great city of Babylon in the olden times. But while ancient Babylon was a "great city," it was also more than a city—it was a country and empire, containing many cities, over which the city of Babylon itself—"the great city"—bore rule. And while Babylon the capital was the mother city of the

empire, all the other cities were as truly Babylon as
was she; for they were an integral part of the empire,
only they were of less importance.

Now, here in the Revelation we have the antitype of
this ancient Babylon. The leading feature of the whole
scene is the capital city itself—"Babylon the Great";
but we must not become so absorbed in viewing her
splendid adornments that we forget that she is in fact
a mother city—"mother of harlots and abominations
of the earth"—and that her influence extends to all
parts of the great empire of Babylon. In other words,
the mother city is but one feature of the great Babylon.
Other cities there are in the empire, with their respective "kings" and institutions, but Babylon "the Great"
is the capital of all. And if the capital city represents
an apostate church, the church of Rome, then the other
cities with which she is compared represent also other
apostate churches of like character.

In chapter XVII of the present work we saw that
the pure light of the primitive gospel was succeeded
by a great universal apostasy which overspread the
earth, East and West. This was "the wilderness" into which the woman, or pure church, fled (Rev. 12:14).
This apostasy was not confined to Rome in the West,
but "affected the church universal," as Dowling said;
and this wilderness was to hold the woman as in captivity, just as the ancient literal Babylon held the Israelites in captivity. Out of this great apostasy, or Babylon
state, arose into prominence certain "cities," or fallen
churches, with "Babylon *the Great*," or the papacy in
the West, leading in importance and exercising rule

over the rest. Therefore from the same original source we have in the East Greek Orthodox, Gregorian (Armenian), Nestorian, Old Syrian, Maronite (later allied with the papal), Abyssinian and Coptic churches, with their subdivisions, as churches of the same great apostasy. For centuries the influence of Rome was exerted over this part of the world; but in the fifth and sixth centuries were established those national churches which arose as a protest against the decisions of the councils of Ephesus and Chalcedon—Nestorian, Armenian, Old Syrian, Coptic, and Abyssinian. The final separation between the Greek and the Latin church (or the East and the West) took place, however, in the eleventh century.

The papal church was Babylon *the Great;* while all these other cities, or churches, were simply Babylon the less: and since Rome was the greatest in extent and influence—the leading church of all the churches of the apostasy—she stands in the prophecies specially symbolized as the "mother" city. In fact, she stands as the representative of the entire Babylon in whatsoever form; in other words, "Babylon the Great" symbolically covers the whole empire of Babylon.

Since the gospel was first planted in the East, it may be that the Greek and the Gregorian churches will object to being classed as "daughters," with the papacy leading as the "mother." Will either of them be willing, then, to take the place of Rome and be reckoned as the "mother of harlots," with Rome as one of their daughters? The relationship, it seems to me, is not very good in either case.

Later, in the West, Rome secured a greater acquire-
ment of "daughters" when Protestantism arose.

A careful study of the prophecy in Rev. 18:1-4 (now
under consideration) in connection with its parallel
prophecy in chap. 14: 8-10, shows that it has particular
reference to the Protestant division of Babylon. The
reason for this is clear—because she contains far the
greater proportion of God's people. Under the reign
of Catholicism the people of God are represented in all
the symbols of the Revelation relating thereto as existing separate from that communion. In fact, the description of this apostate church given in the seventeenth
chapter shows clearly that instead of being partly composed of God's saints, she was their most bitter and
relentless persecutor, yea, was *drunken with the blood
of the saints,* and with the blood of the martyrs of Jesus." This is definite proof that the present phase of
Babylon under consideration is the Protestant division;
and her moral fall and the special message from heaven
are the grand signal for the escape of God's people
who have partly composed her number, as the fall of
ancient Babylon was the signal for the escape of the
Israelites. In their younger days the Protestant organizations ("daughters") were of better character than
the mother church from which they descended. Many
of them started out on reform. While the people of a
movement were spiritual, God worked with them; but
when they made their image to the beast, they suddenly
declined; and this voice from heaven finally declares that
the sects are in a fallen condition and that the people
of God therein *must come out.*

ADMITTED BY PROTESTANTS.

That this application of the term "Babylon," including Protestantism, is correct, and also that the fallen condition ascribed to her is in accordance with the facts, I will prove by the following testimonies of Protestants themselves. The first is from "Vision of the Ages; or, Lectures on the Apocalypse," by B. W. Johnson, member of the Christian sect.

"It is needful to inquire what the term 'Babylon' means. It occurs several times in the New Testament. Here [in the Apocalypse] it is spoken of as 'that great city,' and her fall is doomed 'because she hath made all nations drunk with the wine of her fornication.' In Rev. 17: 5, a scarlet harlot is seen sitting upon the seven-headed and ten-horned monster, and upon her forehead is written, 'Mystery, Babylon the Great.' With this woman the kings of the earth are said to have committed fornication. In chapter 18 the fall of the great city Babylon is detailed at length, and it is again said that all the kings of the earth have committed fornication with her. The harlot with Babylon stamped on her brow, and the great city of fornication styled Babylon, in chapters 14 and 18, are one and the same existence.

"There is an ancient city of Babylon often mentioned in the Old Testament, but ages before John wrote, it had ceased to be inhabited, the only dwellers among its lonely ruins were howling beasts and hissing serpents. It has never been rebuilt to this day and has passed away forever. John refers therefore not to old Babylon, but to some power yet unseen (when he was upon the earth), that should be revealed in due time, and of

which old 'Babylon was a symbol. Let us notice some
of the features of ancient Babylon.

"1. On that site took place the confusion of tongues
which divided those who before had been one speech
and one family into various tribes and schisms at variance with each other and of various tongues. The word
'Babylon,' a memorial of this event, means confusion,
and is derived from Babel.

"2. Old Babylon persecuted the people of God and
destroyed the temple in Jerusalem.

"3. It carried the people of God into captivity.

"4. It was a mighty, restless universal empire. The
antitype, the spiritual Babylon, must correspond. There
is a power that exhibits all these characteristics. By
apostasy from the truth it originated the schism which
has divided the family of God into different sects and
parties which speak a different spiritual language. It has
carried the church into a long captivity by binding upon it
the thraldom of superstition. It has been a constant
persecutor of the saints, and has enjoyed an almost
universal dominion. That power is the woman that
sits upon the seven-headed beast . . . . the false woman,
symbolical of a false church, the great apostate spiritual dominion of Rome. And we may add, out of which
have come—directly or indirectly—*all the religious
sects of the present day.*"

Dr. Barnes says: "The word 'Babylon' became the
emblem of all that was haughty and oppressive, and especially of all that persecuted the church of God. The
word here [Rev. 18: 4] must be used to denote some
power that resembled the ancient and literal Babylon

in these characteristics. The literal. Babylon was no more; but the name might be used properly to denote a similar power."

Wm. Kincaid, in "Bible Doctrine," page 249, says: "I think Christ has a true church upon earth, but its members are scattered among the various denominations, and are more or less under the influence of mystery Babylon and her daughters."

Alexander Campbell says: "The worshiping establishments now in operation throughout Christendom, increased and cemented by their respective voluminous confessions of faith, and their ecclesiastical constitutions, are not churches of Jesus Christ, but the legitimate daughters of that mother of harlots, the church of Rome."

Lorenzo Dow says of the Romish church: "If she be the mother, who are the daughters? It must be the corrupt, national, established churches that came out of her."

In the "Encyclopedia of Religious Knowledge" we read: "An important question, however, says Mr. Jones, still remains for inquiry: Is Antichrist confined to the church of Rome? The answer is readily returned in the affirmative by Protestants in general; and happy had it been for the world had that been the case. But although we are fully warranted to consider that church as the 'mother of harlots,' the truth is that by whatsoever arguments we succeed in fixing that odious charge upon her, we shall, by parity of reasoning, be obliged to allow other national churches to be her unchaste daughters, and for this plain reason, among others, be-

cause in their very constitution and tendency they are
hostile to the nature of the kingdom of Christ."

Mr. Hartly, a learned churchman, has remarked as
follows: "There are many prophecies which declare the
fall of the ecclesiastical powers of the Christian world,
and though each church seems to flatter itself with the
hope of being exempted, yet it is very plain that the
prophetical characters belong to all. They have left
the true, pure, simple religion, and teach for doctrines
the commandments of men."

Says Mr. Simpson in "Plea for Religion": "We
Protestants, too, read the declaration of the third angel
against the worshipers of the beast and his image, and
make ourselves easy under the awful denunciation by
applying it exclusively to the church of Rome; never
dreaming that they are equally applicable not only to
the English, but to every church establishment in Christendom, which retains any of the marks of the beast.
For though the pope and the church of Rome is at the
head of the grand twelve hundred and sixty years' delusion, yet all other churches of whatever denomination,
whether established or tolerated, which partake of the
same spirit, or have instituted doctrines and ceremonies
inimical to the pure and unadulterated gospel of Christ,
shall sooner or later share in the fate of that immense
fabric of human ordinances."

Says Mr. Hopkins: "There is no reason to consider
the antichristian spirit and practises confined to that
which is now called the church of Rome. The Protestant
churches have much of Antichrist in them, and are far
from being wholly reformed from the corruptions and

wickedness, in doctrine and practise, in it. Some churches may be` more pure and may have proceeded farther in a reformation than others; but where can the church be found [that is, the sectarian church], which is thoroughly purged from her abominations? None are wholly clear from an antichristian spirit and the fruits of it . . . . And as the Church of Rome will have a large share in the cup of indignation and wrath which will be poured out, so all the Christian world will have a distinguished portion of it: as the inhabitants of it are much more guilty than others. There is great reason to conclude that the world, particularly that part of it called Christian and Protestant, will yet make greater and more rapid advances in all kinds of moral corruption and open wickedness, till it will come to that state in which it will be fully ripe and prepared to be cut down by the sickle of divine justice and wrath."

Mr. O. Scott (Wesleyan Methodist) says: "The church is as deeply infected with a desire for worldly gain as the world. Most of the denominations of the present day might be called *churches of the world*, with more propriety than churches of Christ. The churches have so far gone from primitive Christianity that they need a fresh regeneration—a new kind of religion."

Robert Atkins, in a sermon preached in London, says: "The truly righteous are diminished from the earth, and no man layeth it to heart. The professors of religion of the present day, in every church, are lovers of the world, conformers to the world. Lovers of creature comfort, and aspirers after respectability. They are called to *suffer* with Christ, but they shrink even from reproach. Apostasy, *apostasy,* APOSTASY, is engraven on the very front of every church; and did they know it, and did they feel it, there might be hope; but alas! they cry, 'We are rich, and increased in goods, and stand in need of nothing.' "

This list might be greatly extended; but this is sufficient to show, upon the testimony of Protestants themselves, that their churches are a part of Babylon and are spiritually in a fallen condition. Then, may God help the honest-hearted everywhere to hear the call of heaven and *"come out of her."*

TESTIMONY OF THE WORD.

But let us appeal to the prophecies to show definitely that this heavenly cry against Babylon really includes Protestantism also.

Returning to the thirteenth chapter of Revelation, we again observe that Catholicism is symbolized by the first beast, and Protestantism, by the second beast, whose religious forms and institutions constitute an *image* to the first beast. Therefore we have in that chapter the twofold form of the apostasy—Papal and Protestant. Now, immediately following, in the fourteenth chapter, we have a parallel and strikingly contrasted description of the true people of God. They are following the Lamb, not wandering after the beast. They are marked by having their "Father's name written in their foreheads," not with the mark and name of the beast. They are worshiping Christ and giving glory to him, not bowing down before the beast or his image. And while under the reign of the second beast the whole

Word of God did not have free course, since none could "buy or sell" it except as he possessed the mark, the name, or number of the beast; thank God! we have here clearly predicted, THE LAST REFORMATION, in which the whole truth is presented to the world. "And I saw another angel fly in the midst of heaven, having the everlasting gospel to preach unto them that dwell on the earth, and to every nation, and kindred, and tongue, and people, saying with a loud voice, Fear God, and give glory to him; for the hour of his judgment is come: *and worship him* [not the beast or his image] that made heaven and earth" (Rev. 14: 6, 7).

BABYLON IS FALLEN.

This restoration of the pure gospel after the reign of the two beasts also synchronizes with the resurrection of the two witnesses in chapter 11, and began, therefore, in the year A. D. 1880. But this is not all of the message; for the same light that reveals the pure word of Heaven's truth, reveals also the fallen condition of sect-Babylon. "And there followed another angel, saying, *Babylon is fallen, is fallen,* that great city, because she made all nations drunk of the wine of the wrath of her fornication. And the third angel followed them, saying with a loud voice, If any man worship the beast *and his image,* and receive his mark in his forehead, or in his hand, the same shall drink of the wine of the wrath of God, which is poured out without mixture into the cup of his indignation" (Rev. 14: 8-10). This fall is a moral one, as in chapter 18.

Here we find that the heavenly message against Baby-

lon, "that great city," is directed against both the beast
and his image. Now, the "image" was made by the second
beast, or Protestantism (chap. 13: 14); therefore the command to come out of Babylon applies to those who are
in Protestantism.

GOD'S PEOPLE CALLED OUT.

Notice, also, that the message of these last two angels are the same, and are in the same order, as those
in chap. 18: 1-4, already noticed. The first one cries,
"Babylon is fallen, is fallen" (verse 8). The next one
warns the people against worshiping the beast or *his
image,* upon the terrible penalty of receiving the wrath
of God. So also in chapter 18. The first angel cries,
"Babylon the Great is fallen, is fallen" (verse 2).
Then is heard *"another voice* from heaven, saying,
COME OUT OF HER, MY PEOPLE, that ye be not
partakers of her sins, and *that ye receive not of her
plagues"* (verse 4.).

The Revelator describes also the result of this message;
for in chapter 15 he says, "And I saw as it were a sea
of glass mingled with fire: and them that had gotten
the victory over the beast, and over his image, and over
his mark, and over the number of his name, stand on the
sea of glass having the harps of God. And they sing
the song of Moses the servant of God, and the song of
the Lamb, saying Great and marvelous are thy works
Lord God Almighty; just and true are thy ways, thou
King of saints" (verses 2, 3).

While the woman, or pure church, in the morning of
this dispensation was driven "into the wilderness," we

thank God that she was not always to remain there; and in this last reformation she is coming forth out of the great wilderness of the apostasy and, as the bride of Christ, is returning to Zion. "Who is this that cometh up from the wilderness, leaning upon her beloved?" (Songs of Sol. 8:5). "Who is this that looketh forth *as the morning,* fair as the moon, *clear as the sun,* and terrible as an army with banners?" (Songs of Sol. 6: 10). Answer: It is the church of God.

But the Revelation is not the only prophecy that describes this last reformation. Zechariah clearly predicts it thus: "And it shall come to pass in that day, that the light shall not be clear nor dark: but it shall be one day which shall be known to the Lord, not day, nor night: but it shall come to pass, that *at evening time it shall be light"* (Zech. 14:6, 7). I will give this verse as rendered in the Septuagint Version, for it is clearer: "And it shall come to pass in that day [the papal day] that there shall be *no light*: and there shall be for one day [the Protestant day] *cold and frost;* and that day shall be known to the Lord; it shall not be day nor night [a mixture of light and darkness]: *but towards evening it shall be light."* Thank God for the light of the evening time!

So also Daniel in prophetic vision saw the rise of the papacy (chap. 7) and the long reign of darkness and apostasy in the Christian dispensation (chap. 12). He desired to understand the matter, therefore made inquiry. I quote from the Septuagint: *"When will be the end* of the wonders which thou hast mentioned? And I heard the man clothed in linen, who was over the water of

the river, and he lifted up his right hand and his left
hand to heaven, and sware by him that lives forever,
that it should be for a time of times and half a time:
when the dispersion is ended they shall know all these
things" (Dan. 12: 6, 7).

"A time and times and the dividing of time" is the
same prophetic period of forty-two months, or 1260
years, the reign of the papacy. This was followed by
a period of "dispersion," and such Protestantism has
been; for the people of God have been scattered in
hundreds of bodies. But thank God! this dispersion was
to be *ended* sometime, when the people of God should
receive light and knowledge, yea "know all these things."

"And I heard, but I understood not: and said I, O
Lord, *what will be the end* of these things? And he said,
Go, Daniel: for the words are closed and sealed up *to
the time of the end*" (verses 8, 9). At the "time of the
end" the people of God were to understand "all these
things," because of their having been fulfilled; and also
at this time the dispersal of God's saints was to come
to an end. This predicts THE LAST REFORMA-
TION, and the nature of its work is shown in the following verses: "Many must be CHOSEN OUT, *and
thoroughly whitened, and tried with fire, and sanctified*" (verse 10). Oh halleluiah!

This same spiritual movement is predicted also by the
prophet Ezekiel. In chapter 34 he describes the people
of God under the figure of sheep. "And ye my flock,
the flock of my pasture, *are men*" (verse 31). These
sheep of the Lord are represented as oppressed, driven
away, abused, and scattered by false shepherds, or

preachers; yea, God says, "My sheep wandered through all the mountains, and upon every high hill [from one sect to another]; yea, my flock was scattered upon all the face of the earth" (verse 6).

Read carefully the chapter itself. It is a perfect picture of the experiences of God's people scattered during the dark and cloudy day of Protestantism. But the work of final reformation is predicted in verses 11, 12: "For thus saith the Lord God; behold I, even I, will both search my sheep, and seek them out. As a shepherd seeketh out his flock in the day that he is among his sheep that are scattered; *so will I seek out my sheep, and wilt deliver them out of all places where they have been scattered in the cloudy and dark day.*"

The people of God can not retain their spiritual life and remain longer in these places. Babylon is now fallen, and those who remain there will fall too. To stay there, yoked up with the multitudes of godless and graceless professors of religion, who are lovers of this world, means to lose spiritual life and finally to lose your soul. Listen to the Word of God: *"Be ye not unequally yoked together with unbelievers:* for what fellowship hath righteousness with unrighteousness? and what communion hath light with darkness? . . . . Wherefore COME OUT FROM AMONG THEM, and *be ye separate,* SAITH THE LORD, and touch not the unclean thing; and I will receive you, and will be a Father unto you, and ye shall be my sons and daughters, saith the Lord Almighty" (2 Cor. 6: 14-18).

The call of God in this last reformation is to come out of sect-Babylon, for she is fallen, fallen. Reader, have you heard this voice from heaven? Says one: "I do not believe in this." Jesus says, "Ye believe not, because ye are not of my sheep . . . . *My sheep hear my voice,* and I know them, AND THEY FOLLOW ME" (John 10:26, 27). These are the ones spoken of by the Lord through the prophet Ezekiel: "So will I seek out *my sheep,* and will deliver them out of all places where they have been scattered in the cloudy and dark day" (Ezek. 34:12).

"The evening sun is shining; the cloudy day is past;
The time of our repining is at an end at last.
The voice of God is calling to unity again;
Division walls are falling, with all the creeds of men.

"Back to the one foundation, from sects and creeds made free,
Come saints of every nation to blessed unity.
Once more the ancient glory shines as in days of old,
And tells the wondrous story—one God, one faith, one fold."

THEY ARE CALLED TO ZION.

Now, when the people of God hear this heavenly message to come out of sect-Babylon, and they obey, where shall they go? Shall they wander around, independently of each other, over the spiritual deserts of the earth? No! Let the Word of God settle this point. The experiences of natural Israel under the Old Testament dispensation is in many respects a type of the experiences of God's spiritual Israel or church in the New Testament dispensation. As Israel was led captive to literal Babylon, so the church has been held captive in spiritual Babylon. As literal Babylon was overthrown, and the Jews made their escape; so spiritual Babylon "is fallen, fallen," and God's people are commanded to "come out of her." What did literal Israel do when

they came out of Babylon? Answer: They made their
way *in a body* direct to Mount Zion, where formerly
stood in magnificent glory the temple of Jehovah; and
they began at once the work of restoration under the
direction and the approval of God. And the work at
Jerusalem prospered, because "the people had a mind
to work" (Neh. 4: 6).

Thus shall it be with those who make their escape
from spiritual Babylon: "The ransomed of the Lord
shall return, and COME TO ZION with songs and everlasting joy upon their heads: they shall obtain joy and
gladness, and sorrow and sighing shall flee away" (Isa.
35: 10). This means the restoration of a pure church,
or temple of God, as in apostolic days; a church dedicated by the Holy Spirit and filled with the power and
glory of God.

This restoration is now being effected by the truly
spiritual, who have a "mind to work," yea, are "*workers
together* with God." The unity of all the saved was
the apostolic condition; and now the special message of
God is, "Gather my saints *together* unto me." When
this is accomplished, it can be said, as of old, "Out of
Zion, the perfection of beauty, God hath shined" (Psa.
50: 5, 2). Some men, Sanballat-like, may at first pre-
tend to want to help, then afterward try to hinder the
restoration; but the work goes forward nevertheless.
It is a twofold work—the gathering of God's people
"in their own land" and the restoration of the temple,
or church of God in its pure state. "He that is not with
me is against me; and he that gathereth not with me
scattereth abroad" (Matt. 12: 30).

Reader, God's work in this period of the world is a gathering work. He is delivering his people out of all the places where they have been scattered. If you do not have a "mind to work" with God in this reformation of Heaven's truth, are not gathering with him, *you are against God,* and may he help you to realize it and feel it. To oppose God's work is to oppose him; and all such opposers will be left outside of heaven, unless they repent and are baptized by his Spirit into the one body, which only is the church. "He that is of God heareth God's words." "Whosoever transgresseth, and abideth not in the doctrine of Christ, hath not God. He that abideth in the doctrine of Christ, he hath both the Father and the Son" (2 John 9).

> "Have you heard a voice from heaven
> Calling in a solemn tone,
> 'Come, my people, from confusion;
> This is not your native home?'
> Yes, I heard, and to my vision
> Zion's glory brightly shone;
> Then I rose and fled the ruin,
> Taking not a Babel stone."

THE PRESENT-DAY REFORMATION.

In exact fulfilment of these prophecies God began in A. D. 1880 to raise up a holy ministry to send forth his word against sect-Babylon, calling his people out, and through them began restoring the church as in apostolic days. The creeds and doctrines of men were ignored, and the cry, "Back to the blessed old Bible," sounded forth. Multitudes of the redeemed everywhere have heard the voice of God calling to unity again, and have forsaken sect-Babylon, and they are now unified in one body, according to the Word.

In the same year, 1880, was begun the publication of *The Gospel Trumpet*, which is a weekly holiness journal, devoted exclusively to the promulgation of this heavenly message. It is published by the Gospel Trumpet Company, Anderson, Indiana, U. S. A. At this printing-office many religious books and tracts, and a number of periodicals in addition to *The Gospel Trumpet*, are sent forth by the thousands and by the tons to all parts of the world. These are prepared by a host of consecrated men and women, all of whom devote their time *without salary* to the work of spreading the gospel in this way. In various parts of the world periodicals, books, and tracts containing this same glorious message are now published in different languages.

This work of publishing literature, however, is only auxiliary to the church itself. Many hundreds of holy ministers, laboring as did the apostles of old, without salary, trusting the Lord to supply their needs, are at this hour preaching the pure Word all over the earth; and it is being accepted by thousands. This preaching appeals to the spiritual-minded everywhere, because it really sets forth the whole gospel. Here we find perfect salvation and deliverance from the power of sin, with the result that pure, holy, sinless lives are led; here we find entire sanctification from the inbred nature of sin, through the baptism of the Holy Ghost taught in the New Testament; when afflicted, we find healing for our bodies, as in the apostolic days; here we find the love, harmony and unity of saints *in one body*, as exemplified in the

New Testament church; *here we find the entire truth.*
Glory to God! And wherever it is thoroughly known
this reformation gathers all of the saved in the one body;
it leaves to sect-Babylon only those worldly, graceless,
pleasure-loving professors who "have a form of godliness, but deny the power thereof" (2 Tim. 3:5). Here
under the preaching of the pure Word, by the power and
inspiration of the Holy Ghost, sinners are melted to
tears, and fall upon their faces, even in the public congregation, and cry to God for salvation. Here believers are baptized with the Holy Spirit and streams
of holy fire descend from heaven into the congregation
of the saints.

"Hallelujah saints are singing,
Vict'ry in Jehovah's might;
Glory! glory! keep it ringing,
We are saved in evening light.

"Free from Babel, in the Spirit,
Free to worship God aright;
Joy and gladness we're receiving;
Oh, how sweet this evening light!"

A WORK DIVINELY CONFIRMED.

The true work of God performed by his direction
has in all ages been confirmed by special manifestations
of divine power. Mark this fact; it is important. Truth
is not to be determined by theory alone. "The kingdom
of God is not in word, *but in power*" (1 Cor. 4:20).
When Solomon completed his temple on Mount Zion,
"the priests could not stand to minister because of the
cloud: *for the glory of the Lord had filled the house of
the Lord*" (1 Kings 8:11). So also at the time of its

restoration after the captivity. When the foundations of the house were laid, the people "shouted with a great shout" (Ezra 3: 10-13). Why? Because of the promise of God, "I will fill this house with glory." "The glory of this latter house shall be greater than of the former" (Hag. 2: 7, 9). When the New Testament church was fully set in order on the day of Pentecost, the sanction and seal of the Almighty was manifested in the glorious outpouring of the Holy Ghost and the performance of signs and wonders by the Spirit of the living God.

Likewise in these last days, when God is restoring the church to its primitive condition, the work is being attested and confirmed by the manifestation of his glorious power. Men who are possessed with devils, men whose cases are as bad as those described in the New Testament —the poor victims lying on the floor, writhing under demon influence, foaming and frothing at the mouth, and uttering horrible cries—are delivered by the power of God through the ministers of this reformation, are restored to their right minds, and made to worship and praise God. God is indeed "confirming the word with signs following" (Mark 16: 20). In this work, the eyes of the blind have been opened, the ears of the deaf unstopped, the lame made to leap as an hart, and the tongue of the dumb to sing. Cancer and consumption, rheumatism and heart-trouble, appendicitis and nervous prostration—these and other diseases of almost every description and name have been, in hundreds and thousands of instances, healed by divine power. The writer has himself witnessed the healing of thousands of diseases too numerous to mention. For proof of a few specific cases, see under Personal Testimonies in the chapter of this work entitled *"Divine Healing."*

That this reformation is the true reformation of God is therefore shown by these facts:

1. *It began at the right time*—the exact time predicted in the prophecies.

2. *It accomplishes the very work* described in these prophecies.

3. *It restores to the people the whole Word of God,* and thus rests upon a solid foundation which can never be superseded or shaken.

4. *It restores a pure church,* bearing every specific characteristic of the apostolic church.

5. *God has set his stamp and seal of approval upon it* by the miraculous manifestation of his mighty power.

TRIUMPHANT OVER THE APOSTASY.

To witness such results, after the long reign of the beast and his image, is enough to start songs of rejoicing among the angels of heaven, and ought to awaken shouts and praises among the redeemed of earth. When the Israelites were in Babylonian bondage, sadly they hung their harps upon the willows by the river-side and wept when they "remembered Zion." Here they were tormented by their captors, who said, "Sing us one of the songs of Zion"; and they answered, despairingly, "How shall we sing the Lord's song in a strange land?" (Psa. 137: 1-4). Zion's songs were *songs of deliverance;* therefore it was not possible to sing them in a strange land.

So also has it been in spiritual Babylon. The truly saved held captive therein during the long reign of apostasy, have had their righteous souls vexed from day to day with pride, worldliness, and ungodliness of surroundings; and there they have wept and groaned when they remembered Zion's primitive condition. At the same time, however, they have been expected to be happy and sing the songs of Zion. How could they sing these songs of deliverance in a strange land? Impossible! It is when "the ransomed of the Lord *return, and come to Zion,*" that the "songs and everlasting joy" break forth again. And this was described by the Revelator: "And I saw as it were a sea of glass mingled with fire: and them that had gotten the victory over the beast, and over his image, and over his mark, and over the number of his name, stand on the sea of glass *having the harps of God.* And they *sing the song of Moses* the servant of God [a song of deliverance], and the song of the Lamb [a song of redemption], saying, Great and marvelous are thy works, Lord God Almighty; just and true are thy ways, thou King of saints" (Rev. 15: 2, 3). Thank God! Since we have returned from Babylon we have our harps once more and are able to sing the songs of Zion. Halleluiah!

"From Babel confusion most gladly I fled,
And came to the heights of fair Zion instead;
I'm feasting this moment on heavenly bread;
  I'll never go back, I'll never go back.
The beast and his image, his mark, and his name,
My love or allegiance no longer can claim,
Though men may exalt them to honor and fame;
  I'll never go back again."

A WORLD-WIDE WORK.

This great movement is also symbolized in the tenth chapter of Revelation: "And I saw another mighty angel come down from heaven, clothed with a cloud: and a rainbow was on his head, and his face was as it were the sun, and his feet as pillars of fire: and he had in his hand a little book open: and he set his right foot upon the sea, and his left foot on the earth, and cried with a loud voice . . . . and sware by him that liveth forever and ever . . . . that there should be time no longer: but in the days of the voice of the seventh angel, when he shall begin to sound, the mystery of God should be finished" (verses 1-7).

It is the seventh angel that ushers in the end of all things. This angel, however, is not the seventh, but is another who appears just before the seventh. He had in his hand a little book, which John was commanded to take and eat (verse 9). This symbolizes the Word of God, which the people of God must accept in these last days, just before the end of time.

But the chief point in this vision which I wish to call attention to is the fact that this message is universal. The angel "set his right foot *upon the sea,* and his left foot *on the earth.*" Sea and earth include the whole world. The first message of the gospel in apostolic days went forth to the then-known world only—the territory of the Roman Empire; but this last message is for all people in all parts of the earth. All must receive the "little book," and take it, and eat it. Therefore the call of God to unite in one body—one glorious church—in this present age, knows no geographical or other limits.

While the special prophecies pertaining to Babylon are directed more particularly toward Roman Catholicism and Protestantism, the gathering together of God's people must not be considered as limited to these, but is to embrace all. The great apostasy out of which the Papacy and Protestantism developed in the West, was reigning in the East also, as we have shown, and it has been perpetuated until the present day. And since this message is universal, it is directed against every form of the apostasy without exceptions—Papal, Protestant, Greek Orthodox, Maronite, Gregorian, Coptic, Abyssinian, etc. Not one of these represents the true, pure church of the Bible, but all are filled up with sin and sinners, and teach for doctrines the commandments of men; therefore God is gathering his true, holy people together in one body out of *and outside of* all of these churches of men. Amen.

COUNTERFEIT MOVEMENTS.

In concluding this chapter I wish to call attention to the fact that there are also certain counterfeit movements in the world and that these tend to confuse the minds of many people—various kinds of so-called holiness movements, most of which still leave the people in their God-dishonoring sects, tongues movement, Russellism, Christian Science, Seventh-Day Adventism, Protestant church federation, etc. These movements are for the most part filled with false or misleading doctrines, and thousands of people, led by false spirits, take refuge therein. True, many good honest people, lacking a clear knowledge of God's work and of his truth have also united with these; but this reformation is calling them out, and they are fleeing from these divisions of Babylon also, and are becoming established in the one body which alone bears the true Bible mark of genuineness.

These other movements did not originate at the right time to fulfil the prophecies. They are not performing the work described in the prophecies. They are not giving the whole Word to the people, but each omits many things of vital importance taught in the New Testament, while all add much error. They are not restoring the one pure, holy, apostolic church. And they are not confirmed by that holy power which gives the stamp and seal of divine authority.

As to the falsity of the doctrines taught in these various movements, this book, by setting forth the truth, refutes most of their principal points; for when truth is presented positively, error must fall. Reader, "buy the *truth*, and sell it not" (Prov. 23:23). The church of God has in it the "discerning of spirits," and by this means a clear line of demarcation is drawn "between the righteous and the wicked; between him that serveth God, and him that serveth him not."

"Are you of the holy remnant, Gathered to the king of peace!
    Have you found a full atonement And abundance of his
        grace?
    Yes, my soul has come to Zion, On the high and holy way,
    And I've seen all darkness flying, Driven by the light of
        day."

DIVINE LAW AND THE
KINGDOM OF GOD.

CHAPTER XX

THE TWO COVENANTS.

"Tell me, ye that desire to be under the law, do ye not hear the law? For it is written, that Abraham had two sons, the one by a bondmaid, the other by a freewoman. But he who was born of the bondwoman was born after the flesh; but he of the freewoman was by promise. Which things are an allegory: for these are the two covenants; the one from the mount Sinai, which gendereth to bondage, which is Agar. For this Agar is mount Sinai in Arabia, and answereth to Jerusalem which now is and is in bondage with her children. But Jerusalem which is above is free, which is the mother of us all. For it is written, Rejoice, thou barren that barest not; break forth and cry, thou that travailest not: for the desolate hath many more children than she which hath an husband. Now we, brethren, as Isaac was, are the children of promise. But as then he that was born after the flesh persecuted him that was born after the Spirit, even so it is now. Nevertheless what saith the Scripture? Cast out the bondwoman and her son: for the son of the bondwoman shall not be heir with the son of the freewoman. So then, brethren, we are not children of the bondwoman, but of the free" (Gal. 4: 21-31).

In this scripture two covenants are brought to view: the first proceeding from Sinai and "gendereth to bondage"; while the second is associated with "Jerusalem, which is above .... the mother of us all." They there-

fore represent the two great systems by which God has
governed his people on earth: first, by the law system,
which originated at Sinai; second, by the gospel, which
came through Christ.

Viewed from this standpoint, these two covenants
are represented as the mothers of God's people, prefigured by the two wives of Abraham. Hagar the bond-
wife represents the law system, and her son Ishmael,
signifies the Jewish nation, the "children" of that covenant; while Sarah the free wife represents the gospel
system, and Isaac, her son, signifies all true believers
in Christ, who are "children," not "of the bondwoman,
but of the *free*." These systems are not to continue
side by side together but the one is the successor of the
other in the Father's favor—the law system, with all of
its "children" (Hagar and Ishmael), being rejected for
the true gospel system (Sarah and Isaac). "Cast out the
bondwoman and her son: for the son of the bondwoman
shall not be heir with the son of the freewoman." "Now
we, brethren [of the gospel dispensation], as Isaac was,
are the children of promise."

MEANING OF COVENANT.

The usual signification of the term "covenant" is,
"A mutual agreement or contract binding two or more
parties." But in order for a contract to be *mutual*, the
parties must be able to meet on the same level, each
giving and receiving, and each being obliged by the
other. But the two covenants under consideration were
not of this nature, as can readily be seen; therefore the
term "covenant" is not here used in its proper, or
ordinary, sense, but in an *analogical* sense, because of

the relative position of the parties. All the benefits are conferred by the one, and all the obligations are sustained by the other. This makes a mutual contract or obligation impossible. God and man are not equal, for they occupy different planes; therefore their relations must not be regarded as identical with the contracts, agreements, and relations of men with men.

A study of the Bible use of the term "covenant," as existing between God and man, shows that it signifies God's promise of unmerited favors and blessings to man, generally through *some particular system* by which they are to be enjoyed. For this reason his covenant is used interchangeably with his "counsel," "oath," or "promise."

"I have made a new covenant with my chosen, I have sworn unto David my servant, Thy seed will I establish forever, and build up thy throne to all generations" (Psa. 89: 3, 4). This covenant was not a mutual agreement, but was simply a sworn *promise*. So also in Psa. 105: 8-11. The "covenant [which] he made with Abraham, and his oath unto Isaac," simply *promises* to give the land of Canaan to the Jews. The entire Abrahamic covenant is thus regarded simply as a divine *promise*, and not in any sense a mutual agreement. For proof see Heb. 6: 13-15; Gal. 3: 14-18; Luke 1: 68-75.

The promise of a coming Redeemer is termed "God's covenant"; yet who would think of suggesting that such was the result of a mutual contract or obligation made between God and man? It is a covenant indeed, yet it is all one-sided, and consists of God's gratuitous blessing. See Isa. 59: 20, 21.

In addition to the foregoing proofs of the meaning of "covenant" when applied to God's relations with men, we have positive proof that it is applied to any God-appointed arrangement with or without human conditions. Thus:

1. *Day and night.* "If ye can break my covenant of the day, and my covenant of the night, and that there should not be day and night in their season" (Jer. 33: 20). Day and night are not the result of an agreement between God and man, but are wholly of divine appointment. Therefore any of God's fixed arrangements, or commandments, or promises may properly be termed his covenant, according to the Bible use of the word.

2. *Sabbath.* "Wherefore the children of Israel shall keep the Sabbath to observe the Sabbath throughout their generations, for a perpetual *covenant*" (Exod. 31:16).

3. *Circumcision.* "Thou shalt keep my covenant therefore, thou, and thy seed after thee in their generations. This is my covenant which ye shall keep . . . . every man-child among you *shall be circumcised*" (Gen. 17: 9, 10).

In these last two scriptures positive commandments are termed God's covenant.

So also a single precept of a system ordained by the Lord, is termed his covenant (see Jer. 34: 13, 14).

We have already shown that God has made two special covenants, each of which embraces an entire system of divine law and government in a distinct dispensation of time. These we desire especially to set forth, showing their establishment, nature, duration, and special relations to each other. Although in one sense they are distinct from each other, yet in another sense they bear a certain relationship with each other. Ishmael and Isaac, by which they are represented, were quite different; for one was the son of a slave, while the other was the son of a freewoman; yet, after all they were half-brothers, for they had the same father. Likewise God is the author of both the systems that they represented. The relation of Abraham with his slave, however, was not a natural one, but was an accommodation to certain existing conditions deemed expedient at that time; but this relation ended when Hagar was dismissed from the family after the birth of Isaac. So also God's relation with the old covenant and its "children" was not entirely a natural one, but was an accommodation to conditions in that age of the world, and therefore *came to an end* with the establishment of the gospel; for "we, brethren, as Isaac was, are the children of promise." And now is fulfilled the command, *"Cast out the bondwoman and her son:* for the son of the bondwoman *shall not be heir* with the son of the freewoman."

THE SINAITIC COVENANT.

The first covenant, the one afterwards "cast out," came, we are told, "from the mount Sinai"; therefore we will consult the Word of God in order to see what constitutes that covenant from Sinai.

I. THE DECALOGUE OR TEN COMMANDMENTS.

"And he was there [in Mount Sinai] . . . . forty days and forty nights; he did neither eat bread, nor drink

water. And he wrote upon the tables the words of the
covenant, the *ten commandments"* (Ex. 34:28, 29).
"And he declared unto you his *covenant,* which he commanded you to perform, *even ten commandments;* and
he wrote them upon two tables of stone" (Deut. 4:13).

These two scriptures declare positively that the ten
commandments, written on tables of stone, constituted
the Sinaitic covenant; but this fact is even more clearly
stated, if possible, in Deut. 5:2-22: "The Lord our
God made a covenant with us in Horeb. The Lord made
not this covenant with our fathers, *but with us,* even
us, who are all of us here alive this day. The Lord
talked with you face to face . . . . saying, I am the
Lord thy God which brought thee out of the land of
Egypt, from the house of bondage. Thou shalt have
none other gods before me." Then follows the words
of all the ten commandments, thus giving the words
of the covenant in full, after which come these words
of Moses: "These words the Lord spake unto all your
assembly in the mount out of the midst of the fire, of
the cloud, and of the thick darkness, with a great voice:
and he added no more. And he wrote them in two tables
of stone, and delivered them unto me."

That the decalogue itself constituted the covenant
proper is further shown by the fact that the violation
of any one of its precepts was termed a breaking of
the covenant. For example:

1. *The commandment forbidding images.* "Take heed
unto yourselves, lest ye forget the *covenant of the Lord*
your God, which he made with you, and make you a

graven image, or the likeness of anything, which the Lord thy God hath forbidden thee" (Deut. 4:23).

2. *The commandment forbidding idolatry.* "Then men shall say, Because they have forsaken the covenant of the Lord God of their fathers . . . . for they went and served other gods, and worshiped them" (Deut. 29: 24-26). So also Deut. 31:16.

3. *The commandments against covetousness and stealing.* When Achan coveted and stole certain things at Jericho, he was taken and destroyed because he had "transgressed the covenant of the Lord" (Josh. 7:15).

II. OTHER PRECEPTS ALSO.

But while the decalogue, as the foregoing scriptures show, constituted the covenant proper, other precepts given on Sinai were also included in that covenant, "I made a covenant with your fathers in the day that I brought them forth from the land of Egypt, out of the house of bondage, saying, At the end of seven years let ye go every man his brother an Hebrew, which hath been sold unto thee" (Jer. 34:13, 14). This last-named precept is from Exod. 21:2, and was therefore contained in the book of the covenant that Moses wrote just after God first spoke on Sinai. At that time God gave the ten commandments, together with certain other laws, statutes, judgments, and ordinances; whereupon "Moses wrote ALL the words of the Lord" (which included the decalogue) in a little book containing what is now the 20th, 21st, 22nd, 23rd chapters of Exodus. After writing it, Moses took this little *"book of the covenant,* and read in the audience of the people: and they said, All that the Lord hath said will we do, and be obedient. And Moses took the blood, and sprinkled upon the people, and said, Behold the blood of the covenant which the Lord hath made with you concerning all these words" (Ex. 24: 4-8). Here the word ":covenant" is expanded, including the little book, for the simple reason that the book contained the covenant proper—the ten commandments. Had they not been included in this writing of Moses, we should know little concerning them; for the stone tables upon which (as we shall see) they were also written have disappeared.

III. THE ENTIRE PENTATEUCH.

At a later time Moses wrote a larger book, the Pentateuch, comprising what is now the first five books of the Bible, and in this he included the little book just mentioned, which forms chapters 20 to 23 of Exodus. Now, since "the book of the covenant," which had been dedicated by blood, was incorporated in the complete writings of Moses, the entire work became known as "the book of the covenant," embracing the whole Mosaic, or law, system—moral, civil, and ceremonial. Thus, the writer of the book of Hebrews states that "the first covenant had *also* ordinances of divine service and a worldly sanctuary" (Heb. 9: 1). These ceremonial things were not the entire covenant, but the "first" covenant had these things "*also.*" Therefore in Ezek. 44: 7 the defiling of the temple is termed a breaking of the covenant. In 2 Cor. 3: 14, 15 Paul regards the old covenant as identical with the writings of Moses—the Pentateuch: "But their minds were blinded: for until

this day remaineth the same vail untaken away in the
reading of the old testament [or covenant]; which vail
is done away in Christ. But even unto this day when
Moses *is read the vail* is upon their hearts." Now, this
is the broadest use of the term "old covenant" that we
have in the Bible. This book of the law is termed "the
covenant" because it contains, is built upon, and centers
in, the covenant proper—the ten commandments (Exod.
34: 28; Deut. 4: 13; 5: 2-22, etc.).

The foregoing scriptures show positively that the
covenant from Sinai was one, and that it included the
decalogue and all other precepts and commandments,
whether civil, moral, or ceremonial.

FALSE CLAIM OF TWO LAWS.

Certain law-teachers of the present day have attempted to build up an ingenious theory that there were two
distinct laws given to the Jews—one the law of God and
the other the law of Moses. The decalogue they exalt
above everything else, constantly calling it "the law of
God," "the law of the Lord," "the moral law," etc.;
the rest of the law they place in an inferior position,
calling it the "law of Moses," "ceremonial law," etc.
Now, this distinction is false and is a mere shift in order
to uphold an unscriptural theory. In not one place in
the Bible is this distinction ever made. The decalogue is
never singled out and called "the law of God," "the law
of the Lord," or "the moral law"; nor is the rest of
Moses' writings ever called "the ceremonial law." On
the contrary, these writings of Moses, aside from the
decalogue, are frequently styled "the law of the Lord."

Thus, in 2 Chron. 31: 3 the burnt offerings, set feasts, etc., are all given as commanded in "the law of the Lord."

"For *God commanded* saying, Honor thy father and mother" (Matt. 15: 4). "For *Moses said*, Honor thy father and thy mother" (Mark 7: 10). Here the same precept of the decalogue is attributed both to God and to Moses. No distinction making two laws.

"Did not Moses give you the law, and yet none of you keepeth the law? Why go ye about to kill me?" (John 7: 19). Here the commandment against murder (in the decalogue) is ascribed to Moses. Now verses 22, 23: "Moses therefore gave unto you circumcision . . . . If a man on the Sabbath-day receive circumcision, that the *law of Moses* should not be broken." No such thing as two laws was known to Christ; he simply attributed all to Moses.

"And when the days of her purification according to the *law of Moses* were accomplished, they brought him to Jerusalem, to present him to the Lord; as it is written in the *law of the Lord*, Every male that openeth the womb shall be called holy" (Luke 2: 22, 23). No distinction is made here between "the law of the Lord" and "the law of Moses," but the two are used in reference to the same thing—a ceremonial precept.

"And they spake unto Ezra the scribe to bring the book of the *law of Moses* . . . . So they read in the book in the *law of God* distinctly, and gave the sense, and caused them to understand the reading" (Neh. 8: 1-8). This "law of Moses" and this "law of God" were the same; and out of this book, "in the *law of God*," Ezra read "from the morning until midday" (verse 3). But why is it called both the law of Moses and the law of God? The answer is clearly given—because it was "the book of the law of Moses, *which the Lord had commanded*" (verse 1). "Ezra . . . . was a ready scribe in the law of Moses, *which the Lord God of Israel had given*" (Ezra 7:6). It was the law of God because God was its author; it was the law of Moses because he gave it to the people. Only one law was given to Israel, simply called "the law," which law included the whole system—every precept, whether moral, civil, or ceremonial.

In the effort to exalt the decalogue above the rest of the law and thus enforce this unscriptural distinction, these crafty teachers of the law exclaim, "But God gave the decalogue himself, whereas the remainder was given by Moses." This statement at first appears correct and innocent enough, but a construction is thus placed upon it that is absolutely false. Reader, mark this fact: The entire law, decalogue and all, proceeded from the same source, was given by God himself, and *in the same way*—he *spoke* it all from heaven. The only difference was in the recording of that law. God recorded the decalogue on stones; whereas Moses recorded the entire book of the law (decalogue included) in hand-writing in a book. The recording was an after-consideration. God first spoke the ten commandments directly to all the people (Deut. 5:4-22; Ex. 20:1-18); and these words, accompanied by supernatural manifestations, so terrified the people that AT THEIR RE-QUEST the Lord did not deliver the rest of his law directly to them, as he probably would have done (Heb.

12:19; Exod. 20:19); therefore Moses "drew near unto the thick darkness where God was" (Ex. 20:21). and received the rest of the statutes, judgments, laws, and ordinances, which, as I have already shown, he wrote in a small book and read to the people, then dedicated it as the "book of the covenant." The assertion that the words of God spoken to Moses privately at the request of the people are inferior to the words spoken publicly is, to say the least, a wretched perversion of the facts in the case. In the New Testament some of the gospel was spoken directly by Christ and recorded afterwards in his own words; while other parts were recorded in the language of the apostles through the inspiration of the Holy Spirit. Are there therefore two gospels in the New Testament? Is one part inferior to the other? Certainly not. So in the Old Testament God gave the entire law in the same way—*he spoke it.* The entire congregation heard only a part of it, but Moses heard it all and wrote it. *One law,* proceeding from one source.

The question may then be asked, "Why did God write the decalogue on the stone tables?" The answer is easy and clear. After Moses dedicated the small book of law referred to, he returned to Mount Sinai and remained there many days, during which time he received all of the law from the mouth of God. "And He gave unto Moses, when He had made an end of communing with him on Mount Sinai, two tables of TESTIMONY, tables of stone, *written with the finger of God*" (Ex. 31:18). This explains the whole matter. Over and over again these tables are called the "testimony." Testimony of what? Why, they were God's witness, attestation, or "testimony" to the rest of the law, which the people had not heard; and as they contained the words, divinely written, which the people knew were divinely given, they therefore constituted the proof or seal that the remainder were also THE WORDS OF GOD HIMSELF. A witness never testifies for himself, but for some one else. The tables were a testimony, not for themselves, but *for the remainder of the law*. All of the rules, regulations, limitations, and penalties pertaining to the ten precepts that the people themselves had heard were given privately to Moses; therefore they needed a divine attestation of some kind.

Furthermore, this method of giving some visible thing as a proof or attestation was in accordance with the customs of the times. "Now this was the manner in former time in Israel concerning redeeming and concerning changing, for to *confirm* all things; a man plucked off his shoe, and gave to his neighbor: and this was a *testimony* in Israel" (Ruth 4:7). Now, this old shoe was not a testimony for itself, but was a proof or witness of the entire business transaction. Again, we read concerning Joshua: "So Joshua *made a covenant* with the people that day, and set them a statute and an ordinance in Shechem. And Joshua *wrote these words* in the book of the law of God, and *took a great stone*, and set it up there under an oak, that was by the sanctuary of the Lord. And Joshua said unto all the people, Behold, *this stone shall be* A WITNESS unto us; *for it hath heard all the words of the Lord which he spake*

unto us; it shall be therefore a witness unto you" (Josh.
24: 25-27).

Was the old shoe superior to the transaction of which
it was a "testimony"? Was the stone of Shechem another
law, or in some way a superior object to that written
covenant of which it was only a "witness"? Let candid
men answer. So also the stone tables were simply a
"testimony" divinely given, witnessing to the authenticity
and divine authorship of the one written law given by
Moses.

A TEMPORARY SYSTEM.

In the third chapter of Galatians, Paul discusses at
length the Abrahamic covenant, proving that it meets
its fulfilment in Christ; therefore he was obliged to
consider the matter of this Mosaic covenant, which was
introduced between the giving of the Abrahamic covenant and the appearing of Christ. In this he clearly
shows the temporary nature of the whole Mosaic law
system.

"And this I say, that the covenant [of Abraham]
that was confirmed before of God in Christ, the law [of
Moses] which was four hundred and thirty years after,
can not disannul, that it should make the promise of
none effect" (verse 17). And since he connects the
Abrahamic covenant and the gospel of Christ, thus dis-
pensing with the law of Moses, which was established
between these dates, he asks the question, "Wherefore
then serveth the law?" or in other words, "Why then
was the law given?" This he answers: "It was added
because of transgressions, *until the seed should come to
whom the promise was made*" (verse 19). "And to thy

seed, *which is Christ*" (verse 16). This shows its temporary nature, as also do verses 24, 25: "Wherefore
the law was our schoolmaster to bring us [the Jews]
unto Christ, that we might be justified by faith. But
after that faith is come [the introduction of the gospel],
we are *no longer under a schoolmaster*."

This scripture shows: 1. That the Sinaitic law,
given four hundred and thirty years after the Abrahamic covenant, was to end with Christ. 2. That it
was given "because of transgressions," which shows
that it was designed to restrain sin, thus being adapted
to a sin-age. "Moreover the law entered that the offense might abound" (Rom. 5:20). Paul distinctly
taught what class of people the law was adapted to.
When certain men were endeavoring to bind the law upon
Christians, he declared that these law-teachers understand 'neither what they said, nor whereof they affirmed';
but he himself asserted that "the law *was not made for
a righteous man*, but for the lawless and disobedient,
for the ungodly and for sinners, for unholy and profane, for murderers of fathers and murderers of mothers,
for menslayers, for whoremongers," etc. (1 Tim. 1:7-9).
And Heb. 10:1-4 shows that the law system was not able
to remove sin from the hearts of the people.

Furthermore, the law system was given only to the
Jewish nation. Paul says that the Gentiles "have not
the law" (Rom 2:14). However, according to Exod.
12:48, 49 it was possible for Gentiles, through circumcision, to become Jewish proselytes, and thus become subject to the jurisdiction of their law. And in
some cases this was done extensively, as we read in the

time of Esther: "And many of the people of the land became Jews, for the fear of the Jews fell upon them" (Esther 8:17). But primarily the law applied to the Jews only, and was their schoolmaster to bring them to Christ.

A NEW COVENANT PREDICTED.

"Behold, the days come, saith the Lord, that I will make a new covenant with the house of Israel, and with the house of Judah: not according to the covenant which I made with their fathers in the day that I took them by the hand to bring them out of the land of Egypt; which my covenant they break, although I was a husband unto them, saith the Lord: but this shall be the covenant that I will make with the house of Israel; After those days, saith the Lord, I will put my law in their inward parts, and write it in their hearts; and will be their God, and they shall be my people. And they shall teach no more every man his neighbor, and every man his brother, saying, Know the Lord: for they shall all know me, from the least of them unto the greatest of them, saith the Lord: for I will forgive their iniquity, and I will remember their sin no more" (Jer. 31:31-34).

This new covenant was established by Jesus Christ. "By so much was Jesus made a surety of a *better testament*" (Heb. 7:22). "But now hath he obtained a more excellent ministry, by how much also he is the mediator of a *better covenant,* which was established upon better promises" (Heb. 8:6). In every respect this new covenant through Christ is better than the old one.

1. *It was established on better promises.*" The

Mosaic covenant was based upon those promises in the original Abrahamic covenant which pertain to the literal Israel, hence was limited—national; whereas the "better covenant" is based upon those promises in the Abrahamic covenant which have universal import, meeting their fulfilment in the gospel of Jesus Christ.

2. *It has a better mediator.* "The law was given by Moses" (John 1:17); whereas Jesus is "the mediator of the new covenant" (Heb. 12:24; 8:6).

3. *It has a better priesthood.* The priests of the law were fallible men, who "were not suffered to continue by reason of death" (Heb. 7:23); whereas Jesus is our high priest, and he is "holy, harmless, undefiled, separate from sinners, and made higher than the heavens," and "because he continueth ever, hath an unchangeable priesthood" (Heb. 7:26, 24).

4. *It has a better sanctuary.* "The first covenant had . . . . a worldly sanctuary" (Heb. 9:1). The new covenant sanctuary, temple, or house of God is his spiritual church (1 Pet. 2:5; Heb. 3:6; 1 Tim. 3:15; Eph. 2:19-22).

5. *It has a better sacrifice.* Instead of the "blood of bulls and of goats," "which can never take away sins," (Heb. 9:13; 10:11) it has "the blood of Christ," which is able to "purge your conscience from dead works to serve the living God" (Heb. 9:14).

FIRST COVENANT ABOLISHED.

Throughout the book of Hebrews these two covenants are placed in sharp contrast. In chapter 9, after speaking of the "first covenant," the apostle represents Christ as "the mediator of the new testament," which is brought into force after his death; just as a "will," or testament, is made effective among men by the death of the testator. The first testament was dedicated by the blood of animals, the blood of which could never "make the comers thereunto perfect" nor "take away sins" (chap. 10:1-4); but the second will, or testament, was dedicated by a divine sacrifice. "Then said he, Lo, I come to do thy will, O God. HE TAKETH AWAY THE FIRST, *that he may establish the second.* By the which WILL we are sanctified through the offering of the body of Jesus Christ once for all" (verses 9, 10).

This weakness of the old covenant was one of the causes of its abolition. "For there is verily a disannulling of the commandment going before for the weakness and unprofitableness thereof. For the law made nothing perfect, but the bringing in of a *better hope* DID; by the which we draw nigh unto God .... By so much was Jesus made a surety of a *better testament*" (Heb. 7:18-22). In the new covenant there is perfect salvation from sin through the blood of Jesus Christ.

The abolition of the first covenant and the establishment of the second covenant is set forth in Heb. 8:6-13 in the plainest manner, as follows: "But now hath he obtained a more excellent ministry, by how much also he is the mediator of a better covenant, which was established upon better promises. For if that first covenant had been faultless, then should no place have been sought for the second. For finding fault with them, he saith, Behold, the days come, saith the Lord, when I will make a new covenant with the house of Israel and with the

house of Judah: not according to the covenant that I
made with their fathers in the day when I took them by
the hand to lead them out of the land of Egypt; because
they continued not in my covenant; and I regarded
them not, saith the Lord. For this is the covenant that
I will make with the house of Israel after those days,
saith the Lord; I will put my laws into their mind, and
write them in their hearts: and I will be to them a God,
and they shall be to me a people: and they shall not
teach every man his neighbor, and every man his brother,
saying, Know the Lord: for all shall know me, from the
least to the greatest. For I will be merciful to their
unrighteousness, and their sins and their iniquities will
I remember no more. In that he saith, A new covenant,
he hath made the first old. Now that which decayeth
and waxeth old is ready to vanish away."

Reader, notice the manner in which these two covenants are placed in contrast, thus: A covenant, "a better
covenant"; "first covenant," "second"; "old covenant,"
"new covenant," etc. The first covenant was faulty in
that it was unable to accomplish God's perfect work,
for it could not "make the comers thereunto perfect"
(chap. 10: 1); it "made nothing perfect" (chap. 7: 19).
However, a law might of itself be perfect, and yet never
make any man perfect. But Paul concludes that since
the first covenant has been superseded by the "second,"
"new," and "better covenant," it now "*decayeth* and
waxeth old, and is ready to *vanish away*" (verse 13).

Now, what was included in this "first," "old," and
abolished covenant? I have already shown by many
scriptures that the first covenant, which came from

Sinai, included the whole law of Moses—moral, civil, and ceremonial—decalogue and all. Now I will add three texts showing that the decalogue constituted this abolished covenant proper, and will challenge any man on earth to answer these three texts in the order given.

1. *Hebrews 8:9.* Here (according to the context already given) the "first," "old," and abolished covenant, which "decayeth" and is "ready to vanish away," is declared to be *"the covenant that I made with their fathers in the day when I took them by the hand to bring them out of the land of Egypt."* What was that covenant?

2. *1 Kings 8:21.* "I have set there a place for the ark, WHEREIN is *the covenant of the Lord, which he made with our fathers, when he brought them out of the land of Egypt."* Reader, mark the identity of the language in these two scriptures. The "first," "old," faulty, abolished covenant that God made with the fathers when he brought them out of the land of Egypt was IN THE ARK. Now, what was in the ark?

3. *Verse 9 of 1 Kings 8:* "There was nothing in the ark save the TWO TABLES OF STONE, which Moses put there at Horeb, when *the Lord made a covenant with the children of Israel, when they came out of the land of Egypt."*

All the "perverse disputings of men of corrupt minds" (1 Tim. 6:5), of law-teachers who "understand neither what they say, nor whereof they affirm" (1 Tim. 1:7), can never alter this truth. They may argue and "affirm" that the decalogue was not abolished with the old covenant, *but they can never answer these last three texts,* which declare it—Heb. 8: 9 with 1 Kings 8: 21, 9. "Let God be true, but every man a liar" (Rom. 3: 4).

But while the decalogue is here pointed out as the abolished covenant, we must remember that it was the "testimony" of the whole Mosaic system, that it simply stands for the whole, and that therefore all came to an end with it. Paul declares that Christ "abolished in his flesh . . . . the *law of commandments* contained in ordinances" (Eph. 2: 15). With the abolished law of ten commandments went also the ordinances, statutes, and judgments of the old law with which it was surrounded and which were sustained by it. For this reason Jeremiah, predicting the establishment of the new covenant, says: "In those days, saith the Lord, they shall say no more, The ark of *the covenant of the Lord;* neither shall it come to mind: neither shall they remember it; neither shall they visit it; neither shall that be done any more. At that time they shall call Jerusalem the throne of the Lord; and all the nations shall be gathered unto it, to the name of the Lord" (Jer. 3: 16, 17). The ark and its covenant contain no sacredness for Christians, except in a mere typical sense. Their worship does not center there. By the command of God they have forgotten it; and all of their devotions, worship, and sacred associations center in "Jerusalem," in that gospel of our Lord which went forth from the Holy City.

These two covenants are also contrasted by the apostle Paul in 2 Cor. 3: 3-14: "Forasmuch as ye are manifestly declared to be the epistle of Christ ministered by us, written not with ink, but with the Spirit of the living God; not in tables of stone, but in fleshy tables of the heart. And such trust have we through Christ to Godward: not that we are sufficient of ourselves to think anything as of ourselves; but our sufficiency is of God; who also hath made us able ministers of the new testament; not of the letter, but of the Spirit: for the letter killeth, but the Spirit giveth life. But if the ministration of death, written and engraven in stones, was glorious, so that the children of Israel could not stedfastly behold the face of Moses for the glory of his countenance; which glory was to be done away: how shall not the ministration of the Spirit be rather glorious? For if the ministration of condemnation be glory, much more doth the ministration of righteousness exceed in glory. For even that which was made glorious had no glory in this respect, by reason of the glory that excelleth. For if that which was done away was glorious, much more that which remaineth was glorious. Seeing then that we have such hope, we use great plainness of speech: and not as Moses, which put a vail over his face, that the children of Israel could not stedfastly look to the end of that which is abolished: but their minds were blinded: for until this day remaineth the same vail untaken away in the reading of the old testament; which vail is done away in Christ."

Here the first covenant is defined as the "old testament," "tables of stone," "the ministration of death," which "was glorious" at that time, the "letter" which "killeth," "the ministration of condemnation," and that which "was written and engraven in stones," which was *"done away"* and "abolished." The second covenant is the "new testament," of which Paul was an able minister; "the Spirit," which "giveth life"; "the ministration of the Spirit"; "the glory that excelleth"; that which "remaineth" and is "written in the fleshy tables of the heart."

In the words of Bro. D. S. Warner: "No Old Testament law-teacher is sent of God. In the present dispensation, He makes men 'ministers of the new testament' only. · It is called 'the ministration of the Spirit'; therefore no one can receive or teach it without the gift of the Holy Spirit, excepting in the letter, which 'killeth.'

"In verse 7 the ten words are called, 'the ministration of death, written and engraven in stones.' And though it was declared 'glorious,' it was 'done away.' 'For if that which is *done away was glorious* [the law written on stones, verse 7], much more that which remaineth is glorious.' (verse 11). 'That which remaineth' is the new testament, of which God made Paul an able minister. 'And not as Moses, which put a vail over his face, that the children of Israel could not look stedfastly to the end of that which is *abolished.*' The abolished law, we are told, was given through Moses, who at the time had his face vailed. Now turn to Ex. 34: 28-33, and you will see that it was when he came down from the mount with the tables of the covenant in his hands that his face shone, and was vailed.

"In verse 14 the abolished law is plainly described to be the 'old testament.' The old testament and the old covenant are the same thing. [Note. The term "old testament" as employed in the Scriptures never means more than the writings of Moses. It did not designate the entire body of ancient Scriptures before Christ, as we now employ the term. The collection of Scriptures written before the Savior were classed as "the law of Moses" (the old testament), "the prophets," and "the Psalms." See Luke 24: 44,] And though we have seen that it [the old covenant] is strictly defined as the ten commandments, yet these being the statute basis of the entire old book, the whole volume is sometimes called the old *diatheke*—testament.

"We can scarcely conceive how it could be possible to employ words that would more explicitly assert the abolition of that covenant which was written in the tables of stone . . . . How very explicit and unmistakable this language! All Bible readers know that nothing but the ten commandments were written in the stone tables, and it is affirmed that the very thing that had been 'written and engraven in stones' is *abolished* and *done away*. Compare verses 7 and 11."

CHAPTER XXI.

"THE LAW OF CHRIST."

As we showed in the preceding chapter, the national law of the Israelites enacted on Mount Sinai constituted the first, or old, covenant and was abolished by Christ at the cross; that is, so far as God's sanction and approval was concerned, it ended then, for it had served its temporary purpose as a standard of duty and judgment among God's people. It was only "added because of transgressions *until* the seed should come unto whom the [Abrahamic] promise was made," "which is Christ" (Gal. 3: 19).

NECESSITY OF LAW.

There still exists, however, the necessity of law as a standard of judgment; because without law there could be no sin, "for sin is the transgression of the law" (John 3: 4). Therefore without a law defining and limiting human actions and conduct there could be no sin, hence no pardon or salvation.

Now, our moral obligations, our conduct and actions, are of a two-fold character, embracing the relationship which we hold to our fellowmen, and also the relationship which we hold to that God whose creatures and subjects we are. For this reason, a perfect law, covering all human conduct and defining sin, *must proceed from God.* Men make laws, but these belong exclusively to the department of human life; and even there they are for the most part simply matters of expediency, being framed in accordance with what appears to be the best for the general good of the state or society. But human laws are unable to obligate the conscience in that higher realm of our accountability to God. In this we feel like exclaiming, with William H. Seward, "There is a higher law than the Constitution."

ONLY DIVINE LAW CAN DEFINE SIN.

Again I say, in order to define sin, a law must proceed from God. Now, since the abolition of the Mosaic system, what law furnishes the standard of judgment for the world? What law are Christians under?

"God, who at sundry times and in divers manners spake in time past unto the fathers by the prophets, hath in these last days spoken unto us by his Son" (Heb. 1: 1, 2). God's requirements can be made known to men only by revelation, and this he has made "unto the fathers by the prophets" *in various ways and at different times.* Do not overlook this fact; it is important. As we showed in a preceding chapter, divine revelation was by necessity a gradual, progressive process, in accommodation to human conditions. For this reason commandments and obligations that God has laid upon men in one period of time have often been superseded, in the order of God's plan, by something of a higher and more perfect nature. If men fail to understand this principle, they may, like the Israelites of old, attempt to perpetuate some of God's appointments long after he himself is done with them. Thus, for hundreds of years the Israelites continued to reverence the brazen serpent, which had served a very good purpose in the wilderness. Hezekiah, however, "brake in pieces the brazen serpent that Moses had made: for unto these days the children of Israel did burn incense to it" (2 Kings 18:4). Circumcision, the passover, sacrifices, and scores of other things are also examples. So also while the whole Mosaic system, with its hundreds of obligatory commandments and regulations adapted to the nation of Israel in that period, was "spoken" by God through Moses, it passed away, being superseded by the "new," "second," and "better covenant." This new covenant is God's law to us—our standard of judgment—and by conforming to its requirements we "fulfil the LAW OF CHRIST" (Gal. 6:2). For while God "in time past" "spoke" his laws and requirements in various ways and at different times, he now "hath in these last days *spoken unto us* BY HIS SON."

CHRIST THE LAWGIVER.

Now, when God speaks to men, is not his word law? Is it right to disobey? And if his word is law, then there can be no higher law than "the law of Christ"; for Jesus himself says, "I and my Father are *one*" (John 10:30). He asserts that "all men should honor the Son *even as they honor the Father*" (John 5:23). So far as authority is concerned, then, Christ is supreme. If he delivered a law, that law must be final, binding upon all, and must be the standard of judgment for the world. God *"hath .... spoken unto us by his Son."*

In the Old Testament we have clearly predicted the coming of another lawgiver. Moses himself the mediator of the old law, understood that his system was to be temporary and prophesied of a change. "The Lord thy God will raise up unto thee a prophet from the midst of them [the Jewish nation], of thy brethren, like unto me; *unto him ye shall harken."* This Moses said. *"And the Lord said* .... I will raise them up a prophet from among their brethren .... and will put my words in his mouth; and he shall speak unto thee all that I shall command him. And it shall come to pass, that whosoever will not harken unto *my words which HE shall speak* in my name, I will require it of him" (Deut. 18:15, 17-19). This scripture teaches that God's words which this prophet should speak would be the standard of judgment for the disobedient—"I will require it of him." In Acts 3:22, 23, Peter quotes this prophecy and applies it directly to Jesus Christ. His word is law—"the law of Christ."

While Moses predicted the coming of this lawgiver, Isaiah, with clear reference to Christ, says, "The isles shall wait for his law" (Isa. 42:4). "His law," "the law of Christ," was not in existence in Isaiah's day, but men were obliged to "wait" for it. After the lapse of many centuries it came, thank God!

Follow this divine lawgiver to the Mount of Transfiguration. Here appear Moses and Elias—Moses representative of the law that he delivered and the lawage that he ushered in; Elias, the foremost man among all the prophets of the old dispensation, representative of all the prophets through whom "God spake in time past unto the fathers." Peter amazed by the supernatural illumination of his Lord and overawed with the splendor of the occasion, said, "Lord, it is good for us to be here: if thou wilt, let us make here three tabernacles; one for thee, and one for Moses, and one for Elias" (Matt. 17:1-4). Peter seemed to think that all three should be accorded equal honor and place in the worship of God. But listen to the rebuke of Heaven at the very suggestion: "While he yet spake, behold, a bright cloud overshadowed them: and behold, a voice out of the cloud, which said, *This is my beloved Son*, in whom I am well pleased, HEAR YE HIM." "And when they had lifted up their eyes, they *saw no man, save* JESUS ONLY" (verses 5, 8).

Moses and the law, Elias and the old prophets, can not stand with Him who claims equality with God— "JESUS ONLY." The first covenant was revealed on Mount Sinai and amid great manifestations; how appropriate, then, that the actual change to the new covenant should be made known on a mountain in this marvelous manner, with the seal and approval of Heaven itself upon the demonstration! "The law was given by Moses; but grace and truth *came by Jesus Christ*" (John 1: 17). "The law and the prophets were until John [who baptized Christ]; *since that time* the kingdom of God is preached" (Luke 16:16). In the order of his plan, God "spake in time past unto the fathers by the prophets," but now he "hath in these last days spoken *unto us* by HIS SON." O children of earth, know ye that God hath spoken *unto us* by his Son. "HEAR YE HIM."

NEW LAW GOD'S STANDARD OF JUDGMENT.

According to the prediction of Moses, God promised to place his words in the mouth of the new prophet, or lawgiver. In fulfilment of this, Jesus says: "I have not spoken of myself; but the Father which sent me, he gave me a commandment what I should say, and what I should speak. And I know that his commandment is life everlasting; whatsoever I speak therefore, even as the Father said unto me, so I speak" (John 12: 49, 50).

. Now, this law of commandments delivered by Christ defines sin and is the present standard of judgment. This is proved by the fact that it is the standard by which we shall be judged in the last great day. "He that rejecteth me, and receiveth not my words, hath one that judgeth him: *the word that I have spoken, the same shall judge him in the last day*" (verse 48). In that day says Paul, " God shall judge the secrets of men by Jesus Christ *according to my gospel*" (Rom. 2: 16). Reader, our responsibility is now rated, not by the decalogue, nor the law of Moses, nor the injunctions of the prophets, but by the "gospel," "the law of Christ." *"Hear. ye him."*

1. *Christ possessed all authority.* "All power is given unto me in heaven and in earth" (Matt. 28: 18).

2. *He taught with authority.* "He taught them as one having authority" (Matt. 7: 29). His teachings throughout show a directness characteristic of an original lawgiver. Not once does he quote law or prophet as *his authority* for his teaching. He quotes them for other purposes, but for his doctrine he claims no authority besides God.

Some people foolishly affirm that in Matthew 5 Christ is simply explaining confirming, and enlarging the scope of the old law. Five minutes' study ought to convince any one that, on the other hand, a series of striking contrasts are here introduced. He refers to the law in the words, "Ye have heard that it hath been said"; whereas he introduces his own teaching thus: *"But I say unto you."* His standard is not the law standard, but another standard, and a higher one, and it proceeds directly from him: "I say unto you." Notice this verse: "Ye have heard that it hath been said, An eye for an eye, and a tooth for a tooth: but I say unto you, that ye resist not evil: but whosoever shall smite thee on thy right cheek, turn to him the other also" (verses 38, 39). Now, is this a mere "confirmation" or "enlargement" of the old law? If so, then in order to enlarge the original we must destroy two eyes or pluck out two teeth, instead of one, or knock down the man who smites us on one cheek. No; the law of Christ, "I say unto you," is another law.

In introducing this higher law Christ paid his respects to the old law and the prophets, that had prepared the way for him, in these words: "Think not that I am come to destroy the law, or the prophets: I am not come to destroy, but to fulfil. For verily I say unto you, Till heaven and earth pass, one jot or one tittle shall in no wise pass from the law, till all be fulfilled" (Matt. 5: 17, 18).

"The law and the prophets were until John" (Luke 16: 16). The law "was added because of transgressions *until* the seed should come" (Gal. 3: 19). Therefore the law did not require an act of destruction in order to remove it, for it naturally expired by limitation; and the plain inference is that it should pass away when fulfilled. But it was still in force when Christ delivered this sermon, for its many types and shadows pointing forward to Christ were not "fulfilled" until the death of Christ; therefore Christ did not and could not set himself in direct opposition to the law or attempt to "destroy" it during his ministry. On the contrary, he respected it. Nevertheless, he gave his doctrine as something other than the law and as something superior to that law which he thus venerated. "And it came to pass, when Jesus had ended these sayings, the people were astonished at *his doctrine*" (Matt. 7: 28).

3. *Christ delivered a law.* "The law of Christ" (Gal. 6: 2).

4. *It was a law of commandments.* "Jesus began to do and to teach until the day in which he was taken up, after that he through the Holy Ghost *had given commandments* unto the apostles whom he had chosen" (Acts 1: 1, 2).

5. *It is binding on Christians..* "Go ye therefore, and teach all nations . . . . teaching them to observe [the law?—No! but] all things WHATSOEVER I HAVE COMMANDED YOU" (Matt. 28: 19, 20). Now, these "commandments" of Christ constitute the message to all nations. Mark states it thus: "And he said unto them, Go ye into all the world, and *preach the gospel* to every creature" (Mark 16: 15). The gospel, then, contains the commandments of God binding on Christians, and they were delivered by Christ. For this reason Paul acknowledged himself as being "under the law to Christ" (1 Cor. 9: 21). "Under the law of the Messiah."— *Syriac Version.*

6. *These commandments we must keep.* "If ye love me, keep *my* commandments" (John 14: 15). "If a man love me, he will keep *my words*" (verse 23). "Ye are my friends, if ye do whatsoever I command you . . . . for all things that I have heard of my Father I have made known unto you" (John 15: 14, 15). Some deluded souls imagine that by observing the decalogue they are keeping the commandments of God. Not so. The commandments of God in the Christian dispensation are quite another thing, being, as we have shown, the "words," the "commandments," yea, "the gospel," of Jesus Christ; and *by it* we shall be judged in the last day (John 12: 48; Rom. 2: 16). This "law of Christ" contains many commandments that are entirely "new," belonging exclusively to this dispensation, such as baptism, the Lord's Supper, feet-washing, etc.

In obedience to the divine commission the apostles delivered this law to the Christian churches. Paul, who was God's apostle in a special sense (Gal. 1: 1), wrote to the Corinthians: "I have received of the Lord that which also I delivered unto you" (1 Cor. 11: 23). And again, "If any man think himself to be a prophet, or spiritual, let him acknowledge that the things that I write unto you *are the commandments of the Lord*" (1 Cor. 14: 37). To the Thessalonians he said, "Ye know what *commandments* we gave you by the Lord Jesus" (1 Thess. 4: 2); and he commended them because they had received his preaching, "not as the word of men, but as it is in truth, *the word of God*" (1 Thess. 2: 13).

A "PERFECT LAW OF LIBERTY."

As we have seen, "the law of Christ" is the standard of judgment. Now, in order to be a perfect law defining sin and covering the entire range of human responsibility, it must prohibit everything that is in its nature wrong and enjoin everything that is right. Has the gospel, or "law of Christ," contained in the New Testament, these essential features? Let us see.

I. It forbids and condemns—

1. Hypocrisy—Jas. 3:17
2. Lying—Eph. 4:25
3. Stealing—Verse 28

In 2 Tim. 3:1-5

4. Covetousness
5. Pride
6. Blasphemy
7. Disobedience to Parents
8. False accusation
9. Love of pleasure

In Gal. 5:19-21

10. Adultery
11. Fornication
12. Uncleanness
13. Lasciviousness
14. Idolatry
15. Witchcraft
16. Hatred
17. Variance
18. Wrath
19. Strife
20. Seditions
21. Heresies
22. Envy
23. Murder
24. Drunkenness
25. Revelings

In Rom. 1:27-31

26. Lust
27. Maliciousness
28. Deceit
29. Backbiting
30. Hatred of God
31. Boasting
32. Unmercifulness

In 1 Tim. 2:9, 10

33. Personal adornment
And a host of other things.

James sums it up as follows: *"Every evil work"* (Jas. 3:16).

II. It gives and enjoins—

In Gal. 5:22, 23

1. Love
2. Joy
3. Peace
4. Long-suffering
5. Gentleness
6. Goodness
7. Faith
8. Meekness
9. Temperance

In other texts

10. Humility
11. Forgiveness
12. Purity
13. Sincerity
14. Godliness
15. Brotherly kindness
16. Giving to the poor
17. Visiting the afflicted
18. Caring for the widows
19. Observing all New Testament ordinances (baptism, the Lord's Supper, feet-washing)
20. Evangelizing the world

And many other things.

Paul sums it up as follows: *"Every good work"* (2 Tim. 2:21).

The gospel standard is the only perfect one. It alone condemns all that is wrong and enjoins all that is right. *It alone is in force.* As the "second" covenant, or "will," it has now superseded *in every respect* the "first" covenant and is the standard of judgment now, and by it we shall be judged in the last day.

A GRADUAL CHANGE.

So far as God's requirements were concerned, the change from the sovereignty of the law system to the authority of the gospel standard took place at the cross. It was impossible, however, for the Jews instantly to comprehend this sweeping revolution; therefore, viewed from a human standpoint, the change had to be effected gradually. Even the disciples themselves were "slow of heart to believe" and to comprehend these things. During his personal ministry Christ introduced the law of his kingdom alongside of the Mosaic law; and he said to his disciples just before his death, "I have yet *many things* to say unto you, but ye can not bear them now. Howbeit when he, the Spirit of truth, is come, he will guide you into all truth" (John 16:12, 13). Now, in searching the records of the apostles after they had received the Spirit, we find nothing new and important except this great change from the law to the gospel. And even it was a gradual reformation. The customs, forms, and prejudices of the Jewish mind had to be as it were outgrown. After the resurrection we find the disciples keeping the Jewish Pentecost (Acts 2).

Even years later they were "preaching the Word to none but unto the Jews only" (Acts 11: 19). This shows that they were slow to comprehend the true, universal character of the gospel outside of Judaism.

It required a special miracle to open up the way and make clear to Peter that he should go to Cornelius, and even then the Jews were "astonished" that God should bestow his great favors upon the Gentiles equally with the Jews (Acts 10:45). And as a result of this action there was much agitation in the Jerusalem church; for they were still observing the old law concerning meats and concerning eating with the uncircumcised (Acts 11: 2, 3). About twenty years after Christ, at the time of the council in Jerusalem (Acts 15), a strong effort was made to bind the Jewish law even on the Gentile Christians, but largely through the efforts of Paul it was defeated. But even this council did not free the Jews. Even as late as A. D. 60 the churches in Judea were still observing the law; and as Paul was a Jew, he felt constrained, when among them, to yield to it himself as a matter of expediency (Acts 21: 20-26).

But any observer of conditions in the early church can see that the effort to perpetuate the law among the Christians was productive of a great deal of trouble. Finally Paul came out boldly in his Epistles and declared, over and over again, that the law was abolished. He shows, as we have seen, that the entire Mosaic system has been "done away," being superseded by "the law of Christ."

This effort to perpetuate the law along with Christianity was also prefigured in the family of Abraham,

from which Paul adduces his type of the two covenants—
Hagar and Sarah, and the children of these covenants,
Ishmael and Isaac. Sarah and Hagar with their children lived for a while in the same family, but there
was always trouble. Eventually Abraham, for the sake
of peace, was obliged to send away the slave and her
son. So also in the beginning of the gospel dispensation the old covenant and its children (those who still
clung to the old law) were for a time retained in the
family after the birth of Isaac; but the Ishmaelites
were a source of constant trouble and annoyance, until,
finally, Paul concluded that the only way to get rid of
the difficulty and have general peace was to fulfil the
scripture, *"Cast out the bondwoman and her son; for
the son of the bondwoman shall not be heir with the
son of the freewoman"* (Gal. 4: 30).

Hagar represented the law, and Paul informs us in
another place that the law was dead (Rom. 7: 4), even
"decaying," in his day (Heb. 8: 13). The Ishmaelites,
however, are not all dead. They are still carrying
around the carcass of their "old" mother, who has been
dead for centuries.

My brethren in the gospel dispensation, let us "stand
fast therefore in the liberty wherewith Christ hath made
us free, and *be not entangled again with the yoke of
bondage"* (Gal. 5: 1). "If ye be led of the Spirit, ye
are not under the law" (verse 18). "The law was given
by Moses; but grace and truth came by Jesus Christ"
(John 1: 17). "Ye are not under the law, but under
grace" (Rom. 6: 14).

Fulfil the *"law of Christ."* "HEAR YE HIM." Amen.

CHAPTER XXII.

THE LAW OF HOLINESS.

The law of Christ and the two covenants have thus far been considered from the objective standpoint only; that is, as revelations made to man. So far as the old covenant is concerned, this is sufficient. Its laws were simply written in a book, and this writing by Moses was sealed and confirmed to Israel by the two "tables of *testimony*" on which God himself wrote that part of the law which all Israel heard him speak. But the new covenant, embodied in our New Testament, is more than an external revelation. It is a *"better* covenant."

Jeremiah was the first inspired writer that distinctly mentioned the new covenant, and this he placed in sharp contrast with the Mosaic covenant. He wrote: "Behold, the days come, saith the Lord, that I will make a new covenant with the house of Israel, and with the house of Judah: *not according to the covenant that I made with their fathers in the day that I took them by the hand to bring them out of the land of Egypt;* which my covenant they brake. . . . . . But *this shall be the covenant* that I will make with the house of Israel; after those days, saith the Lord, *I will put my law in their inward parts, and write it in their hearts;* and will be their God, and they shall be my people. And they shall teach no more every man his neighbor, and every man his brother, saying, Know the Lord: for they shall all know me, from the least of them unto the greatest of them, saith the

Lord: for I will forgive their iniquities and I will remember their sins no more" (Jer. 31:31-34).

According to Hebrews 8, where this prophecy is quoted, Christ established this new covenant. This new covenant is not the decalogue. The "first," "old," "decaying," and abolished covenant, which God made with their fathers in the day that he took them by the hand to bring them out of the land of Egypt (Heb. 8:9 and context), was the decalogue, as 1 Kings 8:21, 9 positively shows. The new covenant, however, was to be "not according to" this abolished one; in fact it is "a *better* covenant" (Heb. 8:6). It consists of moral laws; for only moral laws can be inscribed in the heart, producing moral resolutions in human character.

Originally, this perfect law was written in man's heart—inscribed in his very nature. This is clearly proved by the following facts:

1. It is still revealed, though imperfectly, in the subjective consciousness of all men; otherwise they could not, without external revelation, be regarded as morally responsible. This is confirmed by Paul, who says: "For when the Gentiles, *which have not the law* [the written, revealed law] do by nature the things contained in the law, these, having not the law, are a law unto themselves: *which show the work of the law written in their hearts,* their conscience also bearing witness, and their thoughts the meanwhile accusing or else excusing one another" (Rom. 2:14, 15).

2. By the natural disposition of all men to worship God (Acts 17:24-27). Religion is universal. It is the demand of our nature.

This original law constituted the moral image of God in man, but it became largely effaced from the human heart as a result of the fall; so that men, far from God, do not "know" him in that intimate relationship that existed in Eden. In the "new covenant," however, all this is restored.

1. *The internal writing of God's law.* In perfect salvation the laws of God are written in our hearts. Paul quotes the prediction of Jeremiah concerning this writing and applies its fulfilment thus: "He hath perfected forever *them that are sanctified.* Whereof the Holy Ghost also is a *witness* to us" (Heb. 10:14-17). Under the old covenant the laws of God were placed in the second, or inner, room of the tabernacle; under the new covenant they are placed in our hearts. In the holy of holies of the tabernacle all the laws of God were placed—written in a book, and sealed and confirmed by the divine "tables of *testimony.*" Likewise in sanctification, in addition to the perfect writing of God's laws in our hearts, *"the Holy Ghost also is a* WITNESS *to us."* Our decalogue is the Holy Ghost—the exclusive work of God. Halleluiah!

2. *We know the Lord.* In the new covenant restoration "they shall all know me," saith the Lord. Why should we not know him? The earthly manifestation and dwelling-place of God was in the tabernacle, particularly in the second room. So in salvation we experience again that intimate Edenic relationship with God. "And this is life eternal, *that they might know thee* the only true God, and Jesus Christ, whom thou hast sent" (John 17:3).

3. We are restored to the divine "image." Paul says
that we "have put on the·new man, which is renewed in
knowledge *after the image* of him that created him"
(Col. 3:10). "And that ye put on the new man, which
after God is created in *righteousness and true holiness*"
(Eph. 4:24). This work is completed in us in sanctification, the perfecting grace of God, and is therefore
identical with the restoration of God's law in the soul
(Heb. 10:14-17).

But let us define more particularly this original,
universal, moral law. Since in its restoration it is identified with "righteousness and true holiness" in the
sanctified or perfected soul, evidently in the Edenic state
it was comprehended in man's perfect moral nature. Now
what was it?

Jesus gives us an analysis of this subject in the following conversation: "Then one of them, which was a lawyer, asked him a question, tempting him, and saying,
Master, which is the greatest commandment in the law?
Jesus said unto him, Thou shalt love the Lord thy God
with all thy heart, and with all thy soul, and with all
thy mind. This is the first and great commandment.
And the second is like unto it, Thou shalt love thy
neighbor as thyself. On these two commandments hang
all the law and the prophets" (Matt. 22:35-40).

This is the "great" original law, given in two divisions: First, love to God; second, love to man. Christ
did not quote the decalogue, for these commandments
are not in the decalogue, but he went back to the fountain-head of all truth. The decalogue was neither "first"
nor "great" in comparison with these two fundamental

truths; for upon "these two commandments *hang all the law and the prophets.*" These two commandments comprise the entire sum of man's moral obligations. "He hath showed thee, O man, what is good; but what doth the Lord require of thee, but to do justly, and to love mercy, and to walk humbly with thy God?" (Micah 6:8). "To do justly and to love mercy" covers the ground of our human relations; while "to walk humbly with thy God" describes our divine obligations.

Now, this perfect love—Godward and manward—was the original law of man's being. It was "first," both in importance and in point of time. The new covenant restores to us in perfection this divine principle; for in its writing of the law of God in our hearts we are "made perfect in love" (1 John 4:18), yea, "God dwelleth in us, and his love is perfected in us" (verse 12). "The love of God is shed abroad in our hearts by the Holy Ghost which is given unto us" (Rom. 5:5). So complete, so perfect, is this moral principle within, that the apostle exclaims, "Love is the fulfilling of the law" (Rom. 13:10). Love is the *"more excellent way"* of the gospel (1 Cor. 12:31; 13).

"Oh! write thy *law of holiness*
  In living characters of flame,
That by a life of purity
  I may be worthy of thy name.

"Oh! write thy law, thy *law of love,*
  Within me till my soul shall be,
By bonds no storm can ever break,
  United to thy flock and thee."

OBJECTIVE LAW.

We return again to the words of Jesus in Matt. 22: 35-40. "On these two commandments [comprising the *one* original law of love] *hang all the law and the prophets*" (verse 40). The decalogue was not that original law; it was not "first," but it was only *hung on* that law. The time *when* it was "added," or attached, to that "first" and higher law we shall show later. "All the law and the prophets" did not constitute that higher law, but were only later additions. In other words, all objective revelation of whatsoever form or nature is not that original law, but is *only an expression of that higher law, adapted to human conditions.* Therefore the New Testament itself, as a book, is not that law, but only an expression of it, adapted to the present condition of things. Baptism, the Lord's Supper, feet-washing, healing of the sick, caring for the poor and needy, and scores of other things contained in it are clearly limited to the present order of things, and are not adapted to the angels nor to the redeemed saints in the heavenly world hereafter. For this reason, as I have previously shown, divine revelation has been of necessity progressive; and this also explains why some things commanded of God in one age of the world have been withdrawn at a later date; and why an entire system, like the Mosaic, has been abolished and superseded by another and better system. *"There is made of necessity a change also of the law"* (Heb. 7: 12).

The design of objective revelation, then, is to exhibit the divine principle of love to God and to man. In the Mosaic dispensation this was accomplished (as well as could be done through sinful men) by means of an elaborate politico-religious system adapted to that age. But in the gospel dispensation the law of perfect love is placed in the very hearts of the redeemed; therefore no coercive law is necessary in order to secure its manifestation. "If a man love me, he will keep my words," says Jesus (John 14: 23). Pure love flows out spontaneously to God our Creator, and to all men, even our enemies. This is "righteousness and true holiness."

MORAL LAW.

Now, this original, universal law of holiness is *moral law*. Butler has drawn the following clear line of distinction between moral precepts and other precepts, which he denominates *positive*. He says, "Moral precepts are precepts the reasons of which we see; positive precepts are precepts the reasons of which we do not see." Therefore he goes on to show that "moral duties *arise out of the nature of the case itself, prior to external command*. Positive duties do not arise out of the nature of the case, but from external command; nor would they be duties at all were it not from such command received from him whose creatures and subjects we are."—*Analogy of Revealed Religion*, p 208.

Reader, pause a moment and consider well this distinction. It is immutable. Moral law exists in the nature of things; whereas a law that must first be made by external authority or command in order to become a law at all, *is not a moral law*. Therefore all laws of God that have originated by his command or decree are *ceremonial* or "positive"; for in order to become laws at all they had to be first revealed *objectively* to man. On the other hand, all moral law existed subjectively in man originally, and this primitive writing, as we have shown, has to a great extent remained in him until the present day, and is restored once more to its perfect condition in Bible holiness.

CEREMONIAL HOLINESS.

Since this condition, "righteousness and true holiness," describes man's inward moral nature originally, and also in redemption, it is evident that the term "holy" or "holiness" in its "true" sense belongs exclusively to him, so far as earthly things are concerned. It is noteworthy that under the new covenant this term is applied, almost without exception, to the redeemed person. No external thing can be holy in this moral or true sense.

The holiness of *things,* so often referred to, especially in the Old Testament, was not and never could be more than a mere external, ceremonial holiness, a sort of consecration, or dedication, to a religious use. No actual change was made in the nature of the things thus dedicated. Thus, we read, "holy temple," "holy ark," "holy vessels," "holy altar," "holy vail," "holy sabbath," etc. None of these things were holy in the nature of things, but at some time or other they had to be *made* holy in order to become holy at all; therefore they were not moral in any respect but were simply objects or observances ceremonially holy, made such by God's appointment or decree. To show that these things were not *inherently* holy, I have only to call attention to the possibility of substitution. Another tabernacle might have been made and dedicated by God's command, instead of the particular one mentioned, and it would have been just as holy, or sacred, as the one that was made; or another ark, other vessels, etc.; or, as far as we can see, God might have selected some day other than the seventh for the sabbath, and have made it holy, or sacred, instead; and whichever day he might have selected would have been obligatory upon the people, as was the particular one that he did select. This is positive and unanswerable proof that none of these things possessed moral or inherent holiness, but they were simply *made* holy by divine appointment, hence were holy in a "positive," or ceremonial, sense only.

PARTICULAR EXAMPLE OF CEREMONIAL HOLINESS.

In order to show the plain teachings of the Word and make this subject entirely clear, I will select one particular example of ceremonial holiness—the sabbath. This selection is made for two reasons: first, because it furnishes material for illustrating the entire subject of ceremonial holiness; second, because the sabbath has been misunderstood or perverted by nearly all classes of Christians. I will consider the subject in chronological order—the seventh-day sabbath first, and the first-day sabbath idea next.

The selection of the sabbath as the particular representative of all ceremonial observances is a perfectly natural one; for God himself has thus selected it. The decalogue is an abridgement, or epitome, of the entire covenant, or law, of Moses. As far as I know, this is

admitted by all commentators. For this reason the decalogue alone is pointed out again and again as *the* cov-
·enant that was made at Sinai ·(Exod. 34: 28; Deut.
4: 13; 5: 2-22), and the one that was abolished by Christ
when he established the "new" and "better covenant"
(Heb. 8: 9 with 1 Kings 8: 21, 9). This could not be
true unless the decalogue embraced *in principle* the
entire law, and especially that part of the law pertaining
to ceremonial precepts. Therefore the remainder of the
law, written out by Moses, simply gives in a detailed
form the things thus succinctly stated in the ten commandments.

Now, the sabbath is classed again and again with all
the other holy days, feasts, and ceremonial observances
of the law, *heading the list of sacred days* (see Num.
28; Lev. 23; 1 Chron. 23: 32, 31; 2 Chron. 2: 4; 8: 13;
31: 3; Neh. 10: 33, etc.). On these holy seventh-day
sabbaths all the other "holy" things of the law were
brought into use—priesthood, altar, vessels, tabernacle,
sacrifices, etc., etc. Hence, in harmony with this general
classification, the sabbath stands in the decalogue,
"THE COVENANT," as the representative of all other
ceremonial observances.

At this juncture many Christians will be ready to exclaim,· "The decalogue is the moral law; therefore the
sabbath is a moral commandment, and can not represent ceremonial things." Not one text in the Bible calls
the decalogue the *moral law*, though it may and does
contain moral precepts, as every one will admit. Whether
a precept is moral or positive is determined, not by its
position in writing, in the decalogue or outside of it, but,

as we have shown, *by its own nature.* Laws that have to be established by appointment or decree in order to become obligatory upon men are not moral laws.

Now, taking the sabbath as an example, does it rest upon the basis of nature, or simply upon divine appointment? "The sabbath *was made* for man" (Mark 2: 27). Then, if God had not "made" it a holy sabbath, it would never have been holy time; hence the sabbatic law was positive, not moral; it is never termed "moral" in the Bible. To deny this fundamental and unanswerable truth is to manifest either a gross ignorance of the subject or an inexcusable perverseness. There is nothing in nature making one day to differ from another.

Some say that the sabbath differed from all other days originally, because God rested on the seventh day. That does not alter the matter; for the real difference was in God, *not in the day.* If the simple fact of God's resting on the seventh day made it holy, then every day since that time has been holy; for that rest of God was rest from creation work, and as creation work was at that time all *"finished"* (Gen. 2: 1-3), it has never been resumed. Therefore *in the same sense* that God rested this first time he has rested every day since.

But God's resting did not change the nature of the day, or make it holy. The Bible does not state that the seventh day was holy because God rested on it. It affirms that the day was holy because God "blessed and sanctified it," and that one reason for his thus blessing and sanctifying it was "because that in it he *had* rested from all his work" (Gen. 2: 2, 3). The resting was one thing; the blessing and sanctifying of the day was an-

other thing, and a *later* thing—"he HAD rested."
Reader, observe this fact. The day was not "blessed
and sanctified" *when* God rested at the end of the creational period, but at a later date, as this scripture
clearly shows: "And God blessed the seventh day and
sanctified it: *because* that in it *he HAD rested* from
all his work" (verse 3).

Now, *when* did God "bless and sanctify" the seventh
day, so that it was "made" a sabbath. The only scriptures in the Bible answering this question that proceeds
from Genesis 2, refer to the time of the Israelites in
the wilderness. Listen to the Word: "Wherefore I
caused thee to come forth out of the land of Egypt, and
brought thee into the wilderness, and I gave them my
statutes, and showed them my judgments . . . . moreover
also I gave them my sabbaths, to be a sign between
me and them" (Ezek 20:10-12). Did God *originate*
statutes and judgments in the wilderness? Yes. He
says, "*I gave them* statutes and judgments." Did God
originate the sabbath in the wilderness? Yes. He
says, "*I gave them* my sabbaths." To say that " gave"
means in the one case originated, and in the other case
does not, is to wrest Scripture.

But do the sabbaths mentioned in this text signify the
seventh day? We will see. They were given, this text
says, for "*a sign.*" "And remember that thou wast a
servant in the land of Egypt, and that the Lord thy
God brought thee out thence through a mighty hand
and by an outstretched arm: *therefore the Lord thy God
commanded thee to keep the Sabbath-day*" (Deut. 5:15).
"Thou . . . . gavest them right judgments, and true laws,

good statutes and commandments: and *madest known* unto them thy holy sabbath" (Neh. 9: 13, 14). Then the Israelites did not know the sabbath before this time, for it was "made known" in the wilderness. *"I gave* THEM my sabbaths to be *a sign." "Wherefore the children of Israel shall keep the sabbath* . . . . It is A SIGN *between me and the children of Israel forever"* (Exod. 31: 16, 17). It was "made known" in the wilderness, "given" "to the children of Israel" as a "sign" commemorating their deliverance from Egypt, as well as God's rest at creation. In all the Word of God it can not be shown that one person other than Jews or Jewish proselytes ever had or ever kept the seventh-day sabbath; and in every case where its observance is recorded, it was after the exodus from Egypt.

Now, the book of Genesis was written by Moses after the exodus and after the giving of the Sinaitic law. Paul quotes Gen. 3: 16 as "the law" (1 Cor. 14: 34); therefore Genesis was in the book of the law. "The law was given by Moses" (John 1: 17). But the Scripture shows clearly, as all admit, that the law of Moses came from the wilderness and from Sinai. According to the ordinary chronology, this was many hundreds of years after the events described in Genesis 2. Therefore let us read Gen. 2: 3 in the light of the only scriptures that we have on the subject, which state that the sabbath was "given" and "made known" after the exodus. "And God blessed the seventh day and sanctified it [in the wilderness and at Sinai], *because* that in it he HAD rested [at the close of creational week] from all his work which God created and made." Genesis

2 gives one reason (out of two) *why* the Sabbath was given; for the following scripture, with the others already quoted, gives the other reason why it was given and the time *when* it was given: "And remember that thou wast a servant in the land of Egypt, and that the Lord thy God brought thee out thence through a mighty hand and by an stretched-out arm: THEREFORE *the Lord thy God commanded thee to keep the sabbath-day*" (Deut. 5:15). What can be plainer? The sabbath was given in the wilderness as a double memorial, commemorating particularly their deliverance from Egyptian bondage, and also God's cessation from work at the close of the creative period.

The sabbath subject, however, does not hinge on the matter of a point of time. The time when the sabbath was instituted is only secondary. The Passover was instituted in Egypt, circumcision in the time of Abraham, and sacrifices in the family of Adam; and they were all incorperated into and became a part of that law of Sinai which was abolished at the cross. Hence age alone has little to do with the subject. The determining factor is the nature of the thing considered. I have already shown that the sabbath is "positive," or ceremonial, in its nature; hence it was ceremonial, no matter when instituted. But let us approach the subject from another angle, showing the difference between moral and ceremonial things, and proving that the Sabbath was not moral, thus:

1. *The term "moral" pertains to character, or quality.* When objects are made holy ceremonially, their true character, or quality, is not changed; *only their use is*

changed. Even God can not do contradictory things (see Tit. 1:2). He can not make an object morally holy unless it is first morally *unholy.* Thus, unholy men can be made holy in the true sense. But no day is by nature unholy; therefore no day can be made *morally* holy. This distinction is fundamental; hence this point is simply unanswerable.

2. *Moral principles are universal, binding upon all men and at all times.* Such a thing as an intermittent application of moral principles is absurd. Who would think of arguing that it is wrong to kill men one day, but right for the next six days? *Killing involves moral law,* a law written subjectively in the hearts of men. It is binding upon all. It knows no relaxing. But the sabbath is simply a ceremonial repetition. The thing that is perfectly *right* for six days becomes, on the seventh day, *entirely wrong*; or, what is still more absurd on a round earth, the act that is entirely wrong in one place is altogether right in another place *at the same time,* the difference being occasioned by the well-known difference in time between distant points. How foolish to talk that such is moral law, when the whole subject depends upon the successive manifestation of sunshine!

3. *Moral law, when deeply impressed in the heart of an individual, can never be completely lost.* A person may lose the favor of God and become a most wretched sinner, but his knowledge of what is morally right and wrong remains almost undiminished. Even after the lapse of ages since the original fall, the Gentiles, Paul shows, still have God's law in their hearts to the extent

that it makes them morally responsible (Rom. 2: 14, 15).

Now, a person may, through fever or other causes, become delirious for days; but when reason returns, all moral law is still in his heart as before. But test the sabbath idea by this. The person who has lost his reason for days *can never by himself recover his sabbath,* for his reckoning is lost. This is absolute proof that the sabbatical law is ceremonial; THAT IT IS NOT, AND NEVER CAN BE, WRITTEN IN A MAN'S HEART. The person can have a willingness in his heart to keep sabbath if necessary, just the same as he can be willing to keep the Passover, Pentecost, or any other external ceremonial observance; but the Sabbath itself is not in his heart. Now, the new covenant, as the Word of God declares, is written in the hearts of God's people (Heb. 8: 10); therefore the sabbath *is no part of the new covenant.*

If the sabbath were intended to stand associated with the new covenant as a ceremonial observance, as baptism, the Lord's Supper, feet-washing, etc., it would have to be positively enjoined in the "law of Christ"; for, as we have observed, the old covenant was abolished at the cross. Not one of the Old Testament ceremonial observances has a place in the law of Christ under the new covenant. Even those moral principles contained in the first covenant are not authoritative now on account of their having been formerly associated with the law; but their authority is inherent, underived from any national code in which they have been placed. Moral laws, as I have shown, are the universal, higher law on which "hang all the law and the prophets." They did not arise with the Mosaic system neither did they disappear with the Mosaic system; and, what is more, *they derive no authority whatever from the Mosaic system* after it has been abolished.

If the new covenant is a "better covenant," a *"perfect law of liberty"* (Jas. 1:25), as the Word affirms, it must of necessity reveal moral law in a perfect manner; therefore every moral principle formerly contained in the Mosaic system is also placed in the gospel system; and this system, "the law of Christ," now possesses all authority over men—an authority as direct and independent as though there had never been a law of Moses, moral or ceremonial. We are under no obligations whatever to any principle of whatsoever nature unless it can be shown to be a constituent part of the revealed "law of Christ" under the new covenant.

By arguments which, I confidently assert, will never be answered I have shown in the present chapter that the sabbath was in its nature ceremonial. Over and over again it was classed with the ceremonial observances of the law, heading the list of sacred days. In agreement with its nature and classification, the apostle Paul asserts that it is abolished: "Blotting out the handwriting of ordinances that was against us, which was contrary to us, and took it out of the way, nailing it to his cross, ... Let no man therefore judge you in meat, or in drink, or in respect of an holy day, or of the new moon, or of the sabbath-days: which are a shadow of things to come; but the body is of Christ" (Col. 2:14-17). That this expression "the sabbath-days" means the weekly sabbath I will show by definite scriptures.

1. *Both the singular and the plural of the sabbath are used to designate the seventh day.* "My sabbaths ye shall keep . . . . it is a sign . . . . wherefore the children of Israel shall keep the sabbath" (Exod. 31:13, 16, 17). So Lev. 23:37, 38; Isa. 56: 2, 4; Ezek. 20:12; Matt. 12: 10; Luke 4:31; Acts 17:2. "Have ye not read in the law, how that on the sabbath-days the priests in the temple profane the sabbath, and are blameless?" (Matt. 12: 5). In all these scriptures sabbath-days and sabbath are the same, meaning the weekly seventh day. So Col. 2: 16—"Let no man judge you, ... in respect of . . . . the sabbath-days." In every place where the term "sabbath" occurs in the fourth commandment of the decalogue it is plural in the Greek.

2. *The only Greek word ever used in the Bible for the term "sabbath"—sabbaton—is the very word Paul used here,* where he asserts that the sabbath is abolished.

3. *The identical list of Jewish days which Paul says was abolished is given many times in the Old Testament, and in such a manner as to prove that the sabbath-days mean the weekly sabbath.* As follows:

In Numbers 28 and 29 we have a detailed account of all the offerings required by the law. First, we have the *daily* offerings (verses 3, 4). Secondly, *weekly* offerings. "And on the sabbath-day two lambs of the first year without spot . . . . this is the burnt offering of every sabbath" (verses 9, 10). Thirdly, we have the new moons—*monthly* offerings. "And in the beginning of your months, ye shall offer a burnt offering," etc. (verse 11). Fourthly, we have the *annual* feast-days. "And in the fourteenth day of the first month is the Passover of the Lord" (verse 16). The remainder of chapter 28 and chapter 29 gives the details concerning these feasts. "These things shall ye do unto the Lord in your set feasts" (chap. 29:39). This gives the *daily, weekly, monthly,* and *annual* offerings; or, in other words, those offerings performed every day, on the sabbath-days on the new moons and on the annual feast-days. I will now give a number of texts showing how carefully this list, was observed, and where it is given, time and again, in almost the identical language of Col. 2:16.

1 Chron. 23:30, 31—"To stand every morning to thank and praise the Lord, and likewise at even; and to offer all burnt sacrifices unto the Lord in the sabbaths, in the new moons, and on the set feasts, by number, according to the order commanded unto thee." This follows the exact list given in Numbers 28 and 29, and "the sabbaths" are the weekly sabbaths, as every one can see.

2 Chron. 2:4—"Behold, I build an house to the name of the Lord my God, to dedicate it to him, and to burn before him sweet incense, and for the continual show-bread, and for the burnt offerings morning and evening, on the sabbaths, and on the new moons, and on the solemn feasts of the Lord our God.". Same list again— daily, weekly, monthly, and yearly offerings. But "the sabbaths" are the weekly · sabbaths and nothing else.

The list is exactly the same in 2 Chron. 8:13; Neh. 10:33; also in 2 Chron. 31:3, with "the sabbaths" designating the seventh day.

"Offerings in the feasts, in the new moons, and *in the sabbaths*" (Ezek. 45:17).

"Took it out of the way, nailing it to his cross . . . .
Let no man therefore judge you . . . . in respect of . . . .
a feast-day, or of the new moon, or *of the sabbath-days*
(Col. 2: 14-16, R. V.).

Paul was no novice in the things of the law. He
knew that this classification of the Jewish holy days, and
knew that the expression "the sabbath-days," when thus
classified with new moons and feasts, *always referred
to the seventh-day sabbath.* Now the question comes,
If he knew this, why did he use the expression "sabbath-
days" when speaking of the things abolished by Christ?
The evident answer is, Because he wished to convey
the idea that the seventh-day sabbath was abolished.

Notice how consistent this is with Paul's ministry and
teaching. He was particularly the apostle of the Gentiles. He says that the Gentiles "have not the law"
(Rom. 2: 14). They never kept the sabbath. Now,
if we include Hebrews, Paul wrote fourteen of the New
Testament Epistles; and the most of his Epistles were
either written directly to Gentile churches or else directly
concerned Gentile churches. In his epistles he gives
us over and over again exhaustive lists of evil things
but *not once* does he mention sabbath-breaking as a bad
thing. He also gives us many times long lists of good
things that the churches must do; yet *not once* does
he mention sabbath-keeping as a good thing. His only
direct reference to the sabbath, calling it by name, is
in Col. 2: 16, where he says it was abolished. Is this
the method of a sabbatarian sent to evangelize sabbath-
breakers?

People who are anxious to perpetuate the sabbath

under the gospel dispensation affirm that Christ kept the sabbath and that therefore we must keep it. Christ was "made under the law" (Gal. 4:4); while we "are not under the law, but under grace" (Rom. 6:14). But Christ was circumcised also. The law was not abolished until his death; therefore as he was a Jew, born and brought up under the law, it was perfectly natural that he should pay respect to the law. Can it be shown that Christ kept the sabbath as a moral commandment? Of course, it can not. If it could, Christ would stand convicted of sin, for the Word of God affirms that Christ broke the sabbath on at least one occasion. "Therefore did the Jews persecute Jesus and sought to slay him, because he had done these things on the sabbath-day. But Jesus answered them, My Father worketh hitherto and I work. Therefore the Jews sought the more to kill him because he not only had broken the sabbath, but said also that God was his Father, making himself equal with God" (John 5:16-18). It was not the Jews, but John, who recorded the fact that Christ "had broken the sabbath." But it was a fact, no matter who said it. He commanded the sick man to take up his bed and walk (verse 12); while the old command was, Thou shalt "bear *no burden* on the sabbath-day" (Jer. 17:21, 22). See Neh. 13:19; Exod. 20:10. However, the sabbath was not abolished until the death of Christ; therefore Christ's observing it has no bearing on the sabbath question under the new covenant.

It is sometimes urged that, as the Bible says the sabbath is to be "perpetual," "forever," "everlasting," "throughout your generations," etc., it can never be repealed. But almost every ceremonial thing in the law is stated in the same language. ·Thus, the Passover, incense, burnt offerings, atonement, Pentecost, feast of tabernacles, circumcision, etc., were all to be observed "perpetually," "throughout your generations," "forever," etc., as can be seen by referring to the following scriptures: Exod. 12:14; 30:8; 29:42; 30:10; Lev. 23:21, 41; Gen. 17:13; Exod. 31:16, 17.

The very fact that these time-specifying words are used with reference to these legal enactments proves their "positive," or ceremonial, character. *Moral precepts are never so stated in the Bible,* because they exist not by enactment, but by nature. But in order that these ceremonial things might be maintained without negligence, it was necessary to state that they must be observed "perpetually," etc.; that is, they were to remain intact during the lifetime of that system of which they formed a part. But the New Testament teaches that the old system has been abolished, together with its offerings, incense, sabbath, circumcision, Passover, and all other ceremonial observances. ·

Some people say that since Paul and other Christians kept the sabbath we also must. What has this to do with the subject? I have already shown that the whole church in Judea for a long time after the cross observed all of the law—sabbath, Pentecost, meats, refusing to eat with Gentiles, vows, circumcision and everything. If that makes sabbath-keeping obligatory, it also binds the whole law upon us. *Jewish converts only* kept the sabbath. The reason for this, as I have shown before,

was that they did not at that time understand clearly
the relation existing between law and gospel, and did
not apprehend that the old covenant ceased with the
introduction of the new covenant; therefore they endeavored to keep both together. They tried to keep
Isaac and Ishmael and their mothers in the same family.
It required a special vision to prepare the way for Peter
to go to Cornelius, a Gentile. Even then his Jewish
brethren severely reproved him for going to those uncircumcised and eating with them. But later, at the
council at Jerusalem (Acts 15), they had received sufficient light to free the Gentile converts from obedience
to the law, but they themselves remained under it still.
Later the apostle Paul brought out the clear light concerning the true relation of the two covenants, showing
that the first ceased at the cross. But all could not
appreciate such deep truth immediately; therefore when
necessary Paul adapted himself to the conditions existing. "Unto the Jews I became as a Jew, that I might
gain the Jews" (1 Cor. 9: 20). He went into the Jewish
synagogues on their sabbaths, when they were gathered
together, and preached to them; but in every such instance recorded it was before a Christian church had
been established at the place. *There is no record in the
New Testament of a Christian church meeting together
for divine worship on the seventh day.*

Some law-observers could not see the full gospel
light quickly; therefore Paul was inclined to bear with
them. This is his illustration: "Him that is weak in the
faith receive ye, but not to doubtful disputations. For
one believeth that he may eat all things: another, who is

weak, eateth herbs" (Rom. 14:1, 2). His illustration means that the one who can eat "all things" is the strong man, and the one who can eat only herbs is "weak." This prepares the way for the thought which the apostle wishes to bring out; accordingly he goes on to say: "One man esteemeth one day above another: another esteemeth every day alike. *Let every man be fully persuaded in his own mind"* (verse 5). Paul knew that under the gospel there is no difference in the days themselves; but those who were "strong" in this knowledge were obliged to bear with the "weak" man who was still observing the holy days of the law. After the brethren at Galatia, had gotten out from under the entire law, certain Judaizing teachers came in during Paul's absence and "bewitched" them by "perverting the gospel of Christ" and persuading them to "turn again" to the observance of days. So Paul wrote to them, "Are ye so foolish?" "Ye observe days [sabbath-days] and months [new moons] and times [annual feasts] and years [sabbatical years]. *I am afraid of you,* lest I have bestowed upon you labor in vain" (Gal. 4:10, 11).

Without seeking for the true explanation, some people regard Isa. 66:22, 23 as teaching that the sabbath will be observed in the new world hereafter and that it must therefore be observed in the Christian dispensation. The text reads: "For as the new heavens and the new earth, which I will make, shall remain before me, saith the Lord, so shall your seed and your name remain. And it shall come to pass that from one new moon to another, and from one sabbath to another, shall all flesh come to worship before me, saith the Lord." This text has "new moons" as well as sabbaths, and Paul clearly teaches that new moons are abolished with the sabbath.

Now, even if this scripture from Isaiah is applied to the heavenly world hereafter, it is easy to show that the description of its worship pertaining to days is only symbolic, and not literal. John says, "I saw a new heaven and a new earth: for the first heaven and the first earth were passed away" (Rev. 21:1). Did he see literal new moons and sabbaths in it? "The city had no need of the sun, *neither of the moon*, to shine in it: for the glory of God did lighten it, and the Lamb is the light thereof .... *There shall be no night there*" (Rev. 21:23-25). There will be no new moons in heaven in reality, neither succession of days; therefore sabbaths are impossible.

Isaiah 66 is simply a highly symbolic description, the language being *based on the religious customs of the age in which it was written*. In the immediate context of this verse we have "holy mountain," "Jerusalem," "Israel," "clean vessel," "house of the Lord," "priests," "Levites," and then immediately following, "new moon," "sabbath." Not one of these things will have a literal distinction in heaven. There will not even be a "house of the Lord" there; for John declares, "I saw *no temple* therein" (Rev. 21:22).

OBJECT OF LAW CEREMONIES.

All of the ceremonial observances of the law served a distinct purpose. In Col. 2, where they are summed up as feast-days, new moons, and sabbath-days, Paul says, they "are a shadow of things to come; but the body is of Christ" (verse 16, 17). This shows that they occupy a typical relation. So also the writer of the Hebrews represents the law as "having a shadow of good things to come, but not the very image of the things" thus foreshadowed (Heb. 10:1). Some ceremonies of the law served a double purpose, being memorials of past events as well as types of something future; for example, the Passover, which commemorated the miraculous preservation of the Hebrews from death when the first-born were slain in Egypt; while it also pointed forward to "Christ our passover, who is sacrificed for us" (1 Cor. 5:7). Likewise the sabbath had a sort of threefold signification; it commemorated both the deliverance of Israel from Egyptian bondage, and the rest of God at the close of the creative period; while it was also a "shadow of things to come," meeting a fulfilment under the gospel of Christ, as we shall now see.

A symbol is something that stands as the representative, not of itself, but of something analogous, to which it bears a certain resemblance. The symbol and the thing symbolized stand in different departments, and the thing symbolized is greater than the symbol; therefore the types of the law were not "the very image of the things" that they were intended to represent. The sacrifice of a lamb under the law did not typify the death of another literal lamb, but pointed forward to Christ's sacrificial offering.

Paul names the sabbath as one of the things which were "a shadow of things to come" (Col. 2:17). What

can the sabbath typify? It must symbolize something
in another department that bears a certain analogy to
it. Where shall we look for its fulfilment? Let us
first observe its position in the type; then we can tell
exactly where to look for its position and signification
in the antitype. The sabbath was inscribed on the
tables which were placed in the ark. This is set forth
in the Scriptures as representative of the new covenant
laws *in our hearts* in the gospel age (Heb. 8:9, 10).
Therefore the antitype of the sabbath is also in our
hearts. It can not represent another literal-day sabbath,
for that would destroy the true relation of type and antitype. Besides, as I have already shown, a literal day
can not be written in a person's heart. Not one of the
Old Testament ceremonies represented literal ceremonies
under the gospel, but every one met a *spiritual* fulfilment; accordingly the sabbath commandment reaches
its fulfilment antitypically in something *spiritual* in the
heart. The literal sabbath was bodily rest; the spiritual
sabbath is—what? *Soul-rest.* Praise the Lord! Our
great Redeemer, who has established the new covenant,
said: "Come unto me, all ye that labor and are heavy-
laden and I will give you rest . . . . And ye shall find
rest unto your souls" (Matt. 11:28, 29). "His rest
shall be glorious," exclaimed the prophet (Isa. 11:10),
and all the blood-washed can reply that it is even so.
Glory be to God!

This is the interpretation of the sabbath question
given by the writer of the Hebrews. He first speaks of
the seventh-day sabbath, which he evidently regards as
a type of another "rest," which Christians enter by faith.

"For he spake in a certain place of the seventh day on this wise, And God did rest the seventh day from all his works. And in this place again, If they shall enter into my rest. Seeing therefore that it remaineth that some must enter therein, and they to whom it was first preached entered not in because of unbelief: again he limiteth a certain day, saying in David [the Psalms], Today, after so long a time; as it is said, Today if ye will hear his voice, harden not your hearts. For if Jesus [Joshua, margin] had given them rest, then would he not afterward have spoken of *another day*. THERE REMAINETH THEREFORE A REST TO THE PEOPLE OF GOD. For he that is entered into his rest, he also hath ceased from his own works, as God did from his" (Heb. 4: 4-10). The following facts appear so clear in this scripture that they can not be overlooked:

1. The Israelites, with their seventh day sabbath, did not obtain true rest.

2. Those later, under Joshua, did not obtain it after they were established in Canaan.

3. Therefore David prophesied concerning *"another day,"* which the inspired writer interprets as the gospel day, and which has finally come "after so long a time."

4. "Today"—the gospel day—"there remaineth therefore a rest ["the keeping of a sabbath," margin] to the people of God."

5. This rest, or sabbath, is spiritual in its nature, for it is obtained by faith—*"We which have believed do enter into rest"* (verse 3).

6. This spiritual rest, or sabbath, which "remaineth

to the people of God" is the direct antitype of the seventh-day sabbath. "For he that is entered into his rest, he *also* hath ceased from his own works, *as God did from his."* Notice carefully this sixth point. When God ceased the work of creation, he ceased once for all. Likewise we in obtaining this spiritual sabbath cease perpetually from our own works, as God did from his. This makes our sabbath a perpetual one. Our "own works," from which we must cease forever in order to enter into this rest that "remaineth to the people of God," include everything that is contrary to rest—self, self-efforts, sins, and all. It is by faith that we "enter into rest."

Reader, the true sabbath of the gospel dispensation is not the observance of any literal day. We have a perpetual sabbath, a rest to the soul.

> "How sweet is my rest!
> And how richly I'm blest!
> Oh, how sweet is the rest of my soul!"

Since our sins are all gone and we have indeed "entered into his rest," we are able to "serve him without fear, in *holiness* and righteousness before him, *all the days of our life"* (Luke 1:74, 75). Every day is a day of holiness to the true Christian because in the gospel dispensation holiness is not attached to one day out of seven, but pertains to the man himself; and he must live holily *every day in seven.* And when he really understands the subject, he "esteemeth every day alike" (Rom. 14:5), so far as moral things and moral holiness is concerned.

The removal of the Old Testament system of ceremonial things carried with it also the abolition of its distinctions between meats clean and unclean (Lev. 11). The New Testament knows no such rule. Paul says, "I know, and am persuaded by the Lord Jesus, that there is nothing unclean of itself" (Rom. 14:14). The Christian has liberty to decide every matter of this kind, and to eat any kind of meat that he likes. That this is the New Testament standard can be seen by the following texts: Mark 7:18, 19 (especially in Revised Version); Rom. 14:1-3, 14, 15; 1 Tim. 4:3-5. "Ye are not under the law, but under grace."

NEW TESTAMENT CEREMONIES.

The new covenant, while placed in the hearts of God's people, is not to be hidden there. We have a particular relationship with each other and with a world of sinners. For this reason God has seen fit to give us in this dispensation a system of ceremonial observances designed as channels of expression, through which we manifest openly our redemption, faith, love, and hope, also the spontaneous worship of our hearts.

·The ceremonial observances of the gospel, however, do not possess the rigidity of the law system. Peter describes that system as "a yoke upon the neck of the disciples, which neither our fathers nor we were able to bear" (Acts 15:10). The ceremonies of Christ are no such yoke as that, but they are a yoke nevertheless. "It is good for a man, that he *bear the yoke* in his youth" (Lam. 3:27). Jesus says, "Take my yoke upon you" (Matt. 11:29). There are obligations under the new covenant dispensation, and these we must take. The

Lord, however, has given us this comforting assurance: "My yoke is *easy,* and my burden is *light"* (verse 30).

The great things experienced and enjoyed by the new covenant believer which require open and public manifestation are: 1. Our individual salvation; our private acceptance of Christ and the authority and law of his kingdom. 2. The procuring cause of redemption as experienced in the believer; the ground of all salvation, and the basis of our hopes, present and future—the atonement. 3. The depth of that true and special love which exists between us as the real disciples of Christ. 4. Our worship and our faith. These I will consider in the order given.

1. *Our individual salvation; our private acceptance of Christ and the authority and law of his kingdom.* The external ceremony by which this is manifested publicly to the world is the rite of water-baptism. In this act we testify that our sins are gone; that Christ is our personal Savior; and that we are willing to obey and follow him in all of his commandments. The subject of baptism has been considered at length in Chapter XIII, so that a mere reference to it in this place will suffice.

2. *The procuring cause of redemption; the ground of all salvation, and the basis of our hopes, present and future—the atonement.* The Lord's Supper, or communion, is the outward symbol of this. While in the nature of the case the analogy is not and can not be very prominent, still when it is known that we partake of these natural elements for the express purpose of commemorating

our Lord's sufferings and death, our observing this ordinance shows the reality of our faith in that atonement; that upon it all our hopes are built. For a more complete treatment of this subject, see Chapter XIV.

3. *The depth of that true and special love which exists between us as the real disciples of Christ.* Some one may wonder why an external ceremony should be necessary in order to express this. By what means, then, can it be expressed? If we visit a brother when he is afflicted, do we thereby do any more than sinners? Do they not visit their sick friends? We may give means to help him when he is in distress; sinners do the same by their friends. We may associate closely with him; sinners also form close associations. There is no ordinary act of kindness, respect, or hospitality that will bear convincing proof of the superiority of our brotherly love. How, then, can it be expressed? By our humbly and willingly performing a service for our brethren which sinners do not and will not do.

Here is that New Testament ceremony, in the words of Christ: "If I then, your Lord and Master, have washed your feet: *ye also ought to wash one another's feet.* For I have given you an example *that ye should do as I have done to you*" (John 13: 14, 15). At first Peter objected to this service, but Jesus said to him, "What I do thou knowest not now; but thou shalt know hereafter" (verse 7). Peter did not understand *why* Christ was doing this. After he had finished this work and given the express command that they also should do it (verses 14, 15)—while they were still in the same room and surrounding the same table—he explained .

why he instituted this new service and required it of them. Here are his words: "*A new commandment* I give unto you, That ye love one another *as I have loved you*" (verse 34). The requirement to love, as expressed in ordinary acts of kindness, was not "new"; it is as old as creation. Long before this occasion Christ had given a commandment to love, a commandment so complete as to require them to love even their enemies (Matt. 5:44). But in this place he gave emphatically a "*new commandment,*" and yet a commandment of love. Notice how nicely verse 34 explains verse 15. Verse 15: "ye should do *as I have done to you.*" Verse 34: "Love one another *as I have loved you.*" But why was it given? The next verse explains: "By THIS shall all men know that ye are my disciples, if ye have [such] love one to another" (verse 35). This act truly expresses our deep love for each other, for it is a special act; and at the same time it specially distinguishes us before "all men" as the "disciples" of Christ.

4. *Our worship and our faith.* The worship, praise, and devotion experienced by every saved believer requires external expression, and the faith of the gospel by which he has been saved must be preached to all men, as Christ has commanded; therefore the necessity of public worship. It is certainly in accordance with the law of Christ that his people should at intervals be "gathered together in his name" (Matt. 18:20). In order to accomplish this there must be a *place where* they assemble, and a *time when* they assemble. That the apostolic church had regular public services is shown by the Scriptures. "Not forsaking the assembling of

ourselves together, as the manner of some is" (Heb. 10: 25).

In the old dispensation when the Israelites were established in Palestine, God set his name in Jerusalem, and that city became "the place where men ought to worship" (John 4:20). But Christ taught the woman at the well-side in Samaria that henceforward God's worship would not be localized, either in Jerusalem or in Mount Gerizim, but that the "true worshipers" should "worship the Father in Spirit and in truth" (John 4:21-23). The gospel is to be preached in all the nations. Therefore the New Testament gives us no instructions as to the geographical place where the "true worshipers" are to "assemble together" for divine service. This is left to the judgment of the worshipers themselves.

But as to the *time when* Christians should meet together for public worship, it is possible to have at least a practical uniformity in this respect; therefore the New Testament has left us the example of one particular day in each week, not as a holy sabbath, but as a day of worship. And this is necessary to our spiritual well-being. Men in the world can not assemble together every day for this purpose; so there must be a definite time devoted to the service of God. And when that time is fixed, all Christians must remember the command of the Word, "not forsaking the assembling of ourselves together." Which is the day?

I have already shown that the three preceding ceremonial observances of the New Testament church were established in order to express openly certain things experienced in the heart of the individual believer.

But they also bear a particular relationship with certain facts in the foundation of Christianity itself. Thus, Christian baptism alludes to the death, burial, and resurrection of Christ (Rom. 6: 3-5). Feet-washing among the "saints" (1 Tim. 5: 10) does not stand as an act of brotherly love alone, but we do it *because our Lord did it.* So also the Lord's Supper is not simply the mere communion of saints in a close brotherly bond, but it is also commemorative of the sufferings and death of our Lord Jesus Christ. Then the New Testament day of worship should also bear a particular relation with some fundamental fact in the foundation of Christianity. What shall it commemorate? his atonement? No; that is accomplished by the communion. *His resurrection.*

This "first day of the week" on which our Lord came forth from the dead (Mark 16: 9) was the most glorious day in the history of this world. If it is necessary that there be in the Christian dispensation an institution to commemorate the great fact of Christ's death, then it is positively necessary that there also be in the Christian dispensation something to commemorate the greatest of all events—his resurrection. For "if Christ be not risen, then is our preaching vain, and your faith is also vain" (1 Cor. 15: 14). All the New Testament institutions are distinctively Christian; not one is borrowed from the old dispensation. And if, formerly, the sabbath was given to commemorate the completion of natural creation, how appropriate that the day of Christian worship should commemorate the resurrection of Christ, who thus stands at the head of the new and spiritual creation!

The first meeting of the disciples after the resurrection took place on this day. "Then the same day at evening, *being the first day of the week,* when the doors were shut where the disciples were assembled for fear of the Jews, came Jesus and stood in the midst, and said unto them, Peace be unto you . . . . Then were the disciples glad when they saw the Lord" (John 20: 19, 20).

The second meeting was just one week later. "And after eight days again his disciples were within, and Thomas with them: then came Jesus, the doors being shut, and stood in the midst, and said, Peace be unto you" (verse 26). On this occasion Thomas was glad when he saw the Lord. "After eight days"; that is, after the arrival of the eighth day; the phrase means the same as "the eighth day." This expression, "the eighth day," was so commonly used in the law to signify the completion of one week that it can mean nothing else in this place (see Lev. 23: 35, 36); just as we now mention the eighth tone of the musical scale, meaning the first of the succeeding octave. Nor does the expression *"after* eight days" alter the matter, as we can see by their ordinary mode of expression. Thus, "in three days," "the third day," and *"after* three days" (Matt. 27: 40; Matt. 20: 19; Mark 8: 31) are all used to describe the same period of time. Therefore "in eight days," "the eighth day," and "after eight days" signify the same thing—one week later. Nearly all of the early Christian writers term the resurrection-day the eighth day.

A little later we have the mention of a notable meeting of the church. "And when the day of Pentecost was fully come they were all with one accord in one place" (Acts 2: 1). Pentecost came on the morrow after the Jewish sabbath (Lev. 23:15, 16), therefore was on Sunday, the first day of the week.

We have another meeting of the Christian church on Sunday, which took place at Troas, in Asia Minor. "And upon the first day of the week, when the disciples came together to break bread, Paul preached unto them" (Acts 20: 7). Here we have the communion service on the first day. Now, this meeting did not occur just because the apostle happened to be there that day, for he was there a number of days (see verse 6). But on the first day of the week they came together, and the facts and the language fairly imply that they were in the habit of doing this—"Upon the first day of the week, *when the disciples came together to break bread.*"

While the writer was on a special missionary tour in the Levant, his steamer sailed along the west coast of Asia Minor, following closely the course taken by Paul's ship on the occasion of this visit to Troas; therefore the writer closely observed the typography of the country and the location of these different stopping-places mentioned in Acts 20. The study of these facts throws light on Acts 20: 7. Between Troas and Assos, Cape Baba, the most westerly point in Asia, juts out into the Aegean Sea. Assos is located east of this point, while Troas lies toward the north; the direct distance between these places, across the promontory, being about twenty-two miles. The country here is covered with low ranges of mountains.

According to Acts 20, Paul's trip was from Philippi, in Macedonia, to Jerusalem, and he was evidently in a great hurry, as verse 16 shows. Seven brethren pre-ceded him to Troas and waited for his arrival with Luke. At Troas they waited a number of days, when the eight brethren took ship around this promontory to Assos, leaving Paul behind. "And we went before to ship and sailed unto Assos, there intending to take in Paul: for so had he appointed, minding himself to go afoot. And when he met with us at Assos, we took him in and came to Mitylene" (verses 13, 14).

From this it will be seen that Paul's meeting with the brethren at Troas on the first day of the week was not accidental; because by waiting for this he missed his ship and was obliged to make a long walk of probably twenty-five or thirty miles over the mountains in order to overtake the boat while it waited at Assos on the other side of the promontory. Now, why did Paul choose this laborious alternative? Evidently, because he had a great desire to be at Troas "on the first day of the week, *when the disciples came together* to break bread." On this occasion they probably gathered from the surround-ing country, and the apostle did not want to leave with-out being with them in this general gathering, which would not take place until *"the first day of the week."*

But Paul's waiting here was not because Sunday was so sacred or holy that it would have been a sin to travel then; for Luke, Timothy, Tychicus, Trophimus, and four other brethren went in the ship from Troas, while the apostle remained behind. These facts clearly indicate that "the first day of the week" was their regular meet-ing-day—the day *"when the disciples came together."*

So also the idea of regular meetings on Sunday is

sustained by a proper consideration of 1 Cor. 16:1-4: "Now concerning the collection for the saints as I have given order to the churches of Galatia, even so do ye. *Upon the first day of the week* let every one of you lay by him in store, as God hath prospered him, that there be no gatherings when I come. And when I come, whomsoever ye shall approve by your letters, them will I send to bring your liberality unto Jerusalem. And if it be meet that I go also, they shall go with me." Now, that this collection was a public one and a single one is shown by the fact that it is contrasted with "gatherings when I come." It is also shown by what he wrote to the Roman brethren: "But now I go unto Jerusalem to minister unto the saints. For it hath pleased them of Macedonia and Achaia to make a certain contribution for the poor saints which are at Jerusalem" (Rom. 15:25, 26). This was all the same general effort to raise money, and it was done by "contribution," "collection." The very meaning of "collect" is *to bring together.* Why were the saints at Corinth instructed to bring their offerings together, each one doing his part, on that particular day? The answer is easy, in the light of other scriptures and the practise of the primitive church: Because that was their regular meeting-day. Money thus collected in the "store," or public treasury, would be ready when the apostle came, so that "no gatherings" would be necessary at that time.

This custom, instituted at first for a special purpose, evidently became general in the churches afterwards; for in the second century we find Justin Martyr referring to such regular collection on the first day of the week.

He says: "And on the day called Sunday, all who live in cities or in the country gather together to one place, and the memoirs of the apostles or the writings of the proph- ets are read as long as time permits. And them that are well-to-do and willing, give what each thinks fit: and what is collected is deposited with the president, who succors the orphans and widows, and those . . . . who are in want," etc.—*First Apology of Justin*, Chap. LXVII.

The day of the resurrection was so glorious to the Christian church that it was ever afterwards called "the Lord's day." And it is appropriately thus designated. "The Lord's Supper," commemorating his death, is dis- tinctively Christian; therefore the day of worship, com- memorating his resurrection, must be "the Lord's day." "I was in the Spirit on the Lord's day" (Rev. 1:10). All subsequent Christians called Sunday "the Lord's day." I have before me at this writing many historical evidences, but from lack of space I will refer only to the following writers, all of whom apply the expression "Lord's day" to the first day of the week: "Teaching of the Apostles," A. D. 125; Dionysius, Bishop of Corinth, A. D. 170; Clement of Alexandria, A. D. 194; Origen, A. D. 225; "Apostolical Constitutions," A. D. 250; Antaolius, Bishop of Laodicea, A. D. 270; Victorinus, A. D. 300; Peter, Bishop of Alexandria, A. D. 306; Euse- bius, A. D. 324. No writer has ever once called any day other than Sunday "the Lord's day."

That Sunday was intended to be the worship-day of the Christian church is further shown by the fact that God himself placed his approval and seal upon it, by making it the day of divine revelation, both to the church

itself and to the world. On that day Christ revealed
himself and the most startling facts of his truth to the
assembled disciples (John 20:19). On that day he
revealed himself specially to Thomas, one of the Twelve
(John 20:26-29). On that day the Holy Ghost dispensation began; the Holy Spirit himself was revealed
to the sons of men in a new capacity; the church was
ordained and set in order, clothed with the gifts of the
Spirit. On that day the apostle John in the Isle of Pat-
mos was "in the Spirit," and received the wonderful
visions of the Apocalypse. *Every new, special, and glorious thing on record that God made known to the apostles
in the new dispensation was revealed on the first day of
the week.* It is "the Lord's day," and therefore it was
the Lord's revelation-day.

From this fountain-head of regular weekly worship on
the first day of the week, established by Christ and the
apostles, we can easily trace in a continual stream the
same custom during all of the ages. Space forbids more
than the mere reference to a few.

Pliny, Governor of Bithynia, in Asia Mnor, A. D.
106-108, wrote to the emperor Trajan concerning the
Christians, as following: "They were wont to meet together on a *stated day* before it was light, and sing among
themselves alternately a hymn to Chrst as God." When
was this *"stated day"* that they came together to
worship Christ as God? Eusebius, after referring to a
passage in the Psalms, says, "By this is prophetically
signified the service which is performed very early and
every morning *of the resurrection-day* throughout the
whole world."—*Sabbath Manual,* p 125. This was writ-

ten in Asia Minor, where the churches were thoroughly established by the apostles themselves, and only a few years after the death of the apostles. It was not far from Troas, where the disciples met together for worship "on the first day of the week" when Paul was with them.

Barnabas (A. D. 120) says, "We keep the eighth day with joyfulness, the day, also, on which Jesus rose again from the dead." Chap. XV.

"The Teaching of the Apostles" (A. D. 125) says, "But every Lord's day do ye gather yourselves together, and break bread, and give thanksgiving."

Justin Martyr (A. D. 140) says: "And on the day which is called Sunday, all who live in cities or in the country gather together to one place, and the memoirs of the apostles or the writings of the prophets are read as long as time permits. . . . . *Sunday is the day on which we all hold our common assembly*, because . . . . Jesus Christ, our Savior, on the same day rose from the dead. For he was crucified on the day before that of Saturn [Saturday]; and on the day after that of Saturn, which is the day of the sun [Sunday], having appeared to his apostles and disciples, he taught them these things." —*First Apology of Justin*, Chap. LXVII.

Many other historical quotations might be given, but lack of space forbids.

PERVERSION OF NEW TESTAMENT

CEREMONIES.

Originally, the Lord's day was simply a worship-day. The day itself possessed no more holiness than any other day; therefore the true Christians, in full light, esteemed

"every day alike" in this respect (Rom. 14:5), though
assembling together for worship on the first day of the
week ,as I have shown. Later, however, when the great
apostasy began, and when men began to lose sight of
true spiritual things, they began to attach more and more
importance to external things and attribute to them the
greatest degree of holiness and veneration. In this manner the simple worship-day of the Christians became
idolized as a holy sabbath-day in the place of the Jewish
sabbath of the old dispensation, and almost every text of
Scripture pertaining to the Jewish day was perverted
in its application in order to sustain this extravagant
idea. This has been done by popes, by priests of various
churches, and by Protestant divines. But the saints of
God in this last reformation have learned from the
Scriptures the truth concerning this subject, and we
cling to the simple apostolic standard. Sunday is our
day of special worship, because it was theirs; but true
holiness itself pertains to men, and we must be holy every
day.

The present sectarian conception of holiness, which
centers in sabbath (Sunday) keeping, churches (houses
of worship), and other external things, is the offspring
of the apostasy. And when uncounted thousands, even
millions, of professing Christians live in open sin, pleasure, and revelry all the six days of the week, and then on
the first day walk was careful, solemn tread into their
so-called "holy" churches and perform their "holy"
service on this "holy sabbath-day," it is time for God's
true saints to cry out that such things are an abomination
in the sight of a God who is truly HOLY.

But shall we change our wosrhip from the example set by the apostles, simply because of these extremes concerning Sunday-keeping and Sunday-holiness? Never! The same great apostasy has perverted other institutions of the gospel as well. The Catholic priest takes the bread and wine and (as they say) converts it into the actual body and blood of the Lord, and falls down and worships it. Some Protestants also have adopted nearly the same belief and practise.

If people desire to worship the bread in the sacrament or worship Sunday as a sacred sabbath-day, they may do so on their own responsibility. As for us, we will take the same things and use them in the Bible way, because they are useful and necessary. The bread and the wine in the communion do not differ in their nature from other elements of the same kind; they are merely *put to a different use.* So also the Lord's day is the same to us as are all other days, except in this, that, following the apostolic examples, we *put it to a different use.* Morally there is no difference. No New Testament ordinance or ceremony is termed "holy" in the Bible— not in one single text. New Testament holiness is *"true holiness"* (Eph. 4:24) and pertains not to things, but to redeemed men and women.

"Brethren, ye have been called unto liberty; only use not liberty for an occasion to the flesh, but by love serve one another" (Gal. 5:13). The freedom from legal bondage that we experience must not be allowed to cause us to take extreme positions that will rob us of the true spirit of worship and devotion on the first day of the week, and that will also trample on the religious con-

victions of many who do not have so great a degree of
light and personal freedom. We must learn well and
practise the lesson of Rom. 14: 1-6, so that, though we
"esteem every day alike," we can patiently bear with,
and "despise not," the one who is so "*weak* in the faith"
that he "esteemeth one day above another." Paul set
a good example: "Unto the Jews I became as a Jew,
that I might gain the Jews." This he did for the sake of
his influence, and for the sake of the cause of Christ.
May the Spirit of God so direct us in our conduct on
this day of worship that the precious cause of God will
never, through our indiscretion, suffer reproach. Amen.

CHAPTER XXIII.

THE KINGDOM OF GOD.

The subject of the kingdom of God has been greatly misunderstood by many people. Visionists have dreamed of a coming age of blessedness and earthly glory, while writers have expressed it in loftiest phrase and through highly colored word-pictures, the creations of their own fancy. My purpose, however, is not to set forth a mere theory, no matter how desirable or captivating it may appear, but is to show what the Bible clearly teaches concerning the subject, when all forced and fanciful interpretations are omitted.

THE KINGDOM IN PROPHECY.

During the Babylonish captivity of the Israelites, King Nebuchadnezzar had a dream that directly concerns the subject of the divine kingdom. As the dream passed from the mind of the king, Daniel the prophet was called to make known both the dream and its interpretation. This was a most unreasonable demand, viewed from the human standpoint; yet this circumstance and its results prove to us that the dream was of God. Daniel and his friends prayed earnestly, after which the dream was revealed to the prophet, who thus related it to the king: "Thou, O King, sawest, and behold a great image. This great image, whose brightness was excellent, stood before thee; and the form thereof was terrible. This image's head was of fine gold, his breast and his arms of silver, his belly and his thighs of brass, his legs of iron, his feet part of iron and part of clay. Thou sawest till that a stone was cut out without hands, which smote the image upon his feet that were of iron and clay, and break them to pieces. Then was the iron, the clay, the brass, the silver, and the gold broken to pieces together, and became like the chaff of the summer threshing-floors; and the wind carried them away, that no place was found for them: and the stone that smote the image became a great mountain, and filled the whole earth" (Dan. 2:31-35).

Having made known the dream itself, the prophet then proceeded to show its meaning. "This is the dream; and we will tell the interpretation thereof before the king. Thou, O king, art a king of kings: for the God of heaven hath given thee a kingdom, power, and strength, and glory. And wheresoever the children of men dwell, the beasts of the field and the fowls of the heaven hath he given into thine hand, and hath made thee ruler over them all. *Thou art this head of gold*" (verses 36-38).

So the head of gold represented the Babylonian Empire. Though the prophet addressed the king as this head, yet it is evident that the real signification is the empire itself; for, as we shall see, each of the remaining divisions of this image is treated, not as an individual king, but as a universal empire. At this time the Babylonian kingdom was in the height of its power and glory under Nebuchadnezzar. The city of Babylon was the glory of the East. Its palaces and temples were magnificent; its walls, laid in a square, measured, according to Herodotus, fifteen miles on each side, and rose to the astonishing height of 340 feet and were 85 feet thick.

These with the hanging-gardens were reckoned among the Seven Wonders of the ancient world.

"And after thee shall arise another kingdom inferior to thee" (verse 39). This signifies the Medo-Persian Empire, which conquered Babylon about 538 B. C. and became the second universal empire. "Thy kingdom is divided, and given to the Medes and Persians." "In that night was Belshazzar the king of the Chaldeans slain. And Darius the Median took the kingdom" (Dan. 5: 28, 30, 31).

"And another third kingdom of brass, which shall bear rule over all the earth" (verse 39). This signifies the Greecian Empire which, under Alexander the Great, conquered the Persian Empire, and became the ruling empire of the then-known world.

"And the fourth kingdom shall be strong as iron: forasmuch as iron breaketh in pieces and subdueth all things: and as iron that breaketh all these, shall it break in pieces and bruise. And whereas thou sawest the feet and toes, part of potter's clay, and part of iron, the kingdom shall be divided; but there shall be in it of the strength of the iron, forasmuch as thou sawest the iron mixed with miry clay. And as the toes of the feet were part of iron and part of clay, so the kingdom shall be partly strong, and partly broken. And whereas thou sawest iron mixed with miry clay, they shall mingle themselves with the seed of men: but they shall not cleave one to another, even as iron is not mixed with clay" (verses 40-43). This signifies the Roman Empire, which conquered the Greeks and established itself as the ruling power of the world. This description of Rome includes both her strong and divided condition, but it is all summed up under the one head—"fourth kingdom."

Observe carefully that only four kingdoms are mentioned in this prophecy: 1. "The God of heaven hath given thee a kingdom. . . . . Thou art this head of gold"— Babylonian Empire (verses 37, 38). 2. "After thee shall arise another kingdom"—Medo-Persian (verse 39). 3. "And another third kingdom"—Grecian (verse 39). 4. "And the fourth kingdom"—Roman Empire (verse 40).

"And in the days *of these kings* shall the God of heaven set up a kingdom, which shall never be destroyed: and the kingdom shall not be left to other people, but it shall break in pieces and consume all these kingdoms, and it shall stand forever. Forasmuch as thou sawest that the stone was cut out of the mountain without hands, and that it break in pieces the iron, the brass, the clay, the silver and the gold; the great God hath made known to the king what shall come to pass hereafter: and the dream is certain, and the interpretation thereof sure" (verses 44, 45).

According to this prophecy, the stone which was "cut out without hands" represents the divine kingdom of God as the fifth universal kingdom; and since it smote the fourth division of the image we must therefore look to the time of the reign of the Roman Empire for the establishment of the kingdom of God.

ESTABLISHED BY CHRIST.

The prophet Isaiah also clearly predicts the establishment of this kingdom of God, and he also informs us by whom it is to be established, and *when*. "For unto us a child is born, unto us a son is given: and the government shall be upon his shoulders: and his name shall be called Wonderful, Counselor, The mighty God, The everlasting Father, The Prince of Peace. Of the increase of his government and peace there shall be no end, upon the throne of David, and upon his kingdom, to order it, and to establish it with judgment and with justice from henceforth even forever" (Isa. 9:6, 7).

Now, when this "child is born," when this "son is given," the one who is The mighty God, The Prince of Peace, he will establish *"his kingdom"* "with judgment and with justice," and "of the increase of his government and peace there shall be no end." Every Bible student knows that this refers to Christ. However, let us seal it with the Word. The angel Gabriel said to Mary, the virgin of Nazareth: "Thou shalt conceive in thy womb, and bring forth a son, and thou shalt call his name Jesus. He shall be great, and shall be called the Son of the Highest: and the Lord God shall give unto him the throne of his father David; and he shall reign over the house of Jacob forever; *and of HIS KINGDOM there shall be no end"* (Luke 1:31-33).

Some people are looking for the kingdom of God to come in some future age, but these scriptures clearly locate its coming at the first advent of Christ. It was when he was born into the world as a "son" that he became a king and established his kingdom. He himself taught this during his ministry. When on trial before Pilate, he acknowledged that he had a kingdom, but said, "My kingdom is not of this world." And when Pilate asked, "Art thou a king then?" "Jesus answered, Thou sayest that I am a king. *To this end was I born, and for this cause came I into the world*" (John 18: 36, 37). We must therefore look to his first coming as the time for the establishment of the kingdom. "Now after that John was put in prison, Jesus came into Galilee, preaching the gospel of the kingdom of God, and saying, THE TIME IS FULFILLED, and *the kingdom of God is at hand:* repent ye, and believe the gospel" (Mark 1: 14, 15).

This is in exact accordance with the prophecy of Daniel already given. The "stone" smote the fourth, or Roman, division of the image. So also it was in the days of the Roman Empire that the Christ-child appeared. When this humble babe was born in the city of Bethlehem, Rome was in the height of her glory, and Augustus Cæsar, her proud monarch, ruled over 300,000,000 people. But the kingdom Christ was to establish was destined to overthrow all the kingdoms of pagan darkness and to stand forever.

This kingdom of God on earth was represented by the church of God, and it soon came into conflict with all the vile powers of heathenism enthroned in the Roman Empire. This we have seen and described in chapter XVI. That the application is correct is shown by the twelfth chapter of Revelation. Here the woman, representing the early church, is opposed by the "great dragon, having seven heads, and ten horns" (verse 3). This great dragon, which is easily identified by its heads and horns, symbolizes the Roman Empire under its pagan form. Then appears the warfare of Christ and his angels

against this dragon (verse 7), by which is shown the
early conflict of Christianity with paganism; and the
result is given: "And the great dragon was cast out"
(verse 9). Christianity triumphed over heathenism.
Listen! "And I heard a loud voice saying in heaven,
NOW is come salvation, and strength, *and the kingdom
of our God,* and the power of his Christ: for the accuser of our brethren is cast down. . . . . And they
overcame him by the blood of the Lamb, and by the
word of their testimony; and they loved not their lives
unto the death" (verses 10, 11). How clearly this ful-
fils the prediction of Daniel 2 concerning the stone that
smote the image!

Notice how plainly the time of its accomplishment is
given. It was after the death of Christ, for it was by
the "blood of the Lamb" that the victory was gained.
It was before the papal age, because after this victory
the woman "fled into the wilderness" for the period of
1260 years, during which time the beast ruled (verse 14
and chap. 13: 1-8). In the vision of Daniel the stone
was cut out before it smote the image; so also Christ
appeared and established his gospel a little before its
conflict with heathenism.

The time of the establishment of Christ's kingdom is
also shown in Daniel 2 by another means. The burden
of Nebuchadnezzar's dream was to set forth the truth
concerning the kingdom of God. All the rest is comparatively unimportant, only preliminary to the great climax
when the stone smites the image, breaking it, and itself
becomes a great mountain and fills the whole earth.
The prophet said "There is a God in heaven that re-

vealeth secrets, and maketh known to the king Nebuchadnezzar what shall be *in the latter days*" (verse 28).
The expression "in the latter days," as used by Old
Testament writers, is interpreted by the apostles as
applying to their time. Thus, Peter says, "*This is that*
which was spoken by the prophet Joel; And it shall
come to pass *in the last days*, saith God, I will pour
out of my Spirit upon all flesh" (Acts 2: 16, 17). The
writer of Hebrews says, "God, who at sundry times and
in divers manners spake in time past unto the fathers
by the prophets, hath in *these last days* spoken unto us
by his Son" (Heb. 1: 1, 2).

The message of the kingdom of God was introduced
by John. "In those days came John the Baptist, preaching in the wilderness of Judea, and saying, Repent ye:
for the kingdom of heaven is at hand" (Matt. 3: 1, 2).
And Jesus bore witness to this work of John by saying,
"The law and the prophets were until John: since that
time the kingdom of God is preached, and every man
presseth into it" (Luke 16: 16). Then the same message was taken up by Christ, who preached "the gospel
of the kingdom of God, and saying, *the time is fulfilled*,
and the kingdom of God is at hand: repent ye, and
believe the gospel" (Mark 1: 14, 15).

Many teachers who have accepted the theory of a
coming earthly kingdom find it difficult indeed to evade
the force of all these scriptures that so clearly point
to the first advent of Christ as the time of the establishment of his kingdom. In order to accomplish their end
and save their theory from utter destruction, some of
them try to make a distinction between the kingdom of

heaven and the kingdom of God, saying that one was given when Christ appeared the first time, but that the other is reserved for his second coming. Now, the object of this book is not to combat every theory of men, but to show what the Bible teaches. This I shall do in this case by showing that the New Testament makes no such distinction between the kingdom of heaven and the kingdom of God, but *applies both expressions to the same thing*.

1. John preached, "The kingdom of heaven is at hand" (Matt. 3:1, 2). "The law and the prophets were until John: since that time the kingdom of God is preached" (Luke 16:16).

2. "Blessed are the poor in spirit: for theirs is the kingdom of heaven" (Matt. 5:3). "Blessed be ye poor: for yours is the kingdom of God" (Luke 6:20).

3. Concerning John. "He that is least in the kingdom of heaven is greater than he" (Matt. 11:11). "He that is least in the kingdom of God is greater than he" (Luke 7:28).

4. "It is given unto you to know the mysteries of the kingdom of heaven" (Matt. 13:11). "Unto you it is given to know the mystery of the kingdom of God" (Mark 4:11).

5. "The kingdom of heaven is like to a grain of mustard-seed" (Matt. 13:31). "Whereunto shall I liken the kingdom of God? . . . . It is like a grain of mustard-seed" (Mark 4:30, 31).

6. "The kingdom of heaven is like unto leaven, which a woman took, and hid in three measures of meal" (Matt. 13:33). "Whereunto shall I liken the kingdom of God?

It is like leaven, which a woman took and hid in three measures of meal" (Luke 13:20, 21).

The kingdom of heaven and the kingdom of God are the same thing.

NATURE OF CHRIST'S KINGDOM.

Jesus said, "My kingdom is not of this world" (John 18:36). Earthly kingdoms are of one nature; the kingdom of God is another. Now, we can determine the nature of God's kingdom on earth by what the Scriptures have to say about it.

1. *It is a doctrine.* "Go thou and preach the kingdom of God" (Luke 9:60). "The kingdom, of God is preached, and every man presseth into it" (Luke 16:16). The entire message of the gospel is "preaching the things concerning the kingdom of God" (Acts 8:12). In some manner the kingdom of God is so contained in and expressed by the gospel that the preaching of that gospel is called the preaching of the kingdom of God.

2. *It is an experience.* This is indicated by the fact that we are commanded to seek for it. "But seek ye first the kingdom of God, and his righteousness" (Matt. 6:33). "The kingdom of God is preached, and every man *presseth into it*" (Luke 16:16). This shows that it is an experience to be obtained by earnest effort. It is therefore spiritual in its nature. "And when he was demanded of the Pharisees, when the kingdom of God should come, he answered them and said, The kingdom of God cometh not with observation: neither shall they say, Lo here! or, lo there! for, behold, *the kingdom of God is within you*" (Luke 17:20, 21). What a clear

contrast between the nature of Christ's kingdom and
that of earthly kingdoms! Earthly kingdoms are introduced with great external pomp and display; but Jesus
says, "My kingdom is not of this world." It is not
"here" or "there," for it is not localized in any particular geographical locality, but is spiritual in its nature
and "within you," that is, if you have earnestly sought
it acording to Christ's command and "pressed into it."

> "The kingdom of God is within you
> So the greatest of teachers hath said;
> And the faithful and loving have found it,
> And enjoyed it before they were dead."

3. *It is the present inheritance of the saints.* In the
very first century of Christian grace John testified that
he was *"in the kingdom* and patience of Jesus Christ"
(Rev. 1: 9). Paul instructs the Colossians to give thanks
unto the Father, which hath made us meet to be partakers of the inheritance of the saints in light: who hath
delivered us from the power of darkness, and hath
translated us *into the kingdom of his dear Son"* (Col.
1: 12, 13). Yea, "the kingdom of God is preached,
and *every man presseth into it"* (Luke 16: 16). "For
the kingdom of God is not meat and drink; but *righteousness and peace and joy in the Holy Ghost"* (Rom.
14: 17).

> "There's a theme that is sweet to my mem'ry,
> There's a joy that I can not declare,
> There's a treasure that gladdens my being;
> 'Tis the kingdom of righteousness here.

> "There's a scene of its grandness before me,
> Of its greatness there can be no end;
> It is joy, it is peace, it is glory;
> In my heart, how these riches do blend!

" 'Tis a kingdom of peace, it is reigning within,
    It shall ever increase in my soul;
We possess it right here when he saves from all sin,
    And 'twill last while the ages shall roll."

4. *It is a visible working-force.* "I tell you of a truth,
there be some standing here, which shall not taste of
death, till they see the kingdom of God" (Luke 9:27).
"Verily I say unto you, That there be some of them
that stand here, which shall not taste of death, till they
have *seen the kingdom of God come with power*" (Mark
9:1). It is evident that another phase of the kingdom
is here set forth; for as a doctrine it had already been
preached; as an experience, some had already sought
it and pressed into it. But here is a distinct, visible
phase that was to be manifested during the lifetime of
some who were then present and heard the words of
Christ. This phase of the kingdom is identical with
the church of God as a visible, working-force in the
world; and as, on the day of Pentecost, the church was
fully organized and set in order, and dedicated by a
most wonderful outpouring of the Holy Spirit, they indeed saw the kingdom of God come with power (see
Luke 24:49).

A REIGN ON THE EARTH.*

In this organic form the kingdom of God shone forth
gloriously in the morning of this dispensation. In the
visions of the Apocalypse, John saw this blessed trium-
phal reign of the saints on earth; for at the very open-

*The subject of the kingdom of God, as set forth in the
remainder of this chapter, is well illustrated in the large
diagram entitled "The Church in Prophecy and History,"
which is inserted at the beginning of Chapter XVI. This
should be consulted by the reader.

ing of the plan of redemption by Christ, the blood-washed took up the new song of redemption, saying, "Thou art worthy to take the book, and to open the seals thereof: for thou wast slain, and hast redeemed us to God by thy blood out of every kindred, and tongue, and people, and nation; and hast made us unto our God kings and priests, *and we shall reign on the earth*" (Rev. 5: 9, 10). This does not refer to some future reign on the earth, but describes the reign of righteousness enjoyed by the people of God at the very beginning of the gospel dispensation. They were already kings and priests unto God. Peter describes them thus: "Ye are a chosen generation, a royal priesthood [kingly priesthood; that is, a priesthood of kings], a holy nation, a peculiar people; that ye should show forth the praises of him who hath called you out of darkness into his marvelous light" (1 Pet. 2: 9). And Paul declares that "they which receive abundance of grace and of the gift of righteousness shall *reign in life* by one Jesus Christ" (Rom. 5: 17). This "reign on the earth" was a real, public one, coexistent and coextensive with the triumph of the apostolic church itself. It was when the church conquered paganism that the cry went up, "Now is come salvation, and strength, *and the kingdom of our God,* and the power of his Christ" (Rev. 12: 10).

A REIGN WITH CHRIST.

But this phase of the kingdom, which is identical with the visible church in its organic form, was not to continue thus. In order to understand the teaching of the Word concerning the kingdom subsequent to its estab-

lishment, we must understand the teaching concerning
the church subsequent to its establishment. In Chapter
XVI we showed, from Revelation 12, that the church is
set forth under a double symbol—a woman and her son—
in order to show two phases of her existence during the
apostasy. The phase represented by the man-child who
was "caught up unto God and to his throne" is that
phase of the church which was cut off from the earth
through martyrdom and persecution; while the phase
represented by the woman who "fled into the wilderness"
is that phase of the church which continued on earth, but
was hidden in the great apostasy. With these thoughts
in mind we will approach the twentieth chapter of
Revelation.

The reader should observe that the prophecies of the
Revelation are laid out in parallel series covering the
gospel dispensation; that one theme is taken up and carried through until the end, and then the narrative returns to take up another theme, or a different phase of
the same thing, covering the same ground, and termina-
ting at the same point. Now, the last verses of Revelation 19 ends one series of prophecy, showing the overthrow of certain evil powers in the lake of fire. Then
chapter 20 *begins a new series of prophecy* covering the
gospel dispensation likewise, and ending at the same
point—the lake of fire (verse 15). *Observe this carefully*—that the leading events of this chapter take place
before the second coming of Christ and the judgment-
scene, and not afterwards (verses 11, 12). In other
words, these leading events do not follow the second
coming and judgment described in chapter 19, *but pre-*

cede it; being themselves followed by the second coming and general judgment.

"And I saw an angel come down from heaven, having the key of the bottomless pit and a great chain in his hand. And he laid hold on the dragon, that old serpent, which is the devil, and Satan, and bound him a thousand years, and cast him into the bottomless pit, and shut him up, and set a seal upon him that he should deceive the nations no more, until the thousand years should be fulfilled: and after that he must be loosed a little season" (Rev. 20: 1-2).

Many people who read this scripture just conclude without investigation or reason that the angel represents Christ and that this is his second coming. But, as I have just shown, all this series of prophecy takes place before his second coming and the general resurrection and judgment. Furthermore, in the Revelation an angel is never used to represent Christ, for he who claims equality with God can not be symbolized by a created intelligence. Whenever Christ appears on the symbolic scene, as in chapter 19, he appears in his own character, unrepresented by another. "And he hath on his vesture and on his thigh a name written, KING OF KINGS, AND LORD OF LORDS" (chap. 19:16).

The description of this overthrow of the dragon by a mighty angel is exactly parallel chronologically with the overthrow of the dragon by primitive Christianity, described in chapter 12. There is only one dragon mentioned in the Revelation. In chapter 12, where he first appears, he is described as *a* great red dragon; but in every subsequent place where he is referred to he is mentioned as *the* dragon, showing that it is the same dragon. In chapter 12 the dragon that was "cast out" was termed "that old serpent, *called* the devil, and Satan, which deceiveth the whole world" (verse 9). So also in chapter 20 he is described as "that old serpent, which is the devil, and Satan," and he was "*cast* into the bottomless pit," that he should "deceive the nations no more." Any one can see by comparison that we have here two parallel series, covering in some respects two separate phases of thought, and yet each sustaining and explaining the other.

In chapter 12, after the first triumphs of Christianity a great change takes place. The phase of the church, or kingdom, represented by the man-child is, through persecution and martyrdom, "caught up unto God and to his throne," while the woman flees into obscurity for 1260 years. The beast takes the place of the dragon and destroys God's saints (chap. 13: 1-8), and is in turn succeeded by "another beast," which makes an image to the first one (chap. 13: 11-14).

Here in chapter 20 nothing is said about the woman in the wilderness, but the narrative takes up the other phase (the man-child), which was caught up unto God, and there lived and reigned. "And I saw thrones, and they sat upon them, and judgment was given unto them: and I saw the souls of them that were beheaded for the witness of Jesus, and for the word of God, and which have not worshiped the beast, neither his image, neither had received his mark upon their foreheads, or in their hands; and *they* lived and reigned with Christ a thousand years" (verse 4). Notice carefully the facts:

1. It was the "*souls* of them that were beheaded for the witness of Jesus" that "reigned with Christ."

2. Not one word is said about people's being literally resurrected and reigning. This reign was *before the resurrection of the literal dead,* for the resurrection of these does not take place until *after* the one thousand years, at the end of this series of prophecy, and includes both classes, good and bad; for some are found written in the book of life, while some are not (verses 11-15).

3. There is no reign on the earth mentioned here at all; the reign was "with Christ." How well this agrees with Paul's statement, "I am in a straight betwixt two, having a desire to depart, and to be *with Christ;* which is far better: nevertheless to abide in the flesh is more needful for you" (Phil. 1: 23, 24)!

But let us notice some positive proofs that these individuals were not literally resurrected and were not reigning on the earth at all. John saw them at another time, and describes them thus: "And when he had opened the fifth seal, I saw under the altar the *souls* of them that were slain for the word of God, and for the testimony which they held: and they cried with a loud voice, saying, How long, O Lord, holy and true, dost thou not judge and avenge our blood on them that dwell on the earth? And white robes were given unto every one of them; and it was said unto them that they should rest yet for a little season, until their fellow servants also and their brethren, *that should be killed as they were* should be fulfilled" (Rev. 6: 9-11). Here again we have the same persons symbolized by the man-child of chapter 12. They were souls in a disembodied state. They were not on the earth, but they were in a state of "rest" "with Christ."

These scriptures, considered together, blend in one harmonious whole. First the church reigns publicly on the earth, but this phase is cut off by the apostasy on the one hand and by the persecutions of the beast on the other; and, being thus interrupted on the earth, the scene suddenly changes to the realm of paradise, and we see that the souls of the martyrs are reigning there. They "rest" while they "reign with Christ," and they "wait" for the end of that earthly reign of tyranny and usurpation in which their "fellow servants also and their brethren" are being killed as they were.

The special time, then, during which this reign above is brought to our view is that period during which God's people on earth were martyred for the testimony of Jesus. At the end of this period, as we shall presently show, the scene is again laid upon earth and the triumph of the church and spiritual reign of the kingdom is again manifested. But as the public reign of the apostolic church ceased *gradually*, and as its restoration in the last days also takes place gradually, no exact dates for this phase of the subject can be given; therefor the indefinite period of time that elapsed between the two is simply stated by the term "a thousand years." This is not literally 1,000 years, for that would be less than the reign of the papacy, which was 1260 years; while the period under consideration not only covers that period, but also extends into the Protestant era; for Protestantism, as we have shown, also martyred some of God's witnesses during its earlier days. Furthermore, all the time-periods mentioned in the Revelation are symbolic, not literal. If a literal period of 1,000 years had been intended, the prediction would probably have said "a thousand *days*"; just as the 1260 years are symbolized by "a thousand two hundred and three score *days*."

THE FIRST RESURRECTION.

"But the rest of the dead lived not again until the thousand years were finished. *This is the first resurrection.* Blessed and holy is he that hath part in the first resurrection: on such the second death hath no power, but they shall be priests of God and of Christ, and shall reign with him a thousand years" (Rev. 20: 5, 6).

Here we have a resurrection to life that is called the "first resurrection"; but notice that in verse 5 this first resurrection takes place *after* the one thousand years: "But the rest of the dead lived not again until the thousand years were finished. THIS *is the first resurrection.*" How utterly fatal this is to that millennial heresy which teaches that the first resurrection is the literal resurrection of saints at Christ's coming and that they *afterwards* reign with him a thousand years! But verse 6 teaches also that those who reigned with Christ during the thousand years mentioned had taken part in the first resurrection. This shows positively that the first resurrection is of such a nature as to include people both before and after the period of one thousand years. But I have already shown from the Scriptures that those who reigned with Christ during this thousand years were disembodied souls; still, they had had part in this "first resurrection." Here also we have. definite proof that the "first resurrection" is not a literal one. It is both before and after the one thousand years, and still is all *before* the literal resurrection at Christ's second coming, when "the dead small and great stand before God" (verse 12). In the following chapter I shall show by many texts that are not involved in prophetic interpretations that there is but one literal resurrection of the dead, and that both the righteous and the wicked will be raised at the same time. What, then, is the "first resurrection"?

According to verse 6, the first resurrection makes men "blessed and. *holy.*" According to the Scriptures, men must receive a spiritual resurrection, or quickening, before they can be made *holy;* for they are represented as "*dead* in trespasses and in sins" (Eph. 2: 1). "And you being *dead in your sins* . . . . hath he quickened together with him, having forgiven you all trespasses" (Col. 2: 13). That the act of salvation, which makes us alive in Christ, is Scripturally "the first resurrection" is proved most positively by the words of Christ himself: "Verily, verily, I say unto you, The hour is coming, *and now is,* when the *dead* shall hear the voice of the Son of God: and they that hear shall *live*" (John 5: 25, 24). "WE KNOW that we have *passed from death unto life*" (1 John 3: 14). It was this spiritual resurrection that made the martyrs blessed and holy, and fitted them to "reign with Christ" in a disembodied state in "rest" and peace, while *waiting* for their fellow servants on earth to be killed as they were.

In chapter 20 of the Revelation the people of God who have had "part in the first resurrection" are brought

to view as two great companies: those *before* the period
of the thousand years; and the remainder—symbolized
by "the rest of the dead," verse 5—*after* the close of
that period. Such have been the facts in the case. A
great host of people were saved before the great apostasy, and another mighty host are now being quickened
into spiritual life since the period of the apostasy; but
it is all "the first resurrection," as verses 5 and 6 show.

"And when the thousand years are expired, Satan
shall be loosed out of his prison, and shall go out to deceive the nations which are in the four parts of the earth,
Gog and Magog, to gather them together to battle: the
number of whom is as the sand of the sea. And they
went out on the breadth of the earth, and compassed the
camp of the saints about and the beloved city: and fire
came down from God out of heaven, and devoured them"
(Rev. 20: 7-9).

Now, the dragon that Christianity overthrew originally was paganism as enthroned in the Roman Empire.
It was not the civil power itself that the Christians at-
tacked, but that huge system of false doctrine which
stood opposed, both in nature and in spirit, to the spirit
of Christ and Christianity. So in the release of the
dragon in the last days we must look for some power
that is antichristian both in nature and in spirit. The
forms of paganism were many; so also there may be
divers forms of the same old dragon-power manifested
now; but the object of all is to oppose the true spiritual
standard of Jesus Christ. And considering the fact
that the real truth is now in the world, we may expect
the opposition to be of the most subtle and deceptive kind.

The special efforts of Satan against the truth of the Bible can be traced definitely in modern times since the period of the French Revolution. Just prior to this time the infidel philosophers of France had ridiculed everything in the basis of Christianity, and when the people were persuaded of these things so skilfully presented to them, they determined to cast away the religion of Christ altogether and revel in their madness. But the opposition has not always been in this form. By the most subtle methods Satan has sought to undermine faith in the Bible and Christianity. The very dregs of paganism itself are found in the system of Freemasonry, which is spread broadcast everywhere. Such is only a revival of the ancient pagan mysteries. And spiritualism is the direct work of the devil, a revival of the necromancy and magic of ancient heathenism. Christian Science, "falsely so-called" (1 Tim. 6: 20), is another movement of Satan, in which the fantastic idealism of the Gnostics is revived. The dragon is loose in many forms and is deceiving the nations, and all for the purpose of gathering them together against the real truth and work of God.

"And I saw three unclean spirits like frogs come out of the mouth of the dragon, and out of the mouth of the beast, and out of the mouth of the false prophet. For they are the spirits of devils, working miracles, which go forth unto the kings of the earth and of the whole world, to gather them to the battle of that great day of God almighty" (Rev. 16: 13, 14). The dragon when released in these days is not satisfied to work by himself and oppose Christ directly, but he seeks a union with the vile spirits of the beast and of the false prophet.

May God help every honest soul in Babylon to hear the voice of heaven and "come out" (Rev. 18:4). This last reformation is now gathering together the saints of God into their "beloved city," the true church; while Satan is gathering together all the powers of wickedness and deception.

ANOTHER "REIGN ON THE EARTH."

It will be seen that in Rev. 20:8, 9 the subject is not the reign of the martyrs in paradise, but that we have once more in prominence *"the camp of the saints"* "ON THE EARTH." Here we have the mighty host who have had "part in the first resurrection" *after the close of the thousand-year period,* reigning in triumph and victory; while the powers of evil are gathering together for the final conflict. The scene is brought to a close by the second coming of Christ, the literal resurrection of the dead, and the general judgment (verses 10-15).

The fact that the reign of God's people on earth is divided into two distinct periods is shown also by other prophecies. In the seventh chapter of Daniel is recorded a vision of four great beasts, symbolizing the Babylonian, Medo-Persian, Grecian, and Roman empires. Verse 18, connected with Dan. 2:31-44 (already given in this chapter), shows that the saints were to possess the kingdom of God before the overthrow of these four kingdoms; which are fulfilled, as we have seen, by the establishment of Christianity by Christ during the reign of the Roman Empire. Then follows a description of the rise of the papacy, which was to *"wear out the saints of the Most High"* for a period of 1260 years (verses 19-25). This, as before explained, reaches to A. D. 1530. During this period the public reign of the saints on earth largely ceased. Then, immediately following, it is said, "The judgment shall sit, and they shall take away his dominion, to consume and destroy it *unto the end*" (verse 26). This does not refer to the final judgment; it is a spiritual judgment that commences before that time and continues "unto the end." During the Protestant era spiritual reformations from time to time brought judgment against that beast-power which had for ages "worn out the saints of the Most High." In these spiritual reformations many people were resurrected to spiritual life in Christ. But a little later the real spiritual reign of the saints is perfectly restored in the pure gospel light of the evening time; and now the next verse is fulfilled, which says, "AND THE KINGDOM AND DOMINION, AND THE GREATNESS OF THE KINGDOM UNDER THE WHOLE HEAVEN, SHALL BE GIVEN TO THE PEOPLE OF THE SAINTS OF THE MOST HIGH, WHOSE KINGDOM IS AN EVERLASTING KINGDOM" (verse 27).

"Fear not little flock, it is your Father's good pleasure to give you the kingdom" (Luke 12:32). The little stone of Nebuchadnezzar's vision shall yet "become *a great mountain* and FILL THE WHOLE EARTH."

THE UNIVERSAL KINGDOM.

Thus far we have considered the subject of the kingdom of God chiefly from the standpoint of Christ's spiritual work on the earth, either in the hearts of his people, as a spiritual experience, or in his church, as a visible organic movement. But there is another distinct phase that we must understand in order to harmonize all the facts. This is the universal phase. Christ is now universal King, Lord of heaven and earth. Before his ascension he claimed this dominion, saying, "All power is given unto me in heaven and in earth" (Matt. 28:18). This universal dominion is expressed by Paul thus: "Which he wrought in Christ, when he raised him from the dead, and set him at his own right hand in the heavenly places, far above all principality and power, and might, and dominion, and every name that is named, not only in this world but also in that which is to come: and hath put all things under his feet, and gave him to be head over all things" (Eph. 1:20-22).

Peter describes Christ's universal reign thus: "Who is gone into heaven, and is on the right hand of God; angels and authorities and powers being made subject unto him" (1 Pet. 3:22). Christ is now the universal King, yea, "King of kings, and Lord of lords."

> "The universe is God's domain,
>   He built it all his own;
> Though men and devils do, in vain,
>   Conspire against his throne."

Viewed from this standpoint, the earth as a whole "is the Lord's, and the fulness thereof; the world and them that dwell therein" (Psa. 24:1). The whole earth and universe is his kingdom; therefore all sinners and evil men are in his (universal) kingdom, but they exist as rebels against his throne, dominion, and authority. At one time all the world was in sin. Justice would have

sanctioned the complete destruction of this entire host
of rebels; but love and mercy sought for expression;
therefore the pure elements of heaven were again
brought to earth and planted here, in the form of the
gospel and the spiritual kingdom of God, the object of
which is to give all rebels an opportunity to obtain
mercy by submitting to the divine authority of the great
king of the universe. But this will not always continue. Christ can not long endure in his universal kingdom those who rebel against his law; therefore at his
second coming "the Son of man shall send forth his
angels, and they shall *gather out of his kingdom all*
things that offend, and them which do iniquity; and shall
cast them into a furnace of fire: there shall be wailing
and gnashing of teeth. THEN SHALL THE RIGHT-
EOUS SHINE FORTH AS THE SUN IN THE
KINGDOM OF THEIR FATHER" (Matt. 13:41-43).

This is the grand end of earthly things, when Christ
will be revealed from heaven at the last day, when the
wicked will be banished forever from the universe of God's
dwelling, and our Lord will be "glorified in his saints,"
who will be received into heaven itself (2 Thess. 1:7-
10). Then the present spiritual phase of the earthly
kingdom will be swallowed up in the great universal
kingdom, and thus there will be administered to us an
abundant entrance "into the everlasting kingdom of our
Lord and Savior Jesus Christ" (2 Pet. 1:11).

This final change with reference to the earthly phase
of the kingdom will also be accompanied by a change in
the relationship of Christ as reigning King over the redeemed of earth. "As in Adam all die, even so in

Christ shall all be made alive [raised from the dead]. But every man in his own order: Christ the first-fruits; afterward they that are Christ's at his coming. Then cometh the end, when he shall have delivered up the kingdom to God, even the Father; when he shall have put down all rule and all authority and power. For he must reign, till he hath put all his enemies under his feet. The last enemy that shall be destroyed is death. . . . . And when all things shall be subdued unto him, then shall the Son also himself be subject unto him that put all things under him, that God may be all in all" (1 Cor. 15:22-28). Now notice carefully the facts as brought forth heretofore and as clearly stated in these verses:

1. Christ is now universal King.

2. "He must reign"—continue to reign—"till he hath put all his enemies under his feet."

3. "The *last enemy* that shall be destroyed is death." Now, this destruction will be accomplished by the resurrection. But the entire reign of Christ is to take place *before* this resurrection; for death is "the *last enemy*" that he will conquer. Then "he shall have put down all rule and all authority and power." What, then, takes place at the time of the resurrection and the destruction of the "last enemy?" Answer: *"Then* THE END." The word "cometh" is not in the original. *"Then the end* when he shall have DELIVERED UP THE KING-DOM to God, even the Father" (verse 24). The time when millennialists expect Christ to come, set up a king-dom, and *begin* to reign is the very time Paul points out as the *end* of Christ's personal redemptive reign, when

he "shall have DELIVERED UP THE KINGDOM to God, even the Father."

Our Lord is now the reigning King of earth and heaven. At the cross he conquered sin; through his church he conquered paganism in the Roman Empire; through the Reformation he broke the power of the papacy; through his pure church and restored kingdom he is now conquering the spiritual powers of darkness; and those who do not yield to the persuasive influences of his Spirit when manifested lovingly through a moral system, he will subdue by force and judgment at his coming, at which time "the last enemy"—death—shall be destroyed.

"And when all these things shall be subdued unto him, then shall the Son also himself be subject unto him that put all things under him, that God may be all in all" (verse 28).

DOCTRINE OF FINAL
THINGS.

CHAPTER XXIV

SECOND COMING OF CHRIST.

After his resurrection from the dead Christ remained with his disciples many days, speaking of the things pertaining to the kingdom of God; then he led them out on the mount Olivet, near Bethany, and here gave them the final commission to preach in his name among all the nations. "And when he had spoken these things, while they beheld, he was taken up; and a cloud received him out of their sight. And while they looked steadfastly toward heaven as he went up, behold, two men stood by them in white apparel; which also said, Ye men of Galilee, why stand ye gazing up into heaven? This same Jesus which is taken up from you into heaven *shall so come in like manner as ye have seen him go into heaven*" (Acts 1:9-11). Christ had already informed them of his departure, but said to them, "I WILL COME AGAIN" (John 14:3).

In the New Testament much importance is attached to the second coming of Christ. The Scriptures uniformly point forward to that event as the time when the dead will be raised, when the general judgment will take place and final rewards be meted out to the righteous and to the wicked. "The Son of man shall come in the glory of his Father with his angels, and *then* he shall reward every man according to his works" (Matt. 16:27). 2 Thess. 1:7-11 clearly shows that the wicked "shall be punished with everlasting destruction," and the saints "glorified," "when the Lord Jesus shall be revealed from heaven with his mighty angels."

It is a popular doctrine in the world that men and women receive their final rewards at death; but the Bible nowhere teaches this. The texts last quoted, as well as scores of others, point forward to the second coming as the time when final rewards will be given. And since the Scriptures are harmonious on the point that our final rewards and punishments are not received at death, some teachers go to the opposite extreme and teach that when a person dies that is the last there is of him until the resurrection-day; that this interval, perhaps many thousands of years, is passed in silence and unconsciousness.

THE INTERMEDIATE STATE.

That this last position is entirely wrong I shall proceed to show. In Chapter II of the present work, where the nature of man was discussed, abundant evidences were brought forth from the Scriptures showing that the soul of man survives the death of the body and remains in a *conscious* state hereafter. These proofs do not require repetition in this place. But I wish to give one more thought on that point; namely:

1. *The fact of resurrection itself necessitates the survival of the soul after death.* After death the body decomposes, as we all know, and its elements may enter into and help to compose grass, plants, and trees, or the bodies of other organic beings or else lie in the dust of the earth. Now, if the real man himself, the human spirit, does not survive the decomposition of the body,

how can there be a resurrection of this man? Says one,
"God can bring together the same bodily elements that
decompose." True, God can do such a thing; but if
that is all there is to the subject, would it not be creation
instead of resurrection? The act whereby man was first
formed from the dust and given life is called "creation."
Would not this second act be as truly a creative one as
the first? To bring into existence something that does
not exist is to create; therefore if the man himself does
not really exist between death and the judgment, then
another creation is necessary. The individual in the
second creation might be like the first one, but would it
be the same man?

*Identity of the man himself is not secured through
sameness of bodily elements.* This we can prove in this
world. Our bodies are constantly changing. Physiol-
ogy informs us that we have an entirely new, or different,
body every seven years. But though we possess many
bodies successively there remains throughout a unity and
continuity of the essential *self.* We remember things
which took place many years ago. We know that we
are identically the same persons that we were then. This
proves that identity of self is secured through the spirit,
and not through physical, bodily elements.

Again, *memory requires the continued existence of
that which remembers.* Carbon, potash, iron, and lime
remember nothing; therefore though these and other
identical elements which compose our bodies in this world
are brought together in the second creation, *they can
bring with them no memory of past events.* If they
could, they would be very apt to trouble us with mem-

ories of their association with grass, plants, and animals, when they formed a part of these organisms. But the Bible teaches that the final judgment laid upon the resurrected man will be based on "the things done in his body, according to that he hath done, whether it be good or bad" (2 Cor. 5:10). Where is his memory of past events, and conscience? Bodily elements remember nothing. Non-existence remembers nothing. The poor man, sentenced to eternal doom, has no idea why he is punished. Having no direct connection with a former existence, he remembers nothing; therefore he can have no conscience-pangs.

No, reader, it is not thus. The real man survives in conscious existence, and therefore the same man that committed the offense will be punished, or the same man that served God upon earth will be eternally rewarded.

What, then, is the state of man between natural death and the resurrection? Peter plainly tells us that God hath *"reserved* the unjust unto the day of judgment to be punished" (2 Pet. 2:9). But where has God reserved the wicked? This question is well answered in the following quotation from H. M. Riggle's work "Man: His Present and Future," Pp. 81-87:

"Let the Word answer: 'Reserved in everlasting chains under darkness unto the judgment of the great day' (Jude 6). 'He hath kept in perpetual chains under thick darkness for the judgment of the great day.'—*Emphatic Diaglott.* 'For if God spared not the angels that sinned, but cast them down to hell, and delivered them unto chains of darkness, to be reserved unto judgment' (2 Pet. 2:4). 'For messengers that sinned God spared not, but, consigning them to *the lowest Hades,* to pits of gloom delivered them up, for judgment to be kept' —*Rotherham.* 'Cast them into dungeons.'—*Revised* (note). 'Having cast them to the deepest abyss.'—*Inter-linear.* 'Plunging them into Tartarus, delivering them up in chains to be kept in darkness till the judgment.' —*Sawyer.* 'Confirming them in Tartarus.'—*Campbell, McKnight, Emphatic Diaglott.*

"Whether the word 'messenger' here refers to angelic beings or to fallen ministers, the truth remains the same. Fallen demons have not yet received their punishment (see Matt. 8:29; Rev. 20:10). These, together with the spirits of wicked men, are reserved—kept—in 'chains of thick darkness' in 'the lowest Hades.' There in 'pits of gloom' they await an awful doom, which will fall upon them at the judgment. 'Shall burn unto the lowest hell [Sheol, Hebrew; lowest Hades, Greek]' (Deut. 32:22). 'Delivered my soul from the lowest hell [Hades].' The name lowest Hades is Tartarus. The original word is *Tartaroo.* Confined in Tartarus, wicked spirits and demons are reserved unto the day of judgment to be punished.

"No wonder dying skeptics and sinners have uttered words in their last breath like the following: 'I am taking an awful leap into the dark.' As such are forced out from the clay covering into the spirit-world, and know of a certainty the fearful doom that awaits them, and then view their past life just closed in rebellion against the throne of God, the harvest past, the summer ended, the flames of a guilty conscience already torment them. This is the dark realm into which the rich man passed at death. 'For in hell [Hades] he lift up his eyes, being in torment.' It is an actual 'place of torment' (Luke 16: 23). Lost spirits writhe beneath the piercing gaze of Him whose mercy they have slighted. With the fires of hell already kindled in their bosom, and a fearful 'looking for of judgment,' when they will hear the sentence, 'Depart from me into everlasting fire,' these guilty souls in Hades are already tormented in an awful flame."

"There are three states of human spirits. The second is the state in which human spirits are separated from their animal bodies. This commences at death and terminates with the resurrection of the body, and is precisely what is called 'Hades.' But Hades not only signifies a state, but the place of departed spirits. The third state of human spirits commences with the reunion of the spirit and body at the resurrection and continues ever after. Hades is said to be destroyed when the third state commences. Its termination is clearly foretold by John in these words: 'Death and Hades were cast into the lake of fire. This is the second death' (Rev. 20: 14).

"In anticipation of the termination of Hades, Paul exclaims: 'O death, where is thy sting? O Hades, where is thy victory?' (1 Cor. 15: 55). The passage from which Paul quotes is Hos. 13: 14, and reads: 'I will ransom them from the power of the grave [Hades], I will redeem them from death: O death, I will be thy plagues; O grave [Hades], I will be thy destruction.' The LXX, from which Paul quotes, reads thus: 'I will deliver them from the power of Hades, and will redeem them from death: where is thy penalty,

O death! O Hades, where is thy sting? O death, thy power to separate spirits from their bodies is no more! O Hades, thy dominion over disembodied souls is destroyed.'

"The grave *(geber)* is the receptacle of the body, while 'the unseen world [Hades]' is the receptacle of the soul. By consulting Jewish historians (Josephus and others) it will be seen that this was the doctrine of the Jewish people at the time of Christ. Also by consulting the united testimony of the early Church Fathers, it will be seen that this was their understanding of Scripture. When the Hebrews mingled with the Babylonians, Greeks, and Romans, they naturally came into their use of terms, and adopted them. Thus it was that the terms 'paradise,' 'Abraham's bosom,' 'Tartarus,' etc., came to be commonly used among the Jews when referring to the state of the blessed or the wicked after death.

"In the city of Babylon, where the Hebrews were captives seventy years, there was a place of recreation, or rest, for King Nebuchadnezzar and his court; a place of shady trees and blooming flowers. In this place the king and his court retired for rest and recreation from the hard toil and responsibilities of their business. It was kept under a strong guard of soldiers. That place the Chaldees called 'Paradise.' Also the Greeks and Romans had their gardens and fields of delight in Hades, and Tartarus in the same region. So the Jews, adopting these terms, called the abode of the happy separated spirits paradise, or Abraham's bosom; and the place and abode of wicked spirits and demons they called Tartarus.

These terms were thus introduced into the teachings of Scripture.

"Paul speaks of paradise as a heavenly realm (2 Cor. 12: 2-4). Jesus said to the converted thief, 'Today shalt thou be with me in paradise,' meaning the abode of the pious. And again, he clearly states that at death Lazarus was carried by the angels 'into Abraham's bosom.' There he was comforted. Peter, a Jew, and an apostle of Jesus Christ, says that God cast the angels that sinned down to Tartarus (2 Pet. 2: 4). He clearly teaches that demons and wicked persons are here reserved—kept in chains of darkness until the judgment, when they will receive their full punishment. (2 Pet. 2: 4, 9). This is the very place, the lowest Hades, into which Jesus declared the rich man passed at death, and then lifted up his eyes in torment. . . . . But when righteous men die they are carried by the angels into Abraham's bosom— rest—into the paradise of God."

THE END.

Having shown that the souls of men continue in conscious existence during the interval between natural death and the resurrection, I will return to the direct subject of Christ's second coming and show from the Scriptures the events that will take place when he comes. This is purely a subject of revelation. Theory and speculation amount to nothing with respect to future things; for there is no means of proving anything, except by revelation. Therefore the remainder of this chapter will deal with direct Scripture texts bearing on the subject.

"And as he sat upon the Mount of Olives, the disciples came unto him privately, saying, Tell us, when shall these things be? and what shall be the sign of thy coming, and of the end of the world?" (Matt. 24: 3). The burden of Matthew 24 shows that this question of the disciples relates to the actual end of all earthly things, and this they associated in their question with the second coming. So also in 1 Corinthians 15, where Christ's coming and the resurrection are described, we read in this connection, *"Then the end"* (verse 24). This great event marks the end of time, the end of man's probation, the end of Christ's special redemption reign; yea, as Peter says, "the *end of all things* is at hand" (1 Pet. 4: 7).

THE RESURRECTION.

So also the resurrection will take place at that time. "There shall be a resurrection of the dead, both of the just and unjust" (Acts 24: 15). How many resurrections? One, *"a resurrection of the dead."* And this one resurrection of the dead is to include both the just and the unjust. In the preceding chapter I showed clearly that the prophecies which some people suppose refer to two literal resurrections teach no such thing. In this chapter we shall see that those plain texts which are not involved in prophetic interpretations utterly preclude the idea of two literal resurrections in the future. In the present text it is simply "a resurrection," which includes both just and unjust.

But this text does not state when it will take place. In Rev. 1: 7 we have the time stated: "Behold *he cometh* with clouds; and every eye shall see him, and they also which pierced him: and all kindreds of the earth shall wail because of him." At his coming *"every eye* shall see him." This proves the fact of a general resurrection; and that this resurrection includes the wicked also is shown by the statement that even those who "pierced him" will see him when he comes. The idea of two literal resurrections —one of the righteous and the other of the wicked— is utterly demolished by this text; for when he comes, *"every eye"*—including the wicked who pierced him— shall be awake and see him.

That the resurrection is one, but includes both classes, is shown by the words of Christ himself: "Marvel not at this: for *the hour* is coming, in the which all that are in the graves shall hear his voice, and shall come forth; they that have done good, unto the resurrection of life; and they that have done evil, unto the resurrection of damnation" (John 5: 28, 29). Both classes—good and bad—come forth from their graves in the same *"hour."*

1 Thess. 4: 16 is sometimes referred to as teaching two resurrections —the "dead in Christ shall rise first." But it teaches no such thing, as even a hasty examination shows. The word "first" does not refer to other dead people at all. The text, with the context, simply shows that those who are living on the earth when Christ comes will not ascend to heaven *before* those who are dead in Christ, but that the dead in Christ shall rise *first,* and that then they will both ascend together.

So also Phil. 3: 11—"If by any means I might attain unto the resurrection of the dead"—is sometimes perverted in order to sustain the false doctrine of two future literal resurrections of the dead; for, it is argued, if there were only one unconditional resurrection, Paul would not have sought to attain it. But the Bible represents the single resurrection of the dead as composed of *two classes,* the one receiving the resurrection unto eternal life, and the other a resurrection unto eternal damnation. The object and effort of Paul was to attain to this resurrection of life, which can be obtained only by proper effort; for it applies only to those who are the saved of earth. The context shows this application. In verse 19 he mentions one class "whose end is destruction"; while in the two following verses he speaks of the other class, to which he belonged, and says, "We look for the Savior, the Lord Jesus Christ, who shall change our vile body that it may be fashioned like unto his glorious body."

When Lazarus was dead, Jesus said to Martha, "Thy brother shall rise again. Martha said unto him, I know that he shall rise again in the resurrection *at the last day*" (John 11:23, 24). Now, Lazarus was a good man, and his sister had the idea that his resurrection would take place at the *last* day. Does this accord with the idea of two literal resurrections? No. The millennial idea of two resurrections places the resurrection of the righteous first and the resurrection of the wicked last— one thousand years later. But Martha says, "I know that he shall rise again in *the* resurrection at the *last* day."

Where did Martha get this idea that the righteous would be raised at the last day? Evidently from the words of Christ himself; for he affirms this four times in

one chapter. "And this is the Father's will which hath sent me, that of all which he hath given me I should lose nothing, but should raise it up again at *the last day*" (John 6:39). "Every one which seeth the Son, and believeth on him, may have everlasting life: and I will raise him up at *the last day*" (verse 40). "No man can come to me, except the Father which hath sent me draw him: and I will raise him up at *the last day*" (verse 44). "Whoso eateth my flesh, and drinketh my blood, hath eternal life; and I will raise him up at *the last day*" (verse 54).

These scriptures were presented to a certain woman that believed the millennial heresy, and she, anxious to save her false doctrine that the wicked are the ones who will be raised at *the last day,* while the righteous will be raised one thousand years before—she began to affirm that she could prove there would be two and one-half days after "the *last* day." What ridiculous extremes people are driven to in order to defend a false theory! There will be but one literal resurrection of the dead, and it will include "all that are in their graves"— "both the just and unjust"—and together they will come forth in the same "*hour,*" when Christ comes; for then "*every eye* shall see him, and them also that pierced him; and all kindreds of the earth shall wail because of him" (Rev. 1:7).

THE GENERAL JUDGMENT.

To the Athenians, Paul declared that God "hath appointed a day, in the which he will judge the world in righteousness by that man whom he hath ordained"

(Acts 17:31). This judgment-day is "the last day," the day of resurrection; for Paul says that "the Lord Jesus Christ . . . . shall judge the quick and the dead *at his appearing*" (2 Tim. 4:1). The Revelator connects the general judgment with the resurrection at the second coming: "And I saw a great white throne, and him that sat on it, from whose face the earth and the heaven fled away, and there was found no place for them. And I saw the dead, small and great, stand before God; and the books were opened: and another book was opened, which is the book of life: *and the dead were judged* out of those things which were written in the books according to their works. And the sea gave up the dead which were in it; and death and hell delivered up the dead which were in them: and they were *judged every man* according to their works" (Rev. 20:11-13).

FINAL REWARDS.

The doctrine of final rewards is naturally associated with the second coming and general judgment. "Behold, I come quickly; and my reward is with me, to give every man according as his work shall be" (Rev. 22:12). "For the Son of man shall come in the glory of his Father with his angels; and then shall he reward every man according to his works" (Matt. 16:27).

This will be the day of final rewards for all men. God hath "reserved the unjust unto the day of judgment to be punished" (2 Pet. 2:9). This will be an awful day, and one that we can not escape. "Every eye shall see him" when he comes; for "the Lord Jesus shall be revealed from heaven with his mighty angels, in flaming fire, taking vengeance on them that know not God, and that obey not the gospel of our Lord Jesus Christ; who shall be punished with everlasting destruction from the presence of the Lord, and from the glory of his power; when he shall come to be glorified in his saints" (2 Thess. 1:7-10). The same day that he is "glorified in his saints" will be the day of the everlasting banishment of the wicked.

The same great truth is also taught in Matthew 25 and centers in the second coming. "When the Son of man shall come in his glory, and all the holy angels with him, then shall he sit upon the throne of his glory: and before him shall be gathered all nations: and he shall separate them one from another, as a shepherd divideth his sheep from the goats: and he shall set the sheep on his right hand, but the goats on the left" (Matt. 25:31-33). Here we have all men before the judgment-throne *at the same time;* they are divided into two classes, represented by sheep and goats. This division is made for the purpose of settling their final destiny. "Then shall the King say unto them on his right hand, Come, ye blessed of my Father, inherit the kingdom prepared for you from the foundation of the world" (verse 34). Final reward. "Then shall he say also to them on the left hand, Depart from me, ye cursed, into everlasting fire, prepared for the devil and his angels" (verse 41). Final punishment. And here we have the final destiny of both: "And these shall go into everlasting punishment: but the righteous unto life eternal" (verse 46).

DESTRUCTION OF THE EARTH.

The Word of God clearly teaches that the world which we now inhabit will be destroyed, pass away, and be no more. "Of old hast thou laid the foundation of the earth: and the heavens [aerial and planetary] are the work of thy hands. *They shall perish,* . . . . yea, all of them shall wax old like a garment; as a vesture shalt thou change them, and they shall be changed" (Psa. 102: 25, 26).

"Heaven and earth shall pass away," says Jesus (Matt. 24: 35). Peter describes the manner in which the heavens and earth shall pass away. "The heavens" doubtless refers to the aerial heavens surrounding the earth. "But the heavens and the earth, which are now, by the same word are kept in store, reserved unto fire against the day of judgment and perdition of ungodly men" (2 Pet. 3: 7).

Notice that this destruction of the earth by fire is reserved till " the *day of judgment* and perdition of ungodly men." Millennialists have argued that the fire would come first and simply purify the earth, after which the righteous would reign here for a thousand years before the resurrection of the wicked. But, according to Peter, the fire will not come until the time when the ungodly men shall receive their doom. Peter did not believe the millennial heresy. He knew that when Christ came the end of all things pertaining to earth would take place and that the righteous and the wicked would be rewarded at the same time. Therefore he goes on to say: "But the day of the Lord will come as a thief in the night; in the which the heavens *shall pass away* with a great noise, and the elements shall melt with fervent heat, the earth also and the works that are therein *shall be burned up*. Seeing then that *all these things* shall be *dissolved,* what manner of persons ought ye to be in all holy conversation and godliness, looking for and hasting unto the coming of the day of God, wherein the heavens being on fire shall be dissolved, and the elements shall melt with fervent heat?" (verses 10-12).

Peter does not say that the earth shall be burned over, but that it shall be *"burned up";* that "all these things" shall "melt," be "dissolved," and "pass away." And in direct contrast he mentions in the next verse a "new heavens and a new earth" brought to view after the first one has gone. So also the Revelator describes the passing of this old earth: "And I saw a great white throne, and him that sat on it, from whose face the earth and the heaven fled away; and there was found no place for them" (Rev. 20:11). Then in contrast he says, "And I saw a new heaven and a new earth: for the first heaven and the first earth were passed away; and there was no more sea" (Rev. 21:1). This will be heaven, our future and eternal home.

THE MILLENNIAL THEORY.

With these clear and plain Scriptural statements before us, we can readily see that there is no possibility of a millennium, or earthly reign of righteousness after Christ comes.

1. *There will be NO TIME for a millennium.* The second coming of Christ, when he raises and rewards the righteous, is at "the *last* day." At that time "the

mystery of God shall be *finished,*" and "there shall be *time no longer*" (Rev. 10: 6, 7). There is no one thousand years after the *last* day.

2. *There will be NO PLACE for a millennium.* As we have just seen, the destruction of the earth is to take place at the same time that the wicked are to be punished; and this destruction will be complete, the earth being "dissolved," "burnt up," and passing away. Hence there will be no earthly place for a millennium after Christ comes.

3. *There will be NO NEED of an earthly millennium.* The offers of perfect salvation are all extended in the gospel dispensation. "Behold *now* is the accepted time; behold NOW is the day of salvation" (2 Cor. 6: 2). Every means consistent with moral government and the moral freedom of the individual are now being employed to effect the salvation of men. Furthermore, since at the coming of Christ the wicked are judged and sent to their everlasting doom, there is positively no need of an earthly millennium.

The millenarian doctrine is delusive. It is presented in many forms, according to the fancies and desires of its propagators, but evidently the idea is about the same —that there will be an earthly kingdom and reign of Christ for one thousand years.

This theory was first introduced under Christianity by Cerinthus, who was the worst heretic of the first century. The church historian Eusebius has preserved a fragment of writing from Caius, who lived in the second century, and who thus describes the doctrine of Cerinthus: "But Cerinthus too, through revelations written,

as he would have us believe, by a great apostle, brings
before us marvelous things, which he pretends were shown
him by angels; alleging that after the resurrection the
kingdom of Christ is to be on earth, and that the flesh
dwelling in Jerusalem is again to be subject to desires
and pleasures. And being an enemy to the Scriptures
of God, wishing to deceive men, he says that there is
to be a space of a thousand years for marriage-festivi-
ties." "One of the doctrines that he taught was, that
Christ would have an earthly kingdom." Caius evidently
believed the Sriptural doctrine that the kingdom of God
was set up at Christ's first coming; therefore he brands
Cerinthus as an "enemy of the Scriptures, wishing to
deceive men."

Now, Cerinthus lived in the days of the apostle John.
Irenaeus, who was born A. D. 120, states that while a
boy he often sat at the feet of the venerable Polycarp,
Bishop of Smyrna (who was a disciple of John), and
listened while that aged disciple related incidents which
took place in the earlier days of the apostles (Eusebius: Ecclesiastical History, V: 24). Among the things
thus handed down, Irenæus states that once while John
was at Ephesus he entered a public bath to wash, and
finding that Cerinthus was within, he rushed out of the
building, exhorting the others to do the same, saying, "Let
us flee, lest the bath fall in, as long as Cerinthus that
enemy of the truth, is within."—Eusebius Eccl. Hist.,
III: 28. Millennialists, like Cerinthus, claim that their
doctrine is founded in the Apocalypse of John, but that
apostle rejected him as an *"enemy of the truth."*

Bro. D. S. Warner has stated that the devil works

especially to deceive men in either one of two ways; either, first, *Some other way than Christ;* or second, *Some other time than* NOW. This is true. If men will not accept his deception that some other way will do, then he proceeds at once to delay all important things until the future. Thousands of people have thus grasped the delusive idea that there will be after this dispensation another age of blessedness in which salvation-work will be effected. Such is a rank deception of the devil. "NOW is the accepted time: behold, NOW is the day of salvation."

E. A. Reardon has suggested that the devil has produced a purgatory for Catholics and a millennium for Protestants, but all for the same purpose; namely, in order to delude the millions into a false hope of future opportunities until he can get them across the death-line without real Bible salvation, after which, he well knows, their destiny will be sealed eternally.

> "O poor sinner, don't believe them;
> There will be no age to come:
> If in life you find not Jesus,
> Death will seal your awful doom."

CHAPTER XXV.

DESTINY OF THE WICKED.

The subject of the final destiny of those who persist in a life of wickedness has not been left to the mere opinions of men, but is a matter of revelation in the Christian Scriptures. Furthermore, the knowledge which we possess of the manner of God's dealings with sinful men in the past would lead us to conclude that at some time or other justice would be meted out to the guilty violators of his law.

In the beginning the Creator placed his intelligent creatures under moral law, a law that exacts perfect obedience. This law had a penalty attached, which was determined in accordance with the nature of the offense in the mind of its Author. But God, being infinitely holy, must of necessity be infinitely opposed to unholiness; and therefore the law, which reflects his moral disposition, must be infinitely just and in the same degree opposed to injustice. The reward for obedience would therefore, in accordance with the nature of the law, be infinite; while the penalty for its violation could not in the nature of things be other than infinite punishment. It is an illogical supposition that the nature, requirements, and rewards of a law system can be of one character, and its penalty for disobedience bear no quilitative relation to it, but be regulated by another standard. Infinite punishment must be the penalty for the violation of God's universal law, if the moral government of heaven, which requires perfect obedience, be infinite and eternal. But every one can see that such justice is not dispensed in this world; for we see the wickedest of men continuing in health and prosperity right down to the hour of their death; while on the other hand, the righteous man is ground down and oppressed by poverty, affliction, and persecution, and finally passes out of life, like Lazarus, without even a public notice of his burial. These conditions require a time and place of future judgment.

THEY WILL BE PUNISHED.

There is now in the world a large amount of perverse teaching and sentimental talk against the Bible doctrine of the punishment of the wicked. Men have become so hardened through the deceitfulness of sin, that they imagine that God is altogether such a creature as they are—indifferent as to whether men do good or evil. When men get so far from the truth that sin does not look very bad, and righteousness does not look very good, it is time that they should take warning. Hear the word of the Lord: "And it shall come to pass at that time that I will . . . . punish the men that are settled on their lees: that say in their heart, The Lord will not do good, neither will he do evil" (Zeph. 1:12). This is the false doctrine spread broadcast today—that if the Lord does not do good to the sinner, he will at least not do him evil; therefore men presume on his mercy and go forward in their sins, heaping up "wrath against the day of wrath and revelation of the *righteous judgment* of God; who will render to every man according to his deeds" (Rom. 2:5, 6).

The argument that God is too good to punish men

does not alter the matter. God is good, but his goodness is harmonious with his justice; and justice demands the execution of law against wrong-doers. "Behold therefore the goodness and *severity* of God: on them which fell, severity; but toward thee, goodness, if thou continue in his goodness: otherwise thou also *shalt be cut off*" (Rom. 11:22). The goodness of God is manifested specially toward those "who continue in his goodness." "The Lord is good, a stronghold in the day of trouble; and he knoweth *them that trust in him."* (Nahum 1:7).

Every verse of Psalms 136 contains the words "his mercy endureth forever"; but an examination shows that it is towards *his own people* that his mercy is everlasting. The same Psalm shows that while God was manifesting his mercy toward Israel he at the same time "smote Egypt," "overthrew Pharaoh and his host in the Red Sea," "smote great kings" in the wilderness, etc. The *love of God* therefore demands the eternal separation of the wicked from the righteous—not love for the wicked, but love for his own people. He even threatened the wrong-doers in Israel: "I will punish you for all your iniquities" (Amos 3:2). And again he says, "I will punish the world for their evil, and the wicked for their iniquity" (Isa. 13:11).

Since in time past God has, even in this world, manifested his judgment against wrong-doers, we may rightly infer that he will do so in the future. In fact, if God is without "variableness neither shadow of turning" (Jas. 1:17), it must be this way in the future. And does not the Word of God constantly affirm this fact? The Lord has "reserved the unjust unto the day of judg-

ment *to be punished"* (2 Pet. 2:9). "Of how much
sorer punishment, suppose ye, shall he be thought worthy
who hath trodden under foot the Son of God" (Heb. 10:
29). "Who shall be punished with everlasting destruction" (2 Thess. 1:9). "And these shall go away into
everlasting punishment" (Matt. 25:46).

While God is a God of love, it must be remembered
that *love* is only one of his attributes. Justice is one
of his attributes as truly as is love. Now, since God is
a perfect being we must expect to find in him the perfect and harmonious expression of all of his attributes,
and no manifestation of his attributes in any way reflects upon his character, but simply exhibits his character as it really is.

The idea that the punishment of the wicked reflects
upon the character of God is itself unintelligible and
absurd. The same men who argue thus possess within
themselves the same attributes of love and justice, and
these principles receive their full sanction when expressed in the laws that govern human society. Human laws
are primarily for the protection and benefit of the good
and innocent; and when true justice is executed against
wrong-doers, every one, with the full sanction of his
conscience, is ready to assert that such justice is in itself
right. If God were to take all of earth's vile and im-
penitent sinners to heaven, there to remain the same
evil characters and there to continue the same evil work
against the righteous—this of itself would be, in our
estimation, the grossest *injustice.* No, "God is love,"
therefore he can not permit his people to be thus oppressed throughout eternity. A final separation must and

will be made. This does not reflect upon the character of Christ, for he has made a plan of salvation for all; and it is only through their own wilfulness that sinners go on and are punished.

DEGREES OF PUNISHMENT.

The Bible also teaches that there will be degrees of punishment. Paul says that in the day of judgment Christ will "render to every man according to his deeds" (Rom. 2:5, 6). Men become doubly responsible by the light which they receive. Thus, Jesus says: "If I had not come and spoken unto them, they had not had sin: but now they have no cloak for their sin" (John 15:22). "That sin by the commandment might become *exceeding sinful*" (Rom. 7:13). Pilate did a great wrong in delivering Christ up to be crucified, but Judas was more responsible than Pilate, for he had had more light; therefore Christ said to Pilate, "He that delivered me unto thee *hath the greater sin*" (John 19:10, 11).

Now, since our sins are estimated in accordance with the light received, our punishment also will be regulated accordingly. For this reason Peter says concerning backsliders, "It had been better for them not to have known the way of righteousness, than, after they have known it, to turn from the holy commandment" (2 Pet. 2:21). "For if we sin wilfully after that we have received the knowledge of the truth .... Of how much sorer punishment, suppose ye, shall he be thought worthy, who hath trodden under foot the Son of God?" (Heb. 10:26-29). The greater the light and knowledge possessed, the greater the responsibility when that light is rejected.

"Woe unto you, scribes and Pharisees, hypocrites! for ye devour widows' houses, and for a pretense make long prayers: therefore ye shall receive *the greater damnation*" (Matt. 23:14).

"Then began he to upbraid the cities wherein most of his mighty works were done, because they repented not: woe unto thee, Chorazin! woe unto thee, Bethsaida! .... I say unto you, It shall be *more tolerable* for Tyre and Sidon at the day of judgment than for you. And thou, Capernaum, which art exalted unto heaven, shall be brought down to hell .... It shall be *more tolerable* for the land of Sodom in the day of judgment than for thee" (Matt. 11:20-24).

From the foregoing scriptures we see that men will be rewarded "according to their works"; that some will receive a "sorer punishment" and "greater damnation" than others; and that it will be "more tolerable" for some people than it will be for others. But all these degrees will be in accordance with the light received and rejected.

NOT ANNIHILATION.

It is a favorite theory with some that the wicked will simply be blotted out of existence at the day of judgment and that that time will be their final end. But the Scriptural facts just shown—that at the day of judgment the wicked will be rewarded "according to their works," that some will receive "greater damnation" and "sorer punishment" than others—utterly disproves that false theory; for in the case of annihilation all would receive the same punishment.

There are a few texts of Scripture that speak of men in this world as passing away and being no more, which is all very true of earthly things; but there is no text of Scripture *referring to the state of men after the judgment* in which it is even hinted that men will come to an end and be no more. Obadiah 16 is often quoted in order to sustain the false doctrine of annihilation: "They shall be as though they had not been." Even a most careless examination of this text ought to show any one that it has no reference to the state of the wicked beyond the judgment. The entire chapter is concerning certain men *in this world,* and then it refers to only one class or nation of men. Verse 1: "Thus saith the Lord *concerning Edom."* Verse 3: "The pride of thine heart hath deceived thee." Verse 6: "How are the *things of Edom* searched out?" Verse 8: "Shall I not in that day, saith the Lord, even *destroy the wise men out of Edom?"* Verse 9: "That every one of the mount of Esau may be cut off by slaughter." Verse 16: *"THEY* shall be as though they had not been." Verse 18: "And the house of Jacob shall be a fire, and the house of Joseph a flame, and the house of Esau for stubble, and they shall kindle in them and devour them; *and there shall not be any remaining* [on the earth] OF THE HOUSE OF ESAU." What has this to do with the state of the wicked beyond the judgment? Nothing.

So also Mal. 4: 1 is brought forward as proving annihilation: "For behold, the day cometh, that shall burn as an oven; and all the proud, yea, and all that do wickedly, shall be stubble: and the day that cometh shall burn them up, saith the Lord of hosts, that it shall leave them neither root nor branch." This day of burning, however, does not refer to the future state beyond the judgment at all, but was to meet its fulfilment in the day when "the Sun of righteousness shall arise with healing in his wings," which day was to be ushered in by the coming of Elijah (verses 2-5). This Elijah referred to John the Baptist, as the following scriptures show: Luke 1: 13-17; Matt. 11:13, 14; 17:10-13.

The entire fourth chapter of Malachi depicts the gospel dispensation introduced by John, the day when the "Sun of righteousness" was revealed. It was a glorious day for the people of God, and yet "a great and dreadful day" for the ungodly. The overthrow of the Jewish nation is one general example of the consequences of rejecting the Messiah. And as light received and rejected will rate punishment in the future, the gospel dispensation will indeed constitute a dreadful turning-point in the destiny of the wicked.

The work of Christ in the gospel dispensation is represented as a work of *fire*. In the same book of Malachi it is set forth thus: "Behold, I will send my messenger, and he shall prepare the way before me: and the Lord, whom ye seek, shall suddenly come to his temple, even the messenger of the covenant, whom ye delight in; behold, he shall come, saith the Lord of hosts. But who may abide the day of his coming? and who shall stand when he appeareth? for he is like a refiner's *fire*, and like fullers' soap: and he shall sit as a refiner and purifier of silver: and he shall purify the sons of Levi, and purge them as gold and silver, that they may offer unto the Lord an offering in righteousness. . . . . And I will come near to you to judgment; and I will be a swift witness against the sorcerers, and against the adulterers, and against false swearers, and against those that oppress the hireling in his wages, the widow, and the fatherless, and that turn aside the stranger from his right, and fear not me, saith the Lord of hosts. For I am the Lord, I change not; therefore ye sons of Jacob are not consumed" (Mal. 3:1-6).

"And now also the axe is laid unto the root of the trees: wherefore every tree that bringeth not forth good fruit is hewn down, and cast into the *fire*. I indeed baptize you with water unto repentance: but he that cometh after me is mightier than I, whose shoes I am not worthy to bear: he shall baptize you with the Holy Ghost *and with fire*" (Matt. 3:10, 11). Notice also the following scriptures which describe the fire of God's holiness in the gospel dispensation: Isa. 9:5-7; 33:14; Jer. 5:13, 14; Isa. 4:3-5. This is the fire of God's holiness and truth that in this dispensation is kindled in Zion, his church, and keeps it pure from sin and sinners.

The language of Mal. 4:1 is metaphorical. The fire is no more literal fire than are the wicked people literal stubble. The language is simply *figurative*, as are the fire, wood, stubble, silver, etc., in the other texts just quoted—and *none of them apply to the future state*, as can easily be seen.

FUTURE PUNISHMENT WILL BE IN HELL.

"Fear him which after he hath killed, hath power to cast into hell; yea, I say unto you, Fear him" (Luke 12:5). "The wicked shall be turned into hell, and all the nations that forget God" (Psa. 9:17). From these texts we see that hell is a place. But it is also a *place of fire.* "The angels shall come forth, and sever the wicked from among the just, and shall cast them into the furnace of fire: there shall be wailing and gnashing of teeth" (Matt. 13:49, 50).

Hell, then, is not simply a condition, but is also a place; for into it the wicked will be "turned," yea, "cast into hell," and in that "furnace of fire" there "shall be wailing and gnashing of teeth." It is not the grave, for the righteous as well as the wicked will go into the grave; but "the wicked shall be *turned into hell,"* and there exist in conscious suffering, for *"there shall be wailing and gnashing of teeth,* in that condition and place into which the lost will be "cast."

Yes, hell is a place, a most terrible place—a prepared place. Prepared for whom? "Prepared *for the devil and his angels"* (Matt. 25:41). It was not made for man, but was made "for the devil and his angels." Fallen angels and demons are held in reserve until the day of judgment, when they will be cast into it. "And the angels which kept not their first estate, ... he hath reserved in everlasting chains under darkness unto the judgment of the great day" (Jude 6). The demons know of their coming doom; therefore those in the devil-possessed men cried out, "What have we to do with thee, Jesus thou Son of God? art thou come hither to torment us *before the time?"* (Matt. 8:29). But while hell was not prepared for men, yet if men choose to serve the devil, they will share his fate, for "the wicked shall be turned into hell" (Psa. 9:17). "Depart from me, ye cursed, into

everlasting fire, prepared for the devil and his angels"
(Matt. 25:41). "How can ye escape the damnation of
hell?" (Matt: 23:33). Hell is an actual place; its
punishment will be real.

IT WILL BE EVERLASTING.

I shall now proceed to bring forward the different
expressions used in the Bible to describe the punishment
of the wicked in hell, also the duration of that punishment. Some people think that most of these various expressions are only symbolic, and not real, since some of
them are opposite in character, such as "everlasting fire"
and "outer darkness." Their symbolic character, however, in no wise lessens the force of their application.
According to Paul, the things of paradise are of such an
exalted character that it is *not possible* for a man to
utter" them in ordinary human language (2 Cor. 12:4);
therefore wherever the things of that future world are
described they are of necessity set forth symbolically,
objects of this world being chosen to represent them
analogously. But in this case, as in all cases, the symbol
is inferior to the thing symbolized.

So also, in the nature of the case, the future punishment of the wicked in hell can be truly represented in
the present state only *symbolically,* earthly objects of
a certain character being chosen to set it forth analogously. But remember that objects used as symbols are
always inferior to the things symbolized. Therefore
the symbol argument, instead of making the fires of
hell cooler, only succeeds in making them hotter. Let
us now consider these various expressions, describ-

ing the fate of the wicked. Some of these are only *words*, while others are *things*, therefore symbolic.

1. *"Punishment."* The Lord hath "reserved the unjust unto the day of judgment to be *punished"* (2 Pet. 2:9). They are worthy of a "sorer punishment" than death without mercy (Heb. 10:28, 29).

It will be everlasting. "And these shall go away into everlasting punishment" (Matt. 25:46).

2. *"Death."* "For the wages of sin is death" (Rom. 6:23). The death here mentioned is not that natural death which comes to good and bad alike, but it is that death which is the direct result of sin, for it is contrasted with eternal life. Natural death, as we have shown, is not the end of the soul's conscious existence, but is simply that state in which the human spirit is separated from the body. So also spiritual death is not the cessation of conscious existence, but is simply that state in this world in which the soul is separated from its normal position of communion and fellowship with God (Ezek. 18:20; Isa. 59:1, 2; 1 Tim. 5:6; Eph. 2:1; Col. 2:13 and John 17:3). In like manner the eternal death of the soul is not the end of its conscious existence (which would be contrary to all the other statements and symbols), but is simply its eternal separation from God. But natural death is something repulsive; men shrink from it and seek to evade it. It is chosen—with all its repulsiveness, with all its horrors—to represent that future state of separation from God—*death.*

It will be eternal. "He that believeth on the Son hath everlasting life: and he that believeth not the Son *shall not see life;* but the wrath of God *abideth* on him" (John 3:36).

3. *"Darkness."* "He delivered them into chains of darkness, to be reserved unto judgment" (2 Pet. 2:4). According to the parable of Christ, the wicked "shall be cast out into *outer darkness:* there shall be weeping and gnashing of teeth" (Matt. 8:12). What a fearful thought! To be placed in utter darkness is one of the worst punishments inflicted upon men in this world: A dungeon experience is generally sufficient to break the will of the most stubborn, rebellious criminal. Such is the figure of future punishment. How terrible, then, the reality must be! But this is not all. Instead of being an experience of short duration, as imprisonment in a dungeon,—

It will be forever. "To whom the mist of darkness is reserved forever" (2 Pet. 2:17). "The blackness of darkness forever" (Jude 13). Is there not one ray of future hope for the wicked man? Answer: "When he dieth . . . . he shall go to the generation of his fathers; *they shall NEVER see light"* (Psa. 49:17-19).

4. *"Damnation."* "They that have done good, unto the resurrection of life; and they that have done evil, unto the resurrection of damnation" (John 5:29). This expresses the highest form of condemnation. "Ye shall receive the greater damnation" (Matt. 23:14). "How can ye escape the damnation of hell?" (verse 33).

It will be eternal. "Is in danger of *eternal damnation"* (Mark 3:29).

5. *"Destruction."* This word "destruction," as applied to the wicked, signifies, not the end of their conscious

existence, but their utter misery and ruin. The word is
thus used in the Bible over and over again. For examples, see Exod. 10:7; Prov. 11:9; 18:7; Eccl. 7:16;
Hosea 4:6; 13:9; Gal. 1:13. "For when they shall say,
Peace and safety; then *sudden destruction* cometh upon
them . . . . and they shall not escape." 1 Thess. 5:3.
"Whose end is destruction." Phil. 3:19. All of the sinner's plans and hopes, yea, even his own noble self which
God created for his own glory, is forever blighted, and
gone down into everlasting misery and ruin—*destruction.*

It will be everlasting. "Who shall be punished with
everlasting destruction from the presence of the Lord,
and from the glory of his power" (2 Thess. 1:9). This
everlasting destruction is not the end of their conscious
existence, as the context shows, but is simply their final
and eternal separation and banishment from the "presence of the Lord."

6. *"Fire."* "Shall be in danger of *hell-fire"* (Matt.
5:22). It is "in flaming fire" that the Lord Jesus will
be revealed from heaven against wrong-doers (2 Thess.
1:7-9). It is called: 1. *"A furnace of fire."* "And
shall cast them into a furnace of fire: there shall be
wailing and gnashing of teeth" (Matt. 13:42). 2. A
"lake of fire." "But the fearful, and unbelieving, and the
abominable, and murderers, and whoremongers, and sorcerers, and idolaters, and all liars, shall have their
part in the lake which burneth with fire and brimstone"
(Rev. 21:8). "And whosoever was not found written
in the book of life was cast into the lake of fire" (Rev.
20:15).

It will be never-ending. "Depart from me, ye cursed, into *everlasting fire,* prepared for the devil and his angels" (Matt. 25:41). "Are set forth for an example, suffering the vengeance of *eternal fire*" (Jude 7).

Reader, be not deceived by the false doctrines of men. Obey the Word of God and "FLEE FROM THE WRATH TO COME" (Matt 3:7).

"In the awful day that's coming,
 When heaven's trump shall sound
And call the world to judgment,
 Oh! where shall we be found?
Shall we cry for rocks and mountains
 To hide us in that day
From him who comes in glory,
 With all his bright array?

"Shall we begin to tremble
 While looking on that sight,
And take our march in anguish
 Down to eternal night?
OH, WHAT AN AWFUL PICTURE!
 To some it will come true;
And oh! my brother, sister,
 Shall it be I or you?"

THIS TRUTH FOREVER SETTLED.

There is no way under heaven to evade the force of this multitude of scriptures describing the fearful fate of the ungodly. 1. They apply to the wicked. 2. They apply to time beyond the judgment. 3. If literal, the punishment they depict is terrible. 4. If they are symbolic it is *worse.* The language describes a future state of everlasting punishment—of conscious pain, suffering, torment, and wretchedness, in hell. It either means what it says, or it does not. If it does not mean all this, then why do the Bible writers state it thus? and if they really intended to teach such a doctrine as this, what words, comparisons, and descriptions could they employ to set it forth other than the very words that are here employed? Ponder well this last question. *They have well-nigh exhausted the language in this respect.*

Notice, also, that the very same words that are employed to measure the endless duration of all that is good and holy, are used to set forth the duration of the punishment of the wicked in hell. I will call attention briefly to some of these words and their use in the Bible.

1. *"Forever."* "The Lord shall endure forever" (Psa. 9: 7). "The Lord shall reign forever" (Psa. 146: 10). "The word of our God shall stand forever" (Isa. 40: 8). "Forever, O Lord, thy word is settled in heaven" (Psa. 119: 89). This shows its use on the one side.

Now let us look at the other side: "God shall likewise destroy thee forever" (Psa. 52: 5). "If thou forsake him, he will cast thee off forever" (1 Chron. 28: 9). "To whom the mist of darkness is reserved forever" (2 Pet. 2: 17). "The blackness of darkness forever" (Jude 13). The very same word that measures the duration of God's word, of Christ's reign, yea, of his very existence, is the word used to measure the time during which the wicked will be "cast off" and banished in "the blackness of darkness."

2. *"Forever and ever."* "The Lord shall reign forever and ever" (Exod. 15: 18). The saints shall "possess the kingdom forever and ever" (Dan. 7: 18). "Thy throne, O God, is forever and ever" (Heb. 1: 8). The righteous shall shine "as the stars forever and ever" (Dan. 12: 3).

Now turn to the other side: "And the smoke of their torment ascendeth up forever and ever" (Rev. 14:11). "Shall be tormented day and night forever and ever" (Rev. 20:10). As long as the Lord himself shall reign and his throne in heaven stand, yea, as long as the righteous themselves shall "shine as the stars" in their heavenly home, just so long the wicked shall suffer the torments of hell—"*forever and ever.*"

3. "*Everlasting.*" "Everlasting God" (Isa. 40:28). "Everlasting Father" (Isa. 9:6). "The righteous shall be in everlasting remembrance" (Psa. 112:6).

The other side: "Reserved in everlasting chains under darkness" (Jude 6). "Who shall be punished with everlasting destruction from the presence of the Lord, and from the glory of his power" (2 Thess. 1:9). "Everlasting fire" (Matt. 18:8). "These shall go away into everlasting punishment" (Matt. 25:46).

4. "*Eternal.*" "Eternal God" (Deut. 33:27). "Unto the king eternal, immortal, invisible" (1 Tim. 1:17). "Eternal salvation" (Heb. 5:9). "Eternal Spirit" (Heb. 9:14). "The righteous unto life eternal" (Matt. 25:46).

The other side again: "Eternal judgment" (Heb. 6:2). "In danger of eternal damnation" (Mark 3:29). "Sodom and Gomorrah .... are set forth for an example, suffering the vengeance of eternal fire" (Jude 7).

The very same words throughout that are used to measure the reign of the righteous in heaven, yea, the very continuation of God himself and heaven's throne, are used to describe the duration of the punishment of the wicked in hell. In Matt. 25, where the final reward of the righteous and the punishment of the wicked after the judgment are given, the *same word* is used for each *in the same verse:* "And these shall go away into *everlasting* punishment: but the righteous unto life *eternal*" (verse 46). In the Greek the word *aonios* occurs in both places, being translated *everlasting* in the one case and *eternal* in the other, but the meaning is exactly the same.

> "Oh! what will it be to be lost,
> With God's awful wrath on my soul,
> With demons to make my abode in that lake,
> While ages unending shall roll?"

CHAPTER XXVI.

OUR ETERNAL HOME.

As children of the Most High, we are in the world, yet we are not of this world. As "strangers and pilgrims," we are simply "sojourning here" (1 Pet. 2:11; 1:17). "Our citizenship is in heaven" (Phil. 3:20). For this reason we "set our affections on things above, not on things on the earth" (Col. 3:2). All our hopes, our desires, our aspirations, our longings, are there.

This has ever been the conviction of all true saints here. The patriarchs of the old dispensation knew that their period of earthly existence was transitory; therefore they "confessed that they were strangers and pilgrims on the earth." They were indeed seeking a country, but not an earthly one, for "they desire *a better country, that is, an heavenly*" (Heb. 11:13-16). We also of the new dispensation share with them in the same future hope; "for here have we no continuing city, *but we seek one to come*" (Heb. 13:14). Nor will this desire of God's people during the ages go unsatisfied, "for *he hath prepared for them a city*" (Heb. 11:16). It is not to be found in this world, for all the promises of future blessedness point us away from earth to another country, a *"better country,"* "an heavenly." "Man goeth to his eternal home" (Eccl. 12:5, LXX).

How inspiring this thought amid the trying scenes of life! When tossed by the billows of earthly woe, the soul cries out, "If in this life only we have hope in Christ, we are of all men most miserable" (1 Cor. 15:19); but courage survives and faith brightens in view of 'the hope which is laid up for us *in heaven*' (Col. 1:5). What "strong consolation" is this "hope set before us"! which "hope we have as an anchor of the soul, both sure and steadfast, and which entereth into that within the vail" (Heb. 6:18, 19). When earthly reverses and loses come, we accept them "joyfully," "knowing in ourselves that we have *in heaven* a better and an *enduring* substance" (Heb. 10:34); for we have laid up for ourselves "treasures in heaven, where neither moth nor rust doth corrupt, and where thieves do not break through nor steal" (Matt. 6:20).

We are adjusted to every circumstance. When things go smoothly in life, we rejoice and give God the glory; when fiery trials are our portion, we rejoice also, inspired by the hope from above. "If ye be reproached for the name of Christ, happy are ye; *for the spirit of glory and of God resteth upon you*" (1 Pet. 4:14). What does a little opposition or persecution amount to? "Rejoice and be exceeding glad: for great is your reward *in heaven:* for so persecuted they the prophets which were before you" (Matt. 5:12). The eternal reward comes to those who endure to the end. Such shall have an abundant entrance "into the everlasting kingdom of our Lord and Savior Jesus Christ" (2 Pet. 1:11).

A SURE REWARD.

Are we certain of this happy termination of earthly things? Yes, thank God! "FOR WE KNOW that if our earthly house of this tabernacle were dissolved *we have a building of God, an house not made with hands, eternal in the heavens"* (2 Cor. 5:1). Yes, *"eternal* in the heavens"; "for the things which are seen are temporal; but the things which are not seen *are eternal"* (2 Cor. 4:18). The things of earth that pass before our vision day after day are changeable and are constantly changing. The blooming verdure of springtime matures in summer, perishes in autumn, and is covered from sight by the wintry snow. Man himself, fresh and playful in childhood, strong and vigorous in manhood, ripens for eternity, and with whitened locks and trembling limbs he hastens toward the grave.

> "Change and decay in all around I see,
> Oh, thou who changest not, abide with me."

"The things which are seen are temporal; but the things which are not seen are eternal." We look not at the life which now is, but with eager joy and anticipation we press forward to that life which is to be. "We look for the Savior, the Lord Jesus Christ; who shall change our vile body, that it may be fashioned like unto his glorious body" (Phil. 3:20, 21).

Worldly possessions, which are only "temporal," can not hold our affections: we are "heirs of the kingdom which he hath promised to them that love him" (Jas. 2:5). We have "an inheritance incorruptible, and undefiled, and that *fadeth not away,* reserved IN HEAVEN" for us (1 Pet. 1:4). Away with earthly attractions— Jesus and heaven are ours! The beauties of this world can not charm our souls: we are citizens of another country, "a *better country,*" "an heavenly." Scenes of heavenly beauty and glory have passed before our spiritual vision; celestial music—music the sweetest—has fallen in siren strains upon our ears, and onward we press to that land of eternal rest.

> "O my soul, press on to glory!
> Worlds of bliss invite thee on,
> Evermore to be with Jesus,
> When this walk on earth is done."

When, oh, when! shall we enter this everlasting abode of the righteous? "Let not your heart be troubled: ye believe in God, believe also in me. In my Father's house are many mansions: if it were not so I would have told you. *I go to prepare a place for you.* And if I go and prepare a place for you, I WILL COME AGAIN, AND RECEIVE YOU UNTO MYSELF; that where I am, there ye may be also" (John 14: 1-3). Where did Jesus go? "He was parted from them, and carried up into heaven" (Luke 24: 51). When will he come again to receive us? "The Lord himself shall descend from heaven with a shout, with the voice of the archangel, and with the trump of God: and the dead in Christ shall rise first: then we which are alive and remain shall be caught up together with them in the clouds, to meet the Lord in the air: and *so shall we ever be with the Lord"* (1 Thess. 4: 16, 17).

In the course of this world's history one age has succeeded another, until we are now drawing toward the close of the last dispensation, and soon the second coming of our Lord will end our planet's career. But the plan and purpose of God has been complete in the mind of the omnipotent One from the beginning. Redemption itself has ever been present before him; therefore Christ was a "Lamb slain from the foundation of

the world" (Rev. 13:8); still, its actual fulfilment did
not take place until after the lapse of many centuries.
So also the future and eternal home of the redeemed is
but another part of the same great redemptory plan, and
it has been in the mind and purpose of God from the
beginning; hence it is a "kingdom prepared for you
from the foundation of the world" (Matt. 25:34); still,
its actual preparation was a later accomplishment, for
Jesus says, "I go to prepare a place for you." No man
has yet entered this world of final things. *"I will come
again,* and receive you unto myself," says Jesus. Then,
and not until then, shall the heavenly world be brought
to view.

A NEW HEAVEN AND A NEW EARTH.

This second coming is described by the apostle Peter
thus: "But the day of the Lord will come as a thief in
the night; in the which the heavens shall pass away
with a great noise, and the elements shall melt with
fervent heat, the earth also and the works that are
therein shall be burned up. Seeing then that all these
things shall be dissolved, what manner of persons ought
ye to be in all holy conversation and godliness, looking
for and hasting unto the coming of the day of God,
wherein the heavens being on fire shall be dissolved, and
the elements shall melt with fervent heat? Nevertheless
we, according to his promise, look for *new heavens and
a new earth,* wherein dwelleth righteousness" (2 Pet. 3:
10-13).

When in that last great day our Lord descends from
heaven, the earth itself, wrapped in sheets of flame, shall

flee away from before his presence; and the righteous shall ascend with shouts of joy and praise to meet him in the air, ever to be with him in that future world of bliss. Yes, this "new heaven and a new earth" will be our future and eternal home. All the promises point forward to it. "Blessed are the meek: for they shall inherit the earth" (Matt. 5: 5). And we *"according to his promise, look for new heavens and a new earth, wherein dwelleth righteousness."* The new earth is the earth that we shall inherit; for our "inheritance" is one that is incorruptible, and undefiled, and that *fadeth not away,* RESERVED IN HEAVEN" (1 Pet. 1: 4).

The description given by the Revelator is still plainer. "And I saw a great white throne, and him that sat on it, from whose face the *earth and the heaven fled away;* and there was *found no place for them.* And I saw the dead, small and great, stand before God; and the books were opened: and another book was opened, which is the book of life; and the dead were judged out of those things which were written in the books, according to their works. . . . . And I saw a NEW HEAVEN AND A NEW EARTH; for *the first heaven and the first earth were passed away"* (Rev. 20: 11, 12; 21: 1).

THE GOLDEN CITY.

Again we say, This new heaven and new earth brought to view after the passing of the present earth, will be the place of our future and eternal abode. "For here have we no continuing city, *but we seek one to come"* (Heb. 13: 14). Yea, "God hath prepared for us *a city"* (Heb. 11; 16). And when this heavenly world was opened before the apostle in Apocalyptic vision, he saw therein the eternal dwelling-place of God's saints symbolized after the pattern of a "great city," "the new Jerusalem" (Rev. 21). The actual things of the paradise of God are of such an exalted and transcendent character that it is *not possible* for man to utter them in the ordinary language of earth (2 Cor. 12:4); therefore they must of necessity be represented symbolically, the symbols chosen being, of course, in their nature vastly inferior to the things thus foreshadowed.

What city is this laid out before us in splendor and magnificence? It is "the holy city, new Jerusalem." It is a city of "pure gold." Even its streets are of purest gold. It is surrounded by a "wall great and high," and twelve gates, each a solid pearl, give entrance. This wall is of jasper, built on foundations garnished with all manner of precious stones—jasper, sapphire, chalcedony, emerald, sardonyx, sardius, chrysolyte, beryl, topaz, chrysoprasus, jacinth, and amethyst. The glory of God itself illuminates this city continually. Here is "a pure river of water of life clear as crystal, proceeding out of the throne of God and of the Lamb," and on each side of this beautiful stream stands the tree of life, rich in luscious fruits, and no cherubim with flaming swords are there to guard it. Oh! this is paradise restored. "There shall be no more curse." "Blessed are they that do his commandments, that they may *have right to the tree of life,* and may *enter in through the gates into the city.*" (Rev. 22:14).

OUR HOME ETERNAL.

This will be our eternal home. "There the wicked cease from troubling; and there the weary be at rest" (Job 3: 17). There in the city of light we shall "shine as the brightness of the firmament"; yea, "they that turn many to righteousness" shall shine "as the stars forever and ever" (Dan. 12: 3).

> "Oh, what joy will it be when his face I behold,
> Living gems at his feet to lay down!
> It will sweeten my bliss in the city of gold,
> Should there be any stars in my crown."

Oh bliss of heaven! Joy unspeakable! when we shall sit down with Abraham and Isaac and Jacob and all the prophets, in the kingdom of God; or when we shall gather with the ransomed around the great white throne, and there pour out our anthems of praise and thanksgiving unceasingly. O my soul, press onward! There is nothing in this time-world to hold thy affections. "Pleasures forevermore" beckon thee onward to that land of excellent delights where comes no setting sun! My brethren, take courage! Thrones and dominions, glittering scepters and crowns of dazzling splendor, are the symbols of our glory in the life that is to be. Heed not earth's sorrows. No sickness, no pain, no sorrow, and no death shall mar our happiness in the eternal paradise; for God himself shall wipe away all tears from our eyes. With time behind us, eternity before us, the angels and the redeemed of all ages around us— THIS WILL BE HEAVEN, OUR ETERNAL HOME.

SCRIPTURAL INDEX.

CPSIA information can be obtained
at www.ICGtesting.com
Printed in the USA
LVOW13s0741180917

549078LV00012B/460/P